Manchester Medieval Sources Series

Series editors Jonathan Lyon, Sarah Davis-Secord and Simon MacLean

This series provides translations of key sources that are directly usable in students' own work, with accessible and contextual introductions and helpful annotations throughout. The books meet a growing need amongst students and teachers by providing texts central to medieval studies courses and focus upon the diverse cultural, social and political conditions that affected the functioning of all levels of society. The series welcomes a range of sources from across Europe and the Mediterranean. Volumes can be comprised of one or two longer narrative works or collections of shorter texts, including documents. Proposals for new volumes should be accompanied by sample introductory material and examples of annotated translation.

also available in the series

John H. Arnold and Pete Biller *Heresy and inquisition in France, 1200–1300*

C. E. Beneš *Jacopo da Varagine's* Chronicle of the city of Genoa

Andrew Brown and Graeme Small *Court and civic society in the Burgundian Low Countries c. 1420–1520*

Martin Heale *Monasticism in late medieval England, c.1300–1535*

David Jones *Friars' Tales: Thirteenth-century exempla from the British Isles*

Graham Loud *Roger II and the making of the Kingdom of Sicily*

T. J. H. McCarthy *Chronicles of the Investiture Contest: Frutolf of Michelsberg and his continuators*

A. K. McHardy *The reign of Richard II*

Simon MacLean *History and politics in late Carolingian and Ottonian Europe: The Chronicle of Regino of Prüm and Adalbert of Magdeburg*

Anthony Musson and Edward Powell *Crime, law and society in the later Middle Ages*

Andrew Rabin *The political writings of Archbishop Wulfstan of York*

I. S. Robinson *Eleventh-century Germany: The Swabian Chronicles*

I. S. Robinson *The Annals of Lampert of Hersfeld*

Rachel Stone and Charles West *Hincmar of Rheims: On the divorce of King Lothar and Queen Theutberga*

Craig Taylor *Joan of Arc: La Pucelle*

Diana Webb *Saints and cities in medieval Italy*

The reign of Edward II, 1307–27

Manchester University Press

Medieval Sources *online*

Complementing the printed editions of the Medieval Sources series, Manchester University Press has developed a web-based learning resource which is now available on a yearly subscription basis.

Medieval Sources*online* brings quality history source material to the desktops of students and teachers and allows them open and unrestricted access throughout the entire college or university campus. Designed to be fully integrated with academic courses, this is a one-stop answer for many medieval history students, academics and researchers keeping thousands of pages of source material 'in print' over the Internet for research and teaching.

titles available now at Medieval Sources *online include*

Trevor Dean *The towns of Italy in the later Middle Ages*

John Edwards *The Jews in Western Europe, 1400–1600*

Paul Fouracre and Richard A. Gerberding *Late Merovingian France: History and hagiography 640–720*

Chris Given-Wilson *Chronicles of the Revolution 1397–1400: The reign of Richard II*

P. J. P. Goldberg *Women in England, c. 1275–1525*

Janet Hamilton and Bernard Hamilton *Christian dualist heresies in the Byzantine world, c. 650–c. 1450*

Rosemary Horrox *The Black Death*

David Jones *Friars' Tales: Thirteenth-century exempla from the British Isles*

Graham A. Loud and Thomas Wiedemann *The history of the tyrants of Sicily by 'Hugo Falcandus', 1153–69*

A. K. McHardy *The reign of Richard II: From minority to tyranny 1377–97*

Simon MacLean *History and politics in late Carolingian and Ottonian Europe: The* Chronicle *of Regino of Prüm and Adalbert of Magdeburg*

Anthony Musson with Edward Powell *Crime, law and society in the later Middle Ages*

Janet L. Nelson *The Annals of St-Bertin: Ninth-century histories, volume I*

Timothy Reuter *The Annals of Fulda: Ninth-century histories, volume II*

R. N. Swanson *Catholic England: Faith, religion and observance before the Reformation*

Elisabeth van Houts *The Normans in Europe*

Jennifer Ward *Women of the English nobility and gentry 1066–1500*

For further information and subscription prices, see *www.manchesteruniversitypress.co.uk/manchester-medieval-sources-online*

THE REIGN OF EDWARD II, 1307–27

selected sources translated and edited

by Wendy R. Childs and Phillipp R. Schofield

MANCHESTER UNIVERSITY PRESS

Published by Manchester University Press
Oxford Road, Manchester M13 9PL
www.manchesteruniversitypress.co.uk

British Library Cataloguing-in-Publication Data
A catalogue record for this book is available from the British Library

ISBN 978 1 5261 2024 3 hardback

ISBN 978 1 5261 2025 0 paperback

First published 2022

Typeset by Newgen Publishing UK
Printed in Great Britain by CPI Group (UK) Ltd, Croydon

CONTENTS

ACKNOWLEDGEMENTS

The idea of a collection of documents and commentaries for the reign of Edward II was first discussed more than twenty years ago and we are very pleased that it has seen the light of day in the present publication. We have both, over a number of years, taught final-year 'special subjects' on Edward II to our students at Aberystwyth and at Leeds and it is a pleasure to acknowledge the contribution of our students to the development of ideas and selection of materials that have been gathered here. Thanks are also very much due to the series editors of Manchester Medieval Sources, Rosemary Horrox and Simon MacLean, and, at Manchester University Press, the Senior Commissioning Editor, Meredith Carroll, and the Assistant Editors, Alun Richards and Laura Swift. Meredith and her team have been especially patient with us as we have slowly moved the volume towards publication and we are most grateful for their care and support. We are also very grateful for the careful and encouraging advice of the anonymous external reader which has greatly improved the volume. The responsibility for the final text and any remaining mistakes lies, of course, with us.

We are most grateful to the following publishers who have given permission for existing translations previously published in their publications to be used here:

Nos **1a, 2f, 4a, 5a, 8d (i), 9a, 13b, 17a, 19, 20b, 21c, 22a, 36b, 45, 47b** and **49a** are republished from *Vita Edwardi Secundi*, ed. and trans. W. R. Childs, Oxford Medieval Texts (Oxford: Oxford University Press, 2005) with the permission of Oxford Publishing Limited.

Nos **2d, 2e, 3c, 7c, 16b, 23, 39b, 40a** and **50c** are republished from *English Historical Documents*, III: *1189–1327*, ed. H. Rothwell (London: Eyre and Spottiswoode, 1975) with the permission of Taylor and Francis Group.

No. **16a** is published from W. M. Ormrod, H. Killick and P. Bradford, eds, *Early Common Petitions in the English Parliament, c. 1290–c. 1420*, Camden Society 5th series 52 (2017) with the permission of Cambridge University Press.

Nos **18a** and **32d** are published from N. Pronay and J. Taylor, eds, *Parliamentary Texts of the Later Middle Ages* (Oxford: Oxford University Press, 1980) with the permission of Oxford Publishing Limited.

No. **27c** is published from *Regesta Regum Scottorum, vol. V: The Acts of Robert I, King of Scots, 1306–1329*, ed. A. A. M. Duncan (Edinburgh: Edinburgh University Press, 1988), with the permission of Edinburgh University Press Limited.

No. **28** is published from Stones, *Anglo-Scottish Relations*, with the permission of Oxford Publishing Limited.

Nos **37b, 38b** and **53b** are published from *The Anonimalle Chronicle, 1307–1334 from Brotherton Collection MS 29*, ed. W. R. Childs and J. Taylor, YAS Record Series 147 (1991) with the permission of Cambridge University Press.

ABBREVIATIONS

CCR	*Calendar of Close Rolls*
CFR	*Calendar of Fine Rolls*
CPMR	*Calendar of Plea and Memoranda Rolls*
CPR	*Calendar of Patent Rolls*
EcHR	*Economic History Review*
EHD	*English Historical Documents*
EHR	*English Historical Review*
Foedera	T. Rymer, *Foedera, Conventiones ...*
HBC	*Handbook of British Chronology*
HMSO	Her Majesty's Stationery Office
ODNB	*Oxford Dictionary of National Biography*
PRO	Public Record Office
PROME	*Parliament Rolls of Medieval England*
Rot. Parl.	*Rotuli Parliamentorum*
RS	Rolls Series
Statutes	*Statutes of the Realm*, ed. A. Luders et al., 11 vols. (London, 1810–28)
TNA	The National Archives, Kew
Vita	*Vita Edwardi Secundi*, ed. and trans. W. R. Childs, Oxford Medieval Texts (Oxford: Oxford University Press, 2005)
YAJ	*Yorkshire Archaeological Journal*
YAS	Yorkshire Archaeological Society

INTRODUCTION

Edward's reign is well known for its dramatic political narrative of a wilful king, his reliance on favourites, violent baronial resistance, failure in Scotland and France, and eventually the loss of his throne and his murder, but it is also a reign of considerable institutional and ideological interest. The exploitation of royal wealth, the use of parliament and the belief that opposition needed justification by law, precedent and legitimation all saw significant development. Edward I's new revenues were consolidated under Edward II; financial administration was improved; the increasing frequency of parliament brought in its wake more regular procedures and the growing importance of the commons. The strong need for legitimisation of actions encouraged public statements and sometimes written tracts of constitutional interest. In Edward II's reign the position of English kings became both stronger, with access to greater wealth and more efficient administration, and weaker, through increased need for consent and, ultimately, by the precedent of deposition, for, while the office of king remained intact, the removal of the royal person was no longer unthinkable.

In this volume we will take the opportunity to move between the political narrative of the reign and more thematic and broadly institutional developments, introducing each sub-period or theme as well as presenting a series of documents which help to inform our understanding in each instance. The chronological narrative of the reign is chiefly located in chapters I, V, VI, VIII and IX; these chapters move through a series of stages that have tended to define historians' discussion of the reign. A first chapter on early opposition addresses Edward II's accession in 1307, his political inheritance and the early indications of turmoil, culminating in an increasingly demarcated opposition and the killing of Edward's favourite, Piers Gaveston. In Chapter V the middle years of the reign are explored, a period in which tensions persisted and the king struggled either to engage with his opponents or to bring them wholly under his control. Eventually, as set out in Chapter VI, the situation worsened, with the king's new favourites presenting a focus for opposition, and simmering tension shifted to open hostility and a brief but vicious civil war. Emerging victorious from this civil conflict in the spring of 1322, Edward II was able to gather both wealth and heightened authority. A period of so-called tyranny followed, as discussed in Chapter VIII, the final years of Edward's reign, in which he failed to cement his hold over the country or to annul the threat of his opponents, despite the savage reprisals in the wake of the civil war. This failure meant that his end, when it came, was swift; his opponents, including his queen, Isabella, overthrew him in late 1326 and his reign was ended early in 1327, with the coronation of his son, Edward III, in January of that year. His death, described by near-contemporaries in its awful detail, almost certainly followed later the same year, despite some suggestion that Edward escaped and fled the country, matters discussed in Chapter IX.

As well as the chronological narrative, the volume offers a series of more thematic chapters intended to reflect more fully on particular points of continued relevance throughout the reign. From the moment of Edward's accession, and throughout most of his reign, the pursuit of sufficient funds and authority to function as a king, especially in defence of his realm, remained central to his government; his success and, more especially, his failure was measured by his opponents and contemporary commentators in such terms, as is evident in the articles drawn up to condemn his ultimate failure as monarch in 1327.[1] These themes, and the documents which are especially relevant to discussion of the same, are presented in four chapters. In Chapter II the extent of the king's wealth is examined; this encourages reflection on the sources of the king's wealth but also the varying extent of the flow of that wealth across the reign and the explanations for any variation. Central to the politics of the reign was the insurmountable gulf between the king's expectations of his royal authority and the limits which his opponents wished to place upon it; this was not an issue unique to the reign of Edward II, but there is a clear sense of a developing and increasingly institutional limit on unconstrained royal power, exemplified especially in the development of parliament as an institution of government, as will be examined in Chapter IV. Resort of parliament and parliamentary authority, especially in the raising of finances to support military campaigns, was a fairly constant demand of the opposition to Edward's personal rule, and something he sought to nullify in the later stages of his reign. Two further chapters discuss and present material relevant to Edward's foreign policy and military

1 As in the articles of accusation drawn up in 1327, for which see below [**48**].

campaigns. Fears over Scottish incursion in the northern Marches and the pressing need to organise military campaigns against Robert Bruce are issues of major importance during the first fifteen years of the reign; the campaigns and the later attempts to secure truces and treaties with the Scots are set out in Chapter IV. In Chapter VII, another perennial issue, the homage owed by English kings as vassal to the king of France, is discussed. The homage owed by Edward and the need to attend a new French king to perform this recurred as an issue more than once in the reign; in the earlier years, as in the spring of 1313, Edward even used the excuse of the need to perform homage as an opportunity to absent himself from the tensions of domestic politics. However, towards the end of the reign, the coalescence of the need to perform homage allied to competing territorial claims that spilled over into violence and the mission of Isabella and Prince Edward to France, supposedly intended to restore the situation, helped foment a greater crisis for Edward II which contributed to his downfall.

Sources for the reign of Edward II

The present volume represents then a gathering of materials relevant to our understanding of the political development of the reign of Edward II. As will be evident from the bibliography to this volume and the documentary examples themselves, the bulk of the material presented here – but certainly not all that material – draws upon the major narrative sources for the reign. Antonia Gransden's discussion of historical writing in the period, amongst others, usefully identifies the most important literary sources for the reign, including under this broad term the chroniclers and the annalists, and selections from almost all of these are included in the present volume.[2] There is good reason for focusing upon the narrative sources in a collection such as this, since the chroniclers, such as the author of the *Vita Edwardi Secundi*, the most important chronicle for the reign in terms of its range and insight, offer us an immediate, if undoubtedly flawed, purchase on major political events and the high-status individuals directly involved in those events. Almost all the chronicles for the reign are published, and have been in some instances since the nineteenth century, and a few of these are also available in translation.[3] The selections here offer

2 Gransden, *Historical Writing*, p. 499.

3 For instance, *Vita Edwardi Secundi*; *Lanercost*; *Le Baker*.

a sense of their content, style and argument, but there is plentiful scope for the reader to proceed beyond the examples in this volume.

As T. F. Tout noted many years ago, the chronicles offer us an easy if unreliable guide to the broad narrative structure of the reign, noting that 'the chronicles provide us with the frame within which we can set our picture'.[4] As this quote suggests, he also reflected, in the same paper and elsewhere, that the chronicles and other narrative sources are far from an end to the political history of the period, but rather a context for fuller and deeper study. That fuller study, for Tout and others, comes through the administrative sources, the 'records' as Tout termed them and to the study of which he devoted his career. A generation earlier than Tout, in the later nineteenth century, Bishop Stubbs had recognised that the growth of a centralised bureaucracy and of the institutions of government in the thirteenth century had, by the reign of Edward II, generated a wealth of material – important tranches of which were published in the first years of the nineteenth century – that would direct historians away from the narrative sources. Stubbs noted that the records of parliament, its writs and its rolls, as well as the statute book, begin to offer, by the early fourteenth century, a detailed history of the politics and administration that offers a clarity not to be found in the chronicles and the annals.[5] Seymour Phillips's major biography of the king, published in 2010, offers some sense, in its bibliography, of the array of primary material, both published and unpublished, now available to the historian of the reign. In addition to piecemeal items from various repositories, it is the very large body of material from the National Archive, chiefly the records of the two great medieval organs of government, the chancery and the exchequer, which dominates the administrative materials for the reign.[6] The records of chancery and of parliament are available in calendared form or, in the case of the parliament rolls, in printed and online editions; the materials from the exchequer, equally voluminous, are much less available in published form and pose a daunting challenge for the historian of the reign.[7] In this volume, we have sought to present, where relevant,

4 Tout, 'Medieval chronicles', p. 18.

5 Stubbs, *Constitutional History*, II, p. 311.

6 Phillips, *Edward II*, pp. 614–17.

7 For a sense of the scale of the documentation from chancery, exchequer and the courts of law for the period, see the digitised collection gathered by Robert Palmer and his team at the University of Houston, Texas at http://aalt.law.uh.edu/EdwardII.html (last accessed 26 January 2020).

examples of central administrative and parliamentary material as well as to gather important pronouncements of government, such as the ordinances and statutes. In addition, and again reflective of the extraordinary range of available material, we offer the occasional example drawn from the wealth of the chancery rolls to illustrate instances of everyday government activity. Correspondence between individuals, preserved in central or estate archives, also offers a sense of the interpersonal dealings that also produced a great body of materials relevant to the history of the reign.

There remains much material on the reign that has not been examined in detail, let alone published. T. F. Tout, who, a century ago, drew the value of the administrative sources for the reign to the attention of medieval historians, also recognised major gaps in his own coverage of such material and the vast amount of work still to be done. In the introduction to his study of the administrative history of the reign, he reflected upon not only the range of sources he had been able to consult but also those sources he had chosen or been obliged to neglect. In the case of a certain type of exchequer record, the pipe rolls, he avoided examining them in any detail for the reign 'because their extraordinary bulk has terrified me'.[8] Tout was not the only historian of the reign to reflect upon the wealth of material that survives for the reign of Edward II, much of it not contained in the narrative sources. Half a century later than Tout, John Maddicott, in the preface to his study of Thomas of Lancaster published in 1970, also wrote that 'much basic research, particularly on finance and foreign relations, still remains to be done before a full-scale history of the reign can be written'.[9] This situation to large degree still holds true and there is much work still to be done on the medieval exchequer and its development into the early fourteenth century.[10] In this volume we offer examples of correspondence reflective of the business of the exchequer and its reform as well as the work of the crown associated with taxation, customs, finance and pricing, all areas crucial to the medieval governmental machine.

8 Tout, *Edward II*, p. 3. Phillips also comments on omissions in Tout's use of material relevant to the king's household and the implications of this for aspects of his interpretation, Phillips, 'Tout and the reign of Edward II', pp. 109–10. See http://aalt.law.uh.edu/EdwardII.html and column 'Pipe Rolls' (TNA E372) for a glimpse of the source that so 'terrified' Tout.

9 Maddicott, *Lancaster*, p. vii.

10 Barratt, 'Tout and the exchequer', pp. 183–4.

Other areas, represented in a few instances here, offer other insights; we can seldom come as close as we would like to the popular view of politics, the voice or opinion of the ordinary man or woman. Occasionally though we are offered possible insights, as in the political songs of the period, or occasional individual or collective acts of defiance or support that hint at a wider politics. From time to time we have also sought to represent that broader view of the politics of the reign.

Historians and the reign of Edward II

In relative terms the reign of Edward II has not attracted the degree of attention given to the longer and, by general agreement, more successful reigns of Edward's father and of his son. In terms of a modern historiography, historical writing on the reign falls into a series of phases. In the first instance, in the later nineteenth century, historians of the medieval constitution tended to dismiss Edward and his reign as a disappointing hiatus in an otherwise successful and worthy development of English monarchy at this time. Bishop Stubbs offers an emotive and somewhat excessive account of Edward's reign. In his view, Edward II was his father's son only by name and by blood. He possessed, Stubbs argued, few if any of his father's attributes as a king. While grudgingly acknowledging that 'he is not without some share of the chivalrous qualities that are impersonated in his son [the future Edward III]', Stubbs concludes that

> he has no high aims, no policy beyond the cunning of unscrupulous selfishness. He has no kingly pride or sense of duty, no industry or shame or piety. He is the first king since the Conquest who was not a man of business, well acquainted with the routine of government; he makes amusement the employment of his life; his tastes at best are those of the athlete and the artisan; vulgar pomp, heartless extravagance, lavish improvidence, selfish indolence make him a fit centre of an intriguing court … His reign is a tragedy, but one that lacks in its true form the element of pity: for there is nothing in Edward, miserable as his fate is, that invites or deserves sympathy.[11]

Stubbs's view of Edward was based almost exclusively on the narrative sources, the chronicles and the annals. As such his emphasis is dominated by assessments of personality and discussion of individual strengths, weaknesses, ambitions and desires. The next generation of historians, writing in the first decades of the twentieth century,

11 Stubbs, *Constitutional History*, II, pp. 339–40.

extracted most of the personal politics from discussion of the reign and replaced it instead with the apparently more mundane administrative sources and the workings of the constitution. Two keys works, by Tout and by Conway Davies, stand out in this respect.[12] Davies's detailed discussion of baronial opposition in the reign of Edward II is not so much directed at the particular ambitions of leading magnates and their clashes with the crown as it is an investigation of what Davies terms constitutional 'experiments'. For Davies, the various phases or episodes of the reign reflect different efforts to ease the development of a constitutional monarchy. So, for instance, the issue of the Ordinances in 1311 and the work of the York parliament in 1318 are seen as moments of considered engagement with the nature of monarchy and attempts to redefine or modernise it. One striking, and now largely rejected, example of this is the rise of a 'Middle Party' in the years after Bannockburn, which Davies presents as an attempt to limit Edward's worst instincts. The later rejection of such an assessment reflects both a shift in the historical view of the mechanics of political society in early fourteenth-century England as well as access to a range of sources which were either overlooked by or unavailable to Davies.[13] Tout, the early twentieth century's foremost historian of English medieval government, also uses central government records to examine a new facet of Edward's reign and his government. Focusing in particular on exchequer and household records, he offers a semi-prosopographical discussion which itemises the structure and personnel of the royal household. His work extended beyond household offices to examine important aspects of royal administration. So, for example, he explored in detail sealing practice in government and drew important conclusions from the choices the king and his officers made in confirming the instructions of government. Such actions, Tout realised, were as political as they were administrative and, in drawing our attention to the significance of such apparent ordinariness, he helped to forge a view of medieval politics that escaped the gossip and moralising of the chronicles. It also, of necessity, downplayed the impact of the great and powerful lords and, indeed, of the king. For Tout these figures, often limited in their awareness and remote from the day-to-day of government, were of secondary importance to the 'rank and file' in the running of the country.[14] In fact, Tout saw in the

12 Davies, *Baronial Opposition*; Tout, *Edward II*.

13 Phillips, *Aymer de Valence*; Phillips, 'Tout and the reign of Edward II'.

14 Tout, *Edward II*, p. 24.

weakness and personal failings of Edward II the opportunity by which absolutism was avoided and the constraining edifice of secure institutional structures constructed.[15] Commentators writing in the years and decades after this administrative turn in the history of the reign tended to follow a similar path, either working with or challenging aspects of the administrative/constitutional interpretation but not seeking to overturn it. So, for instance, Trueman's careful investigation of the use of the privy seal in the reign and Wilkinson's examination of key constitutional features and their associated documents also reflect the broad constitutional and administrative thrust of this earlier seam of historical work.[16]

It would take another fifty years and a second wave of work on the reign to shift the emphasis and undermine the broad theses of Tout and Davies. In two doctoral theses, both subsequently published as monographs, J. R. Maddicott and J. R. S. Phillips produced, within a few months of each other in the early 1970s, separate biographical discussions of leading magnates from the reign, respectively Thomas, Earl of Lancaster, and Aymer de Valence, Earl of Pembroke. Both works offered chronological accounts of the political careers of their subjects alongside more thematic accounts of their estates and their wealth. Distinctive in both discussions is the analysis of the role and approach of the earls. Phillips's assessment of the so-called 'Middle Party', proposed by Davies as noted above, usefully illustrates the difference in analysis and conception of the high politics of the reign. For, where Davies saw the lofty ambition to control the weaker political instincts and to steer government in the right direction, Phillips detects an attempt to constrain ambition, an attempt informed by the mutual recognition that all parties involved were, to varying degrees, self-serving. This contradiction between higher constitutional aims and the pursuit of self-interest is, as Maddicott shows, manifest in the career of Thomas of Lancaster. His promotion of the Ordinances and of a monarchy constrained by parliament stand in contrast to his preparedness to single out other magnates for attack, to pursue the acquisition of new territory at the apparent expense of his political imperatives and to collude with the Scots in order to secure his northern estates.[17]

15 On this, see also the useful assessment of Phillips, 'Tout and the reign of Edward II', pp. 107–21.

16 Trueman, 'Privy seal'; Wilkinson, *Constitutional History*.

17 Maddicott, *Lancaster*, pp. 333–4.

In essence, then, these detailed analyses of leading figures from the reign speak to a very different kind of politics from that envisaged by Davies and Tout; the random politics of individual ambition looms large in this newer perspective.[18] Where there is a stated constitutional aspiration, it tends to be presented as a sham, a cynical attempt to adjust the situation to the advantage of the supposed aspirant.

This is a view that has tended to persist in more recent work and there has been no significant return to the constitutionalism of the early twentieth century. The appearance in the past twenty years of major biographies of Edward II, especially that by Phillips,[19] has provided the fullest discussions of the reign offered to date. While the biography of Edward by Haines reflects and is heavily influenced by his interest in some key ecclesiastical figures, Phillips offers a balanced and considered discussion of the reign. In terms of his more general assessment of the nature of politics in the reign, he does not depart greatly from his assessment of the reign as set out in his much earlier biography of Aymer de Valence. Given-Wilson's recent short survey of the reign also takes much the same line.[20] Other, more particular, studies of the reign, as, for example, Fryde's discussion of the period of so-called 'tyranny' at its close or Hamilton's discussion of Gaveston's life and death, have also tended to fall into step with a view of the reign as dominated by the naked ambition of powerful individuals, each vying with the other for power and influence over the king.[21] Discussions directed less at the reign of Edward II or its particular politics but instead at longer-term developments of government and its institutions have also tended to adopt this view of the politics and its motives. Maddicott's discussion of the origins and development of the medieval English parliament, hardly surprisingly, adopts his own

18 It also reflects a perspective shared, much earlier and in more general terms, by Stubbs who was more reliant than Davies and Tout on the narrative sources and the views on personal politics set out there, Stubbs, *Constitutional History*, II, p. 323.

19 Phillips, *Edward II*; Haines, *Edward II*.

20 Given-Wilson, *Edward II*.

21 Fryde, *Tyranny*; Hamilton, *Piers Gaveston*. In this respect, Chaplais's discussion of adoptive brotherhood, rather than a homosexual relationship, as an explanation for Edward's bond with Gaveston is an interesting departure; in exploring the nature of their association and the principles upon which it was founded, Chaplais offers an exercise in the close reading of the relevant sources, such as the grant of the earldom of Cornwall in August 1307, to come closer to one highly particular but clearly significant fragment of Edward's history, Chaplais, *Piers Gaveston*.

earlier position, describing the early fourteenth century as 'predominantly baronial and virulently fractious'.[22] Other studies of politics and government, written since the 1970s, have also tended to adopt the same line, though Harriss's important investigation of public finance in the Middle Ages, published in 1975, very soon after the appearance of the studies by Maddicott, is not so inclined to reject notions aligned more closely with the earlier generation of Davies and Tout.[23]

More general and popular accounts of the reign exist in quite large numbers; these broad narratives have tended not to adjust the direction or range of our understanding of the reign, but offer instead compelling and personal histories for those keen to read about this tumultuous period.[24] In addition, as more than one historian has reflected in recent writing on the reign, Edward II's tragic history is not the preserve of academic historians alone; for centuries, playwrights, and much more recently filmmakers, have taken ownership of Edward, especially in terms of his relationship with his favourites. It is striking, but not perhaps so unusual, that the pursuit of an academic history of the reign has not intersected to any great degree with the topics favoured by the reader approaching the reign out of interest rather than academic inquiry. This may reflect a distinction between the reasonable limits of academic inquiry and the more porous boundaries of literary or more speculative accounts of the reign. This is not to say that historians have shied away from discussion of the sexual nature of Edward's relationship with Gaveston or the younger Despenser, for instance, but only to note that the careful and tentative conclusions typically drawn from such analyses are some distance from the queer history narrative of Derek Jarman's *Edward II* or, indeed, the histories written for a more general readership.[25]

Other contentious elements of Edward's history have attracted some attention. For instance, the question of how Edward died or when he died has involved lively, if inconclusive, debate. These discussions lead in similar directions to those associated with Edward's sexuality; so, the persistent and likely irredeemable uncertainty about how Edward

22 Maddicott, *Origins*, p. 331.

23 Harriss, *King, Parliament*.

24 Hutchison, *Edward II*; Saaler, *Edward II*; Warner, *Edward II*.

25 Ormrod, 'Sexualities' makes the important point that in asking whether Edward was gay we are asking the wrong question, certainly not one that can be sensibly answered. On more general accounts and Edward's sexuality, see, for example, Warner, *Edward II*, ch. 2.

actually died does not prevent a slightly different and fruitful discussion of the narratives constructed by contemporaries and near-contemporaries relating to the nature of his death and his perceived 'degeneracy'.[26] In similar respects, Mortimer's informed exploration of the 'after-life' of Edward II has not shifted most historians of the reign from the standard view that Edward died at Berkeley Castle in September 1327. While neither position can be identified as irrefutable, the more secure historical interest appears to reside in the generation of such 'survival' narratives into the reign of Edward III.[27]

Such topics for investigation are not new. Historians in the early twentieth century wrote enthusiastically about Edward II's 'degeneracy' or his death.[28] As testified by blogs, films and plays, as well as an ever-growing number of popular histories of the reign, there remains an enduring interest in the reign of Edward II.[29] In its failings and turmoil the reign has proved a testing ground for historians eager to explore the dynamics of power and of the nature of constitutional change at a time when the balance of authority was shifting from kings to institutions and their representatives; and in the personal tragedies and political disasters there resides the need, which cannot always be answered, for understanding and resolution.

26 Ormrod, 'Sexualities'; Mortimer, 'Sermons of sodomy'. For a recent gathering of materials relating to Edward's captivity, death, burial and 'after-life', see Barlow et al., *Edward II.*

27 See Mortimer, 'Death of Edward II'; King, 'Death of Edward II'; see also the correspondence between Carpenter and Mortimer on the same at www.lrb.co.uk/the-paper/v29/n11/david-carpenter/what-happened-to-edward-ii#letters (last accessed 21 January 2020).

28 Robinson, 'Was Edward II a degenerate?'; Tout, 'Captivity and death of Edward of Carnarvon'.

29 See, for instance, Phillips, *Edward II*, pp. 30–1.

I: EARLY OPPOSITION

Introduction

Historians have tended to the view that Edward inherited significant problems and then almost immediately set about compounding them.[1] There is, in the first instance, no doubt that Edward's father, Edward I, had bequeathed major political problems to his son. Most of these related in one way or another to war and its financing. Edward I's military endeavours in the last decades of the thirteenth century and the first years of the fourteenth had led to campaigning on a number of fronts. These campaigns had become all-consuming by the 1290s, by which point, with the conquest of Wales completed save for the occasional uprising, Edward had directed his military ventures towards Scotland, Flanders and France. By the end of Edward I's reign, such ventures had proved costly, in terms of both actual money and, as Edward I discovered in the mid-1290s, political goodwill. The cumulative costs of persistent military activity meant that Edward I had to turn to a combination of frequent parliamentary taxation, loans, prises and the military obligations of his baronage in order to meet the demands of his ambitions. By the time of his death, in the summer of 1307, Edward I had accumulated £200,000 of debt, a very large sum by early fourteenth-century standards, and, as importantly, had been obliged to mollify his barons in order to continue his plans of campaign. At the time of the so-called 'crisis of 1297', Edward had been forced to concede in the face of significant baronial resistance to his fiscal demands and, within the wider community of the realm, there was growing resistance to and complaint levelled at what was perceived to be unwarranted and injudicious taxation. In addition, and closely associated with this resistance to unconstrained royal money-raising, there was a persistent political view, which reflected complaints often articulated in the thirteenth century, that royal authority needed to be constrained through the agency of the wider community of the

1 This view is expressed in a number of contexts but most memorably in N. Denholm-Young's introduction to his edition of the *Vita Edward Secundi*, where he writes that Edward 'sat down to the game of kingship with a remarkably poor hand, and he played it very badly', *Vita Edwardi Secundi*, ed. Denholm-Young, p. ix.

realm and, increasingly, through the fledging institution of parliament. Baronial demands, articulated through documents which echoed the claims set out in Magna Carta in the reign of King John and the Provisions of Oxford of Simon de Montfort's baronial opposition in the reign of Henry III, were expressed anew in the last years of the reign of Edward I. This is most evident in the 'Confirmation of the Charters', an agreement aimed at a more consultative style of kingship which was followed by the further conciliatory response of Edward I in the 'Articles upon the Charters' in 1300.[2] This process of complaint and concession is mirrored, often word for word, in the jostling of opposition and counter-opposition in the first years of Edward II's reign; on more than one occasion in the opening years of his reign, Edward II had to behave in ways similar to his thirteenth-century forebears and accept statutes and ordinances aimed at constraining and defining his royal authority. Such constraints were imposed almost from the off and were supported by rebukes and threats, sometimes presented in the guise of considered advice.

Not everything that Edward II inherited from his father displays the same continuity of prevailing conditions. Most obviously, the personnel of government underwent inevitable change, notably in the disappearance through death of an older generation of earls and barons who, typically, came to be replaced by their heirs. Some of the 'old guard' of the political tensions of the 1290s, such as the Earl of Lincoln and the archbishop of Canterbury, Robert Winchelsey, survived into the first years of the reign of Edward II but, generally speaking, it was a new and, initially at least, fairly accommodating body of earls and barons who attended the coronation of their new king in February 1308.[3] However, by that point, less than a year into the reign of Edward II, there were already clear indications of growing tension as well as, and in no small part a product of, Edward's capacity to mismanage.

By early 1308, less than a year after he had succeeded his father, the leading nobles and great ecclesiastics were encouraging Edward to be mindful of his responsibility as king and, above all, to avoid listening to bad advice from poor influences. The so-called Boulogne Agreement of January 1308 [**2c**] offers the first, and relatively mild, indication of a growing concern about Edward's style of kingship, as well as an indication that leading magnates felt able to advise and seek in some

2 Prestwich, *War, Politics and Finance*, pp. 272–7.

3 Maddicott, *Lancaster*, pp. 67–9.

measure to limit royal authority. This was more fully and directly expressed a few weeks later, in April 1308, in the 'articles of the Earl of Lincoln' [**2e**]; this trenchant statement that kings had to be true to their office rather than their whims was coupled with the more immediate criticism of Edward's indulgence of his favourite, Piers Gaveston. As importantly, the articles set out the important position that the king's magnates owed their loyalty to the crown rather than the person of the king.

According to the author of the *Vita*, amongst others, Edward's first act upon becoming king was to recall his great friend and favourite, Piers Gaveston, from exile. Gaveston, perceived as an unworthy companion for his son, had been exiled by Edward I only a few weeks before his own death [**1a**; **1b**]. Gaveston's hasty restoration and consequent extraordinary elevation appears to have been tolerated only briefly, and soon became a focus of deep antagonism and intense criticism of Edward's judgement. The generous and highly irregular grant of the earldom of Cornwall to Gaveston, in August 1307, does not appear to have created a display of criticism on the part of the leading magnates, most of whom appear as witnesses to the grant [**2a**].[4] Nor indeed does Gaveston's marriage to Margaret de Clare, which appears to have been planned at the same time as the grant of the earldom.[5] Within a few weeks, however, the situation had worsened as Edward appeared to promote his favourite to even greater heights. Anticipating his absence from the country to attend his marriage to Isabella, daughter of the French king, Philip IV, Edward opted to leave his favourite in charge of the kingdom in the official capacity of *custos regni* (custodian of the realm) [**2b**]. Contemporary chroniclers raged at this elevation of a low-born individual [**5a–b**] and it is reasonable to assume, given the speed by which criticism of Edward and his relationship grew in early 1308, that their view mirrored that of Edward's magnates. While lurid accounts abound in the chronicles as to Gaveston's indulgence and dishonesty during Edward's absence, including the pilfering of wedding gifts sent ahead of the married couple, the more prosaic record of the chancery rolls, the record of day-to-day activity in the exercise of royal government, suggests that Gaveston was rather more restrained during the period of his custodianship.[6] Whatever the nature of his

4 Maddicott, *Lancaster*, pp. 70–1; on the earldom, see Hamilton, *Piers Gaveston*, pp. 39–43.

5 Chaplais, *Piers Gaveston*, pp. 31–4.

6 Hamilton, *Piers Gaveston*, pp. 45–6; Chaplais, *Piers Gaveston*, pp. 34–42.

actions, it was the symbolism of his promotion, the slight to other potential claimants of such an honour and the evidence this offered as to Edward's poor judgement that all served to heighten tension and encourage criticism and scrutiny of Edward and his rulership.[7]

The tensions surrounding Gaveston were only heightened by Edward's coronation, and in particular the elevation of Gaveston, who held the symbolic sword *curtana* during the ceremony, to a lofty role in the formalities. The raising of such a parvenu 'from a dung-hill', as one contemporary commentator had it, was a genuine cause for consternation.[8] It may also have been an opportunity for leverage as, as more than one chronicler suggests, those who sought to constrain Edward used his desire to promote Gaveston's role in the coronation as cause to wrest concessions from the king. However, the suggestion that the fourth clause of Edward's coronation oath [**2d**], a clause which appears to have placed obligation upon him to heed the advice of his subjects, was an addition included as a quid pro quo for Gaveston's starring role in the coronation itself, may exaggerate the tensions and realpolitik of the coronation and its preceding events.[9] Instead, historians tend to the view that there was a steady and speedy growth in opposition to the king and his favourite, which was encouraged by the arrogant display of Gaveston at the coronation and its celebration.[10]

Certainly, within days Edward was engaged in difficult discussions with his baronage at the Westminster parliament and, by April 1308, the Earl of Lincoln issued his powerful and wholly negative assessment of Edward's approach to kingship in his so-called 'articles' [**2e**]. By the spring of 1308 the association of Gaveston with Edward's perceived misgovernment was clear, as was the threat of armed opposition to the king's rule. In his 'articles', the Earl of Lincoln expressed the view that 'homage and allegiance' were owed not to the person but to the crown; if the rule of the person who wore the crown needed to be corrected, this could be achieved by the constraint of the people. As well as theorising on the limits of royal authority, the 'articles' offer an assault on the king's association with Gaveston, the unnamed 'person who is

7 Phillips, *Edward II*, pp. 145–6.

8 *Annales Paulini*, p. 259

9 See Phillips, *Edward II*, pp. 138–44, for a possible association between the Boulogne declaration and its link to the coronation; Phillips proposes a more constructive context in which the coronation was planned. On the fourth clause, see also *ibid.*, pp. 140–2.

10 Maddicott, *Lancaster*, p. 74.

talked about', and present the unequivocal view that the king should remove him from his presence.

Within weeks Gaveston was indeed sent into exile. He left the country in June 1308 but only as far as Ireland and in the role of lord lieutenant of Ireland; this was an important position into which he appears to have been propelled with precipitate haste and in place of the natural incumbent, Richard de Burgh, the Earl of Ulster. The latter was removed from the post no more than a day after he had been appointed to it [**2g**].[11] Edward's opportunism in protecting and privileging his favourite appears again to have taken precedence over the expectations of good government. Gaveston's exile lasted little more than a year, with Edward making every endeavour to secure his restoration and to overturn the threat of excommunication levelled against his favourite should he return without agreement. In fact, the price Edward had to pay for Gaveston's return was the Statute of Stamford (1309); this, as Phillips makes clear, was a confirmation, at the Stamford parliament of July 1309, of the articles issued by the king's opponents in the Westminster parliament of April the same year.[12] In most respects a restatement of the 'articles upon the charters' (1300) of Edward I's reign, the 1309 articles address such issues as the extraordinary levying of goods by the king's household (prises), the extent of the legal authority of officers of the king's household, the exercise of customs and the use of the privy seal [**3a**]. What may seem an eclectic mix of narrow issues in fact reflects a reasonably concerted effort to limit and contain the authority of the king and his household. It also, as its repetition of articles from the previous reign suggests, speaks to a rich vein of reform and constraint of royal and household government running through the political substrata of this era.[13] It is suggested that the king may have accepted these articles, and the consequent limits to his authority, at the Stamford parliament of August 1309 in return for approval of Gaveston's return from exile.[14] The events of 1309 and the issuing of the Statute of Stamford did not bring the matter to an end.

Gaveston's return seems to have re-established the disequilibrium evident before he left. Edward had spent time, during Gavestson's absence, on cultivating and dividing the opposition with grants, gifts and promises; with

11 Hamilton, *Piers Gaveston*, pp. 56–7.

12 Phillips, *Edward II*, p. 159.

13 Prestwich, *War, Politics and Finance*, p. 274.

14 Phillips, *Edward II*, p. 159; Tout, *Edward II*, p. 84.

Gaveston's return the hopes of other nobles for influence at court were dashed and tensions, also heightened by Gaveston's evident contempt for his peers, were once again enflamed. In such a context, demands for the king to undertake further action in order to restore good governance in his realm were inevitable.[15]

By early 1310, leading magnates and ecclesiastics were able to persuade Edward to allow them to reflect and offer advice on the present state of the realm and the need for reform. In March of that year, Edward, by charter, granted them royal authority to proceed in their work and in the following months the Ordainers, who included the earls of Lancaster, Lincoln, Pembroke, Warwick and Hereford, as well as the archbishop of Canterbury, eventually compiled a set of forty-one Ordinances. These ranged over issues that were both general and specific, including pronouncements on royal finance, the need for the king to call and consult with parliament on matters of state, the reform of the royal household, and the maintenance of fair and accessible justice, in both civil and criminal matters [**3c**]. In most respects they reflect issues that were already familiar from the thirteenth century, with control of royal responsibility and a funnelling of power away from the more arbitrary exercise of personal kingship to a more constrained governance informed by the king's magnates. By October 1311, the Ordainers' main work was done and the Ordinances, with the king's formal approval, were published.

It is clear that the work of the Ordainers was acted upon immediately. Chancery writs and mandates illustrate the range of activity in response to the directions of the Ordinances. So, for instance, the revocation of gifts granted in the early years of the reign is illustrated by recall of grants to individuals such as Henry de Beaumont [**3d**]. The cessation of collection of the new custom was also ordered in October 1311 and exchequer receipts indicate that it was implemented straight away; the new custom on wool would not be collected again until the revocation of the majority of the Ordinances at the York parliament in 1322.[16] Use of the privy seal also declined, possibly revealing some apparent adherence to the principle that the king should not act only according to his own whim and judgement.[17] It is also worth noting that there is some indication that Edward, in an instance of his sometimes provocative approach to kingship and one that he came to apply more than once, turned the implementation of the Ordinances upon

15 See, for instance, Maddicott, *Lancaster*, pp. 106–12.

16 See below; also Ormrod, 'The crown and the English economy', table 5.1.

17 Trueman, 'Privy seal', pp. 611–25.

their authors, the Ordainers. So, for example, on 20 and 21 October 1311, explicitly following the precepts of the Ordinances (cl. 7), he revoked the gift granted to one of the Ordainers, Robert Clifford, an act that has the imprimatur of Edward himself in that it was sealed by privy seal and undertaken at his royal residence of Langley (King's Langley) [**3d**].[18] That the Ordainers sought to counter this by demanding, in the so-called 'household ordinances' – published in November 1311 and not ratified by the crown – that the gifts to Clifford and certain others should be respected illustrates the intersection of broad political agendas with personal claims and ambitions; Edward's return of the grant of Skipton-in-Craven to Clifford almost immediately, also in November 1311, adds to the sense of calculated adjustments in the quest for support and some acquiescence to the will of the Ordainers [**3e**].[19]

In many respects, the Ordinance of greatest immediate importance was the one condemning Gaveston and calling for his permanent exile. The author of the *Vita Edwardi Secundi* quotes only this clause in his account of the Ordinances, noting that he refrained from including the full text of the Ordinances as this 'would break the flow of this narrative and prove tedious to readers'. He also suggested that 'the Ordinance which expelled Piers Gaveston from England seemed more welcome to many than the rest, for when people examined the Ordinances they at once turned to it …'[20] [**3f**] Gaveston was briefly exiled from Dover, Edward accompanying him to his point of departure in October 1311. However, contrary to the Ordinances and in an act sure to enflame Edward's opponents, Gaveston almost immediately broke the terms of his exile and returned to England within a matter of months. Joining Edward at York by Christmas 1311, he celebrated the birth of his daughter; thereafter he and Edward appear to have fled, Edward seeking to preserve his favourite from the vengeful baronage, who had distributed their forces across the country in pursuit of the returned exile. A hasty retreat from Newcastle-upon-Tyne in January

18 *CPR 1307–1313*, p. 395; *CFR 1307–1327*, p. 105.

19 'Clifford, Robert, first Lord Clifford (1274–1314)', *Oxford Dictionary of National Biography*(www.oxforddnb.com/view/10.1093/ref:odnb/9780198614128.001.0001/odnb-9780198614128-e-5658); contrary to the statement there, Clifford was an Ordainer and is identified as such in the Annals of London [**3b**].

20 *Vita Edward Secundi*, ed. Childs, p. 35. On the likely tedium of the Ordinances for readers, see also *Bridlington*, p. 35: 'if it were written down here, because of its long-windedness it might cause readers boredom'.

1312 saw Edward leave significant amounts of jewellery and horses behind to be seized by the Earl of Lancaster, a point of contention in the months after Gaveston's death. Gaveston, briefly secured by Edward in Scarborough castle, surrendered into the custody and protection of the Earl of Pembroke, Aymer de Valence, but soon fell into the hands of the hardliners, including the earls of Warwick, Lancaster and Hereford. Condemned to death by the Ordainers, who in the days and hours before the killing joined in pacts of mutual security [**4c**], Gaveston was marched from Warwick on to the neighbouring lands of the Earl of Lancaster and beheaded. Judging by the tone of the chroniclers and annalists, his death appears to have been widely celebrated, a perspective also reflected in political songs and commentaries [**5a–c**].

Gaveston's execution, or judicial murder, at Blacklow Hill brought to a close the first and tumultuous phase of the reign. The death did not, however, end the dispute between the king and his opponents; instead, as Maddicott notes,[21] it set the seal on the next decade of English politics and would eventually help bring the country to civil war.

1 The death of Edward I and the accession of Edward II

Contemporary chroniclers, such as the authors of the Vita Edward Secundi *and the* Annales Paulini *– as far as can be judged, men of some standing in national administration and in possession, therefore, of a reasonably informed view of medieval government and governance – were quick to identify the incipient weakness in Edward II's first year; they point to the hasty recall of Gaveston as a first and important act of folly. For fuller assessment of Edward in the chronicles, see below [49].*

(a) *Vita Edward Secundi*, pp. 4–5

Edward, the first after the Conquest, died on the day of the translation of St Thomas in the thirty-fifth year of his reign,[22] and his son Edward II began his reign, a strong young man in about his twenty-third year. He did not fulfil his father's ambition, but turned his mind to other things. He recalled Piers Gaveston, who had recently abjured the realm of England at his father's command.

21 Maddicott, *Lancaster*, p. 130.

22 7 July 1307.

(b) *Annales Paulini*, p. 257

In the same year, that is, of grace 1307, and the thirty-fifth of the reign of King Edward, with the King Edward, the fourth of that name, worthy of all praise, dying on the seventh day of the month of July, on the eighth day of the same month his son reigned in his stead, and he was the fifth king called Edward. He immediately recalled Piers Gaveston from exile to England. In which condition, by rejecting the advice of age, like Rehoboam,[23] he accepted the counsel of youths who were with him from adolescence, and chief amongst these and above all others, Piers Gaveston; as a result he was lulled into moderating or rather forgetting altogether that sadness which bereavement had briefly or hardly at all brought to him.

2 The restoration of Piers Gaveston and early signs of tension

(a) The grant of the earldom of Cornwall, 6 August 1307

The grant of the earldom of Cornwall to Gaveston was an act of extraordinary elevation of his favourite by Edward; intended for his eldest half-brother, Thomas of Brotherton, the grant by Edward of such a substantial and lucrative earldom instantly promoted Gaveston to the highest levels. Chaplais's discussion of the diplomatic and marginalia of the grant makes clear it was one half of a policy of promotion, of which the marriage to Margaret de Clare was the other.[24] *It is noteworthy that the later staunch opponents of Gaveston and the king were witnesses to the grant.*

Foedera, II.i, p. 2

The king to the archbishops, bishops, abbots, priors, earls, barons, justices, sheriffs, reeves, ministers, and all bailiffs, and subjects, greetings.

Know that we grant, concede and, by this our charter, confirm, to our chosen and faithful knight, Piers de Gaveston, all our earldom of

23 Rehoboam, the son of King Solomon, rejected the advice of his elders and, as a consequence, lost much of his kingdom, 3 Kings (1 Kings) 12:8; 2 Chronicles 10:8. The message was not lost on a number of contemporary commentators, as, for instance, *Vita Edwardi Secundi*, pp. lvi, 32–3, 62–3.

24 Chaplais, *Piers Gaveston*, pp. 31–4.

Cornwall, with castles, towns, manors, hundreds, demesnes, homages, and free tenements, rents, customaries, villeins, their chattels and off-spring, knights fees, advowsons of churches, abbacies, priories, hospitals, chapels, fairs, markets, warrens, wrecks of sea and all other liberties, free customs, rights and other things whatsoever relating to the abovesaid earldom. And also the office of sheriff of the said county, stannary and all minerals of tin and lead, which were [held by] Edmund, once Earl of Cornwall, in the above earldom.

[a list of particular towns, manors and associated rights follows]

To have and to hold to the same Piers and his heirs, from us and our heirs, with all appurtenances to the abovesaid earldom, castles, manors, towns, honours, lands and tenements, hundreds, sheriff's office, tannaries, minerals and chases pertaining, as abovesaid, in perpetuity, in exactly the same way that the abovesaid Edmund held them at the day of his death and how they came into the hands of the lord Edward once king of England, of celebrated memory, our father.

[The same Piers] to perform for us and our heirs the service of three knights' fees for all our service for us and our heirs.

[further details of the earldom and its extent follow]

In witness of this,
Henry de Lacy, Earl of Lincoln
Thomas, Earl of Lancaster
John de Warenn, Earl of Surrey
Humphrey de Bohun, Earl of Hereford and Essex, and Constable of England
Edmund, Earl of Arundel
John de Brittany, Earl of Richmond
Aymer de Valence, and others.

Given by our hand at Dumfries, the sixth day of August in the first year of our reign [1307].

(b) Authority additional to the appointment of Gaveston as *custos regni*

CPR 1307–1313, p. 43

Jan. 18. Dover. Authority for Peter de Gaveston, Earl of Cornwall, previously appointed keeper of the kingdom during the king's sojourn beyond seas, to issue licences to elect, grant royal assents, make restitutions of temporalities, collate and present to prebends and other ecclesiastical benefices, and deal with wardships and marriages during the king's absence from the kingdom. By K.[25]

(c) Boulogne Agreement, 31 January 1308

Phillips, *Aymer de Valence*, appendix 4.1, pp. 316–17

To all of those etc. Antony, by the Grace of God Patriarch of Jerusalem and Bishop of Durham, Henry de Lacy, Earl of Lincoln, John de Warenne, Earl of Surrey and Sussex, Aymer de Valence, Earl of Pembroke, Humphrey de Bohun, Earl of Hereford and Essex, Robert Clifford, Payn Tybetot, Henry de Grey, John Botetourt, John de Berewyk, greetings to our lord. According to the honour of God and holy church and to the profit of our lord the king of England and his realm we are obliged by fealty to the said lord the king to keep his honour and the rights of his crown, we the abovenamed, being of one will and of common assent, agree to place all our fealty, power, effort and aid in so far as we can and know to guard and maintain the honour of our said lord the king and to redress the things that have been done before this time against his honour and the right of his crown, and the oppressions which have been done and are still done from day to day to his people and these amend to the honour of God and of our lord the king and of all of his abovesaid people. And in order to do these things well and faithfully (in all points as is stated below, we truly the abovenamed and each of us has sworn on the saints and has submitted and each and every one of us submits ourselves to the jurisdiction of the honourable father Sire Anthony by the Grace of God, Patriarch of Jerusalem and Bishop of Durham with power to excommunicate and place outside of communion of holy church he or they who come against the below covenants). In witness of this matter each of us, the above-named, have placed our seals to this document.

25 'By K', a nineteenth-century abbreviation from the editors of the Calendars of Chancery Rolls, indicates that the original chancery writ was sealed with the great seal by the king's express authority: *per ipsum regem, CCR 1307–1313*, pp. v–x.

(d) The coronation oath

Foedera, II.i, p. 36; *EHD*, III, no. 97, pp. 525–6

Sire, are you willing to grant and preserve and by your oath confirm to the people of England the laws and customs granted to them by former kings of England, your righteous and godly predecessors, and particularly the laws, customs and liberties granted to the clergy and the people by the glorious King St Edward, your predecessor.

Response: I grant and promise them.

Sire, will you for God and holy church and for the clergy and for the people keep peace and accord in God, to the best of your ability, intact?

Response: I will.

Sire, will you in all your judgements have impartial and proper justice and discretion done in compassion and truth to the best of your ability?

Response: I will.

Sire, do you agree to maintain and preserve the laws and rightful customs which the community of your realm shall have chosen and will you defend and enforce them to the honour of God to the best of your ability?

Response: I agree and promise.

(e) The articles of the Earl of Lincoln, March to April 1308

EHD, III, no. 98, pp. 525–6

The first undertaking and the ordinance presented by the Earl of Lincoln to the king.

Homage and the oath of allegiance are more in respect of the crown than in respect of the king's person and are more closely related to the crown than to the king's person; and this is evident because, before the right to the crown has descended to the person, no allegiance is due to him. And, therefore, if it should befall that the king is not guided by reason, then, in order that the dignity of the crown may be preserved the lieges are bound by the oath made to the crown to reinstate the king in the dignity of the crown or else they would not have kept their oath. The next question is how the king should be reinstated, whether by an action at law or by constraint. It is not, however, possible by recourse to the law to obtain redress, because there would be no other judges than the royal judges, in which case, if the king's will was not accordant with right reason, the only result would be that error would be maintained and confirmed. Hence, in order that the oath may be saved, when the king will not right a wrong and remove that which is hurtful to the people at large and prejudicial to the crown, and is so adjudged by the people, it requires that the evil must be removed by constraint, for the king is bound by his oath to govern his people, and his lieges are bound to govern with him and in support of him.

As regards the person who is talked about, the people ought to judge him as one not to be suffered because he disinherits the crown and, as far as he is able, impoverishes it. By his counsel he withdraws the king from the counsel of his realm and puts discord between the king and his people, and he draws to himself the allegiance of men by as stringent an oath as does the king, thereby making himself a peer of the king and so enfeebling the crown, for by means of the property of the crown he has gathered to himself and put under his control the power of the crown, so that by his evil deeds it lies solely with him to determine whether the crown should be destroyed and he himself made sovereign of the realm, in treason towards his liege lord and the crown, contrary to his fealty.

Since the lord king has undertaken to maintain him against all men on every point, entirely without regard to right reason, as behoves the king, he cannot be judged or attainted by an action brought according to the law, and therefore seeing he is a robber of the people and a traitor to his liege lord and his realm, the people rate him as a man attainted and judged, and pray the king that, since he is bound by his coronation oath to keep the laws that the people shall choose, he will accept and execute the award of the people.

(f) *Vita Edwardi Secundi*, pp. 10–13

After this, seeing that by such discord the whole country could be put in danger, and thinking of the future, in case the recent turmoil should spread its roots so that, having become rooted, it could not easily be weeded out, those who were of the king's council formed a plan by which the king and his barons might once more be brought together in friendship and harmony. By common consent therefore the earls, barons and other great men of the land were summoned to discuss peace, and they arrived at London with an armed force, as they feared treachery; there the king was waiting for them. Then, when the matter had been discussed and rediscussed for a long time, yet without a settlement (for many, on whose advice and judgement the matter hung, wished to please each side and so wavered), finally, after many and varied circumlocutions, since they could not agree on anything else, the king promised and granted to the barons that Piers Gaveston should leave England. Furthermore, sentence of excommunication was pronounced upon Piers by the archbishops and bishops if he should delay in England beyond the appointed term. Accordingly, the term was fixed, namely St John the Baptist's day, on which same feast a year before the same Piers had first forsworn the same land. When the appointed day arrived therefore, the lord king and Piers set out for Bristol with a great following; and there after a little, having taken leave of the king, Piers crossed the sea with a large household and took himself off to Ireland, and by command of the lord king of England the whole country was subjected to his authority and power.

(g) *CPR 1307–1313*, p. 83

June 15. Reading. Appointment, during pleasure, of Richard de Burgh, Earl of Ulster, to be the king's lieutenant in Ireland.

June 16. Reading. Appointment, during pleasure, of Peter [Piers] de Gavaston [*sic*], Earl of Cornwall, to be the king's lieutenant in Ireland, with power to remove and appoint justices, sheriffs, bailiffs and other ministers.

...

Authority for Peter [Piers] de Gaveston to present to churches and other benefices in Ireland, the right of presentation or collation to which may be in the king.

Memorandum. The above letters were read and sealed before the king, the king himself commanding them to be sealed ...

3 The Ordinances of 1311

(a) The Statute of Stamford, 1309

The Annals of London record the Statute of Stamford and its context; the original text is also available in Statutes, *I, pp. 154–6.*[26]

Annales Londonienses, pp. 157–62

And later in the same year, at a parliament held at Stamford on the Monday after the feast of St James [28 July 1309], it was formally agreed with the assent of certain earls and barons that should he conduct himself well and truly towards everyone he should live in peace. But after a little while, with the wicked past still a strong memory, he returned to his customary behaviour and more, treating the earls and barons almost as his servants and thereby sowed discord between the king and his earls. On account of which, as well as the prises and oppressions exacted by the king's servants, the people were on the verge of rising. In this parliament the earls and barons granted the king a twenty-fifth for his Scottish war, unjustly held as it was by Robert Bruce.[27] And henceforth so that the prises should not be seized, they ordained and made statute as follows:

...

Here begins the Statute of Stamford. These are the articles that the King Edward, father of the present King Edward, at his parliament at Westminster, at Lent, in the twenty-eighth year of his reign [1300], amongst the other things he ordained in an attempt to alleviate the grievances which his people had suffered on account of the wars that have been, and to amend their state and in order that they may be readier in his service and more keen to aid him in so far as is possible, the Ordinances were produced in the following manner:

> In the first place, because there is a great grievance in our realm and incalculable damage on account of the fact that the king and the members of his retinue, including both aliens and denizens, take prises wheresoever they happen to be in the kingdom, and seize the goods of people both clerical and lay either without payment or with payment which is less than the value of the goods, it is ordained that, throughout the realm, no one should takes

26 For the Statute of Stamford, see also *PROME*, Parliaments of April 1309 (Westminster) and July 1309 (Stamford).

27 For the 1309 lay subsidy, see Jurkowski et al., *Lay Taxes*, p. 30.

prises unless it be the king's takers and his purveyors for the king's household, taking no more than is required for the household, and the prises that are taken throughout the land should be for food and drink or for other essentials for the household and payment should be made to or agreement made with those from whom the prises are taken. And each of those of the king's takers, purveyors or buyers, should from now on carry their warranty upon them, either the great seal or the privy seal of the king, containing their authority to take those things which they require as purveyance. They shall show this warrant to those from whom they are to take the prise before they do so. And that these takers, purveyors or buyers of the king take no more than the food and drink which is required for the king and his household and those of his children. And that they take nothing for those who are at wages or for any others and that they report to the household and in the Wardrobe, regarding fully all of the prises collected, without making elsewhere any gifts or payments of the things which were taken as the prises of the king. And if any taker of the king's household, with the warrant which he has, takes prises or payments in any way other than is said above, and complaint is made to the steward or the marshall of the king's household, let the truth be established, and if he shall be convicted, let the plaintiffs be fully recompensed and let him be thrown out of the king's service for ever and be imprisoned at the king's pleasure. And if anyone takes prises without warrant and carries them off against the will of him whose goods they are, let him be immediately arrested by the people of the place where the prise was taken and thrown into the nearest gaol, and if he shall be convicted, let that be done to him as would be done to a thief, should the quantity of goods justify this. And as for making prises in fairs and large towns and ports for the great wardrobe of the king, the takers shall have as their common warrant the great seal and, concerning the things that they are to take, let them have the authority of the seal of the keeper of the wardrobe; and concerning the things taken by these prises, their number and their quantity and their value, let an indenture be made between the takers and the overseers of the fairs, mayor or chief bailiff of the town or port, under the scrutiny of the merchants whose goods were taken as prise, and suffer nothing more to be taken as prise other than that agreed in the indenture, and that this indenture shall be taken to the wardrobe under the seal of the keeper, mayor or bailiffs abovesaid and remain there until the account of the keeper of the king's wardrobe. And if it shall be found that anyone has taken otherwise than they ought to have done, let him be punished upon the account of the keeper of the king's wardrobe according to his desert. And if anyone should take such prises without warrant and shall be convicted of so doing, let be done to him as to those who take prises for the royal household without warrant, as abovesaid. And it is not the intention of the king nor of his council to diminish, by this statute, any right of the king concerning ancient prises, dues and customs, such as those relating to wine or Other goods, but that it be preserved by him fully in all points.

Concerning the state of the steward and the marshall and the pleas which they should hold and in what manner, it is ordained that they should not hold plea of free tenement, nor of debt, nor of covenant, nor of contracts of people in general, but only of trespass against the household and other trespasses committed within the verge, and of contract and covenant that someone of the king's household has made with another of the same household and within the same household, and in no other place. And no plea of trespass shall be made that is not set in motion by them before the king leaves the verge where the trespass was committed. And if, by chance, the matter cannot be determined within the bounds of the verge, the pleas before the steward shall cease and the plaintiffs shall go to common law. The steward shall not consider recognizances of debt nor other matters unless concerning the people of the household as abovesaid; nor shall they hold any other plea by obligation made at the distress of the steward and the marshalls. And if the steward or the marshalls do anything against this Ordinance, what they shall do shall be held as nothing.

Let no writ henceforth issue under privy seal that concerns the common law. The present king, at the request of the good people of this realm, having regard to the undersaid things, wishes and commands that from henceforth these articles shall be fully followed and kept in every respect. As regards the request of the said good people as to the right of trying pleas and doing so at the gates of the king's castles, the constables of these castles should not distrain people to plead before them, neither from outside the county nor from within, other than was accustomed from ancient times.

And as regards the customs that the king receives through his ministers, that is to say for each tun of wine 2 shillings, for each cloth which alien merchants bring into his country 2 shillings and for each pound of merchandise, two pence,[28] the king wishes, at the request of the said good people, that the said customs of wine, cloths, and merchandise, should cease at his will, in order to discover from this advice what profit or advantage will accrue to him and to his people by ceasing the prise and these customs, and then the king will take counsel according to the advantage that he will see, saving always to the king the ancient prises and customs due and approved from ancient times.

As regards the other requests that the said good people made to the king, the king freely grants these and charges his chancellor and his other ministers to keep them carefully. And the king wills that should anyone feel aggrieved in any point, against the said commandment, as regards the said articles granted by him, and brings his plea, that the chancellor shall offer him remedy by writ according to his case and according to that which should be done.

28 The correct custom on general merchandise was actually 3d. in the pound as set out in *Carta Mercatoria* (1303); see Gras, *Early English Customs*, p. 66.

(b) The appointment of the Ordainers

Annales Londonienses, pp. 167–72

... In the same year [1310] the king held a parliament at London, where the abovesaid prelates, earls and barons gathered on the third day before the kalends of March [27 February]. They remained there until Palm Sunday [12 April], discussing the order and the state of the whole realm and they presented the following petitions to the king:

The articles of the prelates, earls and barons

> To our lord the king illustrating the great perils and damages, which grow from day to the day, if they are not quickly redressed, and threaten destruction of the franchises of holy church, the disinheritance and dishonour of yourself and your royal power, the disinheritance of your crown, and the damage of all those of your realm, both rich and poor. And from these perils and damages, neither you nor the good people of your land shall escape unless quick remedy is applied following the advice of prelates, earls and barons and the wisest of your realm:
>
> To begin, given that you are ruler of the land and obliged to maintain peace in your land you are subject to unacceptable counsel and bad advice, for which you are held and esteemed in great shame in all lands; so that you are impoverished and devoid of all manner of treasure so that you have insufficient with which to defend your land or to maintain your household unless you take the goods of holy church and your poor people by the extortions of your ministers, who pay nothing, against the form of the Great Charter, the force of which should be held and maintained.
>
> Also, sire, whereas our lord the king, your father, in the protection of the Lord, left to you all of your lands in their entirety, in England, Ireland, and the greater part of Scotland, in good state, you have almost lost your land of Scotland and your rule has been gravely disrupted in England, Ireland, without the agreement of your baronage and without cause.
>
> Also, sire, the community of your realm has given you the twentieth penny of their goods as aid for your war in Scotland and a twenty-fifth penny in place of prises and other grievances; the which money was fully levied, and by inappropriate counsel foolishly spent and wasted, and your war in no way advanced nor your poor people protected from prises or other grievances, which grow more grievous from one day to the next. Because of which, sire, the said good people humbly pray for the security of you and them and the crown, the which they are obliged to maintain on account of their allegiance, that you will assent to them, that these perils and others can be ejected and redressed by the Ordinance of your baronage.

On account of this, the king granted to certain of them that they could act upon the health and state of the realm, in the following way:

The king's charter

> Edward, by the grace of God king of England, lord of Ireland and Duke of Aquitaine, to all those who see or hear these letters, greetings.
>
> Since we have granted to the honour of God and for the good of our lord the king and of his realm by our free will to the prelates, earls and barons of our said realm that they could select certain persons from amongst themselves and others, of sufficient number, during the time of their power, that being from the feast of Michaelmas next for the year following, to ordain and establish the state of the household of our realm and our household, according to what is right and reasonable, we grant by these our letters, that those so elected from amongst the said prelates, earls and barons, shall have full power to ordain for the state of our realm and household, in such manner that the Ordinances shall be made to the honour of God and to the honour and profit of holy church and to the honour of ourselves and to the profit of our people, according to right and reason, and the oath which we made at our coronation. And we wish that those chosen and all those who are of our lordship and allegiance should hold to and keep in all their points the Ordinances which shall be made by the prelates, earls and barons who will be chosen for this and by those called to them for this; and that they may, for their security, bind each other and swear mutual oaths without challenge from us or our men.
>
> And in case any of the persons so chosen shall be hindered by death or illness or reasonable cause, which God forbid, from making the said Ordinances, that those who shall be present shall have power to proceed with the said Ordinances by themselves, or to call other persons to them to make the Ordinances, according to what they will see to be to the greater honour of us and to the profit of us and of our people. In witness of which we have produced these letters patent. Given at Westminster on the 16th day of March, in the third year of our reign.

Then the prelates and earls and barons wrote the following letter to the lord king:

> To all those who see or hear these letters, Robert, by divine sufferance, Archbishop of Canterbury, primate of all England; Ralph of London, John of Lincoln, Simon of Salisbury, Henry of Winchester, John of Norwich, John of Bath and Wells, Walter of Worcester, Walter of Exeter, David of St David, by the same sufferance, bishops; Gilbert de Clare of Gloucester and Hertford, Thomas of Lancaster, Henry de Lacy of Lincoln and Salisbury, Humphrey de Bohun of Essex and Hereford, John of Brittany and of Richmond, Aymer

de Valence of Pembroke, Guy de Beauchamp of Warwick, Edmund Arundel, earls; Henry Lancaster, Henry Percy, Hugh de Veer, Robert Clifford, Robert fitz Payn, William Marshal, John Lovel, Ralph fitz William, Payn Tybetot, John Botetourt, Bartholomew de Badlesmere, John de Grey, John Crombwell, greetings to our lord. As our very dear lord, Edward, by the grace of God king of England, lord of Ireland and Duke of Aquitaine, to the honour of God and for the good of our lord the king and of his realm has granted by his free will to us and to other prelates, earls and barons of the said realm that we could select certain persons from amongst ourselves and others, of sufficient number, during the time of their power, that being from the feast of Michaelmas next for the year following, to ordain and establish the state of the household of our said lord the king, according to what is right and reasonable, and those so elected shall have full power to ordain for the state of the household and of our said lord the king and his said realm, in such manner that the Ordinances shall be made to the honour of God and to the honour and profit of holy church and to the honour of our said lord the king and to the profit of his people, according to right and reason, and the oath which the king made at his coronation. And moreover the king has willed that the persons chosen and all those of his lordship and of his allegiance shall keep the Ordinances to be used as above in all points, and that they may make security, bind and take oath to do so without challenge from the king or any of his own. And in case any of the persons so chosen shall be hindered by death or illness or reasonably cause, which God forbid, from making the said Ordinances, that those who shall be present shall have power to proceed with the said Ordinances by themselves, or to call other persons to them for this purpose, as shall seem to them good for the honour of the king and the profit of him and the kingdom, as is more fully contained in the letters patent. We grant on behalf of ourselves and our successors and heirs, that the grant which our lord the king has made us in the abovesaid manner, shall not be treated hereafter as custom or usage, nor used in prejudice against law and reason, as is above said, nor that the abovesaid grant shall be interpreted in a way other than appropriate to his consideration and free will, and that the power of the Ordainers to create the Ordinances shall last no longer than the abovesaid term. In witness of which things, we have added our seals to this open letter. Given at London the 17th day of March, the year of grace 1310, and the third year of the reign of the King Edward, son of the King Edward.

Then the great of the realm elected from their number one archbishop and six bishops, as below, eight earls and five barons, below written, namely:

… Bishops: Archbishop of Canterbury, London, Salisbury, Chester, Norwich, St Davids, Llandaff. Earls: Gloucester, Lancaster, Lincoln, Pembroke, Hereford, Warwick, Richmond, Arundel. Barons: Hugh de

Vere, Hugh Courtenay, Robert Clifford, William Marshal, William Martyn.

*A list of six preliminary Ordinances follow, addressing such matters as maintenance of the king's peace and of the principles of Magna Carta, the restriction of gifts, effectively bribes, to the Ordainers or to anyone else, and removal of the advantages enjoyed by alien merchants. These presaged the fuller set of Ordinances that followed later in the next year, as below [**3c**].*

(c) The Ordinances, 1311

*The following offers a selection of the 1311 Ordinances, of which there were forty-one in total. The selection is intended to offer a sense of the core aims of the Ordainers and their more particular targets. Other clauses from the Ordinances, not repeated here, are included elsewhere in this volume [**3f, clause 20; 16b, clauses 29, 40**].*

Statutes, I, 157–67; *EHD*, III, no. 100, pp. 527–39

The new Ordinances made at London in the 5th year of the reign of our lord King Edward son of King Edward [1311]

Edward by the grace of God king of England, lord of Ireland and duke of Aquitaine to all those to whom these letters come, greeting, know that as on 16 March in the 3rd year of our reign to the honour of God and for the good of ourselves and of our realm we granted of our own free will by our letters patent to the prelates, earls and barons of our said realm that they could choose certain persons from the prelates, earls and barons whom they saw fit to call to them, and also granted by the same letters to those who should be chosen, whoever they might be, by the said prelates, earls and barons, full power of ordering the state of our household and of our aforementioned realm in such a way that their Ordinances should be made to the honour of God and the honour and profit of holy church and the honour of ourselves and our profit and the profit of our people in accordance with right and reason and the oath we took at our coronation, as is more fully contained in our said letters; and the honourable father in God Robert by God's grace archbishop of Canterbury, primate of all England, the bishops, earls and barons chosen for this purpose by virtue of our said letters have ordained on the aforesaid things as follows.

Because through evil and deceptive council our lord the king and all his subjects are dishonoured in all lands and in addition the crown is in many respects reduced and dismembered, and his lands of Gascony, Ireland

and Scotland on the point of being lost if God does not give an improvement, and his kingdom of England on the point of rebelling because of oppressions, prises and molestations and these things have been known and shown, our lord the king of his own free will granted to the prelates, earls and barons and other good people of his realm that certain persons should be chosen to order and establish the state of his household and of his realm as appears more fully from the commission of our lord king made on the matter: Wherefor we Robert by the grace of God archbishop of Canterbury, primate of all England, the bishops, earls and barons, chosen by virtue of the said commission, ordain to the honour of God and of holy church and to honour of the king and of his realm as follows.

1 In the first place we ordain that the Ordinances previously made by us and shown to the king be held and kept, which are written next below.[29] In the first place it is ordained that holy church have all its liberties to the extent that she ought to have.

2 Again, it is ordained that the king's peace be firmly kept throughout the realm so that everyone can safely go, come and abide in safety according to the law and usage of the realm.

3 Again, it is ordained to pay off the king's debts and restore his estate and the more honourably maintain it, that no gift of land or rent or liberty or escheat or wardship or marriage or bailiwick be made to any of the said Ordainers during their power under the said Ordinance nor to anyone else without the counsel and assent of the said Ordainers or of the greater part of them …

4 Again, it is ordained that the customs of the king be kept and received by people of the kingdom itself and not by aliens, and that the issue and profits of the said customs … shall come entirely to the king's exchequer … to maintain the household of the king and otherwise for his profit so that the king can live of his own without taking prises other than the ancient due and accustomed ones and that all others shall cease.

5 Again, it is ordained that all alien merchants who have received the profits of the customs of the kingdom … be arrested with all their goods … until they have rendered reasonable account of all that they have received …

6 Again, it is ordained that the Great Charter be kept in all its points in such a way that if there is in the said charter any point that is

29 These first six Ordinances were issued as preliminary Ordinances at the start of the Ordainers' work in the spring of 1310; as noted above, they are included as the first of the 'New Ordinances' of 1311, as also recorded in *Annales Londonienses*, pp. 173–4.

obscure or doubtful, let it be made clear by the said Ordainers ... when they see an opportunity during their power.

7 And then again, because the crown is so reduced and dismembered by divers gifts, we ordain that all gifts, made to the king's detriment ... since we were given our commission, of castles, towns, lands and tenements and bailiwicks, and wardships and marriages, escheats and releases ... be revoked ...

9 Because the king ought not to undertake the act of war against anyone, or go out of his kingdom without the common assent of his baronage for the many perils that could happen to him and his kingdom, we ordain that hereafter the king shall not go out of his kingdom or undertake against anyone the act of war without the common assent of his baronage, and that in parliament, and if he does otherwise and for such undertaking has his feudal service summoned, the summons shall be as null. And if it happens that the king undertakes the act of war against anyone or goes out of the land with the assent of his baronage and needs to appoint a guardian in his kingdom, then he shall appoint him with the common assent of his baronage, and that in parliament.

10 And because it is feared that the people of the land will rise on account of the prises and divers oppressions inflicted before this time, particularly because it was formerly ordained that our lord the king should live of his own without taking prises other than the ancient, due and accustomed ones and that all others should cease, and nevertheless prises are taken every day contrary to this Ordinance as before, we ordain that all prises shall cease from now on saving to the king and to others to whom they are due of right the ancient, rightful, and due prises. And if any prises are taken contrary to the aforesaid Ordinance whoever by or whatever his condition, that is, if any one appearing to purvey for the king's use or anyone else's takes corn, wares, merchandise or other kinds of goods against the will of those to whom they belong and does not immediately render the money to the true value, if he cannot have respite for it with the good will of the seller, in accordance with what is contained in the Great Charter about prises taken by constables of castles and their bailiffs, and leaving out of account as an exception the aforesaid due prises, notwithstanding the commission he has, let the pursuit by hue and cry be raised against him and let him be taken to the nearest gaol of the king and let the common law be applied to him as a robber or thief, if he is convicted of that.

13 And because the king has been badly guided and counselled by evil counsellors, as is said above, we ordain that all the evil counsellors be ejected and dismissed altogether, so that neither they nor others like them shall be near him any more, or retained in the king's service, and that other suitable people be put in their place, and in the same way be it done with the attendants and the servants and others who are in the king's household who are not suitable.

22 Also because Sir Henry de Beaumont has received from our lord the king to the loss and dishonour of the king, since the time of the Ordinance of the Ordainers to which the king agreed, the kingdom of Man and other lands, rents, liberties and bailiwicks and has caused lands and tenements, liberties and bailiwicks to be given to others contrary to this Ordinance, and because he has badly advised the king contrary to this oath, We ordain that he be removed from the king's counsel for ever and that he come no more near the king anywhere – unless it be at the common summons of parliament or in war if the king wishes to have him – save by common assent of the archbishop, bishops, earls and barons and that in full parliament …

32 Because the law of the land and common right have often been impeded by letters issued under the king's privy seal, to the great harm of the people, we ordain that from now on the law of the land and common right be not impeded or interfered with by letters of the said seal, and if anything is done by contrary to right or the law of the land in any offices of the court of our lord the king or elsewhere by such letters issued under the privy seal, it shall avail nothing and be held for nought.

41 Likewise we ordain that the aforementioned Ordinances shall be maintained and kept in all their points, and that our lord the king shall have them put under his great seal and sent into every county of England to be made public, held and firmly kept, as well within liberties as without …

The which Ordinances shown to us and published the Monday before last Michaelmas [27 September 1311] we agree to, accept and affirm; and we will and grant for us and for our heirs that all the said Ordinances and each of them made according to the form of our letters aforesaid shall be published throughout our kingdom and henceforth firmly kept and held. In witness of which things we have caused these our letters patent to be made. Given at London the 5th day of October in the 5th year of our reign [1311].

(d) Chancery enactments of the Ordinances

CFR 1307–1319, p. 108

1311. Oct. 9. London. Order to Henry de Bello Monte[30] or his lieutenant in the land of Man to deliver the said land to Robert de Leyburn, constable of the castle of Cokermuth, with the issues thereof from the time of the grant thereof to him, to be delivered by Robert to Gilbert Makaskil to whom the king has granted the keeping thereof during pleasure; the king by letters patent dated 16 March, 3 Edward II [1310], having granted to the prelates, earls and barons of the realm that certain persons be elected from them to ordain touching the state of the household and of the realm, and R. archbishop of Canterbury and the others elected having ordained among other things that all gifts of castles, towns, lands, bailiwicks, wards, marriages, escheats and remissions, made by the king after the 16 March, in Gascony, Ireland, Wales, Scotland, and England, be revoked, whereby the king has thought fit to resume into his hands the said land of Man which he granted to the said Henry after the said date. By K. and the whole council.

...

October 24. Langley. Order to the escheator beyond Trent, pursuant to the same Ordinance, to resume into the king's hand the castle and manor of Skipton in Cravene, which the king by charter granted to Robert de Clifford after the same 16 March; the king having ordered Robert to deliver the castle to him, and visiting also that all lands assigned to the king by Robert in exchange for the manor be restored to him. By p.s.[31]

(e) 'Household Ordinances'

Annales Londonienses, pp. 198–202

But after the abovesaid Ordinances were published by the lord king and ratified throughout the whole of England, the Ordainers discussed

30 Henry de Beaumont, brother to Isabella de Vescy, a confidante at court of Queen Isabella; see Ordinance clause 22, above, and also clause 23, *EHD*, III, no. 100, p. 534.

31 For which order, see also *CPR 1307–1313*, p. 395. 'By p.s.' indicates the use of the great seal in confirming this order was made through the authority of the king's privy seal; the unrestrained use of the latter by the king was also an issue of complaint for the Ordainers: see [**3c**], Ordinances of 1311, clause 32.

the household and servants of the king, and, in the following form, petitioned the king that these servants should be removed from office:

> Let it be revealed to our lord the king, that he should keep and maintain the Ordinances concerning gifts, excepting the four which were made by agreement; that is to say, to Sir Robert Clifford and Sir Guy Ferre, Sir Edmund de Mauley, and Sir William de Sulleye.
>
> Also in respect of the receipt, it should come to the exchequer, as set out in the Ordinance.
>
> In respect of the alien merchants, who have not accounted in due manner according to the Ordinance, let this matter be remedied by the seizure of their lands, and the bishop of Norwich and Sir Hugh Courtenay shall be auditors of the accounts of the aliens or those of the exchequer;
>
> And that no prises shall be collected henceforth against the Ordinance;
>
> Also that the whole lineage of Piers Gaveston shall be ejected entirely from the realm;
>
> Also that Burgensus de Tilly and his son who is marshall of the exchequer should be ejected from the king and from his service;
>
> Also that all of the Bascles should also be thrown out and returned to their country;
>
> Also that Betrand Caillau and his brother and those of Gascony who are in their company in parts of Cornwall shall leave the land and return to their country because they have brought aid to the king and have fortified castles in breach of the peace;
>
> Also that all of the porters shall be ejected and that he will have no more than in the time of his father;
>
> Also that all of the carters shall be removed from the court, except those which he should expect to have, that is as was in the time of his father;
>
> Also that Robert Lewer, archers and such manner of ribaldry, who are in castles and elsewhere, shall be ejected from the king's pay and not remain in his service, unless he shall be at war, and if any wages shall be owed to them it shall be stopped in order that they make amends to those against whom they have trespassed, either there or wherever they are if anyone brings a plea against them;
>
> Also, because the king has in his household officers who were also in the household of the said Piers Gaveston as much as in his own and that of the queen, let all of those who the steward and custodian of the wardrobe consider unfit be thrown out;

Also that John de Knokyn, his brother, Roger, Ralph de Waltham, and Richard de la Garderobe be ejected;

Also that John de Cherleton, John de la Beche, John de Sapy, William de Vaux, John de Hothum, and Gerard de Salveyn, should be ejected from office and the administration and from the service of the king so that in no way could they come near to him;

Sire, the prelates, earls and barons pray that you do right to the bishop of Chester concerning his lands, buildings and other goods, as according to the Great Charter and the Ordinances;

Also Robert Darcy, Edmund Bacon, and the others who had come out of the palace to pursue Hugh Despenser the Younger should be ejected from the king's Household and from his following, and hold no office under him;

Also that Ingelard de Warle should be ejected from the king, and also Roger de Wellesworth should be ejected, so that in no way could they come near to him;

And also that the sheriffs be ejected and replaced with others according to the Ordinance, and in the manner that was ordained, that is before the Chancellor and Treasurer;

Sire, the prelates, earls and barons pray that you appoint a proper warden for the exchanges, as the present one is inappropriate;

Also it is requested that Robert Turke, John Spereman, Adam de Bray and Ralph Spray be ejected from the king's service because they took prises contrary to the Ordinances, to the damage of the king and of his people;

Also that Emery de Frescobaldi should be banished, following the Ordinance, and his lands seized into the king's hands;

Also Richard Damory should be ejected from the king and from the administration, until his reputation shall be restored, since there are many plaints against him. And let order be made to the steward of Gascony and to the constable of Bordeaux or to their deputies that they should make Hugh Hugelyn come safely by sea to render account at Westminster for the time that he was deputy constable of Bordeaux, also concerning all the matters that pertained to the accounts of the Duchy of Guyenne for the time that the said Emery was constable of Bordeaux;

And because neither the justices nor the other ministers of the forest on both sides of the Trent have not rendered account, they shall be distrained in order that they come to account before the barons and the exchequer on the morrow of the feast of St Hilary [14 January];

And because the said Piers Gaveston holds letters of protection and general attorney, these shall be recalled and nullified because they are contrary to the Ordinances;

Also that the lands of Henry de Beaumont in England and elsewhere shall be seised according to the Ordinance and the kingdom of Man delivered into the custody of a good Englishman;

Also that the castle of Bamburgh shall be seised into the hands of the king, as demanded in the Ordinance;

Also that neither the steward nor the marshall shall hold pleas other than those allowed in the Ordinance, and those pleas which have been held against the Ordinance, since the Ordinance was made, shall count as nothing;

Also that the ministers of the king who have not yet given oath as required by the Ordinances should do so according to the Ordinance;

Also, because it was ordained that the profits of the lands of the Templars should come to the exchequer in their entirety, and in order to achieve this they were given into the custody of certain individuals to respond to the exchequer according to the Ordinance, presently these lands have been regranted into the custody of those held them before contrary to the Ordinance, and these things should be remedied;

Also that the officers of the forests, both on this side and beyond the Trent, which were not seized into the king's hands as required by the Ordinance, shall be seized and that certain good and loyal persons shall be assigned to investigate trespasses and grievances caused by the said officers, and to hear and to determine the pleas according to the form of the Ordinance;

Also since the lands of Piers Gaveston have been taken back into the king's hands and have been regranted even to those who were the officers of the said Piers before now, these officers shall be ejected and others put in their place;

Also that our lord the king appoints the chancellor, chief justice of the one bench and of the other, treasurer, chancellor and chief baron of the exchequer, steward of his household, keeper of the wardrobe, controller, clerk suitable for the keeping of his privy seal, chief keeper of his forests on this side of the Trent and the other, chief clerk of the Common Bench, an escheator for this side of the Trent and another for the other side, a chief keeper of ports and of castles on the coast, and good and sufficient officers in Gascony, Ireland and Scotland, according to the Ordinance.

(f) The Ordinances according to the chroniclers

The author of the Vita Edward Secundi *offers a rather wry assessment of the Ordinances and their interest to a wider readership; he quotes only one clause (20), that relating to Gaveston.*

Vita Edwardi Secundi, pp. 32–7

So the king, moved by their warnings and entreaties, agreed for himself and his successors that the Ordinances, provisions and statutes, by whatever name they may be called, should be held inviolably valid for ever. A copy of the Ordinances was therefore sent under the great seal to every county, and there publicly proclaimed, and commanded to be proclaimed by all. Therefore I did not want to insert them here because it would break the flow of this narrative and prove tedious to readers: but if anyone should say that he is unacquainted with them he will find them in their proper place among the other statutes. However, because the Ordinance which expelled Piers Gaveston from England seemed more welcome to many than the rest, for when people examined the Ordinances they at once turned to it although it did not come first in the list but was tenth or later, and so that the cause of banishment may appear clearly once this Ordinance has been read through, I have therefore inserted that decision in the course of my narrative as very relevant to my theme, word for word as it was read out publicly, in the following form:

> Because it is known and found by the examination of prelates, earls, barons, knights and other good and lawful men of the kingdom, that Piers Gaveston has led the lord king astray, advised the lord king badly and persuaded him deceitfully and in many ways to do wrong; in gathering to himself all the king's treasure which, moreover, he has exported from the country; in attracting to himself men who would remain with him against all people, and this by means of the king's treasure thus acquired from day to day; in lording it over the state of the king and of the crown to the ruin of the king and kingdom; more especially in estranging the lord king's heart from his liege men; in despising their counsel, not permitting good ministers to enforce law and removing good ministers; in appointing from his own circle, both foreigners and others, such persons as, at his command and will, violate justice and the law of the land; in receiving lands and tenements against his homage to the crown, not only before the Ordinances ordained by the Ordainers for the profit of the king and the kingdom, but also afterwards, against the provisions and decrees of the said Ordainers.

Also he maintains robbers and homicides and obtains the lord king's pardons for them, and so encourages other evil-doers to greater boldness in crime. He takes the king into a country at war without the common consent of his barons, to the danger of the king and the destruction of his kingdom; he has blank charters sealed under the king's great seal to the deception and disinheritance of the king and the crown; and all the aforesaid things he did craftily, falsely, and treacherously to the great disgrace and damage of the kingdom, the disinheritance of the crown, and the destruction of the people in many ways.

Moreover, having regard to what was done by the most noble king, father of our present lord king, by whose edict the said Piers abjured and was exiled from the realm of England, and who wished that our lord king his son should renounce the company of this person for all time; bearing in mind, further, that afterwards by the common assent equally of the whole realm and of the king it was decided that the said Piers should leave the realm, and he did leave it, and that he did not return by common assent, but only by the consent of some individuals, who consented to this on condition that after his return he should behave well; and now it is found most certainly that he has behaved badly; for which reason, and on account of his aforesaid wrongdoing, and on account of other things which are likely to happen to the lord king and the people, and in order to foster good harmony between the lord king and his subjects, and to avoid many kinds of discords and dangers, we, the Ordainers, as Ordainers and by virtue of the said royal commission, have decreed that Piers Gaveston, as a public enemy of the king and of the kingdom, shall be utterly cast out and exiled from the kingdom, not only from England, but from Wales, Scotland, Ireland, Gascony, and from every land as well beyond the sea as on this side of the sea subject to the lordship of the king of England, for ever and without return. And that before the feast of All Saints next coming [1 November 1311] he shall leave and completely depart from the kingdom of England and every lordship of the king, and we assign to him in the said form Dover harbour. Nor may he leave the land elsewhere nor from another harbour. And if the said Piers stays in the kingdom of England or elsewhere in the lordship of our king beyond the appointed day, he shall thereafter be treated as an enemy of the kingdom, the king, and the people. And let everyone who shall go against this Ordinance, to delay the said exile, be dealt with as seems expedient when they have been found guilty of it.

And this was the manner of Piers's banishment by decree of the Ordainers.

4 Piers Gaveston: exile and death

(a) *Vita Edwardi Secundi*, pp. 37–9

After the feast of All Saints [1 November 1311], as the king had sworn to stand by the Ordinances of the barons, he arranged for Piers to go into exile, because he planned to provide for him very adequately soon. Before Piers left England, however, on the advice of some who clung to his side, he asked for and obtained from the king letters testifying to his good character and loyalty; and the king put his seal to these letters, and many great men more worthy of reproof than praise for this deed did likewise. Amongst these Gilbert, Earl of Gloucester, a young man moved by the king's entreaties, lent his testimony to these letters. For he confirmed them with his seal, but afterwards, persuaded by wiser counsel and excused on the grounds of his minority, he corrected his mistake and tore the impression of his seal from the letters.

Thus protected by such a testimonial Piers secretly, on account of his enemies, departed to Flanders, almost everyone being ignorant of his destination. After this, the earls, wishing to make further arrangements according to the lord king's Ordinances, declared that Piers's friends and supporters should leave the king's court under penalty of imprisonment, lest they should urge the king to recall Piers once more. At this the king, angered beyond measure that he was not allowed to keep even one member of his household at his own wish, but that, as is provided in the case of an idiot, the ordering of his whole house should depend upon the decision of another, recalled Piers out of hatred for the earls, swearing, as he was wont, on God's soul that he would freely use his own judgement.

And so Piers immediately returned to England at the king's command, by way of Flanders, because he mistrusted the king of France. But though France might be dangerous for him, England was going to be more dangerous. For it so turned out for him that, as is commonly said, 'He falls into Scylla in trying to avoid Charybdis.'

(b) *Annales Londonienses*, pp. 202–8

With these Ordinances now promulgated, neither these nor the first were treated without harm. But the certain Piers Gaveston, of whom mention has been made, judgement having been passed, sought concealment with the lord king and did not quit the realm on the appointed day but on the third day after the feast of All Saints, and not at the stated port but by ship on the river Thames, cutting through a favourably calm sea he touched land *inter Rutenos*,[32] where he remained for a short time. But, before the next Christmas, Piers returned to England and resided at Windsor, and with him came agony for the whole realm. The king, having learnt of his return, and reuniting with Piers, they took the road to York with his household and resided in the north, spending some time here and some there. The lord king organised the arming of the castles in those parts. Also he sent by his writ to the mayor and sheriffs of London informing them that Piers had returned to England under his protection.

> Edward etc. To the mayor and sheriffs of London, Greetings. We send to you by the carrier of these letters under our great seal and we command that you assemble the best men of your jurisdiction, open these letters in their presence and publish the tenor of these letters amongst your said jurisdiction with as much haste as you can muster, as much without the county as within and within franchises as without, so that you do nothing less than that required according to the fealty which you owe us. Given under our privy seal, the 21st day of January in the fifth year of our reign [1312].

> Edward by the Grace of God, etc. to the sheriffs of London:

> Since lord Piers Gaveston, Earl of Cornwall, was recently exiled from our realm against the laws and customs of the same realm, which laws and customs we are obliged to maintain by the oath which we made at our coronation, and that he who was exiled was described as other than good and loyal and that now this same earl shall be returned by our command to this our realm, it is ordered that all those that in any way would challenge the abovesaid laws and customs should come before us. Because we hold him good and loyal to our faith and to our peace, and since we regard him so, we command by our royal power that you do likewise, and that you publish this throughout your jurisdiction. Given at York on the 18th day of January in the fifth year of our reign [1312].

The king also wrote to the mayor and sheriffs of London saying that they should guard the city well against his enemies so that none should enter his city armed without loss of lives and limbs. He addressed all of his towns throughout England and the sea-ports in a similar manner, ordering them to do the same. So when the nobles of

32 The *Ruteni* in classical texts suggest the people living in Aquitaine, centred around Rodez (Aveyron), This may indicate that the author believed, certainly in error, that Piers headed for his Gascon homeland. On the likelihood that he spent part of his exile in Flanders, see Hamilton, *Piers Gaveston*, pp. 91–2.

the realm learnt of such betrayal spreading in the land, and that, given that the king and his underlings now treated the first and second Ordinances with contempt, they had worked in vain, filled with a violent rage they set out to assemble at London in the church of St Paul to decide what should be done. But a little before their arrival, the lord king sent a message to the mayor and sheriffs stating that the nobles should be allowed to come and go freely, safe and sound, to and from the city in such a way that the mayor and sheriffs should keep his city safe for him. These same prelates, earls and barons, ordained that the Earl of Gloucester should be responsible for the whole of Kent, Sussex, and Surrey, as well as London and the south of England, and that the Earl of Hereford should be custodian of Essex and the east whilst the Earl of Lancaster should secure the west and the north of Wales, lest there should be any disorder among the people.[33] Also lord Robert de Clifford and Henry Percy were to guard the border between England and Scotland, to prevent any aid coming from there, in case the king and Piers attempted a treaty with Robert Bruce who had illegally crowned himself king of Scotland during the life of the worthy Edward father of this same Edward and thus reigns there. They also ordained that Aymer de Valence, Earl of Pembroke and John Earl Warenne should follow the king in order to capture the seducer Piers and to advise the king. After this the Earl of Lancaster came with his retinue to Newcastle whilst the king was at Tynemouth with the queen and the said Piers. Those to whom the king had handed the custody of his town, surrendered it to the earl without a siege; the earl entered the town and then the castle where he seized the royal treasure, arms and ninety-seven great horses and arrested all of the king's servants for three days. And when news of this reached the king, he, almost shuddering, immediately took ship with Piers by night and they sailed on a calm sea to Scarborough where they entered the castle and they secured the fortifications. Then the king put the castle, reinforced as it was, into Piers's hands to guard and in order to save his life. From here the king went to the castle of Bromholm and thence to York. Meanwhile Aymer de Valence, John de Warenne and Henry Percy drew near and they besieged the castle of Scarborough, with great force, for three weeks and more; but Piers spoke with them using flattering words and made them act in his favour, the following chirograph recording what was agreed between them:

33 *Venedocia* in the text, the Latin name for the Welsh princedom of Gwynedd.

To all those who hear or see this letter, lord Aymer de Valence, Earl of Pembroke, lord of Wexford and of Montignac, lord John Earl of Warenne and of Surrey, lord Henry Percy, greetings in the name of God.

We wish it to be known that on Friday 19th of May, an agreement made at Scarborough between us and all of the other good people who were there, on behalf of the community of the realm on the one part, at the request of lord Piers Gaveston of the other part; this is to declare that we, the abovesaid earls and barons and good people, have undertaken by our faith, given and affirmed on the body of our lord, that we will conduct, guarding from all manner of damage from us and ours and from all other manner of people, the abovesaid Piers Gaveston, knight, to the Abbey of Our Lady at York, and there the agreement between ourselves and lord Piers Gaveston, knight, will be explained to our lord the king in the presence of the Earl of Lancaster or whosoever that the said earl shall agree to on his behalf, following which, should it so please our lord the king, the agreement shall hold until 1st August next, during which time the archbishops, bishops, earls and barons, and the other good people of the realm will be able to discuss terms, and from this day until the date above he shall remain in our custody under the abovestated terms. And if, by chance, the said lord our king or the abovesaid Piers Gaveston, knight, should not accept the above terms, then we, Aymer de Valence, Earl of Pembroke, lord John, Earl of Warenne, and lord Henry Percy, and the other good people present, will return the abovesaid lord Piers Gaveston to the castle of Scarborough, soundly and safely without injury to his body and without any deception, and the said castle of Scarborough shall not be entered between now and the 1st August nor shall the necessities, provisions or arms be reduced by the part of the said lord Piers Gaveston, knight, or by that of his men in any manner unless he should disturb the above. And that those who remain in the castle should be able to take what they need for their sustenance from the town and elsewhere, paying in cash for these forays. And if it should happen that anyone is struck down by illness or that the people in the said castle are obliged to leave, we grant and request that one is admitted for each one which departs, a Gascon for a Gascon, and Englishman for an Englishman, each person sufficing for the other so that the number of people remains the same in the castle of Scarborough as at the time when the agreement was made. And in order to keep, hold and maintain these things well and faithfully we have sworn on the body of our Lord and the Holy Gospels, that God forbid we act contrary to any of the above terms. We undertake to forfeit to our lord the king all that we have for ourselves and our heirs; and in order that these abovesaid things should be better affirmed, if it should come about in any manner or other point than is written, either by report or by knowledge, we will, from that day forward, consider ourselves to be held as false and disloyal in every respect and that our word should never be trusted. And also we promise that not one of us will attack the castle of our lord the king at Scarborough between this day and the abovesaid day, nor at any that shall

> be there. And the abovesaid lord Piers Gaveston, knight, promises, in good faith and loyalty and without fraud, that he shall not attempt to obtain any further terms from the king or from his ministers but only those points already agreed. In witness of this, we have each placed our seal. Given at Scarborough on the 19th day of May in the fifth year of the reign.

Thus, in the same way, Piers Gaveston surrendered. But, on account of this, the king was greatly annoyed, despite which Piers remained in the custody of the said Aymer. After a while, the said Earl Aymer took him with him and they came to the village of Deddington in Oxfordshire, and to the rectory there. There the earl left him for a few days with his servants so that he could visit Bampton, one of his manors, where his wife was staying. When news of this reached Guy Beauchamp, the Earl of Warwick, he gathered together forty knights and a hundred foot soldiers and pursued Piers by day and night in order to prosecute him as a traitor to England. So when he was approaching Deddington with his force, on the eve of the feast of St Barnabas the Apostle, that is 10 June, just as the sun was rising, a voice was raised in Ramah above Piers, louder than the voice of Rachel when she pleaded more bitterly.[34] And the house in which Piers resided was surrounded. And thus when Piers realised that such misfortune was descending upon him and looking to far and near to see if, by chance, any help should be at hand, and discovering none, he surrendered himself to the abovesaid earl, in bare feet, wearing only a tunic and with his head uncovered. Then the earl seized him and took him to Warwick, to his castle, and put him into the charge of four guards. Meanwhile the earls of Lancaster, Hereford and Arundel, and many others, praised the Earl of Warwick, because of his actions, and debated what they should do next. Indeed their counsel and assent was openly declared by their actions.

Therefore on the Monday after the feast of St John the Baptist, in the abovesaid year, namely on 19th day of June, the abovesaid earls, with their retinues came to Warwick and removed Piers from the custody of the Earl of Warwick, so that the Earl of Warwick handed him over to the earls safe and sound. The earls took Piers out of the town of Warwick and beyond the fief of the said Earl of Warwick to Gaverissweche, between Warwick and Kenilworth, within the lands of the Earl of Lancaster and there he was beheaded, at about midday, by the hands of a certain Welshman in the presence of all

34 Matthew 2:18.

those assembled there. And they all went on their way, leaving the body of Piers where it had been beheaded. Then four shoemakers from Warwick carried the corpse on a ladder in order to bury it there; however, the Earl of Warwick, who for the whole time of the beheading had remained in his castle, made them carry the body back to the same spot where it was beheaded, namely outside his fief. But brothers of St James[35] took the body to Oxford where it was treated with great honour, on account of which they are much in the displeasure of the said earls.

But when Earl Aymer de Valence learnt of this news, he was full of anger and sorrow, and supported by John Earl Warenne, they presented themselves to the king, requesting his mercy. The king gratefully received them because he did not have any supporters ...

(c) Letter patent of the Earl of Lancaster

This formal statement of protection, offered by the Earl of Lancaster to the Earl of Hereford, may be one of a number of such agreements made in anticipation of the events to follow;[36] *it was completed on the eve of Gaveston's killing and suggests a keen awareness of the king's likely response.*

Davies, *Baronial Opposition*, appendix no. 138, p. 598

To all those who see or hear this letter, Thomas Earl of Lancaster and of Leicester, steward of England greetings in our lord. Know that we have undertaken to defend and preserve with all our power against the king and all others lord Humphrey de Bohun, Earl of Hereford and Essex from damages which he could suffer as a result of the quarrel concerning lord Piers de Gaveston both in respect of the king and in respect of all others according to our power. And we will and assent that the said lord Piers shall be as an enemy of the king and of the realm and of his people. And we faithfully promise to live and to die in the aid and defence of the said earl in the abovesaid quarrel. And on this we have given our oath on the Holy Gospels. In witness of these things we have made these letters patent sealed with our seal. Written at Warwick the 18th day of June, in the fifth year of the reign of our lord the King Edward son of the very noble king Edward.

35 The Jacobins were Dominicans, an order of friars for whom Edward, and his mother, had a particular devotion, Phillips, *Edward II*, pp. 64–5.

36 Maddicott, *Lancaster*, pp. 128–9.

5 Piers Gaveston: character and response to his death

The chronicles are unanimous in their strong dislike of Gaveston; they offer or at least propose a more general view of this animosity, which is also reflected in political songs that celebrate his death.

(a) *Vita Edwardi Secundi*, pp. 26–9

This Piers, originating from Gascony, was the son of a certain knight who had been a member of the elder King Edward's household. While Edward the younger was still Prince of Wales, the said Piers was received into his household as a young esquire, and by a pleasing attention to his duties he quickly found the very highest favour in his master's sight. And, to make a long story short, when he had obtained the kingdom of England on the death of his father, our king made Piers Gaveston Earl of Cornwall. But Piers, now Earl of Cornwall, was unwilling to remember that he had once been Piers the humble esquire. For Piers reckoned no one his fellow, no one his equal, except the king alone. In fact his countenance exacted greater deference than the king's. His arrogance was, then, intolerable to the barons and the main cause of both the hatred and the rancour. For it is commonly said,

> You may be rich and wise and handsome,
>
> But insolence could be your ruin.

I therefore believe and firmly maintain that if Piers had behaved discreetly and humbly towards the great men of the land from the beginning, none of them would ever have opposed him. But there was a secondary cause of their hatred, namely that, though of old it has been desirable for all men to find favour in the eyes of kings, Piers alone received the king's favour, welcome, and goodwill, to such an extent that, if an earl or baron entered the king's chamber to speak with the king, while Piers was there the king addressed no one, and showed a friendly countenance to no one except Piers alone. And in truth envy is accustomed frequently to spring from such behaviour. Certainly, I do not remember having heard that one man so loved another. Jonathan cherished David, Achilles loved Patroclus; but we do not read that they went beyond what was usual.[37] Our king, however, was incapable of

37 Chaplais, *Piers Gaveston*, pp. 5, 8, 110.

moderate affection, and on account of Piers was said to forget himself, and so Piers was regarded as a sorcerer.

(b) *Annales Paulini*, p. 259

… as much as the hatred of the worthy people intensified against him who had been raised from a dung-hill, so much also did the ardour of the king for Piers increase. For the king, on account of his excessive love, referred to Piers as his brother. Indeed, he was commonly called the king's idol, for he feared to displease him as if he was his father, and sought to please him as one would a superior. The king, therefore, conferred upon that Piers the control of various forms of grace and favour, which issuing out of the royal prerogative adhered to him alone and no other. For if any of the earls or magnates should require a special grace of the king concerning the settlement of some matter, the king sent him to Piers. And whatsoever Piers should say or order, it would immediately be done, and the king would also accept it. Whence came the indignation of all the people: two kings in one kingdom, ruling together, one in name and the other in deed.

(c) Wright, *Political Songs*, pp. 259–61

Celebrate, my tongue, the death of Peter[38] who disturbed England,
Whom the king in his love for him placed over all Cornwall;
Hence in his pride he will be called earl, and not Peter.
The people of the kingdom was made sorrowful for the fraud upon the treasure,
When Peter becomes wastefully insolent with the treasury,
Not bearing in mind what the future day may produce for him.
This is the work of our salvation that Peter is dead;
All the artfulness of the multifarious traitor has perished;
Henceforth let the good omen rejoice our hearts, for sorrow is past.
When the fulness of time which was fit for the thing came,
His head is cut off from the juncture of the body;
He who raised trouble within the kingdom is now troubled from without.
He who was unwilling to have an equal, clothed in the extreme of pride,

38 Wright's translation of *Petrus* in the Latin text is 'Peter' rather than 'Piers'.

Against his will bends his neck to the executioner;
Of whose merited death this hymn is set forth.
He who placed himself as a head above his equals loses his own head;
Justly his body is pierced, whose heart was so puffed up;
Both land, sea, stars and world rejoice in his fall.
Ferocious and cruel among all men, he ceases now from his pomp;
Now he no longer behaves himself like an earl, or a king;
The unworthy man, worthy of death, undergoes the death which he merits.
This tree with its branches bent falls into a proverb;
For the stiffness which pride gave is softened;
Thus ought the auspicious and aspiring man to be humbled.
May the house of Peter, in which he is held, not be supported in strength;
Many the other place be profane, and may it be in disgrace,
Which the filthy gore spilled from Peter's body has defiled!
Glory be to the Creator! Glory to the earls
Who have made Peter die with his charms!
Henceforth may there be peace and rejoicing throughout England!
Amen.

II: THE KING'S WEALTH

Introduction

One of Edward II's greatest achievements was in royal finance. At his death contemporaries described him as 'the wealthiest king since the Conqueror' [**13a–b**], yet he had started his reign with a large debt and financial departments in disarray. His success had required considerable reorganisation, persistence and luck, but was perhaps not totally surprising given the economic potential of England.

An expanding economy

England was economically wealthy from agricultural and mineral resources. By the beginning of Edward's reign, it had experienced (like the rest of western Europe) two centuries of economic growth. Population and agricultural areas had expanded; markets and towns had increased in numbers and size, and many more towns had clear economic functions; commercial activity increased absolutely and as a proportion of economic activity.[1]

While England's economy remained largely agricultural, its trade connected it directly and indirectly with much of Europe. Its exports, predominantly of wool [**6a**], brought possibly as much as £230,000 in silver into England annually,[2] and this wealth spread from the merchants to wool producers, great and small, and to many ancillary services. The bulk of the wool went to the cloth industries of the Low Countries. Here merchants from all over Europe congregated and in the towns and ports (especially at Bruges), English merchants could buy goods from all over the known world. Trade with other areas thrived too. Direct Scandinavian trade was still active in east coast

1 Three studies are particularly useful: Britnell, *The Commercialisation of English Society*; Britnell and Campbell, *A Commercialising Economy*; Hatcher and Bailey, *Modelling the Middle Ages.*

2 A rough calculation may be made based on average weights, quality and prices: Lloyd, *Wool Prices*, pp. 1–5, 48.

ports; trade to the Rhineland was longstanding and direct trade to the Baltic was growing;[3] Gascony sent wine in return for grain and fish;[4] and direct trade with Castile (the country of Edward's mother) and Portugal took place through southern ports and London.[5] Direct seaborne trade between England and the Mediterranean had also begun in the late 1270s and 1280s, pioneered by Majorcan and Genoese ships, but Italian merchants had long been established in England, coming first via the Champagne fairs and the Low Country towns. The Riccardi of Lucca, the Frescobaldi of Florence and Antonio Pessagno of Genoa were bankers to English kings, and Florence also drew on English wool.[6]

Sources of royal revenue

English kings benefited from the expanding economy through income from their own estates and through new taxes. The royal estates had shrunk since William the Conqueror held half of England, but they were still substantial enough to produce some £10,000–15,000 a year. Relatively little of this income came directly to the exchequer, but it provided the queen's dower, households for the royal children and grants of patronage. Royal estates worth at least 20,000 marks (£13,333 6s. 8d.) were taken over by Queen Isabella in 1327.[7] Alongside the demesne Edward II had a traditional income from a miscellany of royal rights, such as shire farms, profits of justice, feudal dues, mintage, prise and purveyance, which probably amounted to c. £15,000–19,000 annually as it did in 1284 and the 1340s.[8] Some of these rights were expanded by open abuse, especially purveyance, which at its worst had been extended to supply whole armies and for which payment was often late and sometimes never.

Beyond this traditional income, Edward I had found ways of tapping his subjects' increasing wealth through taxes. His greatest success was

3 Lloyd, *Alien Merchants*, pp. 123–56; Lloyd, *England and the German Hanse*, pp. 13–49.

4 James, *Wine Trade*, passim.

5 Childs, *Anglo-Castilian Trade*, pp. 11–39; Childs, 'Anglo-Portuguese relations', pp. 27–33.

6 Lopez, 'Majorcans and Genoese'; Ruddock, *Italian Merchants*, pp. 14–29; Kaeuper, *Bankers*, passim; Kaeuper, 'Frescobaldi'; Prestwich, *Edward I*, pp. 99–100, 239–41, 521–2, 534; Fryde, 'Antonio Pessagno'.

7 Wolff, *Royal Demesne*, pp. 32–7, 54–6; Harriss, *King, Parliament*, pp. 149–50.

8 Mills, 'Exchequer agenda', pp. 232–4; Prestwich, *Edward I*, p. 237; Harriss, *King, Parliament*, pp. 145–9, 524–5.

direct national taxes on trade, which provided a substantial regular income. From 1275 wool exports paid a duty of 6s. 8d. a sack and in 1303 further taxes were levied on all trade handled by foreign merchants, as agreed in the *Carta Mercatoria*.[9] The value of the wool trade to the king is very clear. The tax on c. 25,000 sacks a year in the 1270s brought in more than £8,000 a year.[10] At Edward II's succession exports averaged around 35,000 sacks a year, bringing in nearly £12,000 in revenue. Even when exports dropped substantially after 1315, they were still no lower than in the 1280s. The extra tax on foreign merchants brought in c. £3,000–4,000 annually under Edward II. Total customs revenue thus ran at around £16,000 a year in 1307–11; remained quite high despite the suspension of the 1303 tax at c. £11,800 a year until 1315; fell to between c. £7,000 and £9,000 a year in the worst years of famine and murrain; but recovered to average c. £12,500 after 1322. Overall in Edward II's reign customs duties brought in around £218,000.[11] In addition Edward raised £12,700 in a forced loan on wool in 1317 [**10c**] and £10,000 in an extra wool subsidy in 1322.[12]

Edward I also tapped into his subjects' increasing wealth with direct taxation. He failed completely to impose this on the clergy, but the church and the papacy were willing to provide voluntary gifts to help him rule. He had greater success with direct taxes on the laity, but not carte blanche. Lay taxes had to be for specific needs (often war) and required consent. Parliament provided the facility for consent (which in turn contributed to the increasing role of the commons in parliament). Unlike customs duties, clerical grants and lay subsidies were intermittent, but over Edward II's reign each brought in a similar amount to the regular customs income. The English church provided Edward II with seven grants (agreed in Convocation), assessed in total at £61,700, of which at least £54,600 was paid.[13] The papacy made eleven grants of complete or partial papal tenths based on the valuation of the English church made under Pope Nicholas IV in 1291–2; these amounted to a

9 *EHD*, III, no. 91 (pp. 515–18).

10 Carus-Wilson and Coleman, *Export Trade*, pp. 36–43, 122–3 and Document 6 (a); Mills, 'Exchequer agenda', pp. 232–4.

11 Childs, 'Finance and trade', pp. 22–33; Ramsay, *Revenues*, II, p. 149; Ormrod, 'The crown and the English economy', pp. 168–9; Jenks, *Enrolled Customs Accounts*, I, pp. 64–259.

12 Ormrod, 'Political theory', p. 210.

13 Ormrod, 'The crown and the English economy', pp. 161–2. One request was refused (1323): Buck, 'Reform', pp. 253–4.

total of £241,000, of which at least £194,000 was collected.[14] Over the reign, therefore, the English church, through both types of grant, provided Edward with c. £250,000. In addition, for a while, Edward benefited from the confiscation of Templar lands, potentially worth c. £4,500 annually, but used by Edward largely as a source of patronage.[15] From the laity Edward II received seven subsidies. A new valuation was made at each grant and the fraction demanded varied each time, not settling at a tenth and a fifteenth (from towns and countryside respectively) until the reign of Edward III.[16] Individual assessments ranged from c. £34,000 to c. £42,500 and together they were nominally worth £267,000. Efficient collection ensured that some £252,600 was received.[17] In addition Edward took a tallage in 1312 (which brought in at least £2,000 and possibly nearer £3,700), two scutages in 1314 and 1319 (of which little was collected), and a tax in Wales. He also raised troops at the vills' expense in 1316 and 1322 [**10a–b**].[18]

Edward II thus inherited considerable financial assets in both the expanding economy and his father's new taxes. He also enjoyed the same financial flexibility as his father by anticipating revenue through loans. It is likely that the Riccardi of Lucca advised Edward I on setting up the wool customs in 1275 and they, like subsequent Italian lenders to the crown, received wool revenue directly from customs collectors or held customs offices themselves.[19] Gascon revenues were similarly used to repay Italian loans, and under Edward II Amerigo Frescobaldi and Antonio Pessagno of Genoa held Gascon offices.[20] After the fall of the Frescobaldi, Edward continued to use Italian bankers: Pessagno lent him c. £145,000 between 1310 and 1319, and in the 1320s Edward turned to the Ballardi, Spini and Bardi.[21]

14 Lunt, *Financial Relations*, pp. 392–3, 396, 402, 407, 409–11; Ormrod, 'The crown and the English economy', pp. 163–4. This includes one grant from 1306, which was collected in Edward II's reign.

15 Slavin, 'Templar estates', pp. 210–11, 219; Perkins, 'Wealth of the Knights Templar', pp. 253, 258.

16 Jurkowski et al., *Lay Taxes*, pp. 29–36.

17 Willard, *Parliamentary Taxes*, pp. 344; tabulated by Ormrod, 'The crown and the English economy', p. 153.

18 Hadwin, 'Last royal tallages', pp. 351–3; Jurkowski et al., *Lay Taxes*, pp. 30–2, 34–5.

19 Kaeuper, *Bankers*, pp. 146–51.

20 Tout, *Edward II*, pp. 349–50; Gascon Roll Project online, C61/32: numbers 30–2, 320–3, www.gasconrolls.org/ (last accessed 12 August 2018).

21 Fryde, 'Antonio Pessagno', pp. 168, 170, 173–8; Fryde, *Tyranny*, p. 91; Buck, *Stapeldon*, pp. 193–4.

Problems and chronology

Despite these advantages, Edward II also inherited financial problems: a debt of some £200,000,[22] an exchequer in disarray, discontent among those whom the exchequer pressed for lost revenue, and unpopular royal bankers. Financial concerns are evident in the petitions to Edward II in 1309,[23] and were seen as so pressing that Gaveston was allowed back in return for their remedy in the Statute of Stamford. They remained prominent in the Ordinances in 1311. Edward's reign also faced wider economic problems of inflation and famine. Prices of oxen, wheat, cheese and grain increased by c. 50 per cent in Edward's early years [**6b**] and grain prices soared in the exceptional famine of 1315–17.[24] The causes of inflation were complex and the famine was extreme, as contemporary comment makes all too clear [**9a–b**]; both were impossible for the government to control. Nonetheless, it tried and its efforts to combat inflation in 1309, although they failed, show some sophisticated economic understanding in the use of a trial period [**7a–c**].[25] Similarly the government could do little about victual prices in 1315–17. Price controls introduced in 1315 were withdrawn in 1316 when goods disappeared from the market [**8a–d**], and attempts to limit ale prices in 1317 and to prohibit forestalling (the interception of goods before they reached open market in order to elevate the market price) were little more successful.[26] Edward's letter to his bishops in April 1316, at the height of the famine, requesting that they instruct hoarders of grain to release it on to the market for the benefit of the poor and beggars suggests both an awareness of the disaster as well as the incapacity of government to respond to it [**8b(ii)**].[27] That medieval government could offer only limited response to a food crisis that has been identified as, in real wage terms, the worst event of the past thousand years should hardly surprise us; it is perhaps as striking that Edward and his government attempted to do so and also recognised

22 Prestwich, *War, Politics and Finance*, p. 221; Prestwich, *Edward I*, pp. 535–7.

23 Ormrod et al., *Early Common Petitions*, no. 110: clauses 1–3, 7.

24 Mate, 'High prices'; Farmer, 'Crop yields'.

25 Childs, 'Government and market', pp. 37–44.

26 *Letter Book E*, pp. 43–4; *Foedera*, II.ii, p. 266; *CCR 1313–1318*, p. 227; Britnell, 'Forstall, Forestalling'; Childs, 'Government and market', pp. 44–7; Davis, *Medieval Market Morality*, p. 254.

27 *Register of Richard de Kellawe*, II, pp. 1118–20. The letter and other attempts by Edward's government to control food prices and access to resources are discussed in Sharp, *Famine and Scarcity*, pp. 33–55.

a moral compulsion to make that attempt.[28] Further damage was done to the northern economy in these years by devastating Scottish raids. Despite the hardship, throughout the famine years the government continued to demand and collect revenue. In 1316 stringent regulations were issued on debt collecting and the government experimented with raising armies at the cost of the vill [**10a–b**]. This experiment failed, but the substituted sixteenth brought in more than £38,000, one of the highest subsidy returns of the reign.[29] In 1317 the government experimented again, successfully raising a loan on trade that circumvented the prohibition in the Ordinances on raising taxes without general consent [**10c**]. Despite famine, murrain, sliding customs revenue and Scottish raids, royal finances began to show recovery and Edward became solvent probably sometime between 1315 and 1320.[30]

Reform

After 1322 Edward's revenues benefited further from a thorough overhaul of exchequer procedures, demonstrated in ordinances of 1323, 1324 and 1326.[31] These ran alongside the reform of the household, with separate ordinances in 1318 and 1323.[32] The need for institutional reform in the exchequer had been clear from the beginning of the reign. Earlier theories that the drive for reform was spearheaded by Edward's opponents to undermine the king's conscious avoidance of exchequer control are now rejected, and recent studies emphasise that changes in financial practices were due to practicalities rather than opposing policies. Edward I's use of household departments to speed up war payments backfired when records were left in disarray, and Edward II and his advisers (whether political opponents or supporters) were as one in promoting exchequer reform. From 1316 stringent debt levying and substantial reorganisation of exchequer records are apparent and such measures continued unbroken through the crisis years to the end

28 Sharp, *Famine and Scarcity*, p. 42. On the uniquely poor state of real wages in 1316, see Clarke, 'The long march of history', p. 110.

29 Buck, 'Reform', p. 246; *PROME*, Parliament of January 1316, SC9/20, item 2; Jurkowski et al., *Lay Taxes*, p. 33; Ormrod, 'The crown and the English economy', pp. 153, 155–6.

30 Phillips, *Edward II*, p. 218; Fryde, *Tyranny*, p. 88.

31 *Red Book of the Exchequer*, III, pp. 849–969.

32 Tout, *Edward II*, pp. 244–84.

of the reign.[33] They are illustrated by instructions issued to exchequer officials in 1319 [**11a**] and by major reforms in the ordinances of Cowick (1323) [**11b**] and Westminster (1324 and 1326). The reforms were encouraged by Stapeldon and Hugh Despenser, whose emphasis on spending money wisely appears in his letters on the Gascon war [**42a**], and Edward's own insistent grasping for funds is well attested in instructions and letters. Their success is shown in the receipt rolls for Easter and Michaelmas 1323, which appear to show that available income that year reached nearly £114, 000.[34]

The push for reform included an attempt to assess 'normal' government revenue in 1324 [**12**], which provides an interesting snapshot of crown resources, although it did not include the patrimonial estates. The traditional shire resources provided c. £11,700, and various other dues and traditional income probably amounted to an additional £8,000. These, with escheats and other fines, produced a core income in 1324 similar to that of 1284.[35] The newer resources from customs duties amounted to between £11,000 and £12,000 that year.[36] In addition Gascony was a valuable asset with an expected income of c. £13,000 clear. If this were regularly reached, then during Edward's reign Gascon income would have totalled c. £260,000 (a similar sum to the customs duties and to the lay and clerical subsidies). In addition Edward received two windfalls. Contrariants' lands still in hand in 1324 were estimated to be worth £12,652 a year (a much larger sum than he had drawn from the earlier custody of Templar lands), and in addition he still held most of the parliamentary grant of 1323, of which some £39,300 was collected and not used in a Scottish expedition.[37] These windfalls and the systematic exploitation of all potential revenue enabled Edward to pay off most of his father's debt, pay for the Gascon war, and amass at least £62,000 in cash by 1326.[38]

33 Davies, *Baronial Opposition*, passim (and especially pp. 60, 350–6); Tout, *Edward II*, pp. 83–4; Tout, *Chapters*, II, pp. 84, 188–95, 281, 340–3; Harriss, *King, Parliament*, pp. 208–14; Prestwich, *Edward I*, pp. 137–8; Buck, 'Reform', pp. 241–8; Buck, *Stapeldon*, pp. 163–8.

34 Buck, 'Reform', pp. 249–51; Fryde, *Tyranny*, pp. 98–103; Buck, *Stapeldon*, pp. 163–96, esp. at p. 166 nn. 20, 26, 30, p. 167 nn. 32–3, pp. 174, 193–4.

35 Mills, 'Exchequer agenda', pp. 232–4; Prestwich, *Edward I*, p. 237; Harriss, *King, Parliament*, pp. 145–9.

36 Ramsay, *Revenues*, II, p. 149; Ormrod, 'The crown and the English economy', p. 168.

37 Ormrod, 'The crown and the English economy', p. 153.

38 Fryde, *Tyranny*, pp. 209–10; Buck, *Stapeldon*, p. 193; Phillips, *Edward II*, p. 421.

Edward's government did exceptionally well in reforming the financial system and exploiting resources. This wealth should have made him safer and more independent, but there was a political cost. It became yet another focus for dissatisfaction, bringing not only anger from those pressed for money but sharp criticism that Edward did not use it more wisely [**13a–b**].

6 Examples of contemporary quantitative data

(a) Wool exports

Wool exports brought much wealth to the country and the king. Customs duties were charged at the rate of 6s. and 8d. for a sack of 364lb weight and export figures can be extracted from the customs accounts, which survive from 1275. The gaps for 1275–9 and 1290–4 are because the accounts for this period record not the number of sacks, but only the duties collected and include within them the duties collected on hides. It is likely that wool exports were still high at 25,000–30,000 sacks a year. Low exports in 1294–6 were due to trade disruption by the Anglo-Flemish war.[39]

Figure 1 (a and b) is compiled from the figures in Carus-Wilson and Coleman, *Export Trade*, pp. 36–45.

(b) Grain prices

The grain prices compiled by D. L. Farmer, chiefly from manorial demesne accounts, are given in shillings per quarter (a quarter being roughly equivalent to a year's individual supply of grain) and have been recalculated from Farmer's indexed prices. As will be evident, from Table 1 and Figure 2 using the same data, they reveal considerable fluctuation, with some extreme peaks in prices in the worst of the famine years, the so-called Great Famine of 1315–16. In those years all grain prices tended to move together, suggesting that there was pressure on poorer quality grains and legumes, such as oats and peas, as much on the better-quality food grains, such as wheat. Numerous contemporary commentators reflected upon and used grain price movement as an important index of dearth and famine.[40]

39 Lloyd, *Wool Trade*, pp. 75–96.

40 See below, documents in [**9**] (Famine).

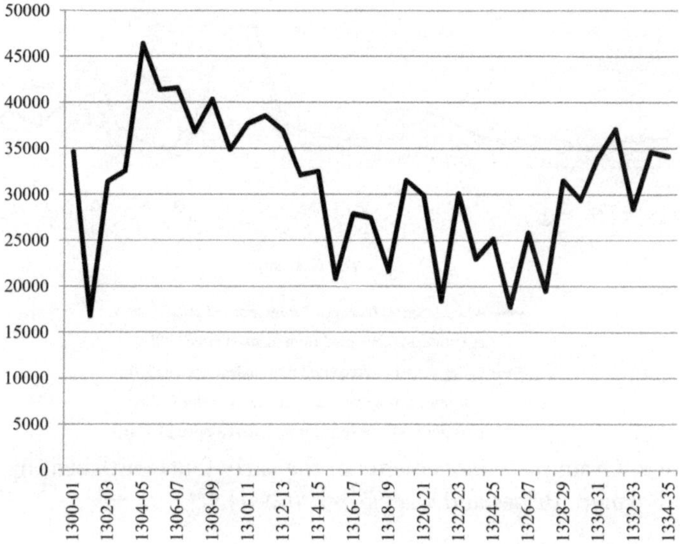

Figure 1(a) Raw wool exports in sacks 1300–1335.

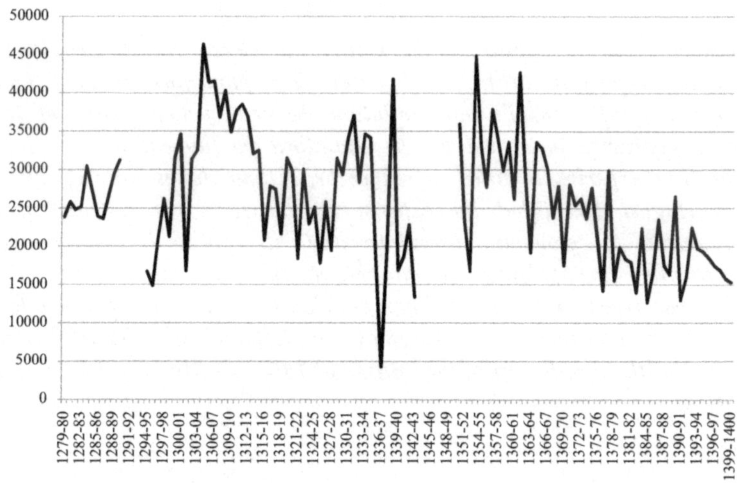

Figure 1(b) Raw wool exports in sacks 1279–1400.

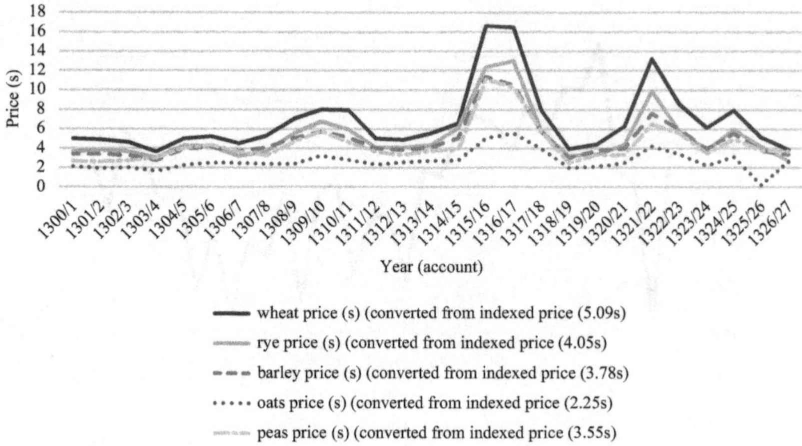

Figure 2 Grain price movements in the early fourteenth century (from Farmer, 'Prices and wages', pp. 790–1).

7 Inflation and the removal of customs dues, 1309–10

Financial concerns appear in the petition of eleven clauses presented to the king in parliament in April 1309: false purveyors, coinage, undue prisage and inflation. To fight inflation the new customs duties of 1303 were temporarily suspended at the Stamford parliament on 20 August 1309. The experiment failed to reduce prices and duties were re-imposed on 2 August 1310, but the experiment illustrates the response of the government to economic pressures and its political and financial sophistication in applying a trial period. In 1311 the removal of the duties was repeated in the Ordinances (clause 11) and justification for it expanded to make references to Magna Carta, London's liberties and baronial assent. For the significance of the petition of 1309, see Maddicott, Lancaster, *pp. 97–9.*

(a) The conditional removal of the petty customs, 1309

Ormrod et al., *Early Common Petitions*, no. 110. (Also *CCR 1307–1313*, p. 175; *Rot Parl.*, I, pp. 443–5. For the Statute of Stamford, see above [**3a**].)

The articles written below were presented to the lord king by the commonalty of his kingdom at his parliament held at Westminster the month after Easter in the second year of his reign. At which parliament

Table 1 Grain price movements in the early fourteenth century

Year	Wheat price(s) (converted from indexed price (5.09s))	Rye price(s) (converted from indexed price (4.05s))	Barley price(s) (converted from indexed price (3.78s))	Oats price(s) (converted from indexed price (2.25s))	Peas price(s) (converted from indexed price (3.55s))
1300/1	4.99	3.65	3.40	2.09	2.66
1301/2	4.89	3.81	3.40	1.91	2.63
1302/3	4.63	3.65	3.29	2.00	2.73
1303/4	3.66	3.04	2.76	1.67	3.02
1304/5	4.99	4.29	3.97	2.25	4.01
1305/6	5.24	4.21	4.12	2.52	4.33
1306/7	4.53	3.20	3.74	2.50	3.66
1307/8	5.29	3.69	4.08	2.41	3.27
1308/9	7.02	5.55	5.07	2.41	4.69
1309/10	7.99	6.76	5.71	3.26	5.79
1310/11	7.94	5.95	5.14	2.79	4.65
1311/12	5.04	4.09	4.01	2.34	3.66
1312/13	4.89	4.09	3.86	2.57	3.34
1313/14	5.55	4.33	4.12	2.75	3.76
1314/15	6.57	6.08	5.07	2.77	3.87

(continued)

Table 1 (Continued)

Year	Wheat price(s) (converted from indexed price (5.09s))	Rye price(s) (converted from indexed price (4.05s))	Barley price(s) (converted from indexed price (3.78s))	Oats price(s) (converted from indexed price (2.25s))	Peas price(s) (converted from indexed price (3.55s))
1315/16	16.64	12.35	11.38	5.04	11.11
1316/17	16.49	13.00	10.51	5.56	10.30
1317/18	7.94	5.79	5.75	3.98	5.75
1318/19	3.97	3.24	3.02	1.98	2.52
1319/20	4.43	3.40	3.78	2.07	3.30
1320/1	6.26	4.37	4.01	2.50	3.34
1321/2	13.23	9.92	7.60	4.23	6.50
1322/3	8.60	5.83	5.97	3.40	5.61
1323/4	6.16	3.85	3.97	2.21	3.48
1324/5	7.94	5.95	5.56	3.11	4.97
1325/6	5.14	4.21	3.74	0.23	3.80
1326/7	3.87	2.71	3.36	2.63	3.69

Source: Farmer, 'Prices and wages', pp. 790–1

the king asked for an aid from his land, and the laity granted the king the twenty-fifth penny on these conditions: that he took counsel and remedied the aforesaid articles.

And the king at his parliament at Stamford, beginning Sunday next after St James in the third year of his reign, ordained reply and remedy to the same articles [27 July 1309]. Which reply and remedy he notified to his people at his said parliament of Stamford, and which are written here below, that is to say, after each article the remedy that was ordained.

> The good people of the kingdom who have come here to parliament beg the king to please have regard to his poor people who feel themselves greatly aggrieved in that they are not treated as they ought to be, namely according to the points of the Great Charter, and they ask remedy for this, if it pleases him. Also they beg our lord king, if it please him, that he be willing to hear the things which have most hurt his people and still newly hurt them day by day by those who call themselves his ministers and to give amendment, if it please him:
>
> ...
>
> [Clause 2] And another thing, that the king by his ministers takes from every ton of wine two shillings; of every cloth that foreign merchants have brought to his land two shillings; and of every pound of avoirdupois[41] three pence, to the damage of his people, for by such prices the people buy at the third penny more than it used to be.
>
> Answer: Our lord the king, at the request of his people, grants that this petty custom on wines, cloths and avoirdupois be suspended and taken off at the king's will, in order to know what profit and advantage will accrue to him and his people by this suspension; and then the king will take counsel according to what he will see, saving always to our lord the king the ancient prises and customs formerly due and approved.

(b) The resumption of collection, 1310

CCR 1307–1313, pp. 275–6

[2 August 1310] To John de Lincoln. Order to collect and pay into the exchequer the payments and customs for the king's use in London and all places on both sides of the Thames to Gravesend from the goods of foreign merchants that he was appointed to collect, to wit three

41 Miscellaneous goods sold by weight.

shillings from each scarlet cloth and cloth dyed in grain and eighteen pence from each cloth in which a part of grain was intermixed, twelve pence from every cloth without grain, three pence from every pound of avoirdupois; which payment the king in his parliament at Stamford on August 20 in the third year of his reign at the request of the community of the kingdom ordered should cease as it is now evident that no advantage has arisen since the cession to the king or his people in better prices of such good and merchandise.

[Similar orders were sent to all other customs collectors.]

(c) The repetition of suspension in the New Ordinances 1311, clause 11

Statutes, I, pp. 159–60; *EHD*, III, no. 100 (pp. 529–30)

11. Likewise new customs have been levied and old ones increased as upon wools, cloths, wines, merchandise sold by weight and other things as a result of which merchants come more seldom and bring fewer goods to the land and foreign merchants stay for a longer time than they used to, so that goods become dearer than they used to be to the detriment of the king and his people. We ordain that customs and maltotes[42] of all kinds levied since the coronation of King Edward son of King Henry shall be removed and entirely abolished for ever, notwithstanding the charter that the said King Edward granted the alien merchants, because this was granted contrary to the Great Charter and to the franchise of the city of London and without the assent of the baronage; and if anyone of whatsoever condition takes or levies anything beyond the ancient, due and rightful customs or creates a disturbance whereby the merchants cannot do as they wish with their goods, and is convicted of this, damages shall be awarded to the plaintiffs having regard to the purchase, to the suit, to the costs and losses they have had, and to the violation of the Great Charter; and the offender shall be imprisoned according to the scale of the offence and according to the discretion of the justices and never be in the king's service; saving nevertheless to the king the customs of wool, fells and hides, that is for every sack of wool half a mark, and for every 300 wool-fells half a mark, and for a last of hides one mark, if he ought to have it; and henceforth

42 'Evil tolls', or impositions; see, for discussion of the term, Gras, *Early English Customs*, p. 89.

foreign merchants shall come, stay, and go in accordance with the ancient customs and in accordance with what they used to do.

8 Price ordinance, enforcement and revocation, 1315–16

Soaring prices during the famine prompted the government to fix victual prices nationally, except for allowing higher poultry prices in London, which reflected those set in 1274: Mun. Gild. Lond., vol. II: Lib. Cust., *p. 82. Enforcement was vigorous enough to stop high prices in open markets, but drove goods on to the black market. It was revoked in 1316.*[43]

(a) Proclamation of the price ordinance in London, 14 March 1315

Foedera, II.i, p. 263 (*CCR 1313–1318*, p. 160)

The king to the mayor and sheriffs of London, greetings. We have received a complaint from our archbishops, bishops, earls, barons and others of the community of our kingdom through their petition shown before us and our council, stating that the expense of oxen, cows, sheep, pigs, geese, hens, capons, young chickens, pigeons and eggs in these days is great and nigh intolerable to the great damage and injury of them and all others of the people within the same kingdom. Because of this they begged us with urgency that we should take care to provide a suitable remedy on this:

We therefore, assenting to the said supplication for the common utility of the said people of the kingdom as it shall seem expedient, have ordained with the counsel and assent of the prelates, earls, and barons and others of our council being in our last parliament held at Westminster, that the better live fat ox for sale, not fed on grain, should be sold henceforth for sixteen shillings and not more; and if it has been fed on grain and is fat it is to be sold for twenty-four shillings at most; and henceforth there should be sold the better cow, live and fat, for twelve shillings; and a fat pig of two years for forty pence; a fat unshorn sheep for twenty pence; a fat shorn sheep for fourteen pence; a

43 For the Price Ordinance, 1315, see also *PROME*, Westminster Parliament of January 1315, and for its revocation, *PROME*, Lincoln Parliament, January 1316, and below [**15i**].

fat goose in our said city for three pence; a good fat capon for two pence halfpenny; a fat hen for a penny halfpenny; two young chickens for a penny halfpenny; three pigeons for one penny and twenty eggs for one penny; and if any person or persons should be found who do not wish to sell goods for sale of this sort for the fixed price set out above then the aforesaid goods for sale shall remain forfeit to us.

And because we wish the aforesaid ordinance to be firmly and inviolably kept from now on in our city, we order you, firmly enjoining you, that in our city aforesaid and its suburb wherever you see it expedient, you should have the ordinance publicly and clearly proclaimed and to be inviolably observed henceforth throughout the whole of your bailiwick in all and every article on pain of the aforesaid forfeiture.

And as you wish to avoid our displeasure and to keep yourselves secure, you should in no way omit to do this. Witnessed by the king at Westminster, 14 March.

[Similar letters were sent to the Sheriff of Lincoln and all other sheriffs the same day, with the following changes after the fat shorn sheep for fourteen pence: a fat goose for two pence halfpenny; a good fat capon for two pence; a fat hen for one penny; two young chickens for one penny; four pigeons for one penny and twenty-four eggs for one penny.]

(b) Enforcement

Enforcement followed quickly, with orders to London officials to attach offenders (20 March) and to prevent forestalling (17 April): Letter Book E, *pp. 43–4. A general order to prevent forestalling was issued on 10 April (below). Requests to ensure the release of supplies followed in 1316.*

i Order against forestalling, 10 April 1315

Foedera, II.i, p. 266 (*CCR 1313–1318*, p. 227), sent to all sheriffs

The king to the Sheriff of Middlesex, greetings.

[the writ recites the ordinance on prices]

And now we understand from the information of our dear and faithful Chancellor, Treasurer and barons of the exchequer and justices and other ministers occupied in our service in our city of London and also from the citizens of the said city and of others coming to that city that diverse forestallers in the royal highways and other diverse places within your bailiwick, after the proclamation and publication of the said ordinance made in your county, plotting to destroy and annul that ordinance, fraudulently and maliciously hinder in various ways merchants and others wishing to come to the said city with all sorts of saleable goods to expose for sale there according to the form of the ordinance, and still have not ceased hindering [them], so that they have not been in a position to bring those victuals for the sustenance of our faithful people at that city and others living there, as they wish.

And they compel the said unwilling merchants and others, who want to bring such victuals to the said city, as is allowed, to hand the victuals to themselves, for the price set for things for sale outside the city, before they can come to the said city; and many times they take them away with force, taking and carrying these saleable things to London or other merchant towns within your bailiwick to sell them there; and they carry them off without making any satisfaction according to the said ordinance or in any other way; and many times they upset and weary those wishing to sell saleable goods; because of these injuries and forestalling those with such goods withdraw from the said city and other merchant towns and are unwilling to come, to the abrogation of the ordinance and to our manifest contempt.

We, not wanting the said ordinance to be invalidated by such fraud and malice, order you, firmly enjoining you, that in the cities, boroughs, merchant towns and other places in your bailiwick, both within and without the liberties, you proclaim in each without delay and have it firmly forbidden on our behalf that no one, of whatever status or condition he should be, should presume under pain of forfeit to impede in any way merchants or others wanting to come to the said city with such saleable goods, nor in any way take any such saleable goods away from them, taking and carrying them off against their will, so that they may not take them to the said city or other merchant towns in your bailiwick to expose them for sale there according to the form of the ordinance.

And if it should happen that those going against our prohibition should be found in your bailiwick then you should promptly send notifications to us of their names to our chancery under your seal, so that we can have them punished according to their deserts and as will be just.

And if you should be without diligence, negligent and remiss, we shall consider you contemptuous of our mandate according to the character of the business in this matter.

Witnessed at Windsor 10 April.

ii Edward's letter to the bishops regarding the hoarding of grain, April 1316

Register of Richard de Kellawe, ed. Hardy, II, pp. 1118–20

Edward, by the grace of God, king of England, lord of Ireland and duke of Aquitaine to the venerable father in Christ, Dom. Richard, by the grace of God bishop of Durham; greetings.

Our realm, which, as we have been told by many, used to be more abundant than other regions in earlier times in a wealth of wheat and other victuals and grain, is now exposed to such deficiency, lack, and unusual scarcity of grain in these days, because of the folly of the times, because of the sins committed by the people entrusted to us, as we fear, at the decision of the Almighty, who by His divine power, as He wills, humbles and punishes the proud and disobedient. Purchasable grain, from which our people will be able to be sustained, cannot be found in the said realm, mostly because some of the same realm, having grain in their granges in no small quantity, and they retain it thus and refuse to expose it for sale, so that later they may sell it more dearly. Because of this the poor and beggars of the said realm, not being able to find any who have the authority to provide food to them, because of this deficiency and scarcity of grain, daily die of hunger and starvation, which we believe is very sufficiently known to you as to others of the said realm. Because of this, not unreasonably, we feel regret and compassion in the innermost places of our heart. Who, therefore, of pious mind, considering and thinking about the abundant fertility of earlier times and the current scarcity and pressing deficiency, would not lament in his inmost thoughts; would not be compassionate to his neighbour dying of hunger and starvation? Wishing therefore to provide for the salvation of our people in the ways and means that we can, as we are obliged to do, we earnestly require your loyal support, and ask you as far as you can, to advise with strong words, those, both of the clergy and the people of your city and diocese, viz those who still have grain in their granges and granaries, inducing them by other ways and means as you see expedient, that they should not hold back from exposing for sale the grain that they have, retaining reasonable sustenance for themselves and their household through to autumn, lest the cause of such death and mortality in the people should be imputed to those having grain and refusing to sell it. If, indeed, men who have saleable grain in your diocese should refuse to obey your admonition in this matter and it becomes known to us, we, because of the pressing necessity, will in no way omit that which we should do in this, to apply a suitable remedy for the greatest sustenance of our people that seems to us should be done with [the advice of] our council.

Westminster 24 April 1316

(c) Revocation, 20 February 1316

Foedera, II.i, p. 286 (*CCR 1313–1318*, p. 325); sent to all sheriffs

1316 February 20: The king to the Sheriff of Lincolnshire, greetings.

Although we recently ordered you to have it publicly proclaimed in the cities, boroughs, merchant towns and other places where you saw it as expedient, that oxen, cows, pigs, sheep, geese, capons, hens, pullets, pigeons, and eggs should be sold for a certain price, nevertheless, because we understand that this proclamation which at the time we believed to be done for the advantage of the people of our realm, has now redounded to their greater damage than to their advantage.

We order you that in the cities boroughs and other places you should have it publicly proclaimed that oxen, cows, pigs, sheep, geese, capons, hens, pullets, pigeons and eggs be sold at a reasonable price as it used to be done before the said first proclamation; making known to all and every one that the aforesaid first proclamation was not made by virtue of the Ordinances recently made by the prelates and nobles of our realm and accepted by us nor is it contained in them.

Witnessed by the king at Lincoln 20 February.

(d) Views of chroniclers on price-fixing

Most chroniclers, if they note the ordinance, do so without comment. Three offer critical opinions: the Vita's *author showed sympathy for buyers, Trokelowe for sellers (London poulterers) and the canon of Bridlington criticised the inanity of trying to overrule God's will.*

i Vita, *pp. 120–1*

1316

The regulations formerly made about food were completely abolished. In fact, those who travelled about the country were suffering much hardship, for, as a result of that statute, little or nothing was exposed for sale in the markets, whereas formerly the market had been full of goods, even though they seemed dear to travellers. But it is better to buy dear than to find there is nothing to buy when you need it. For although scarcity makes produce dearer, subsequent plenty brings back a better time.

ii Trokelowe, *p. 90*

1315

After the provision had been published in this way throughout all the counties of England and serious damage had been inflicted on poulterers and other retailers in London and elsewhere for not observing the provision, the clergy and the people came at the king's summons to London two weeks after Easter to deal with other business ...

[For Trokelowe's further comments on the ordinance, see under Famine, [**9b**].]

iii Bridlington, *pp. 47–8*

1315

Look! What an amazing ordinance, and one not in accord with reason – namely that man should regulate goods for sale and fix a price for them; since it is most certainly evident that the fertility and sterility of the soil and of all plants and also every other thing that grows remains and stays in the sole power of the Divinity; therefore, of necessity, it follows that the price of every single thing follows not from the judgement of men but from the abundance of produce.

9 Famine

The Great Famine of 1315–16 was, by most measures, the most extreme in the Middle Ages and, lasting more than two years, caused great hardship. Price data (as above **6(b)***) show the scale of the problem, but the chronicles reveal the human cost. While the famine has tended to feature less prominently in modern accounts of the reign and its politics, it attracted a good deal of contemporary comment; most of this was directed at identifying the main features of famine: high prices, disruption and the death of poorer people. Occasionally, commentators offered fuller comment and description* (Trokelowe), *as well as a degree of moralising* (Vita).

(a) *Vita*, pp. 110–13, 120–3

1315

By certain other portents the hand of God appears to be raised against us. For in the past year there was such plentiful rain that men could scarcely harvest the wheat or store it safely in the barn. In the present year worse has happened. For the floods of rain have rotted almost all the seed, to such an extent that the prophecy of Isaiah might seem now to be fulfilled, for he says that ten acres of vineyard shall yield one little measure and thirty bushels of seed shall yield three bushels (Isa. 5:10). And in many places the hay lay so long under water that it could neither be mown nor gathered. Sheep commonly died and other animals were killed by a sudden pestilence. It is greatly to be feared that if the Lord finds us incorrigible after these scourges, he will destroy at once both men and beasts; and I firmly believe that if the English church had not interceded for us, we should have perished long ago.

1316

After the celebration of Easter the dearth of grain began to increase greatly. Such a scarcity has not been seen in our time in England, nor heard of for a hundred years. For the bushel of wheat was sold in London and its vicinity for forty pence, and in other less thickly populated parts of the country thirty pence was a common price. Indeed during this time of scarcity a great famine appeared, and after the famine came a severe pestilence, from which many thousands died in different places. I have even heard it said by some, that in Northumbria dogs and horses and other unclean things were consumed as food. There, indeed, on account of the frequent raids of the Scots, people are afflicted with greater hardship as the accursed Scots rob them daily of their food. Alas, land of England! You who out of your abundance once helped other lands, now, poor and needy, are forced to beg. A fruitful land is turned into barrenness; the inclemency of the weather destroys the fatness of the land; wheat is sown and tares are brought forth. All this comes from the wickedness of them that dwell therein.[44] Spare, O Lord, spare thy people![45] They scoff and deride us, who are round about us.[46] Yet those who are wise in astrology say that these storms in the heavens have happened naturally; for Saturn, heedless and cold, brings rough weather that is useless to the seed; in the ascendant now

44 Ps. 106(107):34.

45 From the liturgy: Legg, *Sarum Missal*, pp. 54, 151.

46 Ps. 43(44):14.

for three years he has completed his course, and kindly Jupiter has in turn succeeded him. Henceforth, under Jupiter these floods of rain will cease, the vales shall abound with corn, and the fields shall be filled with plenty;[47] for the Lord will give goodness and our earth shall yield her fruit.[48]

(b) *Trokelowe*, pp. 92–4, 95–6, 104–5

Unheard-of sickness, hunger and dearth

In the year of the lord 1315 in addition to the other misfortunes with which England was afflicted, famine increased in the land, as if God was not pleased with what was in the statutes. For since they had been ordained and promulgated everything was more expensive than usual. For meat began to run out, eggs and other dairy produce disappeared. Capons and geese could hardly be found; sheep were few and far between because of murrain; pigs, in excess before the dearth, could not be fed. For a quarter of wheat, beans and peas was then sold for twenty shillings, malt for a mark[49] and oats for ten shillings. But a quarter of salt was commonly sold for thirty-five shillings; which had hardly been heard of for a century before. So great was the penury that the land had to suffer, that when the king visited St Albans at the next feast of St Laurence [10 August], hardly any bread for sale could be found to sustain his household.

Concerning the journey of the king to other parts

Afterwards the king removed himself to Clipstone in Sherwood where he kept his court at Christmas. And around the feast of the Purification at Lincoln, by the counsel of his barons, the king revoked the above said provisions in their entirety, ordering universally that each and every one may offer for sale his saleable goods at the best marketable price that may be had.

The said dearth began in the month of May, in the year of the Lord 1315 and lasted until the feast of the Nativity of the Blessed Mary [8 September]. Summer rains were so abundant that the crops could not ripen. And until the said day of the Nativity they could hardly

47 Ps. 64(65):14, 12.

48 Ps. 84(85):13.

49 13s. 4d. (or 160d.).

gather enough to bake bread, unless it was first sent to be dried in ovens. Towards the end of autumn this dearth was partly mitigated but around Christmastime it totally returned. Nor did the bread have any power to nourish or the strength that it once did, because the grain had no nutriment from the heat of the summer sun. So those eating it, even if they consumed a great amount of it, were hungry again after a brief time. Nor is it to be doubted that while the poor wasted away by hunger and starvation, so the rich were continually hungry after sumptuous meals.

Therefore, with the dearth prevailing like this, both lay lords and ecclesiastics cut back their courts, withdrew customary alms and reduced their households. As a result these people, thus removed from the courts, accustomed to leading comfortable lives, had no idea how to dig, were ashamed to beg;[50] overcome by the need for food and drink, they were desperate for others' goods and turned to killing and plunder. And thus so many were turned into dishonest people, who were not allowed to live in peace as honest folk.

Thus, having considered and understood the straits and miseries set out above and yet to come, we will be able to see that that prophecy which is spoken in Jeremiah – 'If I go forth into the field, then behold the slain with the sword; and if I enter into the city, then behold them that are sick with famine'[51] – is fulfilled in these days among the English people coming forth into the fields, when we bring to mind the ruin perpetrated on our people at various times in Scotland and Gascony, Wales and Ireland, together with these people whose throats are cut every day in robbers' ambushes. Nonetheless, we might ponder letting those weakened by hunger enter the city, when we see the poor and destitute, oppressed by the same hunger, lying neglected and dead in the streets and highways.

Concerning parliament

In the year of the Lord 1316 the nobility, called by the king's command, gathered in London to discuss the state of the realm, and during that parliament the famine grew ever more fierce. For the quarter of wheat and also of salt was sold at thirty shillings until the feast of St John the Baptist. From that day until the feast of the Assumption it rose to forty shillings. Therefore, with this famine so oppressing the whole land, the death of people followed. For so many destitute people died that the

50 Luke 16:3.

51 Jer. 14:18.

living were scarcely sufficient to bury the dead. For dysentery, caused by the rotten food, infected almost all of them; acute fever or a deadly throat infection followed.

And just as people succumbed, poisoned by the rotten food, so beasts and livestock, infected by the putrid fodder, fell to the ground with murrain. No one remembered having seen such dearth and famine before; nor that such mortality followed. Nor in this plague could the wisdom of doctors discover, as it used to previously through their art, any suitable remedy against the said diseases. For medicinal herbs, which used to bring relief to the sick in a time of high mortality, degraded because of the inclement weather and chaotic clash of the elements, contrary to their nature yielded poison instead of strength.

Concerning the hardship and scarcity that were in England of both food and drink

So that it is clear to those coming after us how harsh life was throughout England then, I am inclined to insert a little in this script here, before the royal edict is described.

In fact, four penny-worth of coarse bread was not sufficient for one single man for one day. Ordinary meat, which is permissible to eat,[52] was very limited; but horseflesh was precious to those who stealthily stole fat dogs; and, as many asserted, in many places both men and women secretly ate their children and those of others. But, what is horrible to bring to the notice of people in the future, prisoners even devoured thieves recently coming among them, still half alive.

But when a man is without drink and empty of victuals, to make mention of drink itself will generate loathing. For the gallon of ale that was then made in England sold for two pennies and the better for three and the best for four. Therefore London, especially afflicted by the hunger and fearing for the future, lest wheat should be further consumed for drink, ordained that for the safety of the ordinary people, a gallon of the better ale should be sold for three half-pence and the rest for one penny and no more. The king, moreover, aroused by the clamour of the people, expressly ordered that ale should be sold according to the statute of London everywhere through his kingdom, both within liberties and without, in cities, boroughs and market towns, and in country villages, for one penny, and forbade that wheat

52 That is, 'clean' flesh, deliberately slaughtered, and not 'dying of itself': Deut. 14:21.

should be henceforth turned into ale under pain of serious forfeit. And this appears through his writ to the Sheriff of Hertfordshire and Essex and directed on by the same sheriff to the bailiffs of the liberty of St Albans in these words. And without this mandate having been promulgated more quickly in this way, the greatest part of the people would have perished from hunger and starvation that year as it had done in the previous year.

[the writ to the sheriff follows ...]

Concerning the sickness of animals

[1319] In the course of the same year a pestilential death of cattle grew in all England on a scale no one remembered seeing before. In this sickness, amazingly this happened: that both the dogs and crows who fed on the corpses of the dead cattle swelled up on the very spot and, infected, died. So that there was no man who dared to taste the meat of cattle, lest by chance he should succumb, poisoned by carrion. It began in the time around Easter in Essex and lasted for one whole year. It is also said that the whole of France was for the same time contaminated by the same destruction.

10 Experimental taxation

Edward II was granted seven lay subsidies, but also experimented with new forms of money-raising, especially during the famine years, notably trying to pass army costs directly to the vills in 1316 and taking a forced loan on wool in 1317.

(a) Grant of one man per vill, 1316

A grant of a fifteenth was made by cities, boroughs and the royal demesne, but in the countryside each vill was to send a man at its own expense to the muster at Newcastle on 8 July. This grant was unsuccessful this year and on 29 July it was converted to a subsidy of a sixteenth. A similar levy in 1322 was more successful and produced seven thousand men (Powicke, *Military Obligation*, pp. 152–3).

PROME, Parliament of 1316, SC 9/20, no. 1: and below [**15**]

[Grant of foot soldiers for the Scottish war]

On the following Friday [20 February] the great men and the community of the kingdom granted the king in aid of his Scottish war, from each town in the kingdom, except from the king's cities, boroughs and demesne, one able and fencible foot soldier; and those foot soldiers will be armed with haketons and bacinets and equipped with swords, bows, arrows, crossbows, lances or other armaments suitable for foot soldiers. And the people will find at their own cost those armaments for the said foot soldiers, and their expenses, until they come to the place where the king will have summoned his army for the said war, and the wages of the same foot soldiers, for a stay of sixty days there from the day when they arrive there, or for proceeding further in the king's service for the same period, that is to say 4d. a day for each foot soldier. And if it is a town where there is a market, which can be charged with a greater number of foot soldiers and their expenses, then it is to be charged more. And the king has granted that he will issue his letters, for himself and his heirs, to the great men and the community of his kingdom, that this grant of foot soldiers will not be prejudicial to them or their heirs, nor is it to bring any consequence in the future.

(b) The substitution of a sixteenth, 1316

*Collectors for the sixteenth were appointed on 5 August 1316 (*CPR 1313–1317, *pp. 529–31). Although rumours of refusals to pay led to enquiries in February 1317 (*CCR 1313–1318, *p. 453), this sixteenth brought in one of the largest subsidy amounts of the reign (Willard,* Parliamentary Taxes, *p. 344; Ormrod, 'The crown and the English economy', p. 153) and shows that the government could effectively collect revenue despite the famine.*

CPR 1313–1317, p. 529

5 August 1316: Appointment of Henry Cobham the younger, Richard de Rokesle and Thomas de Sandwich together with a clerk whom they shall choose to assess and collect in the county of Kent the sixteenth granted by the earls, barons, free men and commonalty of the counties in the parliament at Lincoln on Thursday next after the feast of St James the Apostle [29 July], which was granted to purchase exoneration from the aid of foot soldiers for the war in Scotland, granted in the parliament at Lincoln on the quinzaine of St Hilary [27 January], and also to obtain a confirmation of the perambulations of the forest

already made, and that perambulations should be made in such forests as had not been perambulated before. The money is to be levied and paid into the exchequer, one half on the morrow of All Souls [3 November] and the other on the quinzaine of Easter [17 April 1317].[53]

(c) A loan from merchants, 1317

*This discussion document, put before the Nottingham council in July 1317, stated explicitly that its author was trying to circumvent the Ordinances, which had just been confirmed in 1316. The proposal was accepted and writs to collect the levy were sent out on 24 July (*CFR 1307–1319, *pp. 335–6, 338). By then the merchants had clearly bargained with the crown as rates demanded on wool, fells and hides were lower than in the original proposal. The loan netted £12,747, 2s. 4¾d. (Ormrod, 'Political theory', p. 210).*

TNA C49/4/23: Ormrod, 'Political theory', pp. 214–15

Because God, reason, and right require that, when a king or prince of a land comes sometimes [to need] defence, whether making war or other necessary reasons appertaining to his crown, in view of this fact he should be assisted by his people as well as by strangers who repair to his country like denizens, because of the advantages and profits that they take from his country thanks to the merchandise which they export from the realm and import. On this matter it would be good to look at the most convenient and most suitable way [to do this] so that no trouble or imputation of crime may [*ms damaged*] to the king and his council. And so that the council may be better advised on this matter, the one putting forward these things to the great advantage of the king [*ms damaged*] will show how the king can best raise 100,000 marks without grievance to the people and cry and noise and without murmur of the people and without violating any of the Ordinances, which have been ordained by the ordainers ...

11 Exchequer reform

Reform was badly needed and gathered momentum in the second half of the reign, with ordinances to reform the exchequer in 1323, 1324

53 Given as 25 April 1317 in Jurkowski et al., *Lay Taxes*, p. 33, and repeated in *PROME*; 25 April is the quinzaine of Easter for 1316, not 1317.

and 1326 paralleling household ordinances in 1318 and 1323. Walter Stapeldon (treasurer 1320–1, 1322–5) is given much credit for it, but major reforms began before he became treasurer and Edward II and the Despensers also took a keen, active interest in reform (Buck, Stapeldon, *pp. 163–96).*[54]

(a) Instructions to exchequer officials, 31 October 1319

These instructions illustrate the tightening of financial procedures before Stapeldon became treasurer. They were meant to speed up the presentation of wardrobe and other accounts at the exchequer, punish lax officials, prohibit the discharge of debts without proper authorisation and encourage order in the rolls so that information could be found easily. Members of the king's council were to check on the exchequer at least twice a year.

Davies, *Baronial Opposition*, appendix no 29, pp. 557–9, with comment on p. 529

To the barons on behalf of the king.

Edward by the grace of God, king of England, lord of Ireland and duke of Aquitaine, to the treasurer, barons and chamberlains of our exchequer, greetings.

We order and charge you, firmly enjoining you on the faith that you owe us and the oath that you have made to us, that you should have the estate of our said exchequer, and all the things that are collected to be delivered there for us or in future will be delivered, duly established and supervised; and also that you have [matters] expedited according to the laws and usages of the same place; and that all manner of accounts that are collected to pay there, of the wardrobe, Gascony and Ireland as well as elsewhere, should be dealt with speedily without favour to anyone, of whatever estate he is, unless there is special order from us.

And that you, the treasurer and barons, should make sure clerks and all others of whatever estate they are, who serve or who ought to serve in that place, are to do well and assiduously what is appropriate to each of them; and if there should be anyone who does not do it, he should be duly reproved and chastised for this by you, or totally dismissed if the deed demands it.

54 On reform, cf. Phillips, 'Parliament in the reign of Edward II', pp. 44–5; and Phillips, 'Tout and the reign of Edward II', pp. 119–20.

And we will and charge you that henceforth you do not have any debt terminated which is of farm or fine, nor for anything bought from us nor arrears of account nor other clear debt that can well be levied from the debtor or his mainpernors[55] or pledges, provided that it is without great hardship to them [and] that they have no special order from us; but all the debts which are clearly due to us should be levied by all the means that one ought properly to levy them by, without granting respite on this to anyone unless there is good cause to give respite or unless we of our special grace command it be done.

And indeed make sure among yourselves that such respites should be recorded in our exchequer so that we can find out about them when we want.

To this we command and charge, in the above-said form, you, the treasurer and chamberlains, that among you, you duly carry out your office at the Receipt and do not allow anyone to enter there or into our treasury in any manner, except with reason to enter, nor should anyone see any manner of books, rolls or other memoranda which are set up, except he swears an oath to us.

And have all the things in the treasury, whatever they are, that carry a financial charge viewed and put in such order as befits them; and this in such manner that one can find out what they are and have them and quickly find them at the time when we want to have them, for ourself or someone else, whether to cite as proof or in another manner in which help is needed.

And that henceforth no payment or assignment should be made at our exchequer in any way to anyone without special order from us under our great seal or privy seal, which makes mention of him to whom payment or assignment ought to be made and of how much every time henceforth. If the sheriff, bailiff or another has paid to the keeper of our wardrobe to our use that which he should have paid at our exchequer and for which he has open letters from the keeper to you which bear witness to it, or if the sheriff, bailiff or other, who is held to answer at our exchequer for farm or in other manner has had payment made for costs in purveyance of victuals or other things to our use by our order from the issues of his bailiwick and he accounts for that in the wardrobe and from there he has bill of testimony as is due to him for this reason, make such letters and bills to duly allow this whenever they are presented to our said exchequer

55 Those who stand as surety for an individual, ensuring they meet some or other legal obligation, such as repayment of a debt awarded against them.

and allowance on them demanded, and let this be done without his having any delay in his allowance in such case; but henceforth no assignment nor payment should be made by any other manner at our exchequer if they do not have an order from us in the manner said above.

And know certainly that we have now ordained certain people of our privy council whom it pleases us to assign to be sent each year to our said exchequer, at least twice a year or more according to what we will see as necessary, to observe and learn about the receipt and issue of our same exchequer in the presence of you, the treasurer and chamberlains, and of the barons, whichever of whom it seems to them they should have called for this; and also have them make a memorandum summarily on the estate [of the exchequer] such as it will be found and report to us secretly; and also that they see how this our order will have been kept and maintained on all points, and that they report to us what they will have found to be done, so that we will see what has been reasonably done.

Have this, our command, enrolled at our great exchequer and the exchequer of Receipt in the manner that it may be often seen and understood by you.

And do not omit to do this for anything.

Given under our privy seal at York the last day of October in the thirteenth year of our reign.

(b) The Exchequer Ordinances of Cowick, 1323

These ordinances were sent to the exchequer by the king and council from Cowick on 14 June 1323. They were to be 'carried out in every particular'. Forty-nine chapters deal with recording and auditing accounts at the exchequer and lay down detailed procedures for the Remembrancers' offices.[56] *They are technical not political, and the first three chapters given below indicate their character. For the full text (Latin with translation) see* Red Book of the Exchequer, *pp. 849–907. The further exchequer ordinances of 1324 and 1326 follow there (pp. 908–29, 930–69).*

Red Book of the Exchequer, III, pp. 849–53

56 The two offices of Remembrancer, namely King's and Treasurer's, were increasingly delineated in terms of their principal function, which was to oversee the correct recording of exchequer business, Tout, *Edward II*, pp. 47, 197–8.

These are the articles ordained and provided for the ordering of matters in the exchequer in Trinity Term of the sixteenth year of the reign of King Edward, son of King Edward, to be held and performed and kept in the exchequer aforesaid.

1 That the barons shall not engage on any day in holding any pleas until the sheriff who is accounting be examined by the Pipe[57]; nor hold any pleas unless, etc.

Because the accounts of the sheriffs and the bailiffs of franchises who account at the exchequer (which accounts are made up of all manner of fee-farms and others due to the king annually, as of counties, cities, boroughs, manors, towns, hundreds, assarts[58] and purprestures[59] and other matters let out at rent by the year, and likewise of the great debts which are paid at certain terms, and other debts whereof the sheriffs and bailiffs only charge themselves with a part and which things are all in the Great Roll which is called the Year Roll, whereby these accounts are examined and rendered in full exchequer before the treasurer and barons of the place) cannot be sufficiently rendered, heard or concluded without great diligence and perfect quiet, let not the barons henceforth on any day after their coming into court in any wise engage in hearing or holding any plea or suit until the sheriffs and bailiffs present in court to account are with good examination and good diligence examined before the treasurer and themselves in so far as shall suffice for the day's writing in the Great Roll. And let the barons take heed that no pleas from henceforth be held in the exchequer without the king's special mandate, or unless the pleas concern the king in matters which belong to the place or to his ministers there; and let these things be done in such a manner that the conclusion of the accounts be not delayed nor disturbed.

2 How the examination of accounts of the Foreign Summonses is to be made, and sheriffs and bailiffs put their answers into writing, and what debts are [to be removed] out of the estreats[60] into the Year Roll

As to the examination of accounts of the sheriffs and bailiffs for the other debts of the king, which are not in the great Year Roll and are

57 That is, by the record of the pipe, which Tout defines as the individual membranes of the so-called 'foreign accounts'; for a fuller definition of both 'pipe' and 'foreign accounts', see Tout, *Edward II*, pp. 196–7.

58 Assart: clearing of waste for agriculture.

59 Purpresture: illegal enclosure.

60 Estreat: true copy of original records.

issued by many summonses out of divers estreats, let this examination of accounts be made by the baron and clerk assigned for this, separately, immediately after the other examination of accounts. And let them take heed that they pass no debt, great or small, contained in the said estreats, which has not been examined; and let the sheriff or bailiff remain charged with it if he does not put in a suitable and passable answer as to why he should not be so charged.

And let every sheriff and bailiff from henceforth put in writing his answers which he shall give on the account, both at the examination of accounts in full exchequer and at this latter examination of accounts for every debt with which he alleges that he cannot and ought not to be charged; and let this be delivered to the treasurer's Remembrancer to keep, and to put at the end of the account before the treasurer and barons, [for them] to ordain what shall be done on the king's behalf. And as to this examination of accounts of the estreats aforesaid, no debt contained there shall be removed out of the said estreats nor put in the Great Roll, except a debt with which a sheriff or bailiff shall charge himself in whole or part, or a debt that ought to be allowed by reason of a franchise or otherwise, or any yearly item, if it be found in the said estreat, whereof the king ought to be answered; for the Great Roll has been and is so weighted by copious writing that the settlement of the accounts hath been and is the more delayed.

3 How to write the Year Roll, etc.
And to abridge such writing let it be from henceforth ordained that the Year Roll be made and written in the following manner, that is to say: that therein be written annually all the farms of the counties, as well remainders of farms of the body of the counties, farms of profits and increments, as others whatsoever they be, great or small, or yearly rents due to the king and debts of fixed date and no others, except such as sheriffs and bailiffs shall have charged themselves with in whole or part in their accounts.

12 Balance sheet of 1324

Part of the reforms in 1324 included an estimate of revenue (Bodleian MS North C.26). This is tabulated by Harriss, King, Parliament, *pp. 523–4.*

Table 2 Balance sheet of 1324

	£ s. d.	£ s. d.
Shire revenues (sheriffs, farms, fee farms, etc.)	11,742 12 3	
Ancient custom (clear value)	mutilated	
New custom (clear value)	mutilated	
Fines and amercements in the courts (omitting eyres)	mutilated	
Reliefs, marriage fines, and attermined debts	mutilated	19,496 12 5
North Wales and west Wales	mutilated	
Exchanges of London and Canterbury	no estimate[a]	
Mines in Devonshire	no estimate[b]	
Stannaries in Devonshire (at farm)	mutilated	
Escheatries north and south of Trent		700 0 0
Forests		333 6 8
Prise of wine		400 0 0
Gauges of wine (at farm)		200 0 0
Gascony (clear receipt}		13,000 0 0
Ireland		1,424 0 0
Fines and amercements before the seneschal and marshal and clerk of the market		300 0 0
Issues of the great seal (clear receipt)		300 0 0
Contrariants' lands in England, still in the king's hands		12,652 0 0
Contrariants' land in Wales and Ireland	no estimate	no estimate
Forfeitures of wool per aulnagers	no estimate[c]	no estimate
Total		**60,548 11 4**

[a]Valued at £500 earlier in Edward's reign.

[b]Valued at 400 marks earlier in Edward's reign and later farmed at 200 marks.

[c]Valued at £700 p.a. but sent directly to the wardrobe.

13 Edward's wealth according to the chroniclers

Two very different chronicles note Edward's wealth. The Brut, *often inaccurate on detail, is valuable for reports on contemporary opinions. The author of the* Vita Edwardi Secundi *is close to the court and an informed observer.*

(a) *The Brut*, p. 225

1322

Then the king made Robert Baldock, a false tonsured clerk, chancellor of England through the advice of the foresaid Despensers; and he was a false and covetous villain. And they counselled the king so much that the king had all the goods of the lords that were wrongfully put to death taken into his own keeping, into his own hands; and they took the goods that were within holy church as well as the goods that were without, and had them put into his treasury in London and had them called his forfeit; and by their counsel the king made and disinherited all those that owned the goods; and through their counsel had a tallage raised on all the goods in England; wherefore he was the richest king that ever was in England after William Bastard of Normandy that conquered England. And yet through their counsel, it seemed to him that he had not enough, but he made yet every town of England find a man at arms upon their own costs to go and [make] war on the Scots that were his enemies.[61]

(b) *Vita*, pp. 230–1

1325

Meanwhile the foot soldiers claimed their wages, but they were not given them, because of which they overran the whole countryside, plundering the inhabitants for their food. Everyone was amazed that the king did not pay the infantry, since they could not live properly without wages, and the king's treasure was abundant enough. For many of his forebears amassed money, he alone outstripped them all. However, the king's harshness is blamed on Hugh [Despenser the Younger], like the other evils that take place at court.

61 See above [**10a–b**].

III: PARLIAMENT

Introduction

Consultative assemblies were well established in English political life by the fourteenth century,[1] but Edward II's reign is important for two developments: the increasing role of the commons in parliament and parliament becoming more central to political crises. As parliament was called more frequently, so its practices and processes became regularised, its importance was openly articulated, and it became perceived as the normal gathering to express the views of the full community of the realm.[2]

Kings had great power but were not free to do as they wished. They could not, in practice, govern without widespread consent, and from Magna Carta to the Articles on the Charters, the king's greater subjects established a tradition of limiting royal actions. They continued to do so under Edward II. His opponents used threats, shows of force and open violence, but they preferred the legitimacy offered by law and in parliament, and in crises Edward might face strong baronial pressure to call parliament. The wide consultation possible there was useful not only in crises, but also when government was running well. It was a flexible forum for the king to dispense justice, to take advice, to explain royal policy and to persuade those attending to grant support and financial help. It was also a forum for his subjects to present petitions, both private and for the common good, even against royal ministers. Such petitions were at first presented by the magnates speaking on behalf of the 'community', but during Edward's reign economic, social and political developments made the baronage less convincing as the sole voice of the lay community, and by the 1320s many petitions were clearly brought by the commons themselves.[3]

1 Maddicott, *Origins*, traces developments back to the Anglo-Saxon period, but sees 1215–1327 as the period that gave parliament its distinctive form.

2 For a recent discussion of Edward II's parliaments, see also Phillips, 'Parliament in the reign of Edward II'. For each individual parliament during the reign, see also the Introductions and edited texts in *PROME*.

3 Maddicott, *Origins*, pp. 352–9; Ormrod et al., *Early Common Petitions*, pp. 2–5.

The growing impact of parliament is apparent in all the political crises in Edward's reign, and although the legitimacy gained from its support might prove temporary when power changed, the desire for it remained strong.[4] The major crises reveal the perceived value of parliament in various statements made. For example, in 1311 the Ordinances themselves contained important demands for regular parliaments in a convenient place and for consent in parliament [**16b**]. In 1320 Lancaster stated that parliament should be held openly (*non ... in cameris*).[5] In 1321 the peers claimed that, as peers, they could declare new laws in parliament,[6] and in 1322 Stapeldon and Cobham, faced with the return of the Despensers, told the king that what was done in parliament would be best undone in parliament [**16c**]. The deposition in 1327 was the ultimate political action in parliament, orchestrated by the lords, but providing visible acceptance from all ranks. The deposition was not, however, in any way 'by' parliament and parliament's role caused no concern to Edward III, unlike Henry IV later.[7] The growing use of parliament in its combination of roles – consultation, opposition, redress and taxation – drove it towards a permanent role in government, but as yet, despite baronial influence and the growing role of the commons, parliament remained the king's instrument. He decided when to call it, who should come and what business should be discussed.

The practicalities of parliament

Parliament was still fluid in personnel and process, but more frequent assemblies increasingly brought conventional practices. Twenty-seven assemblies formally called parliaments met in Edward's twenty-year reign,[8] more on average than the one a year demanded by the Ordinances. Westminster was becoming the usual venue. Nearly two-thirds of parliaments were held there and one in London. York provided a second centre with seven parliaments, and one was held in each of Northampton, Stamford and Lincoln. By c. 1321–2 the

4 Dodd, 'Political legitimacy', passim; Maddicott, *Origins*, pp. 336–8.

5 *Vita*, pp. 176–7. This reflects *Modus* cap. 19 (*in loco publico ... non in privato nec in occulto loco*), for which see Pronay and Taylor, *Parliamentary Texts*, pp. 67–79.

6 Pronay and Taylor, *Parliamentary Texts*, pp. 164, 168.

7 Dodd, 'Political legitimacy', pp. 167–70.

8 *PROME* identifies twenty-six assemblies summoned and held by Edward II and the final parliament of January 1327, which was called in his name; three more were summoned by him but not held.

anonymous author of the *Modus Tenendi Parliamentum* conceived parliament as an institution with fixed conventions even down to the number of doormen and the width of the parliament roll (caps 20, 25).[9] Certainly by this time records reveal increasingly standardised practices, especially in summoning parliament. The warning given by writs of summons still varied widely between forty and seventy days,[10] but the forms of the writs were settled [**14a–d**]. Individual writs were sent to the archbishops, bishops, deans and priors of cathedral churches, archdeacons, a selection of greater abbots and priors, the earls, a selection of the barons, and the king's major administrators. The sheriffs organised the representatives of the laity through the county courts (two knights for each county, two citizens or burgesses for each city or borough in the county as selected by the sheriff). Clerical proctors (one for each cathedral chapter or priory and two for each diocese) were organised through the archbishops and bishops. The formula for the commons (lay and clerical) to come with 'full and sufficient power' to bind their communities to decisions agreed in parliaments was set by 1294,[11] and by 1313 the nobility also expected a standard form of summons. Lancaster, Hereford and Warwick justified non-attendance at parliament that year because they were not summoned in the form found in the chancery register [**14g**]. The king not only expected justification for absence but expected attendance to be peaceful. Royal opponents were forbidden, for example in 1310, to attend 'riding and in arms',[12] although some chroniclers saw this as justified self-defence.[13]

A full parliament was potentially a very large gathering. All 21 archbishops and bishops of England and Wales were summoned; the number of abbots summoned varied from 11 to 55, settling at around 45 in Edward's middle years and decreasing to around 28 nearer the end of the reign. The judges and clerks remained a fairly stable group at between 25 and 38. There were usually 8 to 10 earls, depending on deaths and new creations. The numbers of barons fluctuated widely from 39 to 110, depending on the king's need for wider consultation,

9 Pronay and Taylor, *Parliamentary Texts*, pp. 65–91; Weber, 'Purpose'. See also now the discussion in Phillips, 'Parliament in the reign of Edward II, pp. 41–6.

10 *HBC*, pp. 552–6. *Modus* advises forty days (cap. 1).

11 Edwards, '*Plena Potestas*'; Maddicott, *Origins*, pp. 289–90; Denton, 'The clergy', pp. 96–7.

12 See, for example, *CPR 1307–1313*, p. 206; *Foedera*, II.i, p. 103.

13 E.g. 1308: *Annales Paulini*, p. 263 [**17b (i)**]; 1312: *Vita*, pp. 60–1.

but usually lay between the mid-forties and the mid-eighties.[14] There were 74 county representatives at two per county. The list of parliamentary boroughs was not yet fixed and varied from 63 to 82 (potentially 126 to 164 representatives).[15] The cathedral deans and priors, the archdeacons, and the cathedral and diocesan proctors formed a group of 148 lower clergy.[16] Thus some 400–450 people were summoned to Edward II's parliaments in mid-reign. Those who came would bring retinues. Even the shire and borough MPs travelled with servants, so the burden on smaller towns would be great. No wonder the king suggested they deal with business quickly at Lincoln in the famine winter of 1315–16 [**15a**].

The growing role of the commons is marked. Edward summoned knights, citizens and burgesses to nineteen of his parliaments, knights alone to two others and representatives of the Cinque Ports to one other.[17] The author of the *Modus* (cap. 23) emphasised the commons' importance in taxation (although his exact meaning is debated), but in only seven of these meetings did they grant tax.[18] Their role was wider than that. Since they came to parliament with full power to act for those they represented, their support could give legitimacy to actions taken by either side.[19] At the same time, however, their independent interests were becoming more apparent, and recent work has traced the shift towards increasing numbers of parliamentary petitions presented by the commons themselves.[20]

The day-to-day business of most parliaments is difficult to trace. We have a detailed day-to-day narrative only for the 1316 Lincoln parliament [**15**], but there is no reason to think it is untypical in pattern, even if unique in detail. The meeting was less confrontational than many and shows political groups successfully co-operating to find solutions in the statute of sheriffs, the articles of the clergy and the

14 Numbers of those summoned by individual writ are given in the introductions to each parliament in *PROME* and their names are in *Parl. Writs*, II.ii, pp. 1–366. See also Given-Wilson, *Nobility*, p. 58.

15 McKisack, *Parliamentary Representation*, pp. 25–7.

16 Denton, 'The clergy', pp. 92–3.

17 He also held non-parliamentary commons' meetings: of knights concerning forest perambulations and of merchants concerning staples and loans.

18 For parliamentary taxation, see Chapter II: The king's wealth.

19 Dodd, 'Political legitimacy'.

20 Maddicott, *Origins*, pp. 340–1, 347–52; Ormrod et al., *Early Common Petitions*, passim.

arrangements for Lancaster to head the council. The business of other parliaments can be partially reconstructed from a variety of petitions, statutes, ordinances and executive orders, which reveal the concerns raised there. Sometimes arguments deployed can be recovered from chance survivals for other meetings, such as the discussion paper for the forced loan of 1317 [**10c**] or the council agenda and memoranda of 1322.[21] Chroniclers also help. What they chose to report reveals what topics they considered interesting and what was known across the country of parliamentary business. Sometimes, as with Edward's deposition, chronicles may be our most important sources [**50a–e**]; at other times they provide vivid detail, as in 1321 when they report the barons riding to parliament in arms with their supporters in livery of green and saffron.[22]

Attitudes to parliament

Attitudes to parliament were generally favourable at all political levels. The king needed it for taxes, to publicise government strategy, to sound out the country, to show he had support. He expected those summoned to attend or to provide good reasons for absence [**14e; 15b**]. For magnates and prelates (the 'natural counsellors' of the king) parliaments, like councils, were part of the political furniture through which they expected to be consulted. Even if their attendance was sometimes low, they had clear ideas of how to manipulate parliaments in political crises and a growing identity as a group of peers.[23] The Ordinances, for example, contain provisions for baronial assent in parliament, Lancaster avowed its importance in 1317 [**30b**], and in 1321 some barons claimed that they 'had the power, as peers of the land, to promulgate and establish a new law in full parliament in accordance with the customs of the kingdom'.[24] The prelates found parliament a suitable refuge from Lancaster's attempt to stir up support in the north in 1321 [**17c**] and in 1322 Bishops Stapeldon and Cobham articulated the growing sense that what had been done in parliament would be better annulled in parliament

21 Ormrod, 'Agenda', pp. 26–7; Ormrod et al., *Early Common Petitions*, no. 113.

22 *Historia Roffensis* in Pronay and Taylor, *Parliamentary Texts*, pp. 161, 166; *The Brut*, pp. 213–14.

23 Roskell, 'Attendance of the lords', pp. 156–64; Maddicott *Origins*, pp. 350–1.

24 *Historia* Roffensis, fo. 36v, in Pronay and Taylor, *Parliamentary Texts*, pp. 164, 168.

[**16c**]. The commons' liking for parliament is shown in their frequent re-elections and by the first evidence of a disputed election in 1318 [**14f**].[25] Taxation might be a burden, but they could and did make grants conditional (1309, 1315 and 1316)[26] and sometimes refused requests (1324 and possibly 1325).[27] With more frequent and longer parliaments, the commons developed familiarity with its processes and with each other, which fostered co-operation and more effective action. The disarray among the baronage in the last years of the reign possibly encouraged this further.[28] Chronicles also reveal contemporary perceptions of parliaments. Most chroniclers clearly expected parliaments to be useful and criticised them if they did nothing [**17a–e**]; the Lanercost chronicler, writing in the 1340s, thought Lancaster's trial should have been in parliament;[29] and the author of the *Modus*, whatever his purpose might be, clearly viewed parliament as ancient and important.

Conclusion

Over the reign parliament became increasingly standardised in personnel and procedures. The standardisation was driven by increasingly frequent summonses for 'normal business' and by the crises in which parliament was used. Moreover, whenever wider consultation was advisable, a parliament with the commons present was now the obvious choice. A meeting of nobles alone was no longer enough to represent the 'community of the realm' for all purposes. Parliament was, nonetheless, by no means independent. It remained the king's to call; the lords retained the political leadership within it and parliaments may have been weaker after 1322 with so many lords missing.[30] Its role in the deposition, although important for legitimacy, was supplementary, since the decision to remove Edward was taken outside

25 Edwards, 'Personnel'; McKisack, *Parliamentary Representation*; Maddicott, *Origins*, pp. 338, 340–4; Maddicott, 'Constituencies'.

26 Jurkowski et al., *Lay Taxes*, p. 30; *CCR 1313–1318*, pp. 224, 346; Harriss, *King, Parliament*, pp. 107, 115–17.

27 Buck, *Stapeldon*, pp. 145–6, 157–8; Maddicott, *Origins*, pp. 357–9; Dodd, 'Political legitimacy', pp. 171–2.

28 Maddicott, *Origins*, pp. 331–52; Ormrod et al., *Early Common Petitions*, pp. 2–5; Ormrod, 'Agenda', pp. 16–19.

29 *Lanercost*, p. 244 (Maxwell trans. p. 234).

30 Dodd, 'Political legitimacy', pp. 170–2; *Vita*, pp. 230–1.

parliament.[31] Before the end of the century great claims would be made about the rights and powers of parliament; such claims were hardly visible yet, but their roots are perceptible in the use and views of parliament in Edward's reign.

14 Summoning parliament

Writs of summons had become standardised. By 1294 the formula was set for the commons to come with full power to bind their communities, and by 1312 the nobles also expected a standard writ. Writs for the Lincoln parliament of 1316 were typical of the period, although they gave an unusually long period of warning (103 days). Besides the examples below, for this parliament individual writs were sent to the archbishop of York, nineteen bishops, forty-five abbots, three priors, the master of Sempringham, seven other earls, eighty-three barons and thirty-three officials and judges. A full list of names is in Parl. Writs., *pp. 153–4; the brief calendar in* CCR 1313–1318, *pp. 314 errs in counting only forty-seven abbots and priors.*

(a) Writs to churchmen: 1316 to the archbishop of Canterbury

Parl. Writs, II.ii, p. 152

The king to the venerable father in God, Walter, by the same grace archbishop of Canterbury, primate of all England, greetings.

Because, concerning various and important affairs touching us and the state of our realm and especially and most importantly our land of Scotland, we propose to hold our parliament at Lincoln a fortnight after St Hilary next coming and to have a colloquium and discussion with you and with the other prelates, great men and nobles of the said realm; we order you in the faith and love by which you are bound to us, firmly enjoining you, that on the said day and place, setting aside all other things, you should be there in person with us and with the other prelates, great men and abovesaid nobles and give us your counsel on the said affairs. Warning the prior and chapter of your church of Canterbury, the archdeacon, and all the clergy of your diocese that the same prior and archdeacon in their own persons and the chapter by one [suitable proctor] and the same clergy by

31 Valente, 'Deposition', pp. 856–9, 864–5.

two suitable proctors, having full and sufficient power from the chapter and clergy, should be together there and then with you, to do and consent in all ways to the things which then and there by common counsel, with God's favour, should come to be ordained on the affairs mentioned before. And you should in no way fail in this.

Witness myself at Empington 16 October.

(b) Writs to the baronage: 1316 to Thomas, Earl of Lancaster

Parl. Writs, II.ii, pp. 153–4

The king to his faithful kinsman Thomas, Earl of Lancaster, greetings.

Because, concerning various and important affairs, etc. We order you in the fealty and homage by which you are bound to us, firmly enjoining you, that on the said day and place, setting aside all other things, you should be there in person, with us and with the prelates and other great men and nobles of the aforesaid realm, to give us your counsel on the business to be discussed. And you should in no way fail to do this.

Witnessed as above [Empington 16 October].

(c) Writs to the sheriffs, 1316

Parl. Writs, II.ii, p. 154

To the sheriff of Hertfordshire and Essex.

Because, concerning various and important affairs, etc. We order you, firmly enjoining you, that from each of your counties you should cause to be elected two knights from your said counties and two citizens for each city in those counties and two burgesses from each borough from those more discrete and more hard-working, and cause them to come on the said day and place. So that the knights have full and sufficient power for themselves and for the aforesaid counties, and also the said citizens and burgesses for themselves and the communities of the aforesaid cities and boroughs, severally, to do and consent at that time and place to the things, which then by common counsel, with God's favour, should come to be ordained on this aforesaid business.

The like to all sheriffs in England.

(d) Additional writs, 1316

As with all parliaments, writs of later dates show arrangements being adjusted according to specific circumstances.

i Parl. Writs, II.ii, p. 155

14 January 1316

Henry Spigurnel is ordered that, setting all other things aside, he should come in person to the king's parliament which is to be held at Lincoln a fortnight after St Hilary next coming, and not to hold any sessions in the counties in which he is appointed justice of the Bench during the parliament.

Witnessed by the king, at Clipston, 14 January; on the information of William Inge.

ii Parl. Writs, II.ii, p. 156

17 January 1316

The king to his dear and faithful Roger de Mortimer of Wigmore, greetings.

Since, at the time we issued summonses for our parliament at Lincoln a fortnight after St Hilary next coming, you were to have been in Ireland, we did not write requiring you to be present at this parliament, but we understand that you have now returned from Ireland to our realm; we order you in the faith and homage by which you are bound to us that if you are not returning to Ireland before the said parliament, then you should attend our parliament in person on the said day and place to discuss with us and the great men and nobles of our realm and to give your counsel concerning our business and the state of our realm for which we have ordered our parliament to meet. And in no way fail to do this.

Witnessed as above [Clipston, 17 January].

(e) Absence from parliament

Those summoned were expected to attend and absence had to be justified. For the Westminster parliament of 1315 the sheriff of Northumberland returned his writ endorsed as follows:

Return of Members, p. 49 n.

This writ was proclaimed in full county court and reply was there given me that all the knights of my bailiwick would not suffice for the defence of the borders; and a mandate was sent to the bailiffs of the liberty of Newcastle-upon-Tyne, who also replied that all the burgesses of the town were scarcely sufficient for the defence of the town, and so nothing has been done to carry out this writ.

(f) A disputed election in 1318

*Eagerness to attend is indicated by the first disputed election. Crowthorne sat for Exeter city instead of Devon that year (*Return of Members, *p. 55). For comment, see Maddicott 'Constituencies', p. 73.*

PROME, Parliament of 1318, SC 9/21, no. 79

For the petition of Matthew of Crowthorne, the king is shown that when he was recently chosen by the community of the county of Devon to come here to this parliament on behalf of the aforesaid county, the sheriff of that county a little while ago returned here the names of other knights, for which he requests a remedy; this answer is given: he is to have a writ to the treasurer and barons of the exchequer to have the undersheriff appear to answer concerning his false return, etc.

(g) The earls' claim concerning writs of summons, 1313

*Following Gaveston's murder, the earls agreed in December 1312 to submit to the king, but in February 1313 excused themselves from doing so at the next parliament, partly because the form of their writ of summons was unusual. The earls' claim is interesting for its revelation that they expected a set format, but it is not at all clear from the writs as recorded that the form was different (*Parl. Writs, *II.ii. pp. 72, 80, 101). For the December agreement, see below [**29**] and for discussion of the additional articles, see Maddicott,* Lancaster, *pp. 147–8.*

Annales Londonienses, pp. 225 (narrative), 227 (the articles)

… but because the said earls of Lancaster, Hereford and Warwick were not summoned to the parliament of the said king in the same manner as is found in the chancery register, they did not come but, through messengers, they sent the articles written below to the lord king in these words …

... [The articles, cap. 2] Also the reason why they and we demand a suitable day to make the said submission is because it was agreed before the aforesaid that due summons ought to be made from parliament for all to arrive on the third Sunday in Lent [18 March] at Westminster, which summons was to be made to us in the form that has been used for all time, according to what can be found in the register of chancery, which form was not kept to in our case; because of that they and we will not come in person nor by proctors, as to parliament. Therefore we ask for a suitable day to make the said submission.

15 The business of parliament: proceedings in parliament at Lincoln, 1316

Airmyn's roll is the only official narrative of a parliament in Edward's reign. It is written in Latin (as is normal for a formal record), but the form of appointment for Lancaster is in French, reflecting the spoken and working language of much of government. The rubrics are those given in PROME.

PROME, Parliament of 1316, SC 9/20, no. 1[32]

(a) Opening of parliament

The lord king on Wednesday, the day after the aforesaid quinzaine (28 January), entered a certain chamber in the dean of Lincoln's lodgings, where he was then staying, among the prelates, earls and others present there, and had it announced in public by William Inge, one of the king's justices of Common Bench, that the king greatly desired that the aforesaid parliament, which had been summoned for various and difficult matters touching him and the state of his kingdom and especially his land of Scotland, as is contained in the summons, be held with all the haste with which it could conveniently be done, and that the aforesaid business and other things to be discussed at the same parliament might likewise be dealt with swiftly; and that the lord king had a great concern that the said prelates, earls and others had come there from distant regions and that their stay there, if it were long, would be hard and burdensome to them because of the expense of victuals, which in those days was a greater problem than had once been the case.

32 A translation of the Airmyn roll is also to be found in Spufford, *Origins*, pp. 203–10.

(b) Absence of the Earl of Lancaster and other great men

However, because Thomas Earl of Lancaster and certain other great men of the kingdom, with whose counsel the lord king wished to proceed in the said difficult matters, had not yet arrived, the lord king wished to defer discussion of those matters until the arrival of the aforesaid leading men; but nevertheless he ordered the prelates, earls and others present there at that time to meet there on a daily basis and continue the said parliament and deal with other business until [their] arrival ... John of Sandale, the chancellor, was ordered to receive the proxies and excuses of the prelates and others summoned to the said parliament, who had not come; and he and the others whom the lord king would associate with him were to examine them and to allow acceptable excuses, provided that those excusing themselves had suitable proctors; and they were to give the king the names of those who had not come nor excused themselves nor appointed proctors, so that he could order appropriate action to be taken ...

(c) Receiving of petitions

On the same day it was agreed that petitions should be received and dealt with.

[The names of receivers follow. Difficult cases still pending to be brought to parliament in writing.]

(d) Arrangements for hearing petitions; continued absence of Lancaster

On the following Thursday [29 January] it was agreed to proceed on the petitions.

[The names of those appointed to hear the petitions follow, grouped for England; Gascony and the Channel Islands; Wales, Ireland and Scotland.]

(e) Answers to the petitions of the prelates

On the following Saturday [31 January] [answers were given to their petitions].

(f) Appointments to king's council; continued absence of Lancaster

On the following Sunday [1 February] [four bishops were sworn to be of the king's council, and two of them and two earls were sworn as king's lieutenants in his absence from parliament, until Lancaster and other leading men arrived].

(g) Lancaster present; business of parliament explained

Afterwards on 12 February, that is on a Thursday, in the hall of the said dean of Lincoln, the lord king in full parliament in the presence of the Earl of Lancaster and the other leading men who had previously been absent ... had the reason for the summons of the said parliament and the other things noted above, declared [to advise on Scotland and grant an aid].

After this it was agreed that the aforesaid prelates and leading men on the next day, that is on the Friday [13 February], would meet in the chapter house of the church to discuss the matters mentioned above.

(h) Meeting of the prelates and leading men

On Friday 13 February they met in the chapter house and on Saturday 14 February at the house of the brethren of the order of the Blessed Mary of Mount Carmel for further discussion

(i) Proclamation on the price of victuals

On the following Saturday [14 February] it was agreed that a certain proclamation previously made concerning the selling of oxen, cows, sheep, geese, hens and other victuals for a certain price was to be revoked, and that they were to be sold for a reasonable price, as used to be done previously; and writs were issued on this under the king's great seal.[33]

33 See above [**8a**] for the original price-fixing ordinance [1315] and for further references.

(j) Statute concerning sheriffs

On the same day a certain statute was agreed concerning sheriffs and wardens of hundreds, in the form that is contained on another roll.

(k) Observation of the Ordinances; discussion with Lancaster

On the following Tuesday [17 February] the bishop of Norwich [having declared the statute of sheriffs] added that the lord king wished the Ordinances, previously made by the aforesaid prelates and leading men and agreed by him, and the perambulations of the forest made during the time of the Lord Edward, his father, to be observed in all things, saving to the king his arguments against those perambulations. And on this letters and writs were issued as is contained on another roll; and the aforementioned bishop said some things on behalf of the king to the Earl of Lancaster, which are contained on another roll. [See below, **15o**.]

(l) Grant of foot soldiers for Scottish war

On the following Friday [20 February] the great men and the community of the kingdom granted the king in aid of his Scottish war, from each town in the kingdom, except from the king's cities, boroughs and demesne, one able and fencible foot soldier. [Terms are stated and the grant is not to be to the prejudice of the community of the realm or their heirs.][34]

(m) Summons of military service

On the same day [it was agreed all service due was to be at Newcastle-upon-Tyne on 8 July].

(n) Grant of a fifteenth by the citizens, burgesses and knights of the shires

[The terms of the grant are given.][35]

34 See also [**10a**].

35 For which see [**10a**].

(o) The king asks the Earl of Lancaster to be chief of the council

On the Tuesday before Lent [24 February 1316] ... some words were further spoken to Thomas, Earl of Lancaster, on behalf of the lord king, to remove a certain doubt that the said earl was said to have entertained about the said lord king, informing him that the lord king bore a sincere and whole-hearted goodwill towards him and the other leading men of his kingdom and held them in his special royal benevolence as his faithful liege men, as was fitting, and, because the lord king wished the same earl to be the chief of the lord king's council, asking the same earl on behalf of the lord king and that of the prelates and leading men of the kingdom there present, that he might be pleased to assume the role fully and bring fitting counsel and aid to the business of the king and kingdom, as he was bound to do. And the said earl, thanking the lord king for this, humbly begged that he might consider it and answer later. Afterwards the said earl was sworn to the lord king's council in the form given below:

(p) Form of appointment of the Earl of Lancaster

Whereas our lord King Edward, by the Grace of God king of England, has, with the prelates, earls and barons of his land, in his full parliament, requested his dear cousin, Sir Thomas, Earl of Lancaster, that he might be pleased to be chief of his council in all the great or weighty matters concerning him and his kingdom, together with other prelates, earls and barons, so that between our said lord the king and him they might see what is to his advantage and that of his kingdom, the said Sir Thomas, Earl of Lancaster, for the great love that he bears towards his said lord the king and for the common advantage of the kingdom and of the Ordinances, which he has, of his mercy, entirely consented to uphold and to maintain the rightful laws on all points, and in the hope of correcting several unsuitable things connected with the household and estate of his kingdom, has granted that he will be of the council of our lord king with the aforesaid prelates, earls and barons: provided that whenever our lord king does not wish to act with his advice and that of the others of his council in business concerning his household and his kingdom, when these things have been shown to the said king, the earl of Lancaster can leave his council without ill will, challenge or resentment, and that matters concerning him and his realm are not to be put into effect or carried out without his assent and that of the other prelates, earls and barons, who will be appointed to counsel him; and if any of the prelates, earls and barons counsel our said lord king or do any other thing in a way that is not to his advantage and that of his kingdom, they are to be removed at the next parliament in accordance with the advice of our lord king and his own. And so on from parliament to parliament, for them and for each of them, according to the faults found in them. In testimony of which thing this bill attests to the appointment of the said Earl of Lancaster: it is to be entered on the roll of parliament.

The aforesaid bill containing the terms written above was delivered to William Airmyn, clerk, by the hands of Sir Walter of Norwich, the treasurer, and Sir Bartholomew of Badlesmere, ordering the same William on behalf of our lord king to have the same bill enrolled word for word on the roll of parliament. And that bill is nevertheless sewn to this roll.

16 Views of parliament and its functions

(a) 1309 common petition, c. 6

The petitioners see parliament as a route for complaints and reveal the desire for clear procedures. The appointment of receivers and hearers can be seen in Airmyn's roll of the Lincoln parliament, 1316.

Ormrod et al., *Early Common Petitions*, no. 110

Six: that the knights, people of the cities and boroughs and other towns, who have come to his parliament at his command for themselves and for the people, and have petitions to deliver on wrongs and grievances done to them, which cannot be redressed by common law nor in any other way without special authority, cannot find anyone to receive their petitions as there used to be in parliament in the time of their lord king's father, on whom God have mercy; and concerning this they pray for his grace and remedy.

Answer: The king wills that in his parliaments henceforth, people should be assigned to receive petitions and that they are delivered by his council as they used to be in the time of his father.

(b) 1311 Ordinances

The Ordinances show parliament valued as both political and judicial meeting place. Twelve clauses have substantial importance for parliament. Gifts (c. 7) and doubtful points in the Charters (c. 38) are to be reviewed in parliament. The king must have baronial assent in parliament to leave the realm or make war (c. 9), to choose major officials (c. 14–16), to have Beaumont at court (c. 22) and to change the coinage (c. 30). Clauses 24 and 25 emphasise the importance of parliament for petitions, especially against exchequer officials. Clause 29 demands annual parliaments in a convenient place and clause 40 establishes a parliamentary committee to investigate breaches of the Ordinances by royal officials.[36]

Statutes, I, pp. 157–67; *EHD*, III, no. 100, pp. 527–39

Clause 29. Because many people are delayed in their claims to the king's court because the party alleges that the claimants ought not to be answered without the king, and also many people are aggrieved by the king's officers contrary to right, remedy for which grievance cannot be obtained without a common parliament, we ordain that the king hold parliament once a year, or twice if need be, and that in a convenient place, and that in the same parliaments pleas that are delayed in the way mentioned and pleas in which the justices are of different opinions shall be recorded and determined; and in like manner shall bills that are delivered in parliament be determined so far as law and reason require it.

Clause 40. Likewise we ordain that in each parliament one bishop, two earls and two barons shall be assigned to hear and determine all the complaints of those who wish to complain of the king's officers, whoever they are, who have contravened the abovementioned ordinances; and if the said bishop, earls and barons cannot all attend or are prevented from hearing and determining the complaints then three or two of them shall do so, and those that are found to have contravened the said ordinances shall be punished in respect of the king and of the plaintiffs by the discretion of the said persons assigned.

36 Document 3(c) for clauses 7, 9 and 22.

(c) 1322: Stapeldon's second response concerning the Despensers' exile

*For the king's letter, sent on 4 January 1322 to nine bishops requesting their views on the revocation of the Despensers' exile, see below [**33b**]. Stapeldon received Edward's letter on 16 January and replied on 31 January. The king was dissatisfied and wrote again on 10 February, to which Stapeldon replied on 20 February, restating and amplifying his previous view. Cobham, similarly asked, wrote that revocation could be done by the plenitude of royal power, but that it was better done and seen to be done in full parliament [*Register of Thomas Cobham, *p. 119]. The* Historia Roffensis *recorded that others in parliament felt the same but feared to say so [Buck,* Stapeldon, *pp. 137–9].*

Register of Walter de Stapledon, pp. 443–4 (and trans. Wilkinson, *Constitutional History*, III, p. 359)

But as to the counsel which is sought from us in the aforesaid matters, it seems to us, without prejudice to wiser counsel, that the final revocation of the above consideration, which was done in time of parliament, although without the presence and consent of the prelates, could be therefore more honourably, more usefully and more securely made in parliament than anywhere else, if time permits this and it pleases your highness to call it – would that it might be a peaceful assembly, peacefully summoned – at a suitable place for this and other things. And if it should seem expedient to those who are more discreet and more expert in the laws of England, and with an adequate security given to stand to right in the next parliament, the said consideration might meanwhile be revoked or suspended; for, even though the above consideration was made through injustice and error, it nevertheless does not seem to be right that any injustice or error should enter into the making of its revocation in any manner whatsoever.

17 Chroniclers' views of parliament

Many chroniclers recorded parliaments – regularly or occasionally, in detail or cursorily. All are useful in showing what parliamentary information was available across the country and what attitudes were to parliament. Some provide detail not available elsewhere. The Vita, Annales Londonienses, Annales Paulini *and the Bridlington chronicle recorded parliaments most frequently and they clearly expected parliaments to be useful. In contrast, the author of the* Flores *recorded few, and those with derision.*

(a) *Vita*, pp. 86–7 (1314), 177–8 (1320), 230–1 (1325)

The author of the Vita *regularly reported on parliaments after 1310 (which may be when he started to write). Particularly interesting are his reports in 1314 (parliament and the Ordinances), 1320 (Lancaster demanding an open parliament) and 1325 (that the king was undermining parliaments).*

1314

He therefore summoned the earls and barons to come to his aid [for the Scottish campaign]. The earls replied that it would be better for all to meet in parliament and there unanimously to decide what ought to be done in this matter, rather than to proceed thus without consultation; moreover, the Ordinances demand this. But the king said that the present business required the utmost speed and he could not therefore wait for parliament. The earls said that they would not come to fight without parliament, in case they infringed the Ordinances.

[The author recorded similar demands in 1318: pp. 152–3.]

1320

The lord king therefore summoned his barons to York ... The Earl of Lancaster, however, as frequently happened, when summoned, did not come. He stated that it was improper to hold parliament in secret. For he regarded the king and his supporters as suspect and he declared, no longer privately but publicly, that they were his enemies.

1325

The king's harshness has indeed increased so much today that no one, however great and wise, dares to cross the king's will. Thus parliaments, consultations, and councils decide nothing these days. For the nobles of the realm, terrified by threats and the penalties inflicted on others, let the king's will have free rein. Thus today will conquers reason. or whatever pleases the king, though lacking in reason, has the force of law.

(b) *Annales Paulini*, pp. 262–3 (1308), 292–7 (1321), 322 (1327)

The annals briefly record the majority of parliaments held, but they are full and interesting on two Westminster parliaments: the difficult meeting in 1308 and the disruption caused by the size of parliament in 1321. The reference to the deposition parliament is then disappointingly brief.

1308

Then, on the first day of Lent [3 March], the magnates held a parliament in the monks' refectory at Westminster. The king commanded them to discuss among themselves the state of the kingdom, and, if they made recommendations that worked for the honour of God and the church and for the profit of the king and the kingdom, he himself would certainly confirm their arrangement with the protection of his seal. The earls sent back word that he should give them his commission on these matters and from the outset demanded that each for himself, by a sworn pledge, should keep to what the magnates ordained. But the king was slow in agreeing to the demands, and one earl, angered about the requests, spoke like this: 'First show me the articles to which I am about to pledge my assent; if I see that they deserve to be observed I will keep them, otherwise in no way will I give a pledge.' The others answered: 'Know that, without the king's commission at his order, we can arrange nothing concerning the business of the kingdom; and from that it follows that we cannot put into words what has not yet been conceived in the mind.' Then having waited for the royal assent for some days, the earls left the town, after arranging a day for their return a fortnight after Easter [28 April], in case they could at least reach agreement then ... [T]he same King Edward V,[37] a fortnight after Easter [28 April], was at Westminster monastery; and the earls and barons met together in parliament in arms, but for reason of defence not hostility. They discussed the affairs of the kingdom, but the king was by himself in his palace and the earls in the monastery. The king in truth could not bear to exile the person of his adoptive brother, Piers Gaveston, nor to lessen his dignity ... Finally ... Piers returned his charter of enfeoffment for the earldom of Cornwall to the king, and the king gave it to the earls who set fire to it on the spot.

37 This style of counting starts with King Edward the Elder, AD 899–924.

1321

The same year the lord king held parliament at Westminster [on 15 July] ...

Having consulted among themselves ... about what they might lawfully do, and how to remove and destroy the lord king's evil counsellors, [the Marchers] made a written agreement, ordained and approved according to ancient custom, before their arrival at parliament. Then after the magnates had joined in a league by swearing an oath, they travelled to London to the said parliament from a northern direction through St Alban's. The Earl of Lancaster did not come with them, but he sent messengers with excuses in his name. Then they took themselves to Waltham and stayed there and nearby for four days. During this delay the lords, the Earl of Hereford and Roger Mortimer, sent their letters under their seals by a certain dominus John Hereford, a clerk, to the mayor, sheriffs, aldermen and the whole community of London, in these words:

> Greetings and warm friendship. We send to you our dear dominus John Hereford, the bearer of these letters, to tell you about matters agreed by us about some of you coming to us. On this we ask you to believe him and that he may come in safety. God keep you.

That letter was handed over in full husting. The said mayor with certain aldermen left the husting and went up into a room of the Guildhall to confer on this matter. They immediately sent to the lord king at Westminster to ask what should be done about this. He forbade the mayor and citizens to have any communication with those men, but rather that they should keep the city safe as they had previously promised. Afterwards the said earls and magnates left the town of Waltham, that is on the Wednesday after the feast of St James the apostle [29 July], and came to London, for the most part armed and very well equipped. They did not, however, enter the city, but stayed outside in Islington and Smithfield, split up into three troops. Lord Roger Mortimer had lodgings at St John's Clerkenwell with his household. The Earl of Hereford lodged at Holborn in the Earl of Lancaster's houses with his force. Lord Roger Damory was at the New Temple and Lord Hugh Audley took his place at St Bartholomew's Priory in Smithfield. The rest of the magnates found shelter in Smithfield, near Holborn and Fleet Street, and in neighbouring places, and thus each and every one was lodged in peace without trouble. It was commonly reported that the number of magnates was one thousand five hundred in addition to those coming with them and their servants. In the meantime, while delays occurred and days passed, the lords the archbishop of Canterbury and the bishops of London, Ely, Salisbury, Lincoln, Hereford, Exeter, Bath, Chichester, Rochester and many others, together with the clergy and people who had gathered for parliament, busied themselves and showed care in restoring peace between the lord king and his earls. For this purpose they met often, sometimes in the New Temple, sometimes in the Carmelite friary, both before dinner and after it. They went in turn to the king and, afterwards, to the barons to moderate their feelings. On the Wednesday before the feast of St Peter in Chains [29 July], the aforesaid magnates sent a message to the mayor of London saying that they would come to speak to him and others from the city. These now consulted the king about this. The king gave them permission. Then the mayor and community chose Robert Swalclive, the city's recorder, with other worthy and upright men, who on the following Thursday [30 July] went out to the said earl and magnates at the Earl of Lancaster's house in Holborn. Then the Earl of Hereford spoke to them pleasantly and courteously, to explain why they had come, and that they came for the profit and advantage of the king and of the realm. They were concerned to destroy Hugh Despenser the father and the son and their accomplices, because they harmed the king and the kingdom; and he proved this with many reasons. He also said that Hugh the father and Hugh the son themselves had arranged the eyre[38] in the Tower of London to cause the city's ruin and they had done many other outrageous things. On these matters the said Robert Swalclive and the other messengers requested from the said earl and the other magnates present there a delay until the following Thursday [6 August], so that they could hold discussions again with the mayor and community. Afterwards twelve law-worthy men from each ward met, and when these things which the aforesaid earl had said were explained and read out in their presence, it was recommended that these matters should be told to the lord king, before they gave a reply to the earl and the barons. They then chose three suitable men to send to the lord king; when they had put these matters before the lord king, the lord king postponed his reply until the following day. On that day, which was a Friday [7 August], the lord king forbade the community to take an oath with them to support any complaints; and he said it was his wish to destroy every enemy, even if it should be his brother or his son. On the next day, a Saturday

38 Circuit court.

[8 August], at St Bartholomew's Priory at Smithfield the London citizens gave their reply to the earls, barons and magnates gathered there, written down in these words:

> My Lords, the aldermen and good men of the city beg you, since you are well disposed to them, that you hold each and every one of them excused from the bad reports you have been given of them. They are blameless of any evil intent towards you in any way. May it please you not to believe anything to the contrary no matter what you hear. They would have you know that they have no wish to support either of the Despensers, the father or the son, nor any other who is an enemy of the king and of the land, nor do they wish to oppose in any way your undertakings for the benefit of the king and of the realm. The said good men further entreat you not to be angry because they keep watch and ward of the city by day and night for the city's safety and to keep the peace for you and for themselves.

It seemed to the aforesaid messengers that the said earl and barons were well satisfied with those replies given to them. Days passed, with delays caused every day in this parliament by the lord king in this way, whatever he granted one day he revoked the next, and thus parliament lingered on for many days without the said magnates appearing before the king. And this delay was blamed on Lord Hugh Despenser, who was in a great ship of the lord king, full of armed men, lying in the Thames near Gravesend, and who reached the king, sometimes near at hand, sometimes afar, and sometimes by night. Such anger and burning hatred therefore spread among the said magnates that they all proposed to rise against the lord king and to set fire to all the districts from Charing Cross as far as [Westminster][39] because they believed that the said Lord Hugh the son had been secretly in the lord king's chamber and had brought about these delays. The grace of the Holy Spirit intervened, however, and Lord Aymer de Valence, Earl of Pembroke, who had recently come from abroad, and Lord John of Brittany, Earl of Richmond, the archbishop and other prelates, acting as peace-makers between the king and the earls and barons, and even Lady Isabella, queen of England, pleading on bended knee for the people, meanwhile interceded. They spoke seriously to the lord king, so that, as if led by terror or fear, he accepted the petitions and decisions of the earls and barons on the eve of the Assumption of the Blessed Mary, which was a Friday [14 August]. On that day all the earls and barons came into the great hall at Westminster, which was a wonderful sight, and awaited the lord king's presence. After a long delay the king came into the hall, led by the aforesaid earls of

39 *Monasterium* in the text, most probably for *Westmonasterium*.

Richmond and Pembroke; he looked with a sombre expression on the crowd of people, for the said hall and the whole courtyard outside the hall was filled with people on horseback and on foot. At length, after the said earls and barons had greeted the king, certain matters regarding the agreement between the king and the earls were recorded and read out. Finally they left the king, receiving the king's peace and a charter that was granted to them for all their misdeeds.

1327

... a parliament began in London at Westminster ... and there the lord king Edward, through proceedings brought against him, was deposed. Many good things, however, were ordered and established there. All those who had fled and been disinherited were restored to the lands, properties, and fiefs of their fathers in the said parliament. They also granted, confirmed and increased the liberties of the city of London.

(c) Bridlington, *Gesta Edwardi*, pp. 64–5

*The canon of Bridlington frequently mentions the business done in parliaments (1308, 1309, 1311, 1315, 1316, 1318, 1319, 1322, 1327), and he is particularly valuable for recording the views of Lancaster (1317) and the prelates, as in the example below which sets out their answer to Lancaster's articles presented at Sherburn in Elmet (1321) on the importance of using parliaments for certain matters. For Lancaster's letter excusing himself for absence from the council meeting at Nottingham because the business would be better dealt with in parliament, see below [**30b**]. For the canon's account of the meetings before Sherburn, see below [**32b**].*

When the articles had been read, the earl asked all the prelates to withdraw for an hour and to reply to the case put forward at their pleasure. A copy of the articles was handed to them and they went to the house of the rector of the church and, drawing up the answer that follows immediately below, they replied to the earl:

> Revered lord, the prelates and clergy of this diocese and province who have met here all together because of your request, thank you humbly and from the heart that so much love for the kingdom and this country possesses your heart; and because they all dread an attack by the Scots to destroy the country, as they have ruined it before these times, and if they come in (God forbid) to do evil as before, all agreed to help as far as they can, together with you and other great men and the assembled community, so that the wickedness of the enemy may be restrained, saving always the

> estate of the clergy and the church. Also as to some disturbances recently set in motion in the kingdom, they humbly and faithfully beg your revered lordship and others, whosoever they are who are joined with you here, that, for the reverence and honour of God and the holy church, the safety of the kingdom, and the tranquillity of the people, there should be forbearance in respect of the said disturbances, and that in the next parliament, through peaceful discussions in Christ, friendly accord and unity should be ordained between the lord king and his lieges, whatever it will seem more fitting to arrange. When this is done, all believe that concerning the articles presented here, with God's favour, a timely remedy will be arranged in the said parliament.

This written reply was read out before the earl, and he gave the clergy and prelates special thanks and so, given leave, each one departed.

(d) *Flores Historiarum*, pp. 143–4 (1309), 173 (1316)

This anonymous author was bitterly opposed to Edward and saw parliaments as a further and unnecessary instrument of the king. Unlike other chroniclers he expected nothing from them.

1309

At the turn of this year, there took place many sophistical and rather ridiculous parliaments in England, because under the reeds of fraud and deceit sounded the reed-pipe of falsity and the shriek of the cheat; under whose many and violent noises the lyre of truth and honesty meanwhile lay silent; many came to these gatherings 'dull of heart, loving vanity and seeking lies' [Psalm 4:3]; but men of worth who have 'not walked in the counsel of the ungodly' [Psalm 1:1] withdrew from them, leaving the judgments of the ungodly, hoping for peace and not finding it, and they sought good things and 'behold trouble' [Isaiah 17:14].

1316

At the parliament in Lincoln, which he ridiculously ordered to be held there ... he feigned to be arranging peace with his cousin, the Earl of Lancaster.

18 Tracts

Two theoretical tracts survive from the politics of the early 1320s. The Modus Tenendi Parliamentum *may be the work of an administrator or lawyer, seeking to make sense of or rationalise an evolving institution as much as to justify its use in specific political crises. The tract on the steward may have a more immediate political purpose.*

(a) *Modus Tenendi Parliamentum*, c. 1320–2

The date of the Modus is generally accepted as c. 1321–2, but its author is unknown and its purpose unclear. The chronology and business of parliament in the text show some parallels with Airmyn's roll, but no parliament can be shown to have worked with this schematic precision. Some details are correct (cap. 25 on the parliament roll); some are fiction (cap. 9 on amercements). The tract's views of parliament's antiquity, of its regularised organisation, of the roles of the commons (cap. 23) and of the steward (caps 14, 17), that it should be open (caps 19–21), and that its discussions must be audible (caps 11, 22), are important ones and are, Weber suggested, perhaps the aspirations of an administrative clerk to whom parliament was important but who believed it could be improved.[40]

Pronay and Taylor, *Parliamentary Texts*, pp. 67–79, trans. pp. 80–91; partial trans. also in Wilkinson, *Constitutional History*, III, pp. 351–58

The manner of holding parliament

Here is described the manner in which the parliament of the king of England and of his Englishmen was held in the time of King Edward, the son of King Ethelred; which manner was related by the more distinguished men of the kingdom before William, Duke of Normandy, conqueror and king of England. By the Conqueror's own command and through his approval it was used in his times and in the time of his successors, the kings of England.

Cap. 13. Concerning the king's absence in parliament

The king is in every way bound to be personally present in parliament unless he is detained by physical illness, in which case he may stay in his chamber, provided that he does not lie outside the manor or at least the vill in which parliament is held; and then he ought to send for twelve of the greater and worthier persons summoned to parliament, two bishops, two earls, two barons, two knights of the shires, two citizens and two burgesses, to view his person and testify to his condition. In their presence he ought to commission the archbishop of

40 Maddicott, *Origins*, pp. 364–6; Weber, 'Purpose', pp. 169–75.

the place, the steward and his chief justice so that they jointly and severally open and carry on the parliament in his name, stating expressly in that commission the reason for his absence, which ought to be sufficient, and advising the rest of the nobles and great men of the parliament together with the open testimony of the aforesaid twelve peers. The reason is that there used to be uproar and murmurings in parliament because of the absence of the king, because it is a damaging and dangerous matter for the whole community of parliament and the kingdom when the king is absent from parliament, nor ought he nor can he absent himself from parliament except in the case mentioned above.

Cap. 18. Concerning the order of business of parliament

The business for which parliament has been summoned ought to be considered according to the calendar of parliament, and according to the order of petitions lodged and filed, without respect of the manner of people, but who first proposed, pleads first. In the calendar of parliament all parliamentary business ought to be listed in this order: first, concerning war, if there is a war, and other matters concerning the persons of the king, queen and their children; secondly, the matters of common concern to the kingdom, so that laws shall be enacted against the defects of customary law, judicial law and executive law, after judgments, which are the chief business, have been given; thirdly, private concerns should be brought up and this according to the order of petitions filed, as aforesaid.

Cap. 23. Concerning aids to the king

The king used not to demand aid from his kingdom except for imminent war or knighting his sons or marrying his daughters, and then such aids ought to be requested in full parliament and these requests delivered in writing to each grade of peers of parliament and given a written reply. And it should be known that for the granting of such aids it is necessary that all the peers of parliament consent. It is to be understood that two knights who come to parliament for the same shire have a greater voice in granting and denying than the greatest earl of England, and in the same manner the proctors of the clergy from one diocese, if they be agreed, have a greater voice in parliament than the bishop himself; and this in everything that ought to be granted, denied or done in parliament. And this is evident because the king can hold parliament with the community of his kingdom without bishops, earls and barons, provided they have been summoned to parliament, even though no bishop, earl or baron come in response to his summons; because at one time there was no bishop, no earl, no baron, and yet the kings held their parliaments then. But it is different the other way round. Allow that the communities, clerical and lay, are summoned to parliament, as by right they should be, and for certain reasons are not willing to come, if, for example, they argue that the king does not govern them as he should, and mention specifically in certain articles how he has not ruled correctly, then there would be no parliament at all, even though all the archbishops, bishops, earls and barons and all their peers were present with the king; and therefore it is necessary that all matters which ought to be confirmed or rejected, granted or denied, or done by parliament ought to be granted by the community of parliament, which is composed of three grades or orders of parliament, that is to say of the proctors of the clergy, the knights of the shires, the citizens and burgesses, who represent the whole community of England, and not of the great men, because each of these is at parliament for his own individual person and for no one else.

Cap. 26. Concerning the grades of peers of parliament

The king is the head, the beginning and the end of parliament ... But it must be realised that if any one of the grades below the king be absent, provided that they have all been forewarned by due and correct summons of parliament, nonetheless it shall be considered to be complete.

(b) Tract on the steward, c. 1321

Harcourt dated the tract to c. 1326, but it is more likely c. 1321. The tract's exaltation of the steward's political and legal role was closely aligned with the aims of Lancaster, who had shown his interest in the stewardship from 1307 and firmly raised his claim to be hereditary steward from 1317–18 (Maddicott, Lancaster, *pp. 76–7, 208, 233, 241–2; Phillips,* Edward II, *pp. 334, 338–9, 381–2). The tract sits alongside caps 14 and 17 of the* Modus.

Vernon Harcourt, *His Grace the Steward*, pp. 148–51

The stewardship of England belongs to the earldom of Leicester, and has belonged to it from ancient times.

And it should be known that his office is to supervise and regulate, under the king and immediately after the king, the whole kingdom of

England and all the officers of laws within the same kingdom in times of peace and war, as follows.

The manner in which and when he ought and is bound to exercise his office by service and by his oath of homage and fealty is such: when any man or woman shall come to the lord king's court, whatever court it may be, and possibly to the king, to have and obtain remedy for injustice done to him [or her], and he or she shall not be able to obtain suitable remedy, then the steward of England ought and is bound to receive such petitions and complaints to keep safe until the next parliament to be held thereafter, and to give and assign to such complainants, if they so wish, a day there for prosecuting their petitions, and, in full parliament in the presence of the king, to censure and accuse the officer or officers, whoever they be, who thus have failed in doing justice and to call them to account in respect thereof.

In such a case everyone throughout the kingdom is bound to answer to him, the king only excepted; so that if the chancellor of England has failed in providing the original remedy, and the justices, treasurers, barons and chamberlains of the exchequer, steward of the king's household, escheators, coroners, sheriffs, clerks, bailiffs and other officers, of whatsoever localities or places they be, shall fail or cease doing justice in their processes, judgments and executions of judgments, to the favour of one side and loss of the other, because of gifts, bribes or other means of corrupt provision; and further if any justices, when both parties pleading before them have come to judgment, shall by such corrupt provisions defer and delay such judgments contrary to justice and the law and custom of the realm; and if the chancellor of England, in such case, or any other officer of law, shall allege in parliament and say for their excuse that in such case such hardness and ambiguity of the law arose when the same was heard before them, that neither he nor the court of chancery, nor any other courts wherein he is an officer, were able or knew how to attain the safe determination of the law, then shall he declare the same difficulty and ambiguity in parliament. If then it be found that the law was doubtful in that case, the chancellor and such like officer shall be held excused. And then the steward of England together with the constable of England, in the presence of the king and others of the parliament, shall choose twenty-five persons, or more or less according to what the case shall require, together with other similar cases referred to the same parliament; amongst these shall be earls, barons, knights of the shires, citizens and burgesses, who there shall ordain, make and establish a remedy of law, in all such cases to last for ever. And these laws shall then be recited, written and approved in full parliament and sealed with the great seal and delivered to all places of justice, being thenceforth held for laws, and to public places where it shall seem expedient for the commonalty, to be proclaimed and made public, as everyone is held to know common laws and especially statute laws publicly proclaimed throughout the realm.

And if by chance there was already such a case, either common law or statute law, in which the king, the steward and others of the parliament might understand and see that such defaults and delays occur in processes and judgments and take place through such officers (whence the corruption or malice of such officers plainly and often may be presumed), then he shall be removed from office and some other suitable officer shall be appointed in his place; and if the presumption is against the justices and such like officers, but they, by way of excusing themselves, shall say that they have not until now been aware that they themselves or the courts in which they act have deliberated in such cases, or that they have perhaps been negligent; then they ought to be admonished by the steward on behalf of the king and parliament to study and look more closely at the common laws, so that no such ignorance nor negligence be found in them in similar or other cases afterwards. And if it shall happen again, then they shall be removed from their offices and other more discreet and diligent persons shall be appointed by the king and his council.

[The final paragraphs deal with the steward's right to remove evil counsellors from the king.]

IV: THE SCOTTISH WAR

Introduction

Scotland was, until the Anglo-Scottish truce of 1323, a persistent thorn in Edward's side and a major examination of the effectiveness of his government and of his personal judgement. By any reasonable estimate Scotland was a test that Edward failed and failed repeatedly. In the process of deposition in 1327 one of the chief accusations levelled against him was that 'through lack of good government he has lost the realm of Scotland'.[1] While this was an over-statement, given Edward I had not secured Scotland before his death, it did reflect a widely held view that Edward II had lost the initiative in Scotland. When his father, Edward I, died at Burgh-upon-Sands whilst on campaign against the Scots in July 1307, Edward's first inclination was to withdraw from campaigning. The threat from Scotland could not, however, be ignored and the northern Marches demanded Edward's attention time and again from 1307 until 1323.

Why was Scotland of such concern to Edward II? Campaigning against the Scots was not unique to his reign and the northern border between England and Scotland witnessed extensive but intermittent military operations throughout the Middle Ages and into the early modern period. It was in certain respects Edward II's misfortune to rule at a point of severe dislocation in Anglo-Scottish relations, though his own failure to engage militarily with the Scots in the early years of his reign made him, in part at least, architect of his own misfortune. Scotland was an independent kingdom to which the English crown had laid claim since Edward I had rejected John Balliol's right to rule in 1296. Robert Bruce's violent seizure of the Scottish throne in 1306 and his insistence on Scottish independence from the English crown heralded years of cross-border warfare that tested both Edward's capacity and his authority. As such, Bruce's ambitions for Scotland were used repeatedly by Edward's opponents as a rebuke, his inability to subdue the Scots or even to constrain them from their raids into northern England seen as evidence writ large of his incompetence and

1 See below, [**48**].

incapacity. Furthermore, Edward had frequently to adjust his political ambitions in England in order to secure the necessary support to wage war in Scotland. This also meant that he had increasingly to rely upon parliament and systems of taxation granted by parliament, notably the lay subsidy, to generate the revenue necessary for such endeavours.

Having sought initially to withdraw from active campaigning in Scotland, Edward campaigned for the first time in his reign in 1310. His force was limited as the leading magnates involved in preparing the Ordinances of 1311 refused to campaign with him, a reflection of their commitment to the view that the king should not go to war without the assent of his baronage as granted through parliament.[2] Seen by contemporaries as more an attempt to keep his and Gaveston's distance from the Ordainers in London than to strike a significant blow against the Scots, the 1310 campaign was not a success.[3] It failed to bring the Scots to battle and indeed the English force was harried with some success by Bruce and his forces who, avoiding pitched battles, employed guerrilla tactics to attack the English and inflict significant casualties.[4]

The years following were taken up, in England, with feuding between the king and his opponents which left the country on the brink of civil war and, as the author of the *Vita Edwardi Secundi* notes, distracted the king from his assault on Bruce [**19**]. This presented an opportunity for Bruce to run amok in the Scottish lowlands and the northern Marches, an opportunity he did not overlook. Taking major English towns in southern Scotland, such as Perth, Edinburgh, Linlithgow and Roxburgh, Robert Bruce and his forces extended their military ambition into northern England. Here the ambition was not to secure towns and land but to raid and disrupt. From 1311 onwards, Scots rampaged across Cumberland, Northumberland and County Durham, attacking major towns such as Durham.

This was a situation that could not be tolerated by the English crown. A temporary reduction in the tensions between the king and the killers of Piers Gaveston allowed Edward, in 1313, to secure parliamentary support for a campaign against the Scots. A second parliament, planned for April 1314, did not meet because, according to the king,

2 For a fairly recent discussion of the 1310–11 campaign, see Simkin, 'English army and the Scottish campaign'.

3 *Ibid.*, pp. 15–17.

4 *Vita*, pp. 21–7.

the deteriorating situation in Scotland required a hasty response; as the 1314 parliament failed to gather as planned, Ordainers such as Lancaster were presented with the pretext to claim that the campaign had been called without the support of parliament and so they refused to attend.[5] The campaign against the Scots in 1314 could have provided Edward with the perfect opportunity to cement his authority and reduce that of his opponents in England. There is some indication that had he been victorious he would have employed his enhanced position to destroy those, such as Lancaster, whom he presently had to accommodate. That, however, was not to be. The crushing defeat at Bannockburn is recounted in a number of contemporary or near-contemporary chronicles [**20a–c**].

The siege of Stirling Castle by Edward Bruce, brother of Robert, and his agreement with the town's commander that, should the town not be relieved by English forces by midsummer, the English would surrender the town, goaded Edward into action.[6] The calamitous defeat that followed at nearby Bannockburn is recounted in more than one contemporary source and illustrates a lack of tactical regard on the part of the English, a superior force of heavy cavalry faced with Scottish foot soldiers, allied with the fatal bickering of Edward's magnates. The battle was fought over two days, 23 and 24 June, and the first day's fighting with the Scots led to uncertainty and some loss in the English ranks, including the nephew of the Earl of Hereford killed by Bruce himself; on the second day, a desperate bid to undo the errors and failings of the first encounter served only to make matters far worse. The intemperate charge of the Earl of Gloucester, resulting in his death, may, as the author of the *Vita* suggests, have been prompted by the king's derisive rejection of his advice to avoid battle on that day or competition with the Earl of Hereford regarding the right to lead the vanguard [**20b**].[7] Gloucester was the most important of the English nobility to lose his life, but other leading nobles died, including the baron and Ordainer Robert Clifford and a number of knights of Edward's household [**20c**].[8] Edward was led from the field by the Earl

5 *PROME*, Westminster parliament, September 1313; *Vita*, pp. 86–7, for which see also above [**17a(i)**]; see also Ordinance, clause 9, above [**3c**].

6 While a summer 1314 campaign in Scotland was already being planned in the autumn of 1313, the date was brought forward by the siege of Stirling. The siege began in late March 1314 and not the summer of 1313, as was once believed: Phillips, *Edward II*, pp. 217–19, 223–4

7 For discussion of which, see also Barrow, *Robert the Bruce*, p. 217.

8 *Ibid.*, p. 230.

of Pembroke, who prevented the king, in his grief and frustration, from sacrificing himself in a pointless act of defiance.

The defeat at Bannockburn had a number of serious consequences. In the first place it further weakened Edward's authority in England and forced him to seek the support of those he would have preferred to remove, such as Lancaster. Furthermore, the deaths of leading English lords, especially the Earl of Gloucester, created fissures in the tenurial and political landscape of the early fourteenth century that continued to cause disruption and misalignment for many years, not least in eventually aiding the rise of Hugh Despenser the Younger. Finally, the Scottish victory at Bannockburn provided Bruce and his forces with the latitude to continue their military activity in the northern Marches with greater confidence.

In the years after Bannockburn, Bruce took the fight to the English with even greater force. In Ireland his brother Edward led a campaign against Anglo-Irish lords and sought to disrupt supply lines, especially of grain, to England. The Scottish campaign in Ireland, though, was far more than an attempt merely to disrupt English supplies for use in Scotland, also being intended to achieve a conquest of the entire Lordship of Ireland.[9] However, Edward Bruce was unable to foment a Celtic alliance against the English and instead was drawn into a series of struggles with Anglo-Irish magnates; he was killed in battle near Dundalk in October 1318 [**21**]. Meanwhile, Scottish raiding in the north of England was increasingly venturesome and effective; striking further and further south, the military and political benefits of such raids were also matched by the financial returns for Bruce. Individual truces or tributes paid by English towns and lordships to avoid attack were increasingly common and may have amounted to more than £20,000 paid by the English to Bruce at around this time.[10]

An English response was needed and the work of the Lincoln parliament of January 1316 included an unusual grant of foot soldiers from each town to form the next expedition against the Scots.[11] However, the difficulties of gathering men and resources during this famine year became evident and the campaign was abandoned. Edward's alleged

9 See Phillips, *Edward II*, pp. 253–64; see also Frame, *Ireland and Britain*, pp. 71–98; Phillips, 'Edward II and Ireland', pp. 1–18.

10 McNamee, *The Wars of the Bruces*, pp. 129–40. For an earlier example (1312) of such a truce, between Bruce and 'the people of the community of the bishopric of Durham', see Stones, *Anglo-Scottish Relations*, pp. 289–91.

11 See [**10a**] and [**15**].

attempts to use extraordinary forms of taxation, such as prises and purveyance, to help gather resources for the campaign were also railed against by Lancaster. Local court records from Wakefield (Yorks.) in the autumn of 1316 illustrate the lack of willingness to join the king on campaign, with a series of excuses for non-attendances and disappearances.[12] The failure of the plans at Lincoln to mature into an actual campaign was not the only instance of abortive campaigns during Edward's reign. In fact, similar attempts also collapsed in 1308, 1309, 1317, 1318 and 1323.[13] While the proposed campaign of 1316 faced uniquely difficult conditions, it illustrates the major logistical and political challenges Edward faced in mounting any concerted effort against the Scots.

It would take more than two years for a campaign against the Scots to actually take place. The 1319 campaign to retake the town of Berwick, which had fallen into the hands of the Scots in 1318, proved as fruitless as had earlier English efforts during the reign. The siege collapsed amidst claims of incompetence, as well as treachery on the part of Lancaster; the Scots, avoiding pitched battle with the English, perhaps with the support of Lancaster, raided deep into Yorkshire, routed a rag-tag force of townsmen and clergy at the so-called 'Chapter of Myton',[14] and came close to capturing Queen Isabella [**22**]. A two-year truce followed, a period consumed, in England, with political tension and internecine warfare. In Scotland, where Bruce had already been in a tense stand-off with the papacy over his reluctance to agree terms with the English – a resistance for which he and his clergy had paid with the papal issuance of bulls of excommunication – a measure of the flowering of Scottish independence came in the Declaration of Arbroath (April 1320) [**23**]. In a diplomatic offensive aimed both at assuring Pope John XXII that the Scots wished to secure peace – and thereby facilitate a papal crusade against the Turks – and at insisting Bruce be regarded as a king rather than a usurper, Bruce had proclaimed that a treaty with the English would not be possible until the English crown recognised his own right to rule in Scotland.[15] In the Declaration this position, 'the most eloquent statement of the

12 *Court Rolls of the Manor of Wakefield*, IV, pp. 139–40. And this despite the fact that Scots raided into Yorkshire in 1316, McNamee, *The Wars of the Bruces*, p. 82.

13 McNamee, *The Wars of the Bruces*, p. 125.

14 The battle was known as the 'Chapter' of Myton because of the large number of clergy who fought – and died – on the English side.

15 Barrow, *Robert the Bruce*, pp. 245–8. See also Cowan, *For Freedom Alone*.

case for national independence to be produced anywhere in medieval Europe',[16] was set out with enthusiasm and a case made that the Scots wished to live in peace and not be harried by the English and their territorial ambitions.[17]

The deliberations, truces and treaties that followed the Declaration of Arbroath repeat, to varying degrees, Bruce's aim for recognition and the reluctance of the English crown to concede in this respect. The failure in 1323 of the newly created Earl of Carlisle, Andrew Harclay, was to presume to negotiate a peace treaty, rather than a truce, on behalf of the English crown and one which acknowledged the legitimate rule of Bruce over Scotland. A treaty that proposed 'that the king of Scotland in future may hold his kingdom for himself and his heirs wholly, freely and peacefully' and that 'those not wishing to join this agreement, should be destroyed as disturbers of the peace and tranquillity of the people, and notorious enemies of each kingdom' both removed the English claim to Scotland and made the English crown an enemy in its own state [**25a–c**].[18] That Harclay paid for his mistake with his life is not wholly surprising [**26**]. Edward's thirteen-year truce with Bruce, which followed Harclay's rejected truce, is in certain respects similar but what distinguishes it is the lack of acknowledgement by the English of Scottish independence and of Bruce's right to rule [**27b–c**].[19] Both Harclay's attempt at a treaty and the 1323 truce followed, and may even have been inspired by, one further miserable failure of a campaign in the winter of 1322 [**24**]. A combination of broken supply lines, intelligent Scottish harrying tactics, and the disease and starvation of the English force suggested that, for Edward, a successful venture against Bruce and his forces was no more likely with his domestic opponents defeated. Thereafter, Edward's direct involvement in Scotland was at an end; for the remaining few years of his reign his attention was elsewhere and it was left to his son, Edward III, to come to a more permanent settlement with Bruce and the Scots in 1327/8 with the Treaty of Edinburgh. This treaty, concluded a year before Bruce's death, comes close in its approach and emphases to the

16 Barrow, *Robert the Bruce*, p. 308.

17 Compare also the contemporary Irish Remonstrance: for a modern edition and translation, see *Scotichronicon*, VI, pp. 384–404 (text and translation), pp. 467–83 (notes).

18 Barrow, *Robert the Bruce*, pp. 248–9.

19 In the English enrolment of the truce, Bruce is referred to only as 'sire Robert de Brus' throughout; see *Foedera*, II.i, p. 521. Bruce's own letter patent of the truce identifies him as king of Scotland, with regnal year and a realm over which to rule.

treaty arranged by Harclay in 1323; Bruce's authority as 'the illustrious king of Scots, our ally and dearest friend' was recognised [**28**].

19 Edward's first Scottish campaign, 1310–11

The author of the Vita *reflects on the difficulties, domestic and military, that faced Edward in trying to defeat Bruce. Edward's first foray into Scotland, in 1310–11, produced no positive outcome for the English crown and subjected the English forces to random attack; it was also characterised by a reluctance on the part of his baronage to attend and to act in full support of the king. This combined problem of an obdurate opponent and limited capacity to organise campaigns was a pattern often repeated in the reign.*

(a) *Vita*, pp. 25–7

So the king stayed in Scotland throughout the winter and until the following feast of the nativity of St John the Baptist [24 June 1311], and had his castles put in a state of defence and restocked with all necessary provisions. He went round the cities, towns and castles, and obtained supplies of all things. But Robert Bruce stood afar off, that he might see the end, for there seemed no safe place for him in such a neighbourhood, but always as the army approached he kept to the trackless boggy mountain places, into which such an army could not easily penetrate. And indeed even if the king of England were to lay siege to Scotland for seven years, being shorthanded as he was, he would never commit Robert Bruce to his prison. For the king was really occupied with two projects: one was the defeat of Robert Bruce, in which he acted feebly, because the greater part of the English baronage gave no help in the affair; the other was keeping Piers Gaveston with him, for whose expulsion and exile almost all the barons of England were working together. In these two matters the king, worried and very distressed, could not attain one on account of the other. As has been well said:

He who hunts two hares together,
Will lose now one, and then the other.

20 The second campaign: Stirling and Bannockburn, 1314

(a) *Lanercost*, pp. 206–8

Now about the feast of Pentecost [26 May] the king of England approached the March of Scotland; also the Earl of Gloucester, the Earl of Hereford, the Earl of Pembroke, and the Earl of Angus, Sir Robert de Clifford, Sir John Comyn (son of the murdered John), Sir Henry de Beaumont, Sir John de Segrave, Sir Pagan de Typtoft, Sir Edmund de Mauley, Sir Ingelram de Umfraville, with other barons, knights, and a splendid and numerous army, if only they had had the Lord as ally. But the Earl of Lancaster and the other English earls who were of his party remained at home with their men (except those with whom they were bound in strict obligation to furnish the king in war), because the king as yet had refused to agree with them or to perform what he had promised before. And whereas when his noble father Edward went on a campaign in Scotland, he used to visit on his march [the shrines of] the English saints, Thomas of Canterbury, Edmund, Hugh, William, and Cuthbert, offering fair oblations, commending himself to their prayers, and also bestowing liberal gifts to monasteries and the poor, this [king] did none of these things; but marching with great pomp and elaborate state, he took goods from the monasteries on his journey, and, as was reported, did and said things to the prejudice and injury of the saints. In consequence of this and other things it is not surprising that confusion and everlasting shame overtook him and his army, which was foretold at the time by certain religious men of England.

Thus before the feast of the Nativity of St John the Baptist [24 June], the king, having massed his army, advanced with the aforesaid pomp towards Stirling Castle, to relieve it from siege and to engage the Scots, who were assembled there in all their strength. On the vigil of the aforesaid Nativity [23 June] the king's army arrived after dinner near Torwood; and, upon information that there were Scots in the wood, the king's advanced guard, commanded by Lord de Clifford, began to make a circuit of the wood to prevent the Scots escaping by flight. The Scots did not interfere until they [the English] were far ahead of the main body, when they showed themselves, and, cutting off the king's advanced guard from the middle and rear columns, they charged and killed some of them and put the rest to flight. From that moment began a panic among the English and the Scots grew bolder.

On the next day – an evil, miserable and calamitous day for the English – when both sides had made themselves ready for battle, the English archers were thrown forward before the line, and the Scottish archers engaged them, a few being killed and wounded on either side; but the king of England's archers quickly put the others to flight. Now when the two armies had approached very near each other, all the Scots fell on their knees to repeat *Pater noster*, commending themselves to God and seeking help from heaven; after which they advanced boldly against the English. They had so arranged their army that two columns went abreast in advance of the third, so that neither should be in advance of the other; and the third followed, in which was Robert. Of a truth, when both armies engaged each other, and the great horses of the English charged the pikes of the Scots, as it were into a dense forest, there arose a great and terrible crash of spears broken and of destriers wounded to the death; and so they remained without movement for a while. Now the English in the rear could not reach the Scots because the leading division was in the way, nor could they do anything to help themselves, wherefore there was nothing for it but to take to flight. This account I heard from a trustworthy person who was present as eye-witness.

In the leading division were killed the Earl of Gloucester, Sir John Comyn, Sir Pagan de Typtoft, Sir Edmund de Mauley and many other nobles, besides foot soldiers who fell in great numbers. Another calamity which befell the English was that, whereas they had shortly before crossed a great ditch called Bannockburn, into which the tide flows, and now wanted to recross it in confusion, many nobles and others fell into it with their horses in the crush, while others escaped with much difficulty, and many were never able to extricate themselves from the ditch; thus Bannockburn was spoken about for many years in English throats.

(b) *Vita*, pp. 87–95

When all the necessary supplies had been collected, the king and the other great men of the land with a great multitude of carts and baggage wagons set out for Scotland. When the lord king had reached Berwick, he made a short halt there to await the arrival of the army. However, the Earl of Lancaster, Earl Warenne, the Earl of Arundel and the Earl of Warwick did not come, but sent knights equipped to do their due service for them in the army. On the sixth or seventh day before the feast of St John the Baptist [17/18 June 1314], our king with his whole army left Berwick and made his way towards Stirling. The men-at-arms numbered more than two thousand, without counting a very large troop of foot soldiers. There were in that company quite sufficient to penetrate the whole of Scotland, and some thought if the whole strength of Scotland had been gathered together, they would not have stayed to face the king's army. Indeed all who were present agreed that never in our time has such an army marched out from England. The great number of wagons, if they had been placed end to end, would have stretched for twenty leagues.

The king therefore took confidence and courage from so great and fine an army and hurried day after day to the appointed place, not as if he was leading an army to battle but rather as if he was going to Santiago.[20] Short were the halts for sleep, shorter still were those for food; hence horses, horsemen and infantry were worn out with toil and hunger, and if they did not bear themselves well it was not their fault.

The Earl of Gloucester and the Earl of Hereford commanded the first line. On Sunday, which was the day before St John's day [23 June], when they had passed a certain wood and were approaching Stirling Castle, the Scots were seen straggling under the trees as if in flight, and a certain knight, Henry Bo[h]un, pursued them with the Welsh to the edge of the wood. For he had in mind that if he found Robert Bruce there he would either kill him or carry him off captive. But when he had come there, Robert himself came suddenly out of his hiding place in the wood, and the said Henry seeing that he could not resist the crowd of Scots, turned his horse intending to return to his companions; but Robert opposed him and struck him on the head with an axe that he carried in his hand. His squire, trying to protect or rescue his lord, was overwhelmed by the Scots.

This is the beginning of their troubles! On the same day a sharp action takes place, in which the Earl of Gloucester is thrown from his horse, and Robert Clifford is disgracefully put to flight, and though our men long pursue the Scots, many are killed on each side. Because now the day was over, the whole army gathered at the place where it was to rest that night. But there was no rest; for they spent the whole night sleepless, expecting the Scots rather to attack by night than to wait for battle by day. At daybreak it was abundantly clear that the Scots were

20 I.e. as if on pilgrimage rather than on a military campaign.

ready for the conflict with a great force of armed men. Therefore our men, that is the veteran knights and those who were more experienced, advised that we should not fight that day, but rather wait for the next day, both on account of the importance of the feast and their previous exertion. This practical and honourable advice was rejected by the younger men as lethargic and cowardly.

The Earl of Gloucester, on the other hand, counselled the king not to go forth to battle that day, but rather to rest on account of the feast, and let his army recuperate as much as possible. But the king scorned the earl's advice, and grew very heated with him, charging him with treachery and deceit. 'Today,' said the earl, 'it will be clear that I am neither a traitor nor a liar,' and at once prepared himself for battle. Meanwhile Robert Bruce briefed his company and drew them up in battle array, gave them bread and wine, and heartened them as best he could; when he learned that the English line had reached the field, he led his whole army out from the wood. He brought about forty thousand men with him, and split them into three divisions; and not one of them was on horseback, but each was furnished with light armour, which a sword would not easily penetrate. They had axes at their sides and carried lances in their hands. They advanced like a thick-set hedge, and such a troop could not easily be broken. When, however, it had come to the point that the two sides must meet, James Douglas, who commanded the first division of the Scots, vigorously attacked the Earl of Gloucester's line. The earl withstood him manfully, once and again penetrated their wedge, and would without doubt have been victorious if he had had faithful companions. But look! At a sudden rush of Scots, the earl's horse is killed and the earl falls to the ground. Furthermore, without a defender and burdened by the weight of its body he could not easily rise, and of the five hundred men-at-arms whom he had led to battle at his own expense, almost only he was killed. For when they saw their lord thrown from his horse, they stood stunned and did not help him. Cursed be the knighthood whose courage fails in the hour of greatest need!

Alas! Twenty armed knights might have saved the earl, but among some five hundred, not one was of any use. May the Lord confound them! Some said that the Earl of Gloucester had perished suddenly by reason of his rash attack. For there was rivalry between him and the Earl of Hereford, over who should take precedence over the other in the line, and the Earl of Hereford said that this was lawfully his by right, because he was constable of England. The other replied that his forebears had always led the van, and therefore this was his by custom. Then, while they argued in this fashion, and the Scottish forces were approaching rapidly, Earl Gilbert dashed forward in disorder, seeking to carry off the glory of the first clash; but see! the earl is met by the onrushing Scots and his horse immediately killed; because there was no one to defend him when he was thrown from his horse, he was pierced by many wounds, and was shamefully killed. Alas! Twenty armed knights might have saved the earl, but among some five hundred not one was of any use. May the Lord confound them!

While he was in command of the king's rein, Giles Argentein, an active knight and very experienced in the art of war, saw the earl's misfortune and rushed there, eager and anxious to help the earl, but he could not. Yet he did what he could, and fell together with the earl, thinking it more honourable to perish with so great a man than to escape death by flight; for those who fall in battle for their country are known to live in everlasting glory. On the same day Robert Clifford, Payn Tibetot, William Marshal, famous, powerful and active knights, overcome by the Scots, died there.

When those who were with our king saw that the earl's line was broken and his men ready to run, they said that it would be dangerous to remain longer and safer for the king to retreat. On their advice the king left the battlefield and hurried towards the castle. Then, when the royal standard was seen to depart, the whole army quickly scattered. Two hundred knights and more, who had neither drawn their swords nor even struck a blow, were reduced to flight.

Oh! Famous race unconquered through the ages, why do you, who used to conquer knights, flee from foot soldiers? At Berwick, Dunbar and Falkirk you carried off the victory,[21] and now you have turned your backs to Scottish infantry. But whatever others may say, the hand of the Lord was not with you.

(c) *Annales Londonienses*, pp. 230–1

In the same year after Easter the king and his men travelled to Scotland with their army to oppose Robert Bruce who for many years had kept our king of England from Scotland by main force and falsely. The English king went from the town of Berwick on Tweed to Stirling Castle, which is about sixty miles away. It is situated on the water of

21 In the reign of Edward I.

Forth, which is also called Queensferry, and twenty-four miles away from Edinburgh to the west. The castle was under siege by the Scots, and when the king with his army arrived, a fearful battle was joined between the two sides, but, grievous to relate, the Scots were victorious. They killed Gilbert de Clare, the Earl of Gloucester, Robert Clifford, a baron, Payn Tybetot, William Marshal, Giles Argentein, and many other noble knights. The king of England only just escaped to Berwick by sea. The Earl of Hereford was captured there and later ransomed. All this happened because of the very great sins of the English, namely because of overweening pride, lechery, gluttony, greed and other vices.

Names of the English knights killed at the battle of Stirling:

In the first place Gilbert de Clare, Earl of Gloucester, aged about twenty-three years; his sisters had his inheritance as is related later; he rests at Tewkesbury. Robert Clifford, a baron, Payn Tybetot, William Marshal, Anselm Marshal, John de Montfort, Henry de Bohun, John Rivers, Edmund Mauley, the king's steward, John Comyn, Robert Hastele, Edmund Comyn, William Deyncourt, Giles Argentein, John Lovell 'le Riche', Edmund Hastings, Robert Botevilyn, Oliver Picton, Gerard del Idel, John Gosorald, Hugh Scales, John Elsefeld, John Henebregge, Robert Pulford, Thomas Bosford, Reginald Deyncourt, Robert Applyndene, Thomas Conrad, Thomas of St Legier, Reginald Lem, Robert Bertram, Miles Beauchamp, John Cabery, Thomas Archdeacon [Ercedekene], Nicholas Vipont, Miles Stapelton, Miles Poinings, William Gosyngtone. The greater part of the English foot soldiers and squires were not killed, but God's vengeance and pursuit were incalculable. And certainly that day was punishment for the wickedness of the English, for all had been as if without heart, and all who could fled. Aymer de Valence, Earl of Pembroke, fled barefoot, and the Earl of Hereford fled truly with a thousand armed men; but in the end, through being separated, he was captured and later ransomed. And the greatest number were captured but afterwards, if they could, they ransomed themselves.

21 Bruce and Ireland

(a) *Lanercost*, pp. 212–13, 225–6

1315

The Scots, therefore, unduly elated, as much by their victory in the field as by the devastation of the march of England and the receipt of very large sums of money, were not satisfied with their own frontiers, but fitted out ships and sailed to Ireland in the month of May, to reduce that country to subjection if they could. Their commanders were my Lord Edward Bruce, the king's brother, and his kinsman my Lord Thomas Randolf, Earl of Moray, both enterprising and valiant knights, having a very strong force with them. Landing in Ireland, and receiving some slight aid from the Irish, they captured from the king of England's dominion much land and many towns, and so prevailed as to have my Lord Edward made king by the Irish. Let us leave him reigning there for the present, just as many kinglets reign there, till we shall describe elsewhere how he came to be beheaded, and let us return to Scotland.

1318

Let us now hear what happened to his brother Edward in Ireland. Within fifteen days after the feast of St Michael [14 October 1318], he came to the town of Dundalk with his Irish adherents and a great army of Scots which had newly arrived in Ireland to enable him to invade and lay waste that land and [to harass] the king of England's people to the best of their power. But by God's help, nearly all these were killed by a few of the commonalty, excepting only those who saved themselves by flight; for they were in three columns at such a distance from each other that the first was done with before the second came up, and then the second before the third, with which Edward was marching, could render any aid. Thus the third column was routed, just as the two preceding ones had been. Edward fell at the same time and was beheaded after death; his body being divided into four quarters, which quarters were sent to the four chief towns of Ireland.

(b) *Scalacronica*, p. 57

Edward Bruce, brother to Robert king of Scotland, desiring to be a king [also], passed out of Scotland into Ireland with a great army in hopes of conquering it. He remained there two and a half years, performing here feats of arms, inflicting great destruction both upon provender and in other ways, and conquering much territory, which would form a splendid romance were it all recounted. He proclaimed himself king of the kings of Ireland; [but] he was defeated and slain at Dundalk by the English of that country, [because] through over-confidence he would not wait for reinforcements, which had lately arrived, and were not more than six leagues distant.

(c) *Vita*, pp. 106–7, 154–5

1315

He had also sent his brother Edward to Ireland with a picked force of knights, to stir up that people against the king of England, and subject the country, if he could, to his authority. And there was a rumour that, if he gained his desire there, he would at once cross to Wales, and raise the Welsh likewise against our king. For these two races are easily roused to rebellion; they bear the yoke of slavery reluctantly, and curse the lordship of the English.

1318

God gave us victory over our enemies in Ireland. Edward Bruce and his knights, who now for two years had usurped lordship there, approaching Dundalk to take the town, came up against our army; but when battle was joined Edward fell before our men that day, and five hundred stout-hearted men-at-arms with him.

22 The third campaign: Berwick and Myton-on-Swale (the 'Chapter' of Myton), 1319

(a) *Vita*, pp. 160–7

After Easter all the great men of the land met the lord king at York, and, having held council, they unanimously agreed that all should muster in arms at Newcastle on St Mary Magdalen's day [22 July], and then, God willing, happily make a start on the preparations for a campaign. The nobles also granted to the lord king the eighteenth penny from all England as a war-subsidy.

When these things had been thus arranged, the lord king sent envoys to Scotland to claim the kingdom, offer peace, and allow safety in life and limb to Robert Bruce. For it is fitting for a king to act thus, and to attack his enemies when peace is refused … Robert Bruce replied that he did not much care for the king of England's peace; the kingdom of Scotland was his and belonged to him both by hereditary right and by right of battle. He said that he was justified by these titles, and protested that he neither ought to nor would acknowledge any superior or earthly lord.

At the date arranged the king, earls and barons assembled at Newcastle. There were present Thomas, Earl of Lancaster, the Earl of Pembroke, the Earl of Arundel, and the Earl of Hereford, Earl Warenne, and the lord king's brother, the earl marshal. Present, too, were Hugh Despenser, Roger Damory and Hugh Audley, and these three in place of the Earl of Gloucester; for these three had married three sisters who by a family arrangement had divided the earldom of Gloucester between themselves. The other English barons, who are bound to render a fixed service to the lord king, were there too; and many thousands of infantry likewise had assembled; and all these came voluntarily, because the lord king had granted to each man as much of the enemies' goods as he could seize up to the value of a hundred pounds without restitution. Also the lord king granted to all the sailors, so that they should eagerly attack the enemy by sea, that they might increase their own possessions with as much booty from the enemy as they could take. This right to plunder the Scots certainly roused many volunteers to arms, because they need not fear the restitution which was frequently made after a truce.

Then the lord king set out for Scotland and came first to Berwick with his whole army, and decided on advice that this should be the first place to be besieged, both because it had withdrawn from his authority, and so that they should not expose themselves to danger by leaving an unconquered enemy in their rear. The army was therefore disposed about the town on the landward side, and they began to prepare fortifications and siege-works against it. By sea the sailors in charge of the Cinque Ports' fleet kept so close a watch on the entrances and exits, that no one at all could come out.

While this was happening in Scotland, and it seemed as if there was nothing to fear from enemies in England, James Douglas and his supporters, always ready for intrigue, would have inflicted great loss and immeasurable damage upon us, had not God, the Lord of all, provided for us. For according to the advice of Ahitophel he had chosen ten thousand men,[22] and had resolved to carry off the queen of England, who was staying near York. Indeed if the queen had at that time been captured, I believe that Scotland would have bought peace for herself. But the counsel of the traitor Ahitophel came to nought, and the God of Israel did not suffer so great a peril to fall upon us.[23]

22 See 2 Kings (2 Sam.) 17:1.

23 See 2 Kings (2 Sam.) 17:14.

For one day a certain spy was captured at York; and when he saw that he would be interrogated, he promised, if he should be allowed to escape punishment, to disclose the whole conspiracy of the Scots; this bargain pleased the greater men of the city; the archbishop of York and the king's chancellor, at that time the bishop of Ely, were there too. That spy explained that our enemy James Douglas was to come there secretly with his chosen band, to abduct the queen and also kill all those whom he should take unawares. 'They will hide,' he said, 'on such a day and in such a place, and when they see the appropriate moment, they will carry out their plan.' There was hardly anyone who believed this story, because the lord king of England was already beginning to lay waste the lands of the Scots, and it seemed more necessary for such an army to defend its own frontiers than to seek battle a hundred miles outside its own territory. However, the spy added that if what happened did not bear out his words, he would willingly submit to capital punishment.

Then the archbishop and the chancellor went forth from the city, with their combined retinue, the sheriff and the burgesses and their followers, the monks and canons and other regulars, as well as all the others who were found able to handle a weapon, and they brought the queen back into the city; then she was taken by water to Nottingham. That was a safer place for the queen where neither James nor his traps were to be feared.

The next day, on which, according to the spy, the Scots would be found in their hiding places, the laymen, clerks and men of religion went out again from the city of York. They went stealthily and without noise to take the enemy by surprise, lest, if they were forewarned, they should perhaps take flight. Even so, they were well enough warned, but they did not flee. For when they saw our men advancing without military order, they said: 'These are not soldiers but huntsmen; they will not achieve much.' So the Scots set fire to a large amount of hay that had been gathered there, and the smoke rose, spreading widely in the air. The smoke made it difficult for our men to see, so that those whom they thought had fled they found ready for battle. They were indeed men picked from the whole of Scotland, fit for fighting, fit for every task. Many of our men, on the other hand, were untrained in the art of war, and were readier to flee than to fight. Therefore, when battle was joined many of our men were killed and many more taken prisoner; but the Scots returned unharmed to Scotland with their captives, etc.

Word of this came to the king of England and to our army remaining at the siege, and at once by someone's advice the siege was completely raised. Indeed, the king tried to cut off the retreating Scots by one road and the Earl of Lancaster by the other. In truth, the Scots, in possession of a fortunate permit to pass, returned by the other road to their territory. But why was a siege given up that had cost so much labour to begin? Some say that Robert Bruce had friends. Certainly David would not have escaped the hand of King Saul had he not had his friends amongst the household.[24] That the king raised the siege was blamed on the Earl of Lancaster; he was also blamed for the Scots coming to seize the queen, and the king's enemies returning unscathed to their own country. Some evidence of treachery was openly spoken of, from which the reputation of the earl and his followers was seriously damaged.[25] For it was commonly said that the earl received forty thousand pounds from Robert Bruce to help him and his men secretly, and that at the siege, while everyone was attacking the wall, none of the earl's retinue assaulted it, and that the town of Berwick would have surrendered if the earl's scheming had not hindered this, and that James Douglas on his way back to Scotland passed through the earl's lines, and that the earl went unarmed through the midst of the Scots.

(b) *Lanercost*, pp. 226–8

Meanwhile my Lord Thomas Randolf, Earl of Moray and Sir James of Douglas, not daring to encounter the king of England and the earl [of Lancaster], invaded England with an army, burning the country and taking captives and booty of cattle, and so pressed as far as Boroughbridge. When the citizens of York heard of this, without knowledge of the country people and led by my lord archbishop William de Meltoun and my lord the bishop of Ely, with a great number of priests and clerics, among whom were sundry religious men, both beneficed and mendicant, they attacked the Scots one day after dinner near the town of Myton, about twelve miles north of York; but, as men unskilled in war, they marched all scattered through the fields and in no kind of array. When the Scots beheld men rushing to fight against them, they formed up according to their custom in a single schiltrom,[26] and

24 See 1 Kings (1 Sam.) 19:1–2, 11–12.

25 For the lament that follows, see [**36b**].

26 A pike formation.

then uttered together a tremendous shout to terrify the English, who straightway began to take to their heels at the sound. Then the Scots, breaking up their schiltrom wherein they were massed, mounted their horses and pursued the English, killing both clergy and laymen, so that about four thousand were slain, among whom fell the mayor of the town, and about one thousand, it was said, were drowned in the water of Swale. Had not night come on, hardly a single Englishman would have escaped. Also many were taken alive, carried off to Scotland and ransomed at a heavy price. When the king of England, occupied in the siege of Berwick, heard of such transactions in his own country, he wished to send part of his forces to attack the Scots still remaining in England, and to maintain the siege with the rest of his people; but by advice of his nobles, who objected either to divide their forces or to fight the Scots, he raised the siege and marched his army into England, expecting to encounter the Scots. But they got wind of this and entered Scotland with their captives and booty of cattle by way of Stanemoor, Gilsland and all those western parts. Then the king disbanded his army, allowing everyone to return home, without any good business done.

But the excommunicate Scots, not satisfied with the aforesaid misdeeds, invaded England with any army commanded by the aforesaid two leaders, to wit, Thomas Randolf and James of Douglas, about the feast of All Saints [1 November], when the crop had been stored in barns, and burnt the whole of Gilsland, both the corn upon which the people depended for sustenance during that year and in the houses wherein they had been able to take refuge; also, they carried off with them both men and cattle. And so, marching as far as Borough under Stanemoor, they laid all waste, and then returned through Westmorland, doing there as they had done in Gilsland, or worse. Then, after ten or twelve days, they fared through part of Cumberland, which they burnt on their march, and returned to Scotland with a very large spoil of men and cattle. Howbeit, before the Nativity of our Lord, the wise men of both nations met, and by common consent arranged a truce between the kingdoms, to last for two years, and that truce was proclaimed on the march on the octave of the Nativity of our Lord [1 January].

(c) *The Brut*, pp. 211–12

And it was not long afterwards that the king summoned a parliament at York; and there Sir Hugh Despenser's son was made chamberlain. And in the meantime, while the war lasted, the king went again into

Scotland, which was an astonishing thing to learn, and besieged the town of Berwick; but the Scots crossed the Solway Firth, which was three miles from the king's army and secretly they stole away by night and came into England and robbed and destroyed all that they could, and spared no manner of thing until they came to York. And when the Englishmen that were left at home knew of this, all those who could fight – even monks and priests and friars and canons and seculars – came and met with the Scots at Myton on Swale on 12 October. Alas! What sorrow, for the English husbandmen, who knew nothing of war, were killed there and drowned in the River Swale. And their commanders, Sir William Melton, archbishop of York, and the abbot of Selby and their war-horses fled and came to York. And it was their own folly that they had this misfortune, for they crossed the River Swale and the Scots set fire to three haystacks and the smoke from that was so huge that the English could not see the Scots. And when the English had crossed the water then the Scots came with their wing, in the manner of a shield, and came towards the English in a rank; and the Englishmen fled for they had hardly any men-of-arms, for the king had lost almost all of them at the siege of Berwick; and the Scottish hobblers[27] went between the bridge and the Englishmen. And when the great army had come up with them, the Englishmen fled between the hobblers and the great army and the Englishmen were almost all slain there. And anyone who might cross the water was saved, but many were drowned. Alas, for sorrow! For there were killed there many men, religious and secular and even priests and clerks. And with much distress the archbishop escaped. And therefore the Scots called it 'the white battle'.

23 Declaration of Arbroath

EHD, III, pp. 541–3[28]

To the most Holy Father and Lord in Christ, the Lord John, by divine providence Supreme Pontiff of the Holy Roman and Universal Church, his humble and devoted sons Duncan, Earl of Fife, Thomas Randolph,

27 Or hobelars: light cavalry.

28 With additional reference to a more recent edition and translation of the Declaration, based upon the earlier editions of Sir James Fergusson and A. A. M. Duncan and published online by National Records of Scotland. www.nrscotland.gov.uk/files//research/declaration-of-arbroath/declaration-of-arbroath-transcription-and-translation.pdf (last accessed 19 April 2022).

Earl of Moray, Lord of Man and of Annandale, Patrick Dunbar, Earl of March, Malise, Earl of Strathearn, Malcolm, Earl of Lennox, William, Earl of Ross, Magnus, Earl of Caithness and Orkney, and William, Earl of Sutherland, Walter, Steward of Scotland, William Soules, Butler of Scotland, James, Lord of Douglas, Roger Mowbray, David, Lord of Brechin, David Graham, Ingram Umfraville, John Menteith, guardian of the earldom of Menteith, Alexander Fraser, Gilbert Hay, Constable of Scotland, Robert Keith, Marischal of Scotland, Henry Sinclair, John Graham, David Lindsay, William Oliphant, Patrick Graham, John Fenton, William Abernethy, David Wemyss, William Mushet, Fergus of Ardrossan, Eustace Maxwell, William Ramsay, William Mowat, Alan Murray, Donald Campbell, John Cameron, Reginald Cheyne, Alexander Seton, Andrew Leslie, Alexander Straiton, and the other barons and freeholders and the whole community of the realm of Scotland send all manner of filial reverence, with devout kisses of the blessed feet.

Most Holy Father, we know and from the chronicles and books of the ancients we gather that among other famous nations our own, that is, the Scots, has been distinguished by many tributes to its fame. Crossing from Greater Scythia by way of the Tyrrhenian Sea and through the Pillars of Hercules, and residing for a long course of time in Spain among the most savage of peoples, but by none of them anywhere, however barbarous, could it be subdued. From there, twelve hundred years after the people of Israel crossed the Red Sea, to its home in the west where it still lives today, it came and after expelling the Britons and completely destroying the Picts, and, even though very often assailed by the Norwegians, the Danes and the English, it took possession of that home with many victories and untold efforts; and, as the histories of the ancients bear witness, it has held it free of all servitude ever since. Within their realm one hundred and thirteen kings of their own royal stock have reigned, the line unbroken by a single foreigner. The nobility and worth of these people, were they not otherwise manifest, shine out clearly enough from the fact that the King of kings and Lord of lords, our Lord Jesus Christ, after His Passion and Resurrection, called them, even though settled at the very ends of the earth, almost the first to His most holy faith. Nor did He wish them to be confirmed in that faith by anyone save the first-called of His Apostles (though second or third in rank), namely the most gentle St Andrew, the Blessed Peter's brother, whom he willed to keep them under his protection as their patron for ever more.

The Most Holy Fathers your predecessors, weighing these things carefully in their minds, fortified this same kingdom and people with many favours and numerous privileges, as being the particular property of the Blessed Peter's brother. Thus our people under their protection did indeed live in freedom and undisturbed until that eminent prince the king of the English, Edward, the father of the king who now is, in a guise of friend and ally but in unfriendly fashion, harassed our kingdom when it was headless and the people conscious of no malice or treachery and at that time unused to wars or invasions. The wrongs, the slaughter, violence, pillage, arson, imprisoning of prelates, burning down of monasteries, robbing and killing monks and nuns and other innumerable outrage which he perpetrated on this people, sparing neither age nor sex, religion nor order, no one could describe nor fully comprehend unless he had experienced them.

But from innumerable evils, by the help of Him who though He wounds yet cures and heals, we have been delivered by our most strenuous prince, king and lord, the lord Robert, who, that he might free his people and his heritage from the hands of foes, cheerfully endured toil and weariness, hunger and peril, like another Maccabaeus or Joshua. Divine providence, rightful succession according to our laws and customs which we shall maintain to the death, and the due consent and assent of us all have made our prince and king. To him, as the man through whom salvation has been wrought in our people, we are bound both by his right and as what he deserves for preserving our freedom, and to him we will in all things adhere.

Yet if he were to desist from what he has undertaken and be willing to make us or our kingdom subject to the king of England or the English, we would strive to expel him immediately as our enemy and a subverter of his own right and ours, and make someone else who was well able to defend us our king; for, as long as a hundred of us remain alive, never will we on any conditions be subjected to the lordship of the English. It is in truth not for glory, nor riches, nor honours that we fight, but only for liberty, which no honest man loses but with his life.

Therefore it is, Reverend Father and Lord, that we most earnestly pray and on bended knees and from our hearts entreat your Holiness to recollect, in all sincerity and piety, that, since with Him whose vicegerent on earth you are there is neither weighing nor distinction of Jew and Greek, Scotsman or Englishman, you will look with the eyes of a father on the tribulations and distress brought by the English upon us and upon the Church of God. May it please you to admonish and exhort the king of the English, who should rest content with what he has since England used once to be enough for seven or more kings, to leave us Scots in peace, who live in this poor little Scotland, beyond which there is no dwelling place at all, and covet nothing but our own. Whatsoever we can do to preserve our peace where he is concerned, with due consideration to our position, that we are indeed willing to do.

To do this, Holy Father, is your concern, for you see the savagery of the heathen raging against the Christians, as the sins of Christians have indeed deserved, and the frontiers of Christendom are contracted every day; and how much it will tarnish your Holiness's memory if (which God forbid) the Church suffers eclipse or scandal in any branch of it during your time, you must see for yourself. Therefore rouse the Christian princes who, alleging a non-cause as a cause, pretend that they cannot go to the help of the Holy Land because of wars they have with their neighbours. The real reason that prevents them is that they reckon it more profitable and easier to make war on their smaller neighbours. But how joyfully the said lord our king and we too would go there if the king of the English would leave us in peace, He from whom nothing is hidden knows full well; and we declare and testify it to the Vicar of Christ and to all Christendom.

If your Holiness, too ready to believe the tales the English tell, will not give sincere belief to all this, nor refrain from favouring them to our undoing, then the loss of life, the perdition of souls and all the other evils which follow, inflicted by them on us and by us on them, will, we believe, be attributed by the Most High to you.

Inasmuch as we are and shall ever be in duty bound to do your will in all things, as obedient sons to you as His Vicar, and to Him as the Supreme King and Judge we entrust our cause, casting our cares on Him and firmly expecting that He will endow us with fortitude and bring our enemies to nothing. May the Most High keep you to His holy church in holiness and health for many days to come.

Given at the monastery of Arbroath in Scotland on the sixth day of the month of April in the year of grace thirteen hundred and twenty and the fifteenth year of the reign of our aforesaid king.

24 The fourth campaign, 1322–3

(a) *Lanercost*, pp. 238–40

The king of England came to Newcastle about the feast of St Peter ad Vincula [1 August], and shortly afterwards invaded Scotland with his earls, barons, knights and a very great army; but the Scots retired before him in their usual way, not daring to give him battle. Thus the English were compelled to evacuate Scottish ground before the Nativity of the Glorious Virgin [8 September], owing as much to want of provender as to pestilence in the army; for famine killed as many soldiers as did dysentery.

After the retreat of the king of England, the king of Scotland collected all his forces, both on this side of the Scottish sea and beyond it, and from the Isles and from Bute and Arran, and on the day after the feast of St Michael [30 September] he invaded England by the Solway and lay for five days at Beaumont, about three miles from Carlisle, and during that time sent the greater part of his force to lay waste the country all around; after which he marched into England to Blackmoor (where he had never gone before nor laid waste to those parts, because of their difficulty of access), having learned for a certainty from his scouts that the king of England was there. The king, however, hearing of his approach, wrote to the new Earl of Carlisle [Andrew Harclay], commanding him to muster all the northern forces, horse and foot, of his county of Lancaster, that were fit for war, and to come to his aid against the Scots. This he [Carlisle] did, having taken command of the county of Lancaster, so that he had 30,000 men ready for battle; and whereas the Scots were in the eastern district, he brought his forces by the western district so as to reach the king. But the Scots burnt the villages and manors in Blackmoor, and laid waste all that they could, taking men away as prisoners, together with much booty and cattle.

Now my Lord John of Brittany, Earl of Richmond, having been detached with his division by the king to reconnoitre the army of the Scots from a certain height between Byland Abbey and Rievaulx Abbey, and being suddenly attacked and surprised by them, attempted by making his people hurl stones to repel their assault by a certain narrow and steep pass in the hill; but the Scots forced their way fiercely and courageously against them; many English escaped by flight and many were made prisoners, including the aforesaid earl. Justly, indeed, did he incur that punishment, seeing that it was he himself who had prevented peace being made between the realms.

25 Andrew Harclay's treaty with the Scots, 1323

A number of chroniclers describe, in varying degrees of detail, Andrew Harclay's fateful treaty with the Scots in 1323. The rise and precipitous fall of Harclay, as well as the nature of his death – hanged, drawn and quartered by the order of a vengeful king – is an account that few chroniclers could ignore. The treaty itself survives in three versions of varying length and detail, one of which is recorded in the Bridlington chronicle as follows.[29]

(a) *Bridlington*, pp. 82–3

Also the same Andrew made an agreement and negotiated with Robert Bruce, king of Scotland, on certain articles opposed to the right of the king of England, as ⌜is seen⌝ in indentures about this made between them, of which a copy is written in the other book among the *Incidentia Cronicorum*; and because repetition of words often occurs in the same, I will briefly indicate the substance of the articles; thus the first article went as follows:

> Since the inhabitants of each region, namely England and Scotland, living close together, carried on richly and actively while each kingdom was being ruled separately from the other by a king of its own nation and by the laws and ancient customs of the country, therefore the same practice should be kept henceforth; and all followers of such an agreement should show careful vigilance, with all counsel and aid so that the king of Scotland in future may hold his kingdom for himself and his heirs wholly, freely and peacefully. Those, however, not wishing to join this agreement, should be destroyed as disturbers of the peace and tranquillity of the people, and notorious enemies of each kingdom. To those, therefore, who are willing to pledge themselves and agree to a convention of this kind, the aforesaid king of Scotland professes himself willing to affirm and give security that he will be a good lord to them in help, advice and defence, in all and every thing which can arise for the inhabitants of either kingdom, to the general profit and honour of the kingdom in accordance with the declaration and judgement of twelve persons, of whom six should be chosen by the king of Scotland and six by the said earl, to ordain and determine all things which touch the advantage and peace of the aforesaid kingdoms. Also the aforesaid king of Scotland will have a similar guarantee from all those who wish to participate in such an agreement as the aforesaid shall arrange. All the

29 For the three texts, see *Regesta Regum Scottorum*, V, ed. Duncan, pp. 480–5. For an English translation of the longer French text from the Exchequer Memoranda Rolls, see also Stones, *Anglo-Scottish Relations*, pp. 309–15.

upholders, supporters and parties to the same convention, together with the aforesaid king, will not fail to ruin anyone who does not wish to agree to give that surety, he being thus against [the convention]. Also if the lord king of England within the following year should be willing to agree to such a covenant, namely that the aforesaid king of Scotland should have and hold his kingdom for himself and his heirs freely and independently, as said above, then the said king of Scotland will have a certain monastery built within the kingdom of Scotland with an annual income of five hundred marks sterling for the souls of all killed in the aforesaid wars; added to this he will pay the king of England within the next ten years forty thousand marks, namely four thousand marks sterling each year. The same king of England will also have the right of giving in marriage the male heir of the aforesaid king of Scotland for marriage into his own family, if it shall seem to the above noted twelve persons that it will be to the advantage of the people of both kingdoms.

(b) *Adae Murimuth*, pp. 38–9

AD 1322 the seventh year of the said Pope John, and sixteenth of the said king Edward, about the feast of the Purification, Lord Andrew Harclay, recently made Earl of Carlisle, as has been written, on the pretext of making peace, arranged for himself to marry Robert Bruce's sister; the king of England, declaring him a traitor, had him seized for this by Lord Anthony Lucy, who was the earl's most intimate friend, and in whom he fully trusted. The earl was afterwards in the same town, on 3 March [1323], hanged and quartered; his head was sent to London, and the four quarters to four parts of England.

(c) *Lanercost*, pp. 241–3

Wherefore, when the said Earl of Carlisle perceived that the king of England neither knew how to rule his realm nor was able to defend it against the Scot, who year by year laid it more and more waste, he feared lest at last he [the king] should lose the entire kingdom; so he chose the lesser of two evils, and considered how much better it would be for the community of each realm if each king should possess his own kingdom freely and peacefully without any homage, instead of so many homicides and arsons, captivities, plunderings and raidings taking place every year. Therefore, on 3 January [1323] the said Earl of Carlisle went secretly to Robert Bruce at Lochmaben and, after holding long conference and protracted discussion with him, at length, to his own perdition, came to agreement with him in the following bond. The earl firmly pledged himself, his heirs and their adherents to advise and assist with all their might in maintaining the said Robert as king of Scotland, his heirs and successors, in the aforesaid independence, and to oppose with all their force all those who would not join in nor even consent to the said treaty, as hinderers of the public and common welfare. And the said Robert, king of Scotland, pledged himself upon honour to assist and protect with all his might the said earl and all his heirs and their adherents according to the aforesaid compact, which he was willing should be confirmed by six persons in each [kingdom] to be nominated by the aforesaid king and earl. And if the king of England should give his assent to the said treaty within a year, then the king of Scots should cause a monastery to be built in Scotland, the rental whereof should be five hundred merks, for the perpetual commemoration of and prayer for the souls of those slain in the war between England and Scotland, and should pay to the king of England within ten years 80,000 merks of silver, and that the king of England should have the heir male of the king of Scotland in order to marry him to any lady of his blood.

On behalf of the king of Scotland my Lord Thomas Randolf, Earl of Moray, swore to the faithful fulfilment of all these conditions without fraud, and the said Earl of Carlisle in his own person, touching the sacred gospels; and written indentures having been made out, their seals were sent thereto mutually.

Now the Earl of Carlisle made the aforesaid convention and treaty with the Scots without the knowledge and consent of the king of England and of the kingdom in parliament; nor was he more than a single individual, none of whose business it was to transact such affairs. But the said earl, returning soon after from Scotland, caused all the chief men in his earldom to be summoned to Carlisle, both regulars and laymen, and there, more from fear than from any liking, they made him their oath that they would help him faithfully to fulfil all the things aforesaid. But after all these things had been made known for certain to the king and kingdom of England, the poor folk, middle class and farmers in the northern parts were not a little delighted that the king of Scotland should freely possess his own kingdom on such terms that they themselves might live in peace. But the king and his council were exceedingly put out (and no wonder!) because he whom the king had made an earl so lately had allied himself to the Scots, an excommunicated enemy, to the prejudice of the realm and crown, and would compel the lieges of the king of England to rebel with him against the king; wherefore they [the king and council] publicly proclaimed him as a traitor.

26 The trial of Adam Harclay

(a) *Lanercost*, pp. 244–5

... a messenger was sent to the king at York, to announce to him the earl's arrest and all that had taken place, that he might send word to Sir Antony how he wished the oft-mentioned earl to be dealt with.

... On the feast of St Cedda Bishop [2 March] (that is, on the sixth day after the earl's arrest), there arrived in Carlisle from the king a number of men-at-arms, with whom was the justiciary Sir Geoffrey de Scrope, who on the next day, namely 3 March, sat in judgment in the castle, and pronounced sentence upon the earl as if from the mouth and in the words of the king, condemning him first to be degraded and stripped of the dignity of earldom by being deprived of the sword given him by the king, and in like manner of knightly rank by striking off from his heels the gilded spurs, and thereafter to be drawn by horses from the castle through the town to the gallows of Harraby and there to be hanged and afterwards beheaded; to be disembowelled and his entrails burnt; his head to be taken and suspended on the Tower of London; his body to be divided into four parts, one part to be suspended on the tower of Carlisle, another at Newcastle-upon-Tyne, a third at Bristol and the fourth at Dover.

When this sentence was pronounced the earl made answer: 'Ye have divided my carcass according to your pleasure, and I commend my soul to God.' And so, with most steadfast countenance and bold spirit, as it seemed to the bystanders, he went to suffer all these pains, and, while being drawn through the town, he gazed upon the heavens, with hands clasped and held aloft and likewise his eyes directed on high. Then under the gallows, whole in body, strong and fiery in spirit and powerful in speech, he explained to all men the purpose he had in making the aforesaid convention with the Scots, and so yielded himself to undergo the aforesaid punishment.

27 Anglo-Scottish Truce, 1323

(a) *Bridlington*, p. 84

In the year of the Lord 1323, through the agency and endeavours of Lord Henry Sully at Newcastle there was a certain negotiation, with the knowledge of the kings of England and Scotland, between the Earl of Pembroke, Hugh Despenser the son, Master Robert Baldock, archdeacon of Middlesex, Lord William Herle, knight, William Airmyn, canon of the church of the Blessed Peter at York, and Geoffrey le Scrope on the king of England's side, and William, bishop of St Andrew's, Thomas Randolf, Earl of Moray, John de Menteith, and Robert Lowther, knights, Master William Twynham, clerk, envoys of the king of Scotland on the other side, about establishing a perpetual peace between the kingdoms of England and Scotland. But because it seemed to them, when many and various arguments had been put forward hither and thither, that so arduous and burdensome a business could not be duly completed without greater counsel and deliberation, with the assent of the aforesaid parties a truce was entered on for the next thirteen years following, in the hope that meanwhile a perpetual peace could be arranged between the aforesaid kingdoms. And because the truce contains various points within it, a copy of it is put in the other book among the *Incidentia Cronicorum.*

(b) *Foedera*, II.i, p. 521

The opening clause from the English record of the 1323 truce illustrates the English representation of Bruce and his authority.

The 30th May, in the year of grace MCCCXXIII, and of our reign sixteen, by the agreement of archbishops, bishops, earls and barons of our realm, it is agreed

Between us, and on behalf of us, and on behalf of our lands of England, Wales, Gascony, and Ireland together with their appurtenances, and our subjects, adherents and allies of the one part, and the said representatives of Scotland, on behalf of the said Lord Robert of Bruce, his subjects, adherents and allies, and on behalf of the land of Scotland together with their appurtenances of the other part;

[There is to be a] cessation of hostilities and truce to last from the twelfth of June next following, and from this day for the next thirteen years …

(c) *Regesta Regum Scottorum*, V, ed. Duncan, pp. 500–1

The opening clause from the Scottish record of the 1323 truce identifies the realm (rather than the land) of Scotland as held by Bruce, as well as his regnal year.

The 30th May, in the year of grace MCCCXXIII, and of our reign seventeen, by the agreement of archbishops, bishops, earls and barons of the realm of England, it was agreed

Between the said king of England, and on behalf of himself, and on behalf of his lands of England, Wales, Gascony and Ireland together with their appurtenances, and on behalf of their subjects, adherents and allies of the one part, and our said representatives of Scotland, on behalf of us, our subjects, adherents and allies, and on behalf of our realm of Scotland together with its appurtenances of the other part;

[There is to be a] cessation of hostilities and truce to last from the twelfth of June next following, and from this day for the next thirteen years …

For the full Scottish version of the truce, and discussion of its variants, see Regesta Regum Scottorum, *V, ed. Duncan, pp. 499–503.*

28 Anglo-Scottish Treaty, 1327/1328

This is the opening section of a quitclaim sealed by Edward III at York in March 1328; a prior agreement made at Edinburgh in March 1327 includes the main detail of the treaty. The treaty is typically referred to as the Treaty of Edinburgh, where the terms were negotiated, but is also known as the Treaty of Northampton, where the treaty was confirmed. For the full text, see Stones, Anglo-Scottish Relations, *pp. 323–41.*

Stones, *Anglo-Scottish Relations*, pp. 323–5

We, Edward, by the grace of God, king of England, lord of Ireland, and duke of Aquitaine, give eternal greeting in the Lord to all who shall inspect the present letter. We, and certain of our predecessors as kings of England, tried to assert rights of rule, dominion or superiority over the realm of Scotland, and in consequence a grievous burden of wars has long afflicted the realms of England and Scotland: therefore, considering the killings, slaughter, crimes, destruction of churches and ills innumerable which so often befell the inhabitants of each realm, by reason of these wars, and the advantages which would accrue to each kingdom, to their mutual gain, if they were joined by the stability of perpetual peace, and thus enjoyed greater security against the evil attempts of those within or without desiring to rebel or to attack them, we wish and grant by the present letter, on behalf of ourselves, our heirs and all our successors, with the common counsel, assent and consent of the prelates, magnates, earls, barons and communities of our realm assembled in our parliament, that the realm of Scotland, defined by its true marches as they existed in the time of Alexander, of worthy memory, the late king of Scotland, shall remain for ever to the eminent prince Lord Robert, by the grace of God the illustrious king of Scots, our ally and dearest friend, and to his heirs and successors, divided in all things from the realm of England, entire, free and quit, and without any subjection, servitude, claim or demand. Any right in the realm of Scotland which we or our ancestors have sought in past times, in any manners, we renounce and surrender, by the present letter, to the king of Scotland and his heirs and successors.

V: THE MIDDLE YEARS

Introduction

The death of Gaveston in June 1312 has been described by historians of the reign as a watershed moment, defining the following decade's politics and leading, if not inexorably then with at least the inevitably afforded by hindsight, to civil war and the death of Gaveston's own killers. In the months after Gaveston was killed, Edward set about weakening and dividing the opposition. The act of killing Gaveston drove some of that group back to Edward; notably, the Earl of Pembroke, angered at the death and the breach of his own act of good faith, abandoned the opponents of the king and restored himself to Edward's side. There was the real possibility of open warfare in the late summer and early autumn of 1312, and both sides, the king and his opponents, maintained a war footing. Papal nuncios arrived in England in the autumn intending to help re-establish relations between the parties and, over a period of some months, during which both the king and the leading earls, especially Lancaster, displayed their obduracy, a degree of settlement was reached and was recorded in an eventual royal pardon of those responsible for Gaveston's death [**29**]. Rather than being a measure of success for the king's opponents, the grant of a pardon, eventually achieved by the autumn of 1313, is best seen as a limited victory for Edward.[1] The text of the pardon, unlike earlier documents, such as the first attempt at a treaty, drafted in the autumn of 1312 and issued in pursuance of a rapprochement between the king and his opponents, affords Gaveston's killers no credit for their act or justification under the pretext of the Ordinances of 1311. In fact, the very issuance of a pardon makes clear that their action was beyond, rather than according to, the law.[2]

The restoration of formal relations between Edward and his opponents permitted and, indeed, demanded some return to the normal business of government. Most important in that respect was a renewed endeavour in the north and the urgent need for a campaign against the Scots. The Westminster parliament of September 1313 provided the king with

1 Schriber, 'Edward II and the tactics of kingship'.

2 *CPR 1313–1317*, pp. 21–6; *Foedera*, II.i, pp. 230–1; Maddicott, *Lancaster*, pp. 150–1.

the assent and resources to mount such a campaign, and the following year, 1314, he led his forces against the Scots.

The battle at Bannockburn is discussed in more detail in Chapter IV. Here we need note only that it was a resounding victory for the Scottish forces under Robert Bruce and accounted for the death or capture of a number of leading English nobles, the most significant of whom was the Earl of Gloucester, who was killed on the second day of fighting. His death, and the eventual division of his earldom between his three sisters and their husbands, redrew the map of the political landscape, and the king's relations with his magnates, both opponents and allies, were necessarily redefined in the months and years after Bannockburn. Defeat by the Scots added nothing to Edward's lustre, while a further material consequence was the death of the Earl of Gloucester and a redistribution and division of his earldom. Without the support of any particular favourite – none such emerging after the killing of Gaveston in 1312 – Edward had instead to engineer support from established magnates, including erstwhile allies and enemies, notably the earls of Pembroke and Lancaster. He also looked to a newly emerging cohort of younger barons, including the husbands or soon-to-be husbands of the Gloucester heiresses – Hugh Despenser the Younger, Hugh Audley and Roger Damory – in order to bolster his authority. Chiefly through a distribution of largesse, Edward sought to reconstruct about him a new and 'loyal' party of magnates; the lack of a central and dominant recipient of his patronage also led to uncertainty and a degree of turmoil as leading magnates competed for proximity to the throne and its concomitant advantages.[3] We are aware of two significant developments emerging from this uncertainty. The first was a brief period of partial rapprochement between Edward and Lancaster, which reached its highest point in early 1316 at the Lincoln parliament [**15**]; the second was a jostling for position and a series of realignments amongst lesser and up-and-coming nobles.

The Lincoln parliament of January 1316 is notable not just for the evidence of Lancaster's rising star. In terms of the documentation of English medieval parliaments, the record of this parliament – a surviving parliament roll which narrates much of the business done – is our earliest and best example of such a record, a point discussed in more detail in a previous chapter.[4] It is this early survival which

3 Maddicott, *Lancaster*, pp. 192–6.

4 The Lincoln parliament of 1316 is discussed more fully and selected passages from the roll are given in Chapter III: Parliament.

also offers us an important insight into the changing authority of the Earl of Lancaster. Well before the parliament at Lincoln and in the immediate aftermath of Bannockburn, it was evident that Edward recognised the need to modify his stance and soften his approach to his opponents. The parliament at York in the autumn of 1314 had approved again the Ordinances of 1311 and accepted some removal of royal supporters from court. By the autumn of 1315 we find Edward even writing to Lancaster for advice on baronial assemblies in the north and receiving a rather disdainful response [**30a**]. By early 1316, therefore, Lancaster's attendance at Lincoln was a mark both of his confidence and of Edward's incapacity; that the main business of the parliament was postponed until Lancaster's arrival [**15b**], and that he could condescend to accept the proposal made there that he head the king's council [**15o**], both underline the dramatic growth in his authority. In fact, this was the high point of his formal authority; thereafter a decline in relations set in which saw little significant respite and led ultimately to conflict and the earl's execution in 1322. For a few brief months, after the Lincoln parliament, through the summer of 1316, there was, however, the possibility that Edward and Lancaster might co-operate in matters of government. The gathering at the Lincoln parliament was intended to promote a new campaign against the Scots; an unusual combination of lay subsidy and military levy was announced to support an expedition in the late summer of 1316 [**15l**; **10a**].

Despite his newfound proximity to the throne, Lancaster was not an energetic ally of Edward and remained at heart a critic of the king's governance, especially when Edward sought to raise funds for the proposed campaign through extraordinary taxation, including the much-maligned prises and purveyance. Edward's failure to implement further changes to the personnel of his household was also a rebuke to Lancaster and his adherents. That the plans for a new Scottish campaign eventually foundered cannot, however, be explained only by Lancaster's prevarication and limited support as well as Edward's intransigence: plans were as much or more defeated by the prevailing economic conditions in 1315 and 1316, of which dearth and famine, discussed in an earlier section, were the most prominent.[5] In addition, sporadic uprisings, by Adam Banaster in south Lancashire in the autumn of 1315 and by Llywelyn Bren in south Wales in the first months of 1316, and by the citizens of Bristol – which also came to a head in 1316, while chiefly levelled at local authority and lordship

5 See above, Chapter II: The king's wealth.

rather than at the crown – added to a sense of disunity, tension and fractured government.[6] The failure to bring about a Scottish campaign in 1316, as proposed at Lincoln, served to confirm the weaknesses at the heart of government and soon helped shift Lancaster beyond Edward's orbit. By August 1316 Lancaster had effectively withdrawn from Edward's council. His allegation that the king had resorted to prises and purveyance, the much-maligned forms of taxation against which the Ordainers had railed in 1311, and Edward's continued resistance to reform of his household, provided Lancaster with the excuse to distance himself even further from the crown.[7] His correspondence with the king, explaining his refusal to attend council in July 1317, for instance, allowed him to set out such concerns and to pursue the moral high ground [**30b**].

By the end of 1316, alienated from the king once again, Lancaster was also busy isolating himself from a good number of his peers, notably in a number of disputes with various earls and barons; these included some of the new generation of leading nobles, such as the husbands of the Gloucester heiresses, namely Hugh Despenser the Younger, Hugh Audley and Roger Damory, as well as Lancaster's contemporaries, including the Earl of Pembroke and the Earl Warenne. In the case of the latter, a dispute over Warenne's proposed divorce from his wife spilled over into violent disorder and Warenne's abduction of Lancaster's own wife, Alice de Lacy, in May 1317. The death of the Earl of Warwick in 1315 also reduced the number of leading nobles most closely aligned to Lancaster. Lancaster's aggressive behaviour, such as his attacks on Warenne's property in south Yorkshire in late 1317, extended not only towards his peers; the employment of retainers and northern knights, such as Gilbert de Middleton, to disrupt the election of the bishop of Durham by kidnapping Louis de Beaumont in September 1317 challenged royal authority in the north of England.[8]

In the meantime, Edward, through a series of written contracts or indentures, was seeking to bolster his support amongst both the old guard, such as Pembroke, and the upcoming nobles, such as Audley, Damory and the younger Despenser. An indenture drawn up in November 1317 between Damory, Pembroke and another of Edward's newly indentured supporters, Bartholomew Badlesmere, illustrates the

6 Tupling, *South Lancashire*; Maddicott, *Lancaster*, pp. 174–7; Smith, 'Rebellion of Llywelyn Bren'; Fuller, 'Tallage of 6 Edward II', pp. 175–87.

7 Maddicott, *Lancaster*, pp. 187–90.

8 *Ibid.*, pp. 204–6.

precariousness of the situation [31a]. Once seen as an attempt by the three courtiers to create a block or 'middle party', and thereby to restore some control to the king's actions and to thwart the ambitions of Lancaster, the intention behind the indenture has been more recently characterised as an effort by two of the parties, Pembroke and Badlesmere, to control the ruthless ambition of the third, Damory.[9] As such, the indenture stands as evidence for the competitive nature of early fourteenth-century noble society, with individuals vying for proximity to the king and the benefits that such proximity might bestow, as well as the contemporary view of Edward's likely poor management of such a situation.

The tension between Lancaster, the king and other leading nobles was temporarily resolved in August 1318 by the Treaty of Leake, an agreement negotiated through the agency of the country's leading ecclesiastics and intended to restore a working relationship between the king and his leading tenants-in-chief [31b].[10] The provisions of the treaty included a commitment to maintain a body of leading churchmen and nobles with the king for intervals of three months. This immediate and ever-present council did not include Lancaster in person – he was, though, to be represented by one of his leading retainers – but reflected a broad constituency of the political elite. As such, the Leake Treaty fulfilled a similar remit to that intended by the November 1317 indenture between Pembroke, Badlesmere and Damory in reducing the opportunity for a single noble to enjoy special favour from the king.

The rapprochement at Leake was confirmed at the York parliament in 1318 and paved the way, via a further parliament at York in May 1319, for a concerted effort against the Scots in 1319. This culminated, however, in further military embarrassment, the collapse of the siege of Berwick, Scottish raids into England and accusations of treachery levelled at Lancaster.[11] The latter was, it was claimed, in secret agreement with the Scots and facilitated their retreat from their assault in England in order to protect his own interests in the north. By the end of 1319, with tensions and rivalries abundant amongst his own nobles, Edward agreed a two-year truce with the Scots; in the meantime, Lancaster distanced himself further from Edward and refused to

9 Davies, *Baronial Opposition*, pp. 425–43; Phillips, *Aymer de Valence*, pp. 136–77.

10 Phillips, *Edward II*, p. 320.

11 These events and the events of the 1319 campaign are discussed more fully in Chapter IV: The Scottish war.

attend the January 1320 parliament on the spurious grounds that the parliament was being held in secret. The divide between the parties was also evident when the royal entourage, heading south to London a few weeks later, was abused by Lancaster's retainers as they proceeded past Lancaster's stronghold at Pontefract.[12]

Lancaster's retreat from closer engagement with Edward helped pave the way for other opportunists, most especially Hugh Despenser the Younger. From the mêlée of competing nobles in the middle years of the reign, it was the Despensers, Hugh the elder and his son, Hugh the Younger, who emerged triumphant.[13] Their headway in the Welsh Marches saw Hugh Despenser the Younger acquire lands to which other lords, including Humphrey de Bohun, the Earl of Hereford, a key ally of Lancaster, had at the very least competing claims. Such aggrandisements, aided and abetted by the crown, caused consternation and encouraged plotting to secure the downfall of the Despensers. The 1321 accusations levelled against them are certainly far from fanciful, though there is also undoubtedly some degree of over-statement. What is generally accepted is that Hugh Despenser the Younger employed the energy of his ambition and his proximity to the king to his considerable advantage. In so doing, and especially in his successful attempt to secure the lordship of Gower, he drew the ire of those with competing claims as well as that of the Marcher lords who were defensive of their own rights against the crown. In taking Gower in 1320 the younger Despenser's actions, and the support offered by the king in facilitating them, confirmed to his opponents that the balance of power had tipped dangerously in favour of the Despensers.[14]

The rise to power of Hugh Despenser the Younger, and of his father, prompted an inevitable and violent response. By the spring of 1321 plans were being prepared to remove the Despensers from their position of power, a fact also recognised by the younger Despenser who, in correspondence with one of his stewards in the late winter and spring of 1321, expressed his concern regarding the growing opposition and ordered preparations for armed conflict.[15] The Earl of Hereford's request in April 1321 that the younger Despenser be handed over to Lancaster while matters were resolved and to allow him to approach

12 Phillips, *Edward II*, p. 355.

13 Phillips, *Edward II*, pp. 363–6; Fryde, *Tyranny*, pp. 27–36.

14 Davies, 'The Despenser war in Glamorgan'; Fryde, *Tyranny*, pp. 43–5.

15 Goronwy Edwards, *Calendar of Ancient Correspondence*, pp. 219, 220, 259.

the king in safety was met with a haughty rebuff [**32a**]. At the same time, the opponents of Despenser and of the king gathered around the Earl of Lancaster, who arranged meetings at Doncaster, Pontefract and, subsequently, at Sherburn in Elmet, not many miles from his Pontefract stronghold [**32b–d**].[16] These gatherings, reminiscent of similar meetings held in the earliest years of the reign to confront the threat of Edward's favouritism towards Piers Gaveston, were as notable for the early evidence of the fragility of the alliance against the king and the Despensers as for those who attended and indicated some level of support. The indenture witnessed at Sherburn in Elmet in late June 1321 stated the opposition to the perceived misdeeds of the Despensers, but it was chiefly the retainers of Lancaster who committed to action [**32c**]. The greater earls and barons, including the Earl of Hereford and the Mortimers, were present at the discussions but were not identified amongst those who were expected to 'sustain' the complaints against the Despensers.

Attacks on the property of the Despensers in the Welsh Marches were already underway by late spring of 1321; much of this activity suggests wanton destruction more than a scheme for permanent reallocation of tenure.[17] There is, in fact, plentiful evidence of uncertainty in the plans of the opponents. While the intention to remove the Despensers from their positions of power and influence was central to the ambitions of the opposition, quite how this might be achieved and the charges to be levelled against them were less well defined. It is clear that the formulation of the accusations went through a number of iterations between the first gatherings in the spring of 1321 and the parliamentary act of exile at the end of the summer [**32e(i)–(ii)**]. The clumsy repurposing of the Earl of Lincoln's articles regarding 'homage and oath of allegiance', originally a statement of principle but subsequently an illustration of the Despensers' treachery, suggests more than a degree of fabrication and improvisation on the part of the opposition, and more particularly of Bartholomew Badlesmere, a recent recruit from the royalist side.[18] However, a combination of argument and attacks on Despenser property did, briefly, lead to success, and the king, faced

16 Wilkinson, 'Sherburn indenture'; Wilkinson, *Constitutional History*, II, pp. 134–56.

17 For a valuable discussion of the attacks on the Despensers in 1321, see Wells-Furby, 'Gower prelude'.

18 For a different view of the use/misuse of the 'homage et serment' declaration and one that finds some ground for accepting the charge against the younger Despenser in this respect, see Phillips, *Edward II*, pp. 390–1.

with significant opposition, was obliged to concede and to accept the exile of the Despensers.[19] As the chroniclers note, however, any exile was brief and a prelude to armed conflict and civil war.

29 The aftermath of the death of Gaveston

In the months following the death of Gaveston, tension was high and the potential for military conflict considerable; instead, a series of protracted negotiations overseen by leading ecclesiastics brought the parties to some measure of agreement by October 1313. The Annals of London recounts this activity in some detail and records some of the detail of the formal discussion.

Annales Londonienses, pp. 209–10, 221–5

1312

Meanwhile the king made to summon each of the prelates, earls, barons and the community of England to his parliament, which was to be held around the feast of the Assumption of the Blessed Mary in the sixth year of his reign, at Westminster; and in the meantime the king went to Dover and fortified the castle and received the fealty of the Cinque Ports. He also sent a message to the French king through the emissary of Aymer de Valence that he should send help; and thus the king, having assembled a large force for the conflict to come, returned to London.

Whilst these forces were being assembled, the Earls Lancaster, Hereford, Warwick and Arundel, with a large force, were heading towards the king, but they waited for fifteen days at Ware. There the king ordered that on pain of life and limb they were not to come to his parliament as if they were ready and armed for war, lest at that time each side, unless prevented by the grace of God, should destroy the other as if they were enemies. However, the opposing groups were calmed by the Earl of Gloucester who acted as mediator between the king and the earls; however, he was obliged by oath to the earls to serve and protect the Ordinances. Given that that was the case, there arrived in England Lord Louis, count of Evreux, the brother of the king of France, and Lord Arnold, cardinal, and Lord Arnold, bishop of Poitiers, who had been sent by the pope and the king of France to pacify the situation and bring about a general peace. They first issued the following:

19 *PROME*, Parliament of July 1321, Westminster.

The first discussions aimed at achieving peace

Because the Earls of Gloucester, Lancaster, Richmond, Pembroke, Warenne, Hereford, Warwick, Arundel have heard from the talk of others that our lord the king is set against them and against their allies and followers, and these same in desiring his good will in such manner that they can and should have, shall come in reverence of him to the great hall at Westminster, where the great people congregate on behalf of the whole of the community, and humbly, if it so please him, request from him, on bended knee, that he will release them from all misdeeds and quarrels and receive them as his liegemen. And that they shall be received in that form. And that our lord the king will receive the prelates in the same way and their allies and followers. And that he will offer such security as they and their counsel shall ordain ... And in order more quickly to gain his good will for his first expedition into Scotland by the assent of his magnates, the magnates shall grant in aid to him and for his aforesaid war, four hundred men-at-arms who shall go wherever he goes, and their costs for half a year, if the king stays for so long ... And that the lands and tenements, bailiwicks, custodies and castles, or all of their profits, from which men have been ousted by our lord the king and his ministers without due process, shall be entirely regranted. And the men taken and imprisoned by will against the form of law shall be released. And that the goods and chattels which were taken at Newcastle-upon-Tyne and elsewhere by reason that Piers Gaveston was a common enemy of the king and of the realm, so that his allies and followers shall not be able to make use of these goods nor complain of their detention, these goods should be returned to the king ... And that the goods and chattels taken from holy church and from people against their will, since the making of the Ordinances, shall be given back willingly. And that the Ordinances shall be maintained in all respects. And that in parliament, as well as the Ordinances and the laws and customs of the land, shall be done that which should be done for our lord the king, as is required by homage and allegiance to him. And that the evil counsellors and their attendants who are in the vicinity of the king shall be ousted, according to the Ordinances, and that they should respond to plaintiffs for torts and misdemeanours committed both before the Ordinances and after. As for agreeing to the granting of a common aid in the next parliament, when they will have their peers more fully with them and the whole community, they will put every effort into ensuring that the king is suitably aided for his next Scottish campaign; and in order to foster good peace and agreement in the land, they, on each side, should dismiss all manner of grievances and irritations, saving those contravening the Ordinances. And that they should respond to all those who wish to plead, and punish malefactors according to the Ordinances.

...

In the same year [1312], before Christmas, certain of the king's party and of the earls gathered in order to bring about a peace, in this way:

This is the peace treaty concerning certain annoyances and causes for anger which the king feels towards the earls of Lancaster, Hereford and Warwick and certain other barons and other great men of this realm, on account of certain things done and agreed, in the presence of the venerable fathers in Christ, Lord Arnold, by the grace of God, cardinal of St Prisca, and Arnold, bishop of Poitiers, who have been sent to England on behalf of the Pontiff, and in the presence of Louis of France, count of Evreux, and the earls of Gloucester and Richmond; by the Earl of Hereford, Robert de Clifford, John Botetourt, who have been sent to London with sufficient power to discuss and agree this treaty, as much for themselves as for the earls of Lancaster and of Warwick, and by the Earl of Pembroke, Hugh Despenser and Nicholas de Segrave, on behalf of the king, who were to hear the said treaty and then report to the king concerning the following:

Firstly, the said earls and barons shall come before the king in his great hall at Westminster, where with great humility, upon bended knee, they shall offer him their oath of allegiance and shall make oath, should he require it, that that which they have done, for which they understand the king holds them in ill regard, they did not do in despite of him, and they will humbly request that he shall release them from his indignation and annoyance and that he shall receive them into his good will; and they shall restore to him whatsoever was captured at Newcastle-upon-Tyne or elsewhere on account of Piers Gaveston, wheresoever the goods shall be, namely all of the jewels and the horses which as yet have been unaccounted for, and all of the other things whatever they are, these to be restored in the town of St Albans on the feast of St Hilary next coming. And if any of the horses shall be dead, they shall return instead at that place and at that time the price and estimate of the said dead horses which could not be accounted for, and it falls to the king to send, on that day, sufficient men to receive these things and with sufficient power to hand over the king's letters of acquittance for that which they shall receive.

Also be it known that it is discussed and agreed that the next parliament shall be held on the third Sunday of Lent next, at Westminster; at the commencement of that parliament, it will be necessary to grant security for the said earls and barons, their followers, their household and their allies, in the following form:

Edward by the grace of God king of England, lord of Ireland, duke of Aquitaine, to all those who see or hear this letter, greetings in God. Know all that by sureties and agreements made in our parliament at Westminster on such a day and such a year, it is provided and guaranteed by us and by the archbishops, bishops, abbots, priors, earls, barons and the community of our realm, there by our order assembled, of one assent and accord, that no one, be they of whatsoever estate or condition, shall in the future be called upon or challenged on account of the taking, detention or death of Piers Gaveston, nor on account of the death of the same, shall they be taken, imprisoned, impeded, molested, ill-treated nor judged by us or by others prosecuted through our suit or by the suit of any others, either in our courts or elsewhere. And we will that this guarantee and accord shall hold firm and binding in all its points and that each of these shall be held and kept in perpetuity. And that it shall be enrolled in our chancery, our High Bench, our Common Bench, and in our exchequer, and in this we shall issue letters patent under our great seal and they shall be sent to all of the counties of our realm where they shall be read aloud, published, held and kept in perpetuity; and all of those who wish to have our letters patent concerning this thing shall come to our chancery and they shall have them and they shall pay nothing.

Which security, although it seems sufficient to the aforesaid three representatives of the earls and barons, however, as much as it is suitable for themselves, as for its suitability for the said earls of Lancaster and of Warwick whose envoys they were, they are unsure until they will have fully discussed the matter with the said earls, and that when they will have spoken with them, they take it upon themselves to write back in a short time to the aforesaid cardinal and bishop, and the earls of Gloucester and Richmond, and to let them know their will in this matter. And in addition, it is agreed that the king shall release and quitclaim the said earls and barons and their followers, household and allies, from all annoyances and grievances and causes for anger, actions, obligations, quarrels and accusations arising from the matter of Piers Gaveston, in whatsoever manner since the time that he married his dear companion Isabella, queen of England, or that shall be by reason of the taking, detention or death of the said Piers, or of entry into towns or castle, or of sieges or the carrying of arms or the seizing of persons or in any manner whatsoever which in any way concerns or has regard to the person or events which arose from the said lord Piers Gaveston.

Also it is well agreed that, should the said pardon satisfy the said earls and barons, and that they shall not wish to attend parliament in person, that they shall send proxies with sufficient power to discuss and to agree to the said pardon on their behalf and, further, with sufficient power to consent to a pardon which shall be offered in the said parliament for the adherents and supporters of Piers Gaveston, which pardon was discussed and agreed in the following form:

It is granted that no one, of whatsoever station and condition, shall, at no time in the future, be challenged, imprisoned, impeded, molested, ill-treated nor judged by us or by others prosecuted through our suit or by the suit of any others, either in our courts or elsewhere, because of the return of the said Piers to England nor by reason of the aid, maintenance, adherence, counsel, support or alliance made to the same in writing or otherwise, nor of reason of time in his company nor in his service in any times passed. And it is required of the said representatives that they should bring this pardon to the attention of the said earls and discover their views concerning it.

Also the said representatives agreed well that, in the next parliament, there should be provision by the king and by the common assent of the prelates, earls and barons that in all parliaments, meetings and other gatherings which shall be henceforth and for always in the realm of England, that men should come without force and arms, calmly and peaceably to the honour of the king and the peace of him and his realm. And the three representatives promise that they will make every effort they can as regards the earls of Lancaster and Warwick in order that the said proxies who shall come to parliament for the said pardons, shall have sufficient power to consent and agree on their behalfs to the said provision, and it seemed to them good that this should be done. And it was generally recognised that at this parliament nothing other should be done than that concerning the said pardons and the said provision, and that none should come with arms until the said submission shall have been made, which having been made the other matters of the said parliament shall be discussed, according to what shall be reasonable.

Also the said representatives fully promise that, the said reconciliation having been made, when they shall be in parliament with their peers, they shall apply all of their efforts in order that the king shall have sufficient aid from the whole of his realm for his Scottish war.

Also, because the three representatives plead that, after the safe conduct had been given to them and their adherents, the king had seized many goods and lands of a certain Griffin de la Pole who was, as he says, in possession of these at the time of the safe-conduct. If it please the king, two justices, above suspicion, should be sent by him to the place to test the truth of this, and if they discover that the said Griffin has been wrongfully dispossessed since the time of the said safe-conduct given to the Earl of Lancaster, they should be restored to him. And, in order to achieve this, they shall summon the parties, and having heard their arguments, they shall swiftly pass judgment in the matters of contention, applying whatever law shall be suitable. And further, if the said Griffin wishes to plead concerning any other grievances, acts of force or violence which he may have suffered before the time of the safe-conduct, the said justices shall hear his case and offer him their judgment. And since Fulk Lestrange pleads that he suffered ills and was wrongfully dispossessed after the said conduct, the said justices, having called the king's men and Fulk, and having heard their arguments, shall offer them their verdict, in the above form.

Also if it please the king, the goods of Henry Percy, which were seized into the king's hands, shall be restored to him by pledges until the next parliament. The said justices shall have the power to do the abovesaid things before the 20th day after Christmas. Also it is discussed and agreed by our lord the king that all manner of people from England (and from other lands with which we are not at war) may pass throughout the realm, safe and sound, in the safeguard and safe-conduct of the king, according to the law, in order to carry out their business in such a way that they should not come with force and arms. And this safe-conduct and security shall last until next Pentecost, and in this the earls and barons shall be given letters under the great seal of the king for themselves and their followers.

The compilation of this indenture was read out in the year of grace 1312, on the Wednesday before Christmas [20 December], in the cardinal's room at London, in the presence of the said cardinal, the bishop of Poitiers, the bishop of Worcester, the Earl of Pembroke, John Crombwelle, masters Gerard de Curton, Richard Tibetot, clerks of the king of France, master Raymond Sibirain, William de Newcastle, knight, Robert de Northburghe, John Walwayn and Michael de Meldon. In witness of these things, one part of the said indenture shall remain with the king's representatives whilst the other shall be taken by the abovesaid John and Michael to the said earls and barons.

30 Negotiations with Lancaster

(a) Letter from the Earl of Lancaster to the king

Davies, *Baronial Opposition*, appendix no. 101, pp. 587–8[20]

To his most honourable lord if it should please him from his Earl of Lancaster, all possible honours and reverences. Most dear sire we have received your letter by way of your messenger at our castle of Donnington on the Sunday after the feast of St Luke [19 October, if 1315] and we have listened, sire, to what Lord William de Melton and Lord Hugh Audley have said to us regarding yourself and we send, most dear sire, to your dignity as below a document containing our response by the said messenger which seems to us by our understanding the best advice. Very dear sire, our Lord keep you always in honour. Written at our castle of Donnington on the 20th day of October.

Indenture

As regards that our lord the king has heard that the great lords will not pay for themselves to come to the north as was agreed at Lincoln[21] for the common profit of the realm, it seems to the earl that he does

20 The year of this document is uncertain; Maddicott, *Lancaster*, p. 344, suggests 1315.

21 The council of magnates, to which this seems to refer, met with the king at Lincoln at the very end of August and the start of September 1315, for discussion of which see Phillips, *Edward II*, pp. 250, 264–5.

not know how best to counsel on this point until he will have received certain responses from our lord the king.

As regards assemblies made by the great lords. It appears to the said earl that our lord the king should not prevent this unless they should threaten either himself or the kingdom, the which thing he had not heard as likely and if he should hear he would make every effort to save the lord king and to disrupt such gatherings in the best manner that he could.

As regards the fact that the treasurer reports that there is insufficient money to cover the costs of the lord king for his stay in the north this winter, it seems to the said earl that it is as well for our lord the king to stay in the north as in the south. And it was understood that a stay in the north would not be more expensive ...

And the said earl wishes it to be known to our lord the king that he is prepared to remain in the north in the manner that was agreed at Lincoln.

(b) *Bridlington*, pp. 50–2

In the year of the lord 1317 around the feast of the blessed Mary Magdalene [22 July] the king of England, through his letters sent to the Earl of Lancaster, censured the earl himself for summoning private assemblies of magnates and people without just cause, and also for retaining armed men at unwonted and excessive wages, at which the people were struck with considerable fear, and for other things which can appear from his replies, which follow next. Because of their long-windedness, we have put together the following points from the earl's letters of reply, which were written in French. After the words of greeting he states thus:

> May it please your revered lordship to know that we did not summon any assemblies by which the people should be disturbed or frightened; nor are we maintaining any men for disturbance of the kingdom nor for the obstruction of peace, but for the tranquillity of the people and the establishment of peace, and also to preserve especially and entirely the advantage and honour of your crown. And it is not without considerable reason that we are surprised that you should charge us about our retinue at this time, since you recently wrote to us that we should come in person to you at Newcastle on the day after St Lawrence [10 August] with our service, improved and strengthened as far as we can. Because of this, as far as we

are able, we will be ready to go with you with our armed men wherever you may wish, if the earl's life and God allow it.

With respect to the other letters, through which you told us to come to you at Nottingham on 21 July to deliberate with you and others of your council who are to meet there about the arrival of your Scottish enemies, who have come into the kingdom of England, attacking it in a hostile manner, please excuse our absence for this day, because we are not well and not strong enough to work in any way. On this, revered lord, you should remember that in the last parliament held at Lincoln, because your kingdom was seen to be ruled by incompetent and unsuitable persons, you freely granted that the lord of Canterbury with other bishops and earls together with ourselves and Lord Bartholomew Badlesmere, through the careful and prudent judgement of other nobles sworn on to your council, should direct and improve the rule of your kingdom so that dishonest and unruly officials, law-breakers who give pleasing rather than sound advice, were to be banished from your side, and were not in future to serve you further in any office; and that that ordinance of yours should be valid and in force for ever; and on this matter we came to London to the wiser and more prudent men of your council, with whom we ordained exactly what seemed to be necessary for your household and for the rule of your kingdom, and we sent them to your grace in writing by the lords Bartholomew Badlesmere and William Inge; but in truth up to now they are not being in any way observed. Moreover, revered lord, in the ordinances made by Lord Robert, archbishop of Canterbury, of honoured memory, it was shown that many persons remaining as your confidential advisers and in other offices, both public and private, were receivers of benefices and rewards, and were corruptors of truth and justice, and also incompetent and unsuitable to serve in royal offices; it was ordained that you should entirely dismiss all such men from you and from your service, which in truth you have refused to do, but held them so much the more dear; and you have drawn in others of the same sort, worse than them, on more friendly terms, despite the fact that you confirmed the aforesaid ordinances in your letters patent, and also bound prelates, earls and barons and other royal officers by the bond of a sworn oath to keep them in all their articles, as would appear from your letters made before us and before other nobles of the kingdom present there, when, however, nothing in the work has effectively been implemented. And on the matter that we did not come to you on the appointed day, we beg you not to be surprised, because the business on which you wanted our advice and consent according to the tenor of your letters should be put truly before parliament and discussed there with the peers of the land present. We all swore to observe this, as you yourself know, and you should not want to decide and discuss outside parliament what should be determined in parliament. Concerning those matters about which you told us in your last letters to us, that your Scottish enemies have again come into England to attack in a hostile manner, and on which you ask for our assent and advice, we believe that your counsel has already been taken and determined for the future, in that you have instructed us and other chief men of the kingdom by writs that each of us with his service is to be with you at Newcastle on a specified day, prepared to set out further if there should be need; on which day, if you yourself are there, we wish to be among your gathering by God's grace.

31 The 'Middle Party' and the Treaty of Leake

(a) Indenture between Pembroke, Badlesmere and Damory, November 1317

Phillips, *Aymer de Valence*, Appendix 4.3, pp. 317–18; also Davies, *Baronial Opposition*, Appendix n. 42, pp. 563–4

Made to record that on the day of the date of this indenture, Lord Roger Damory, knight, promises in good faith as a loyal knight to the noblemen, Lord Aymer de Valence, Earl of Pembroke, and to Sir Bartholomew de Badlesmere as is contained in what follows. It is to be known that he will put all of his diligence and loyalty to the advantage of our lord the king in that he will allow himself to be led and governed by the counsel of the said earl and Sir Bartholomew and that he will accept the counsel of these two above that of all others, considering that which they advise as good and loyal to the honour of the king and of his crown and his realm, and that by this same advice the said Sir Roger shall govern himself and will not diverge from them in any regard. And that he will not procure by himself or by other nor consent to the king's granting to any living man land worth more than twenty pounds without the permission of the said earl and Sir Bartholomew nor that should the king do anything of great significance which shall be prejudicial to him or to the crown in any case. And if afterwards it shall happen that our lord the king would give land other than the above value to anyone or engage in any important business which should be to his prejudice or that of the crown or of his realm in the absence of the said earl and Sir Bartholomew, the said Sir Roger shall put all of his best efforts to interfere with the same. And if it shall be impossible in any way to interfere, he will make it be known to the said earl and Sir Bartholomew before any effect can result so that all three of them shall of one accord try to change the will of the king. And if the said Sir Roger shall feel that anyone shall speak to or act in any way towards our lord the king which shall be prejudicial or bring dishonour or cause damage to the said earl and Sir Bartholomew in that their status should be lowered in the king's opinion, he will warn them without any delay and will disturb the attempt with all his power. And in order that this agreement shall be well and lawfully maintained and acted upon in the ways set out above and to do nothing or never to come against this, the said Sir Roger makes oath on the body of Christ and further obligates himself to the sum of ten thousand pounds sterling to be paid to the said earl and Sir Bartholomew at their request lest he should say, do or act in any way contrary to the above agreements. And the said earl and Sir Bartholomew are as one in their good faith that, as loyal knights, they shall defend, guarantee and maintain the said Sir Roger against all men of whatsoever condition they shall be, excepting the allegiance which they owe to our lord the king in so far as the said Sir Roger will keep and fully maintain the above covenants. And in this they obligate their heirs, their executors and all their goods, both moveable and immoveable, present and future, to the will of the said Sir Roger. In witness of which things one part of this indenture is sealed by the seals of the said earl and Sir Bartholomew and the other with the seal of the said Sir Roger respectively. Given at Westminster the 24th day of November in the eleventh year of our lord the King Edward.

(b) The Treaty of Leake, 1318

PROME, parliament roll for 20 October 1318, York, SC9/21; *CCR 1318–1323*, pp. 112–13

Firstly, whereas the prelates, earls and barons of the realm assembled at this parliament had debated among themselves the manner of the commencement of the same parliament, it seemed to all that, firstly, the most important thing would be to ask our lord the king to confirm the articles contained in an indenture made at Leake on 9 August last, between the envoys of our lord the king, sent on his behalf to the Earl of Lancaster, on the one hand, and the same earl on the other, the tenor of which indenture is written below: as a result of which this request was made to our said lord the king on behalf of them all, and he willingly granted it, ordering that their request and his grant be enrolled in the following form:

> Be it remembered that whereas certain prelates, earls and barons, at the will of our lord the king and with the assent of the majority of the magnates of

the realm, and of others of the king's council then present at Northampton, recently travelled to the Earl of Lancaster, to discuss and negotiate with him concerning the advantage and the honour of our lord the king and of his realm, and in the discussion and negotiation which took place between the said prelates, earls and barons and the said Earl of Lancaster, it was agreed and arranged that bishops, earls and barons were to remain with our lord the king to counsel him in the matters which concerned him until his next parliament, and concerning this and other things an indenture was made in the following form:

This indenture attests how the honourable fathers the archbishop of Dublin and the bishops of Norwich, Ely and Chichester, and the earls of Pembroke and Arundel, Sir Roger de Mortimer, Sir John Somery, Sir Bartholomew of Badlesmere, Sir Ralph Basset and Sir John Botetourt, of the will and assent of our said lord the king have held discussions with the Earl of Lancaster on matters concerning the advantage of our lord the king and of the realm in the following form: that is that he will be pleased to name the bishops of Norwich, Chichester, Ely, Salisbury, St David's, Carlisle, Hereford and Worcester, the earls of Pembroke, Richmond, Hereford and Arundel, Sir Hugh de Courtenay, Sir Roger de Mortimer, Sir John of Seagrave, Sir John de Grey, and one of the Earl of Lancaster's bannerets, to remain with our lord the king for a quarter until the next parliament, so that two of the bishops, one of the earls, one of the barons and one of the said Earl of Lancaster's bannerets, at least, are to remain with the king constantly, and that all noteworthy things which can and should be done without parliament, are to be done with their assent, and if it is done otherwise, it is to be held to be void, and corrected in parliament by the judgment of the peers, and all suitable matters are to be rectified by them, and at parliament people are to be chosen from among them and from others who are to remain with our lord the king by quarters, according to the terms of their choosing, and they are to be appointed in parliament to act and to counsel our lord the king in the aforesaid form. And the aforesaid prelates, earls and barons, with the will and assent of our said lord the king, have undertaken that the king will give the said Earl of Lancaster, and his people, and his household, releases and acquittances for all manner of felonies and trespasses committed against his peace until St James's day this year, and that the charters of release and acquittances are to be simple and without condition, and if a better guarantee can be found for them at the said next parliament, it is to be done for them and confirmed there before our lord the king and his baronage. And the aforesaid Earl of Lancaster has granted that he will give a release and acquittance to all those who are followers of our lord the king, who wish to ask for it, for things which he is able to grant with regard to trespasses committed against his person, and he will do this as soon as these aforesaid things have been confirmed, and he will not bring suit of felony against any of them from the time when they are in possession of his letters, saving to the Earl of Lancaster all the complaints, actions and suits which he has against the Earl Warenne, and against all those who conspired and helped to commit the felonies and trespasses which the said Earl Warenne has committed against him, contrary to the peace of our lord the king. And the Ordinances are to be kept and observed in the form in which they are found under the great seal of our lord the king. And that these aforesaid things will be done and observed in all points as has been said above, has been loyally undertaken with the will and consent of our said lord the king, by the honourable fathers in God the archbishops of Canterbury and Dublin and the bishops of Norwich, Ely, Chichester, Salisbury, Chester, Winchester, Hereford, and Worcester, and the earl marshal, Edmund his brother and the earls of Pembroke, Richmond, Hereford, Ulster, Arundel and Angus, Sir Roger de Mortimer, Sir John Somery, Sir John Hastings, Sir John of Seagrave, Sir Henry de Beaumont, Sir Hugh le Despenser the son, Sir John de Grey, Sir Richard de Grey, Sir Bartholomew of Badlesmere, Sir Robert de Mohaut, Sir Ralph Basset and Sir Walter of Norwich. In testimony of which thing, the aforesaid prelates, earls and barons have put their seals to one part of this indenture, and the said Earl of Lancaster has put his seal to the other part. Written at Leake, 9 August, in the twelfth year of the reign of the said King Edward [1318].

32 The growth of opposition and the accusations against the Despensers

(a) *CCR 1318–1323*, pp. 367–8

1321. April 23. Bristol. To Humphrey de Bohoun, Earl of Hereford and Essex. Whereas the king lately enjoined him to come to him at Gloucester at a certain day to take counsel with the king and with the other magnates and others of the king's council concerning the assemblies of men-at-arms in Wales and the Marches, and the earl did not come at that time, but signified to the king by John de Somery and Robert de Kendale that he would not come to the king so long as Hugh le Despenser, the younger, remained in the king's company; and the abbot of Dore afterwards came to the king and explained, on the earl's behalf, that the earl would willingly come to the king by his orders, but that he feared to do so whilst the aforesaid Hugh was in the king's company, and requested the king to remove Hugh from his company, and to summon a parliament at a suitable time and place, where the earl and Hugh might come securely to propound their complaints and to receive judgment, and that the king would in the meantime commit Hugh to the custody of Thomas, Earl of Lancaster, stating that Humphrey would mainpern[22], under forfeiture of all that he could forfeit, to take Hugh to the Earl of Lancaster and to bring him back to the parliament in safety, adding that Humphrey would come to the king at Gloucester before he left those parts in hope that the king would grant his aforesaid request; and as it was not evident to the king that the abbot was charged by Humphrey to present the proposals, because he did not bring with him any letters from Humphrey, the king sent his clerk William de Leycestre with his letters to Humphrey, in order that Humphrey might certify the king by his letters if the abbot had been requested to present the proposals by him; and Humphrey has written that he requested the abbot to tell the king the proposals on Humphrey's behalf; the king, understanding Humphrey's request, not without great wonder, considers his excuse for not coming to the king whilst Hugh is in his company as insufficient, because Hugh was appointed the king's chamberlain by the counsel of the prelates, earls and barons, and *proceres* of the realm and by Humphrey's counsel at full parliament at York, and no complaint has been hitherto made against him afterwards in any other parliament by Humphrey or by others, and Humphrey cannot be ignorant that the king's orders are a protection and defence to all and singular coming to him by such orders, as they ought to be according to the law and custom of the realm. It would be unfitting and dishonest to remove Hugh from the king's company, after assuming such an office, as suddenly as Humphrey desires, and it would be an unjust and pernicious example to other ministers of the king if the king so removed him without cause. The king had, before the arrival of the aforesaid abbot, disposed to have treaty with Humphrey and certain others of his subjects at Oxford in three weeks from Easter next, as well concerning a day and place for holding a parliament as upon other affairs of the realm. The king cannot and ought not to commit Hugh or any other person to custody without cause, since this would be contrary to Magna Carta, and the common law of the realm, and also contrary to the Ordinances, which Humphrey is bound by oath to observe, and also contrary to the king's oath, binding him to exhibit justice to all and singular; for Hugh has offered himself openly and publicly before the king to answer in parliament and elsewhere to the complaints of all and singular making complaints of him, and to stand to right therein, and the king is and will be prepared to do justice to Humphrey and to all others, complaining of Hugh or of

22 Stand as surety.

others, as befits his royal dignity; wherefore the king orders Humphrey to be with him in person at Oxford on Sunday in three weeks from Easter aforesaid, putting aside all excuse, to treat with the king and his other magnates upon the premises and to give his counsel.

(b) *Bridlington*, pp. 61–2

1321

Also on Sunday after the feast of St Dunstan, the bishop [24 May], in the fourteenth year of King Edward's reign, in the chapter house of Pontefract Priory, at the Earl of Lancaster's command, all the lords listed below met in the said earl's presence: namely the earl himself first with his men, Thomas Multon, Thomas Furnival, Edmund Deyncourt, Henry fitz Hugh, Ralph Greystoke, Gilbert Acton, Marmaduke Thweng, Nicholas Menill, Henry Percy, John Marmion, Philip Darcy, William fitz William, John Fauconberg, John Deyncourt and Lord Robert Constable of Flamborough, barons and bannerets, who, all and every one with unanimous consent and will, for themselves and for their friends and allies whom they can draw into their agreement, granted that because many disturbances had already occurred in various parts of the kingdom, by which the peace of the land could be upset to the dishonour of the king and of the kingdom and also to no small loss and injury of the people, they all and everyone wanted, and each for himself faithfully promised and agreed, to be of one assent and accord to defend their lands and countryside, so that, if anyone, whoever he might be, should rise against the said earl or against any one of them in any way to the injury and dishonour of them or any one of them, they were all ready [to give] support and defence against all those wishing to attack them in any way with evil intent and to do this with vigour, so that everyone should make himself ready in the best and strongest way he could, so that the universal peace of the land should more effectively be fostered, and the tranquillity and profit of the people should be much more securely maintained. Then every lord aforesaid confirmed that compact, or rather that confederacy, written in similar words in French, by appending their seals. And because it seemed to the aforesaid lords that the aforesaid matter needed the counsel of the magnates and especially the prelates, the Earl of Lancaster wrote to the archbishop and to all other prelates of the province and diocese of York, that, on Sunday after the feast of the Nativity of St John the Baptist

[28 June], they should all meet in like manner at Sherburn in Elmet to discuss with them matters touching the advantage and tranquillity of the people. On this day the archbishop, the bishops of Durham and Carlisle, the earls of Lancaster and Hereford, abbots and priors, and very many barons, bannerets and knights, from the south and the north, met in the parish church of Sherburn …

(c) Sherburn Indenture, June 1321

Wilkinson, 'Sherburn Indenture', Appendix III, pp. 21–2
(Manuscript A with variations in Manuscript B included)

This indenture witnesses that on the Sunday after the feast of the Nativity of St John the Baptist in the year xiiii [28 June 1321] at Sherburn in Elmet in the presence of the honourable fathers in God, the archbishop of York and the bishops of Durham and Carlisle and the earls of Lancaster and of Angus, it was suggested that Sir Hugh Despenser the father and the son had badly advised and led our lord the king into dishonour and the damage of himself and of his realm, and having heard and understood the reasons of the Earl of Hereford, Sir Roger de Mortimer, nephew and uncle, Sir Hugh Daudley, father and son, Sir Roger Dammory, Sir John de Mowbray, Sir Maurice de Berkeley, Sir Roger de Clifford, Sir Thomas Mauduit, Sir Henry le Tyeys, Sir John Giffard, Sir Gilbert Taleboth and the other great men and others of that March; it was advised by the earls of Lancaster and of Angus, Sir Robert de Holland, Sir Fulk Lestrange, Sir Stephen de Segrave, Sir William Latimer, Sir John Devory, Sir John de Haverington, Sir Adam de Swillington, Sir William de Kyme, Sir Marmaduke de Twenge, Sir Richard Walleys, Sir Robert Pierpoint, Sir Randulf Drake, Sir Edmund Deyncourt, Sir Thomas de Willeby, Sir William de Pennington, Sir Ralph de Neville, Sir Giles de Tromppetone, Sir John de Beker', Sir Adam de Hodelestone, Sir Michael de Haverington, Sir Adam de Everingham, Sir William Trossell, Sir Robert de Rigat, Sir Robert de Richer, Sir John de Clifford, Sir Henry de Bradebourne, Sir Nicholas de Langford, Sir John de Brakeworth, Sir Thomas Wyther, Sir John de Clif', Sir Thomas de Longeuilers, Sir Edmund de Neville, Sir Gasselin Dainel, that what the Earl of Hereford, Sir Roger de [*sic*] le Mortimer and the other great men of the March and the other abovenamed have begun concerning the abovesaid Sir Hugh the father and the son has been done for the honour of God and the honour and profit of our lord the king and his realm. And it seemed to all those that the actions of Hugh Despenser father and son have brought about the oppressions which the people suffer from day to day, maliciously, increasingly, and would not be reduced without compulsion. And with one accord of all those who were present that the plaints abovenamed shall be maintained to the honour of God and of holy church and the profit of our lord the king and of the kingdom and of those children and for the salvation of the crown and the people. And since the said Earl of Lancaster and the other great men who have begun the plaints wish to sustain them, the Earl of Angus and all the others named after him shall sustain them in so far as they have the power to do so. And at that point that the Earl of Lancaster and the other magnates cease the quarrels which have commenced, so may the Earl of Angus and all the others cease without challenge and to maintain these things the Earl of Angus and all of the other after him have placed their seals.

(d) A Rochester account concerning disputes during the parliament of 1321

As well as describing the growing animosity and acts of aggression aimed at the Despensers in 1321, this extract from the Rochester chronicle also provides an unusual account of Bartholomew Badlesmere's misuse of the 1308 Articles of the Earl of Lincoln (for which see also above, [**2e**]), an apparently ill-judged attempt to associate the 'Homage and Oath' articles with Despenser the Younger's plotting against the king and in a manner contrary to the intentions of Lancaster, Maddicott, *Lancaster*, pp. 280ff. For a different view of the use/misuse of the 'homage et serment' declaration, see Phillips, *Edward II*, pp. 387–91.

Historia Roffensis, in Pronay and Taylor, *Parliamentary Texts*, pp. 165–9

... the Earl of Lancaster summoned to Sherburn in Elmet all the prelates north of the Trent, as well as the Earl of Hereford, and together with the lords abovementioned, they mutually bound themselves to prosecute as traitors of the realm the aforementioned Hugh, father and son, adding that it was in the interest of the king. While the prelates and leading men of the kingdom were assembling at Westminster for the parliament appointed for the third week after the feast of St John the Baptist [i.e. three weeks after 24 June], the Earl of Hereford, Lords Roger and Roger Mortimer, J[ohn] Mowbray, John Giffard of Brimpsfield, Roger

Clifford, Henry Tyes, Roger Samory, Henry Sandale, Bartholomew Badlesmere, with about twenty-five other bannerets who supported them, sent a request to Lord J[ohn] Grey and other magnates in the vicinity that they should come to their help. In addition, they laid waste their lands and places. All their supporters appeared dressed in green tunics of which a quarter part of the right arm was saffron coloured, as if they had been 'quartered' by the said father and son. Coming to parliament they destroyed all the countryside en route. The abbots, priors, rectors, citizens, merchants and other richer people of the country being present from the Marches, were constrained to make contributions to them, impoverishing everywhere the churches and the land. They finally arrived in the city of London with a thousand mounted men and a large multitude of foot soldiers, and helping them was the Earl of Lancaster who always absented himself from parliament. On the Monday next after the feast of St James the Apostle [27 July 1321], after the prelates and the earls of Richmond, Pembroke, Warenne and Arundel had been summoned to Clerkenwell, they requested them that for the honour of the lord king and for the profit of the realm they join them. After they readily assented, the earls confirmed it with an oath. The prelates, however, refused to take the oath. Having considered these matters for a considerable time they decided to send the prelates and the aforementioned earls to the king together with two knights whom they were sending along with the petitions which they were to present to the lord king. These were the petitions. 'Sire, our masters tell you that they hold both Lord Hugh Despenser, and his son, enemies and traitors to you and to the kingdom, and for this they wish them to be removed from here. And because of this they ask you that you have them brought before parliament to answer, and to restore by award of the peers that which they have destroyed. Ensure that they come, and that they are exiled out of the land for all time and they and their heirs are disinherited as false and traitorous criminals. and spies.' This having been said, the lord king asked the knights whether they had letters of authority; they replied that they had not. The king ordered that their authority be put in writing, and after this had been done the knights retired. The king was very concerned. After the prelates and lords had assembled at the Carmelite friary, Bartholomew Badlesmere, the leader and initiator of the whole undertaking, proposed on behalf of and in the name of all, that Hugh Despenser, the son, was proved to be a manifest traitor and enemy of the king and the kingdom, by the fact that he had conspired against the king, conjoining his liege men against the king. As evidence for the truth of this, he brought forward as witnesses,

Lord Richard Grey, John Giffard of Brimpsfield, barons, and Robert of Shirland, knight, saying that Lord Hugh had shown them a certain parchment the tenor of which was as follows:

> Homage and the oath of allegiance are more by reason of the crown than by reason of the king, and are attached more to the crown than to the person. And this is apparent because before the estate of the crown has descended no allegiance is due to the person. Wherefore if the king in certain cases is not led by reason, regarding the estate of the crown, his liege subjects are bound by the oath made to the crown to guide the king back and to amend the estate of the crown by reason. Otherwise the oath is not kept. Then it must be asked, how is one to guide the king, whether by form of law or by force? By the course of the law one cannot obtain redress, for there are no judges who are not made by the king. In which case, if the wish of the king does not accord with reason, he will have only the error maintained and confirmed, and damaging for the crown and the people. And for this, it is judged that the matter be settled by force. He is bound by his oath to be governed by the people, and his liege subjects are bound to govern with him and support him. As regards the person of Piers Gaveston, the people judge him not to be suffered because he destroys the crown, and has done this for his own power. He has by his advice removed the king from the counsel of his realm, and created discord between him and his people. He has attracted to himself the allegiance of men by as solemn an oath as if he were the king, making himself the peer of the king, and enfeebling the crown. By the wealth of the crown which he had taken to himself through his power, the strength of the crown has thus passed to him, so that the crown is disinherited by this, and he himself against his oath sovereign of the realm by his wickedness and his treason to his liege lord and to the crown.

This argument was invented in 1311, and put into the Ordinances for Piers Gaveston. Removing the name of Piers, they then imputed this to the said Hugh, the son, to colour his deeds. Marvelling greatly at this, the bishop of Rochester asked Lord Richard Grey whether he had received this parchment from Lord Hugh; he [Lord Richard Grey] said that he had found it in his wallet among other parchments. From that time the bishop of Rochester detested their actions and held them in suspicion. The Lord Edmund Woodstock, the brother of the king, was then made Earl of Kent, to which earldom Bartholomew Badlesmere had aspired with all his heart. The barons, acting through the Earl of Pembroke, who made all his speeches in their interest and against that of the king, moved instantly that Hugh, the father and son, should be sent into exile and their heirs disinherited. The king replied that this was unjust and contrary to his oath to disinherit anyone without a hearing. It would be better that they should remain for a time in Ireland until the anger of the magnates had cooled. Although they had behaved badly towards the magnates, he did not consider them traitors. It was to be regretted that well-born and noble men should have judgment passed on them in this way. Then the Earl of Pembroke replied that the king must choose one of two alternatives, either war with his people or the exile of the two, and he must of necessity accomplish one. The king preferred to spare the mass of the people rather than the two. He was persuaded not so much by the prayers of the leading prelates, earls, barons, justices, who were assembled, as under compulsion as he publicly stated from violence, fear and duress, and was forced against his will into conceding, agreeing to and granting their demands. When this was done, he retired, embittered and very unhappy. And so on Friday on the eve of the assumption of the Blessed Mary [14 August 1321], when the earls and barons were assembled in the great hall of the king at Westminster in the presence of the king, the prelates remaining in the large chamber, the barons as previously sought the exile of the aforementioned Hugh and Hugh on the grounds that they were traitors and enemies of the king and of the realm. They declared that if the law of the land did not make this provision, they had the power, since they were peers of the realm, to promulgate and establish a new law in full parliament in accordance with the custom of the realm, following which custom they immediately afterwards determined and decreed that the said Hugh and Hugh should be exiled by due process without hope of returning and with their heirs be disinherited for all time. After the Earl of Hereford had read the statute, Lord Hugh the father who was then at Canterbury immediately he heard this crossed the sea. After this the king, anxious and sad, went to his chamber having said farewell to the bishops. As the bishop of Rochester returned for breakfast the next day, and for celebrating his mass, the king joined him, the bishops having declared that they in no way agreed to his [i.e. Despenser's] exile. The next day when the bishop of Rochester sat at the king's table, the king whispered to him complaining that the father and son had been condemned unjustly, to which when the bishop had replied that the king could totally amend that defeat, the king said that he would within half a year make such an amend that the whole world would hear of it and tremble.

(e) Articles against the Despensers

There are four surviving versions of the list of accusations against the Despensers, drawn up at various points in early to mid-1321. It is evident that the organisation and detail of the accusations underwent some *adjustment between the initial version or versions, compiled in the north of England in the spring and early summer of 1321, and the final version, reflecting negotiations in London later in the summer, and presented to parliament and accepted by the king not as a statute but as an 'award'. Two versions are offered here: the record of the proceedings in the Bridlington chronicle and the final official version, enrolled in the Parliament and Close Rolls. A key difference is the treatment of the 'homage and oath of allegiance' clause, presented as a statement of principle in the initial version (**i**), but transformed into evidence of the younger Despenser's plotting against the king's authority by the time the articles were presented to the king and parliament (**ii**).*

i Bridlington, *pp. 65–9*

Proceedings against the lords Despenser, father and son, in the same year in the parliament held in London three weeks after the feast of the Nativity of St John the Baptist: the earls presented to the lord king the following articles against the two Despensers:

> In the first place, homage, the oath and allegiance are more by reason of the crown than the person of the king, and the people are bound more to the crown than to the person of the king, and this is clear because before the estate of the kingdom is descended to anyone there is no allegiance in regard or respect to the person, whence it may be asked whether the king should be drawn back from error through the sweetness of law or through harshness; by no means through sweetness, because there are no judges except the king's, in which case, if the king's will should be out of harmony with reason, nothing would come of it except error confirmed; whence, if the king will not correct what would be harmful to the crown and damaging to the people, it is adjudged that in order to keep the oath it should be stopped in the end by harshness. For the king is bound by oath to govern the people well; similarly, the nobles of the kingdom themselves are held by their sworn oath to govern with him and to help him in government and also to put right the king's failure.

Then twelve articles follow whose language is verbose, but the whole intention turns upon the annihilation and destruction of both Despensers, namely father and son. With the help of the Lord I will shorten the words, while keeping their meaning:

Therefore, the earls and barons declared before the king against the aforementioned father and son that, when Hugh Despenser the son was nominated and appointed in the parliament at York to give service to the lord king in the office of chamberlain, where also it was ordained that certain dependable persons and other great men, without whose knowledge and counsel no difficult business was to be put in hand, ought to stay near the king for certain fixed periods of the year, the aforesaid Hugh the son drew to him his own father, when it had not been agreed in the same place that he should in any way dwell near the king. Now, moreover, taking the leadership of the kingdom and royal authority for themselves, to the dishonour of the king, the harm of the crown and the destruction of the people and the magnates, they have done the evil deeds which follow, thinking to estrange the king's heart from the peers of the land, so that they themselves alone might have between them the power to govern the kingdom, to such an extent that they do not allow the lord king to show a smiling face or a gracious spirit either to greater men or to lesser or to make any answer to them, save at the pleasure of the same [Despensers]; and thus they draw the hearts of the subjects away from their lord and the heart of the king away from the magnates and the people.

Also, the same do not allow the greater men of the land to come near to speak with the king in order to offer him sound and faithful advice, except in their presence and hearing, or that of one of them, driving away the magnates and good counsellors from their liege lord, and drawing to themselves royal power, authority and pre-eminence above the king's person, to the disinheriting and danger of the king, the kingdom, and equally of the crown.

Also, to satisfy their greed by disinheriting and destroying the people and the magnates, the same have removed the counsellors and good officers chosen by general agreement and have brought in others of their own opinion who are evil and deceitful, namely Master Robert Baldock, keeper of the king's privy seal, Lord William de Cusaunce, a foreigner, a personal clerk of Hugh the son, the keeper of the great wardrobe, and Lord William Cliff, likewise the same Hugh's clerk, and caused them to be sworn of the king's council, that they would not allow any writ affecting or in respect of the aforesaid father and son and any others whatsoever, whose business they wish to advance or also to hinder, to go out of the chancery, that place above all where no justice should be denied.

Also, the same have had appointed as sheriffs, escheators, constables of castles and others men less fit for working in royal service, and also had men appointed as judges insufficiently learned in the laws of the land, namely Hugh Despenser the father, Ralph Basset, Ralph Camoise, John Inge and others bound and sworn particularly to them, to hear and determine cases and matters affecting the people and the magnates; indeed through such officers they caused their deceitful accusers and accomplices and lying jurors to judge the chief men of the land, for example, the Earl of Hereford, John Giffard of Brimpsfield, Robert Mohaut and other noble men because of greed for their goods and lands.

Also the same most falsely and maliciously caused the lord king to go with horses and weapons to the region of Gloucester and there to ride against good and faithful men with armed knights, against the Great Charter and the will and decision of the magnates, to the confusion of the people.

Also when the Earl of Hereford and Lord Roger Mortimer of Wigmore were sent under an instruction to attack Llywelyn Bren, who had risen in a warlike manner against the king in Glamorgan, while the lands in fact were in the hand of the king due to the death of the Earl of Gloucester, the said Llywelyn surrendered to the aforesaid lords and to royal mercy and will; and those men who were promising him mercy handed him over on such a stipulation to the lord king who then received the same under the same terms. The same father and son, drawing royal power to themselves, seized the aforesaid Llywelyn and took him to Cardiff, after the said Hugh had been seised of his share, usurping jurisdiction for themselves where they had not been able to win in any reasonable way in such a cause, and there they decreed that he should be drawn, hanged, beheaded and quartered, to the disinheriting of the king and crown and to the disparagement of the aforesaid lords.

Also, the same evilly counselled the lord king to take into his own hand the lands and castles of Lord Hugh Audley, the son, whom they ousted from his lands without due process, so that they could afterwards procure them for themselves, and also through their deceitful machinations contrived to acquire the lands of Lord Roger Damory in order that they thus might have been strong enough to lay hands on the whole of the earldom of Gloucester to the disinheriting of the peers of the land.

Also, where the lord king had granted to the Earl of Warwick by his letters patent in a parliament in London that, if he himself should happen to meet his death, his executors should hold the lands until his heir was of full age, which concession the lord king indeed confirmed in parliament at Lincoln after the earl's death at the request of the chief men of the land, the aforesaid Hugh the father, with the son urging and instigating the affair, without cause persuaded the lord king to revoke what had been done and to hand over to the same Hugh custody of the same, with ownership of the profits of the lands, by annulling the king's grant made in parliament, against the established laws and entirely against reason.

Also the same do not allow our lord king to take reasonable fines from the peers of the land and others entering a fief in these days as used to be done in times already past, but because of their greed to acquire lands in this way, through the royal authority they had seized for themselves, they had undue burdens brought in to such affairs, charging that such lands were forfeit, as from Lord John Mowbray for lands of Gower, and from other magnates, to the dishonour of the king and against the old established laws of the land.

[Additional accusations follow which relate to claims against the lands of the Templars, the presentations of leading ecclesiastics and more particular offences relating to individuals]

Indeed these wicked counsels and offences noted above, were proved and publicly pointed out by an inquiry by the prelates, earls, barons and many other peers of the realm, and for that reason, the prelates, earls and barons, and the community of the land begged the lord king that the aforesaid Despensers, father and son, as deceitful and most evil counsellors of the king, disinheritors of the crown and destroyers of the people, be exiled from the kingdom of England and never afterwards return, and that on these matters there should be made in the present parliament one statute as a perpetual remembrance of the matter and an example of evil counsellors, lest any should dare to offend in a similar manner in the future.

On that account, we, the peers of the land, earls and barons in the presence of our lord king deem that the oft-times mentioned lords, Hugh Despenser the father and Hugh Despenser the son, as disinheritors of the crown should themselves be disinherited in perpetuity, and that they should be exiled from the kingdom of England and should never afterwards return, except by agreement of our lord king and the magnates, and this in a parliament duly summoned, and we give them the port of Dover and not elsewhere for crossing the sea and leaving the kingdom of England before the feast of the Decollation of St John the Baptist next coming, with that day reckoned in [29 August]. And if the aforesaid Hugh and Hugh Despenser should extend their stay within the kingdom of England beyond the date given them for leaving or should ever return to the same except as set out above, then let them be treated as public enemies of the king and kingdom.

ii PROME, *parliament roll for 15 July 1321, Westminster, no. 2;* CCR 1318–1323, *pp. 494–4*

To the honour of God, and of holy church, and of our lord the king, and to the profit of him and of his realm, and to maintain peace and quiet among his people, and for the maintenance of the estate of the crown, the prelates, earls, barons and other peers of the land, and the community of the realm, demonstrate to him, against Sir Hugh le Despenser the son and Sir Hugh le Despenser the father, that whereas, at the parliament at York, the said Sir Hugh the son was chosen for, and it was agreed that he should be admitted to, the office of our lord the king's chamberlain, to serve in that office, as was deemed appropriate; at which parliament it was also agreed that certain prelates and other great men of the realm should remain close to the king through the seasons of the year, to better counsel our lord the king, without whom no important matter of business ought to be conducted; [however], the said Sir Hugh the son drew over to his side Sir Hugh his father, for whom there was neither assent nor agreement in parliament that he should remain close to the king in this way, and between them usurping to themselves royal power over the king, his ministers and the government of his realm, to the dishonour of the king, the detriment of the crown and the destruction of the realm, and of the great men and of the people, and they carried out the misdeeds set out below, plotting to turn the heart of our lord the king from the peers of the land so as to have sole government of the realm between the two of them.

Firstly, Sir Hugh le Despenser the son was angry with the king, and because of this anger made a bill, with the which bill he sought to make an alliance with Sir John Giffard of Brimpsfield, and Sir Richard de Grey, and others, to lead the king to do his will by force, with the result that he did not forgive him when he did not do it. The tenor of the bill follows below:

> Homage and oath of allegiance are more by reason of the crown than by reason of the king's person, and attach more to the crown than to the person. And so it seems that before the estate of the crown is descended, no allegiance relates to the person: so that if the king by chance does not act according to reason, with regard to the crown, the lieges are bound by the oath made to the crown to restore the king and the estate of the crown by reason. Otherwise the oath would not be upheld at all. Now let it be

> asked how one should move the king, by suit of law or by force? A man cannot gain redress by suit of law, since he would have no judges if this is not on behalf of the king. In which case, if the king's will does not accord with reason, he gains nothing except the maintenance and confirmation of the error. Thus it is necessary, to save the oath, that whenever the king will not redress something or oust that which is wicked and dangerous for the common people, and for the crown, it be decided that the matter be removed by force. Since he is bound by his oath to govern the people and his lieges, and his lieges are bound to govern in support of him, and in default of him.

And also, by their scheming and misdeeds, they led and badly counselled our lord the king, so that his presence, which it is his duty to show to the great men and to his people, and to the graces and right which they might ask him to answer, was not shown by him at all, except at the will and at the bidding of the said Sir Hugh and Sir Hugh, which ousted the king from his duty, contrary to his oath, and the hearts of the great men and people from their liege lord.

[The remaining clauses follow the tenor and structure of the earlier form of the accusations, namely the restricting of access to the king; the ousting of good and suitable ministers and their replacement by those unlearned in the law of the land; advising the king to ride into the region of Gloucester; the arbitrary treatment of Llywelyn Bren; the plots to seize the lands of Hugh Audley and Roger Damory; the reallocation of rights to the lands of the Earl of Warwick, and so on.]

VI: CIVIL WAR AND THE STATUTE OF YORK, 1322

Introduction

Even before the restoration of the Despensers and the revocation of their order of exile, Edward had begun his assault upon the opposition. In what was undoubtedly a contrived situation, Edward first laid siege to Leeds Castle; in doing so, he was apparently responding to 'disobedience and contempt'[1] aimed at his queen who had been denied entry to the castle, which was held by Bartholomew Badlesmere, a recent but prominent addition to the opponents of the Despensers [**34a**; **34b**]. The bloody end to the siege in the autumn of 1321, which saw the summary executions of members of the garrison and the imprisonment of Badlesmere's wife and children, set the tone for the following months of conflict and brutal reprisal. The events at Leeds Castle also speak to the disunity of the baronial opposition; while some of the king's opponents wished to come to Badlesmere's aid during the siege, Lancaster forbad it, his personal animus towards Badlesmere – a former king's man and one-time steward of England, a title that Lancaster claimed as his own – seemingly outstripping any greater tactical imperatives. This lack of cohesion was to be all too evident in the months that followed.

Despite that lack of unity, we are also aware of some gathering of the opposition and a restatement of anti-Despenser sentiment in the early winter of 1321. The so-called 'Doncaster Petition', drawn up by Lancaster and the Marcher lords, chided the king for supporting the exiled Despensers and renewed accusations against their unlawful disregard for the rights and property of others;[2] such complaints fell on deaf ears, however. Soon after the conclusion of the siege at Leeds Castle, the king had in fact set about overturning the exile of the Despensers; in the circumstances, a recourse to parliament

1 *CCR 1318–1323*, p. 504.

2 Haskins, 'Doncaster Petition, 1321'. As Phillips notes, this was Lancaster's last attempt to use the Treatise on the Steward to justify his opposition to the king: Phillips, *Edward II*, p. 399.

was inconceivable, so Edward looked instead to the more favourably inclined of his bishops [**33b**]. The argument, the identification of a series of errors in the judgment of exile, had been rehearsed at the time of the Westminster parliament of July 1321, as the Bridlington chronicler makes clear [**33a**]; there, the case against exile set out by the Despensers was rejected by their opponents. The same or similar arguments were evidently repeated in support of the recall of the Despensers in late 1321. With some reluctance, evident through both excuses against attendance at convocation and the unwelcome advice of Walter Stapeldon, the bishop of Exeter, that a ruling of parliament was the correct means by which the Despensers' exile should be annulled [**16c**], the bishops granted Edward his wish.[3]

During the winter of 1321/2, with the Despensers restored to the realm, Edward led his forces west across England towards the Marcher strongholds on the border with Wales; despite some resistance at Bridgnorth and further south in Gloucestershire, leading opponents, or contrariants as they came to be known, such as the Mortimers and Maurice de Berkeley, soon surrendered to the king. By February Edward had turned north and east, collected his forces at Coventry, and advanced upon Lancaster and the remnants of the contrariant opposition, including Audley, Damory and the Earl of Hereford, gathered with him [**34**]. It is striking that Lancaster had not moved significantly from his northern base in the preceding months and each of the king's opponents was left to resist alone as the king moved from lordship to lordship. In the Marches, Edward had also been able to mobilise the support of native Welsh lords, such as Gruffydd Llwyd, and thereby to press his opponents from both east and west.[4] An attempt by Lancaster's forces to resist the royal advance failed at Burton upon Trent; a desperate attempt to escape to the north and to the Scots was thwarted by Andrew Harclay, a noble loyal to the king and soon to be, albeit briefly, Earl of Carlisle.[5] Lancaster, Hereford and their supporters were brought to battle at Boroughbridge in March 1322, where Hereford was killed and Lancaster surrendered, having already seen some of his forces, including leading retainers such as Robert de Holland, desert to the royalist side.

3 The same issue would resurface once again in May 1322 when, perhaps minding the earlier advice of Stapeldon, the original judgment of exile was wholly revoked at the York parliament: *CCR 1318–1323*, pp. 541–6. Phillips, *Edward II*, p. 422; see also below.

4 On the Welsh support for Edward, see Smith, 'Gruffydd Llwyd'; Smith, 'Edward II and the allegiance of Wales'.

5 For Harclay's rise and, more especially, his fall, see above [**25–26**].

Lancaster's trial, a brief affair at which he was allowed no defence, illustrates the legacy of the previous decade's politics and the opportunity Edward took for revenge (see [**35a–b**] for descriptions by the chroniclers). Not only were the most recent events of the civil war rehearsed but a long history of Thomas's slights and challenges to royal authority was set out. These included his pursuit of the king and Gaveston and the seizure of the king's jewels and horses in early 1312, actions which were already, as was recognised in the indictment, the subject of the king's earlier pardon, in October 1313 [**35c**]. Lancaster was condemned to death by hanging, quartering and beheading, a sentence that was immediately adjusted to beheading, to reflect the status and lineage of the condemned man. The execution took place immediately after the verdict, Thomas led to his death on a mule and pelted with snowballs by a crowd of onlookers.[6]

The death of Lancaster was not the end of the blood-letting. A number of his supporters were executed on the same day, while still others were executed in the weeks that followed.[7] Many were hanged, drawn and quartered; Bartholomew Badlesmere, Edward's initial target at the outset of his campaign, was dragged by horse from Canterbury to a nearby crossroads where he was beheaded and his severed head set on a spike. In some cases, corpses of hanged contrariants were left on gallows for a year and more until the king was persuaded to remove them [**38a–b**]. In other instances, contrariants paid often extortionate sums, sometimes more than £1,000, to secure their release and the return of their lands [**38d**].[8] Family members, including the wives and widows, of contrariants, such as Alice de Lacy, Lancaster's widow, or Elizabeth de Burgh, the widow of Roger Damory, were treated with varying degrees of cruelty and subject to the rapacity of Edward and his favourites. The younger Despenser's attempts to draw together the lands of the Gloucester heiresses by forcing them into the surrender of their own illegitimate rights to estates is the most blatant of such instances.[9]

The extent of Edward's and the Despensers' aggression and rapacity were widely noted and commented upon by contemporaries. The execution of a leading noble, a blood relation of the king and uniquely

6 *The Brut*, I, p. 223.

7 See also below, Chapter VIII: Tyranny and deposition.

8 Fryde, *Tyranny*, pp. 70–7.

9 See, for instance, Holmes, 'Protest'.

wealthy in his tenure of five earldoms, was an extraordinary act (see [**36a–b**] for contemporary assessment of Thomas's wealth and lineage). The chroniclers generally decried the greed and violence levelled at opponents and their families. The execution of Thomas of Lancaster soon provoked a sympathetic reaction amongst the population more generally; poems [**37a**] and other forms of artistic expression, such as wall paintings,[10] celebrating his perceived sacrifice, his saintliness and his likeness to St Thomas of Canterbury, appeared fairly speedily. Though the author of the *Vita Edwardi Secundi* detected a moral lesson in the perils of inconstancy in Lancaster's death [**36b**, re. 1322], failures of judgement, leadership and moral rectitude, set out with élan by commentators during Thomas's life [**36b**, re. 1319; **39c**], were now generally overlooked. Instead, pilgrims attended his tomb at Pontefract as well as the site of his memorial to the Ordinances at St Pauls in London; at both locations, miracles were attested [**37b**].[11] Despite Edward's attempts to shut down the cult as soon as possible, as an order to the bishop of London in June 1323 makes clear,[12] pilgrimages to the new 'St Thomas' continued throughout the reign and into the next, as the unusual survival of a peasant will from Walsham-le-Willows (Suffolk) illustrates [**37c**].

By May 1322 Edward was also taking stock of the vast estate that had fallen into his hands and considering how best to profit from it [**38c**]. Weeks before, and within a day or two of the execution of Lancaster and other rebels, the king had appointed commissioners to oversee the forfeited land.[13] By June 1322, the properties on at least some of the confiscated estates had been farmed out to lessees, with the profits of the leases to be reported to the king by his county administrators.[14] Receipts to the exchequer quickly grew, a product of the property now in the king's hands as well as the fines paid by contrariants to recover their liberty and their lands. Between July and September 1322, almost £15,000 was paid into the exchequer, mostly, it seems likely, from confiscated properties; given the balance of the treasury in May 1322

10 As at South Newington (Oxon.), for which see Tristram, *English Wall Painting*, pp. 72–3 and plates 17–18.

11 On political sanctity in this period, see Walker, 'Political saints'. For a particularly detailed account of miracles at the place of Lancaster's death, see *The Brut*, pp. 228–31.

12 *Foedera*, II.i, p. 525.

13 *Foedera*, II.i, pp. 480–1.

14 *Foedera*, II.i, pp. 490–1. On this process, see Fryde, *Tyranny*, pp. 80–1.

was a little over £1,000, this was an extraordinary change in the condition of the royal finances.[15]

His overwhelming victory in 1322 offered Edward the opportunity to rule, for the first time, as he chose. A first and significant act was to repeal the Ordinances of 1311, a symbol of restraint on his authority and opposition to his rule which Edward now rejected with contemptuous haste. The main work of the York parliament of May 1322, for which no parliament roll survives, was organised around this action, as an agenda for the parliament makes clear [**39a**].[16] The first agenda items were for the repeal of the 1311 Ordinances and the preservation of those Ordinances worth retaining. Overall the work of the parliament, which the king wished to be as brief as possible – a desire reflective less of his regard for the inconvenience of those attending than of his antipathy towards parliaments[17] – was intended to consider amendments to the law for the profit of the king and his people. The principle outcome of the parliament, the Statute of York [**39b**], was a rejection of 'all manner of ordinances or provisions' that might seek to reduce the authority of the king or his estate. Any future deliberations touching on such matters, as is made clear in the statute, were to 'be treated, agreed and established in parliaments, by our lord the king, and by the assent of the prelates, earls and barons, and the commonalty of the realm; as has been accustomed formerly'. The statute is not now considered as constitutionally significant as was once held to be the case. Rather than a statement of intent for the new role of parliament or of the commons within parliament, historians tend to the view that Edward was 'trying to turn the clock back to before 1310–11' and reassert the authority of the king over parliament and his baronage.[18] As such the 'assent' of the political elite and the wider community of the realm was required only, in reality, to affirm the royal will. The reissue of six of the original Ordinances for 'the good keeping of his peace and the tranquillity of his people' is also perceived as a conscious statement of royal authority, Edward selecting a small number of the Ordinances as 'good points' but rejecting all else [**39c**].

15 Fryde, *Tyranny*, pp. 92–3.

16 See Ormrod, 'Agenda' for an important discussion of the wider political context of the agenda.

17 Phillips, *Edward II*, p. 424.

18 Phillips, *Edward II*, p. 423; Fryde, *Tyranny*, pp. 65–6.

33 The return of the Despensers

(a) *Bridlington*, pp. 70–1

The counterclaim of the aforesaid father and son

Errors. The two often-mentioned lords Despenser pointed out errors in the preceding process, which follow immediately:

First, they proceeded to trial with one side not called to reply, as a result of which it is not fit for them by law to record a sentence against anyone.

Secondly, that they have not been found guilty on the criminal articles charged against them.

Thirdly, that out of all the matters set against them, nothing involves felony or treason, without which or without the second of which, nobody should be outlawed and also should not be exiled.

Fourthly, that they proceeded to judgment against the record of our lord king, for our lord king recorded against the aforementioned articles, which he was more competent than any other to know about.

Fifthly, because their decision was given without the clergy, and no judgment falling within a variety of laws should be determined without common assent.

Sixthly, that they came in arms to parliament in a time of peace into the presence of our lord king. And the manner of their entrance terrified the hearts of those attending, and stole from them the will to judge.

Seventhly, that all those by whom the judgment was given were their chief enemies, according to the saying 'our enemies are judges', and that appears plainly in the aforesaid articles.

Eighthly, that the greater part of the same were forced by harshness to accept the will of those men.

Ninthly, because our lord king did not consent to their judgment; this was because they proceeded wholly against the tenor of the Great Charter, which is affirmed by the Statute of Marlborough and by the Ordinances, and because he desires that no one be exiled or proscribed unless by judgment of his peers and by the old established laws of the kingdom, and those who shall have presumed to do anything against the Charter were excommunicated four times in a year.

Upon which [grounds] the aforesaid lords Despenser, father and son, beg the lord king, inasmuch as he is bound by right of his crown and his given oath to rule and support all men in justice and to correct all injustices and errors, that he should have the record and process of the aforesaid decision brought before himself, and examined carefully and faithfully; and if errors of any sort were to be found in the aforesaid record and process may it please him further graciously to do what right and reason demand and require. And the said father and son were ready to answer the accusations of all men. Moreover his royal highness may wish to consider that the Earl of Hereford and others who have been the chief authors of the aforesaid articles and proceedings should not in their own suit take the place of party and of judge, unless this meets canon and civil law and also the laws of the kingdom.

(b) *CCR 1318–1323*, pp. 510–11

Jan. 4 [1322]. Worcester.

To J. Bishop of Norwich. Whereas Hugh le Despenser, the elder, and Hugh le Despenser, the younger, were lately, at the pursuit of certain magnates of this realm, exiled from the realm and disinherited by a consideration made by the said magnates, and said Hugh and Hugh have suggested by petition before the king that there were many errors in the aforesaid consideration, by reason whereof it ought to be annulled, and they have prayed the king to do them justice in this matter, as the king is bound to do justice by his coronation oath and by Magna Carta and by the Ordinances; which petition the king caused to be delivered to W. archbishop of Canterbury[19] and the other prelates and clergy of the province of Canterbury … and he enjoined them to examine its contents and to advise him what he ought to of right in the matter; and they replied that it seemed to them that the consideration as to exile and disinheritance of the said Hugh and Hugh was wholly erroneous and unjust, wherefore the said archbishops and bishops, as spiritual fathers, advised and prayed the king, and consented and agree, as peers of the realm, that the king should cause the consideration to be revoked and annulled, adding that neither they nor any of them ever consented to the consideration, but that each of them protested in writing at the time that they would not and could not consent thereto; and the king afterwards caused the petition and the above answer to be recited publicly before him … By K.

19 Walter Reynolds.

*The entry in the rolls also records that the same was read before leading nobles, including the earls of Kent, Richmond, Pembroke and Arundel, as well as 'justices and others of his council'; letters were also written to the other bishops not present for their response, requesting that they 'write to the king without delay' each stating 'what he thinks of the matter and what he would do and what he would advise to be done by the king'. For Stapeldon's reply to the letter, see [**16c**].*

34 The civil war as recounted in the chronicles

(a) *Bridlington*, pp. 73–6

Also in the same year [1321], Lord Bartholomew Badlesmere through his men held Leeds Castle in Kent by force and arms against our lord king; but before Christmas the king took it, ordered that thirteen esquires be beheaded, and the knights and ladies found there be committed to prison. Also Lord John Hothum, the bishop of Ely, was attached, called to London and charged with certain matters laid against him, and fined. Also before Christmas the Scots again laid waste with fire and the sword the countryside everywhere down to the River Tees. Also about the beginning of Lent after the lords Despenser, father and son, had been recalled by the lord king and restored to their former position, he undertook a journey to the north with them and a great number of armed men. First, however, in Shropshire he took captive the two lords Mortimer, uncle and nephew, and Lord Hugh Audley the elder, with many others, whom he committed to safe custody because they took certain cities and towns in the Marches, struck down knights and other lieges and officials of the king, and committed other crimes until the king came upon them without warning and scattered their troops. Afterwards Lord John Giffard with a substantial force of armed men entered the lord king's town and castle of Gloucester and they occupied it against his peace and will, and both there and in the king's town of Bridgnorth they committed robberies, arson, homicide and other crimes, but when they were warned of the king's approach, struck by terror, giving up the aforesaid lands, towns and castle, they went to the Earl of Lancaster who was staying at Pontefract, as if to their main place of safety. From there they went to the king's castle of Tickhill, taking siege engines with them and attacking it they besieged it for three weeks, assaulting it ceaselessly, and they killed certain of the king's men there. Nor were the aforesaid evil deeds sufficient for them, but Thomas, Earl of Lancaster, the earl of Hereford, lords Mowbray and Clifford, and many other barons and bannerets, with a great number of foot soldiers and other armed men, fell into such madness that at Burton upon Trent, meeting the lord their king with banners unfurled, for three whole days by force and arms they prevented him and his men from crossing the river; there in the second week of Lent, on Wednesday next before the feast of St Gregory the pope [10 March 1322], on the sixth day before the ides of March [10 March 1322], in the fifteenth year of King Edward's reign, and the thirteen hundred and twenty-first year of the Lord's Incarnation,[20] with the Dominical letter C,[21] seizing the town and bridge of Burton with a multitude of men, they killed certain men. The lord king therefore, considering that his earls, drawn up in battle-lines, were prepared for a fight as with an enemy, decided to fight with them, and, guided to a certain ford, he crossed the river towards them, and with his men drawn up for battle, he wished to unfurl his banner, and immediately Lord Hugh Despenser the son leapt down from his war horse, and stretching his arms out on the snow, which then covered the surface of the earth, he prostrated himself before the king, saying, 'Spare, O lord, spare thy people, and for God's mercy let not the king's power but his mercy direct your actions. My lord king, those whom you strive to conquer are nobles of the kingdom and your lieges, led not by sober counsel but spurred on by youthful ardour, they have set their hand to undue violence, and if, my lord king, your banner should be unfurled, universal war will disturb the whole land everywhere, and you will scarcely be able to restrain it in your lifetime. However, your royal highness should continue as you have begun, so that, if by chance they should see fortune to be against them, they will repent and, with God's help, recover their senses about what they have started.'

But the earls, seeing the king's approach, terrified by fear and, having set fire to certain houses in Burton, fleeing in the smoke, hastily made their way to Pontefract. When it was known that the earls had scattered and were in flight, the king took the earl's castle of Tutbury, where Lord Roger Damory was found and other wounded men. From there the king pursued the fleeing earls and they, hearing of the king's approach,

20 The Bridlington chronicler is presumably using the Annunciation (25 March) *after* Christmas as the start of the year; hence the 1322nd year since the incarnation would commence with the feast of the Annunciation, 25 March 1322; see Cheney, *Handbook of Dates*, p. 5.

21 The first Sunday of 1322 falling on the third day of the year, hence 'C'; for explanation of Dominical Letters, see, for instance, *ibid.*, pp. 8–9.

quickly made their way from Pontefract to Boroughbridge; laying waste the countryside and committing other crimes, they arrived there on the eighth day after they had retreated in disorder from Burton; there a certain northern knight, Andrew Harclay, a warlike and vigorous man, by virtue of the royal commission made out to him, which was to oppose and check those in rebellion against the king, leading with him armed men and foot soldiers assembled in those parts, met the fugitives and blocked the crossing at the bridge. Which direction the aforesaid earls wanted to have taken is unknown to most people; the common opinion of the people was, however, that they were disposed to hasten to Scotland. And since the earls despised the small numbers of the northerners, the Earl of Hereford and others engaged in battle with them on the bridge; and [Hereford] also died there; two knights and the earl's standard-bearer likewise lost their lives fighting. Roger de Clifford and many others, being wounded, retired from the battle.

Behold how our sins increase the number of evil days for us, as it is written in the Apocalypse: 'and there went out a red horse and to him that sat thereon it was given that he might take peace from the earth and that they should kill one another'.[22] So, at present, because Englishmen are already fighting among themselves and because the days just now are evil, we fear that future days will be worse …

(b) *Adae Murimuth*, pp. 34–6

The castle of Leeds is besieged. The Despensers are restored. War between the king and the barons breaks out. The earl of Lancaster is beheaded.

In the year of the lord 1321, the sixth year of the pontificate of Pope John and the fifteenth of the reign of King Edward, around Michaelmas, Queen Isabella, with the agreement of the king, came to Leeds Castle in Kent, which was then held by Bartholomew de Badlesmere; he was, however, not there, but his wife, together with his sons and others deputed to look after the castle, were in residence. The queen sought entry to spend the night but was denied access. On account of this the king ordered that the castle be besieged by all the people thereabouts, and by those from the Cinque Ports, as well as some of those from London and Essex. During the siege, the earls and barons gathered at Kingston on the eve of the feast of the Apostles Simon and Jude

22 Rev. 6:4.

[27 October 1321], and with the support of the whole body, they sent the archbishop of Canterbury, the bishop of London and the Earl of Pembroke, in order to relieve the king's anger and to request that the siege should be removed until the next parliament, so that, once parliament was held, the castle would be returned to him. The king chose not to accede to their requests, and they returned, senselessly, to their positions; finally, the castle was returned to the king's grace, together with the people within it. With this done, twelve brave men, who held the castle, were immediately hanged there, namely Walter Culpepper and all; but the wife and sister of Bartholomew Badlesmere, as well as B[artholomew] de Burwassch and certain others, were sent to the Tower of London. And around the feast of Advent, the king headed off towards the March of Wales with a large force. And around 10 December, the archbishop called a council at London, to which few came because of fear and location and the brevity of the time; at this council it was declared by the few prelates present that the process of the exile of the Despensers was in error, and the king with his council pronounced that the exile was not to be respected, and they were restored. At Christmas, the king was at Cirencester but was unable to go to Gloucester because the town was held by certain barons; so, avoiding that way, he travelled through Worcester and those parts to Shrewsbury, and sent some ahead to prepare his way through Bridgnorth. He descended from another region and seized the castle, killing some, whilst others were put to flight; and then the king outlawed those who were there and ruled that their lands should be seized throughout the whole of England. And afterwards he came to Shrewsbury by another way; there, the two Roger Mortimers came to him through the fraudulent mediation of the Earl of Pembroke, the Earl of Richmond, the earls Marshal and Warenne, who made them many promises, but in what form it is not known. And afterwards certain others, namely Maurice Berkeley, Hugh Audley senior, Master Rhys, surrendered themselves to the king. And the king sent the Mortimers to the Tower of London, Berkeley to Wallingford, Rhys to Dover. But the Earl of Hereford, Gilbert Talbot, Roger Dammory, and all the others of that alignment, headed towards the north to join the Earl of Lancaster, who was said to have received them. So the lord king gathered together a great army and headed into the northern parts at the beginning of spring and brought the earls of Lancaster and Hereford to battle at Burton upon Trent, from which the earls and their followers fled. At Boroughbridge, they encountered a great part of the Northumberland force led by Andrew Harclay; there in a terrible battle, on 16 March, the Earl of Hereford was killed and the Earl of Lancaster and sixteen barons were captured. And on Monday 22, before the feast of the Passion, the Earl of Lancaster was beheaded on his own lands at Pontefract, and six barons were drawn and hanged. Also, at York, R[oger] Clifford and J[ohn] Mowbray were drawn and hanged, along with certain others, as were, in London, Lord H[enry] Tyes, and at Canterbury, B. de Badlesmere, at Gloucester, J[ohn] Giffard, at Bristol, H[enry] de Wyntone and certain others. And a parliament was convened at York, as is described below.

35 The trial of the Earl of Lancaster

The trial of the Earl of Lancaster is described with varying degrees of detail and some inconsistency in terms of persons present in a number of chronicle accounts. The chronicler John de Trokelowe offers a full transcript of the proceedings, as below; a closely similar transcript is also recorded in Foedera, *II.i, pp. 478–9. Most chroniclers express some shock at the arbitrary process, as in the example from the Lanercost chronicler quoted below, and at the execution that followed. There has been some debate as to whether the speedy and one-sided process reflected the application of martial law; it seems unlikely, however, that martial law could have been employed in this instance as the king's forces had, at no point, unfurled their banners against the enemy, an act that would have been a formal declaration of war.*[23] *Instead, contemporaries often referred to the events of 1321–2 as a 'dubious war', a reflection perhaps of the same technical issues.*

(a) *Bridlington*, pp. 76–8

When Thomas Earl of Lancaster heard of the death of the Earl of Hereford, he sought peace and a truce until the next day; and in the night that followed almost all his retinue spurned him and deserted. On the next day Lord Simon Warde, sheriff of York, with four hundred armed men quickly came there and without delay the Earl of Lancaster, John Mowbray, Roger Clifford and many others were captured and led to York; and from there they were brought to Pontefract at the king's command on Sunday in mid-Lent, which was the day of St Benedict

23 Fryde, *Tyranny*, pp. 58–9.

[21 March]; and on the following day they were presented for their appearance [before a tribunal].

Therefore on the Monday before the feast of the Annunciation of the Blessed Virgin Mary [22 March] in the castle at Pontefract, with the lord king sitting to give judgment, and with the earls of Kent, Richmond, Pembroke, Warenne and Surrey, Arundel, Athol and Angus, and also barons, bannerets and other magnates of the kingdom as assessors, Thomas Earl of Lancaster was called to judgment and, with him standing present there, it was placed on record that the same Thomas against his fealty, homage and allegiance had come with hostile intent and with banners unfurled at Burton upon Trent together with Humphrey Bohun, Earl of Hereford, with all the proceedings as have been set out above. These treasons, homicides, arsons, plunderings, felonies and hostile acts of war with horses and weapons and unfurled banners are notorious to the earls, barons and other magnates, since they are manifest to all people. And judgment was therefore given that the same Earl Thomas should be drawn for his treasons, hanged for the homicides, plunderings and felonies, and beheaded for the aforesaid flight. But in the end the lord king, out of respect for the excellent and noble family into which the same Thomas had been born, that is as the son of the king's uncle Edmund, out of his special royal grace remitted to the aforesaid earl the carrying out of two of the penalties to which he had been sentenced, namely that he should not be drawn nor hanged; but that the only execution to be carried out on the same Thomas was that he should be beheaded. And when this was done, he was handed over to the monks of the town for burial.

Oh grief indeed! that such a man should be accused of such deeds, and should take part in actions of this sort. And immediately the lords Warin de Lisle, William Tuchet, Thomas Mauduit, Henry Bradbourne, William fitz William and William Cheyney by the same record and process were drawn and hanged there. Also on the next day at York, John Mowbray, Roger Clifford and Goscelin Deyville were by the same record and process drawn and hanged in iron chains. Also, at Gloucester, Lord John Giffard [was executed] because, against his fealty, homage and allegiance and through treachery, he took the town of Gloucester, and also set fire to the town of Bridgnorth and broke the bridge and committed there robberies, homicides and felonies, and from there, laying waste the countryside by force and arms, he went in a hostile manner to the lord king's castle of Tickhill, which he besieged with many others, and afterwards at Burton and Pontefract he opposed the lord king and fought with his liege men with banners unfurled; by the king's record, as set out above, he was drawn and hanged together with Roger Elmerigge, as was required by the above said faults. Anyone indeed who should wish to read or hear the complete record and process made and pronounced against the aforesaid lords will be able to find it all in the other book among the *Incidentia Cronicorum*, just as it was declared in the judgment above; there he may find the names of the lords and of other knights arrested as a result of the aforesaid rebellion, and also the places where they suffered the punishment of death. And in the same place, written in the said process, is contained the letter of credence for a certain John Denome, to expound on behalf of the aforesaid earls to Robert Bruce and the Scots, the making of a league and alliance with the same. That last matter I do not positively confirm, for whether it is true or not I do not know. God knew.

(b) *Lanercost*, pp. 234–5

The king, then, greatly delighted by the capture of these persons, sent for the earl to come to Pontefract, where he remained still in the castle of the same earl; and there, in revenge for the death of Piers de Gaveston (whom the earl had caused to be beheaded), at the instance of the earl's rivals (especially of Sir Hugh Despenser the Younger), without holding a parliament or taking the advice of the majority, caused sentence to be pronounced that he should be drawn, hanged and beheaded. But, forasmuch as he was the queen's uncle and son of the king's uncle, the first two penalties were commuted, so that he was neither drawn nor hanged, only beheaded in like manner as this same Earl Thomas had caused Piers de Gaveston to be beheaded. Howbeit, other adequate cause was brought forward and alleged, to wit, that he had borne arms against the king of England in his own realm; but those who best knew the king's mind declared that the earl never would have been summarily beheaded without the advice of parliament, nor so badly treated, had not that other cause prevailed, but that he would have been imprisoned for life or sent into exile.

This man, then, said to be of most eminent birth and noblest of Christians, as well as the wealthiest earl in the world, inasmuch as he owned five earldoms, to wit, Lancaster, Lincoln, Salisbury, Leicester and Ferrers,[24] was taken on the morrow of St Benedict Abbot [22

24 The Ferrers earldom of Derby: Maddicott, *Lancaster*, p. 9.

March 1322] in Lent and beheaded like any thief or vilest rascal upon a certain hillock outside the town, where now, because of the great miracles which it is said God works in his honour, there is a great concourse of pilgrims, and a chapel has been built. In the aforesaid town Sir Garin de l'Isle, a king's baron, also was drawn and hanged, and three knights with him. But the aforesaid Sir Andrew [Harclay] was made Earl of Carlisle for his good service and courage.

(c) *Trokelowe*, pp. 112–24

Concerning the legal record against Thomas of Lancaster

Edward etc. to all those who these letters should reach, greetings. We have examined the record and process of the justices in our presence against Thomas, once Earl of Lancaster, and certain other of our enemies and rebels, returned, in these words: 'The pleas of the crown in the presence of the lord Edward the king, son of the lord Edward the king, held in the presence of the said lord Edward at Pontefract on the Monday after the feast of the Annunciation of the Blessed Virgin Mary in the fifteenth year of the reign [29 March 1322]. With Thomas of Lancaster, seized for treasons, homicides, robberies, arsons and other various depradations and felonies, led into the presence of the lord king, with Edmund Earl of Kent, Hugh the Earl of Winchester,[25] Aymer the Earl of Pembroke, John de Warenne, the Earl of Surrey, Edmund the Earl of Arundel, David the Earl of Athol, Robert the Earl of Angus, barons and others of the king's magnates also present, the lord king recorded that the same Thomas, a liege man of the same lord king, came to Burton upon Trent, namely with Humphrey de Bohoun, one-time Earl of Hereford, a known traitor of the king and of the realm, with standards raised, at Boroughbridge in armed conflict against the king where he [Humphrey] was killed. Also there was Roger Damory, an adjudged traitor, along with certain other traitors and enemies of the king and realm, who, with standards unfurled as in a war, resisted with hostility and impeded the same lord king, his men and their associates for three days in a row, so that they could not cross the bridge at the said town of Burton, as they sought, and feloniously killed certain of the same lord king's men. On account of which, the same lord king, in order to constrain the abovesaid malice and resistance of the

25 John, the Earl of Richmond, in *Foedera*, II.i, p. 478.

abovesaid earls and others and to preserve the tranquility and peace of his people and realm and to maintain the authority of his crown and in order to repel and remove the abovesaid force, gathered so seditiously, he sought another way to cross the waters of the Trent and hence rode with purpose against the abovesaid earls and others. And the abovesaid Thomas, on becoming aware of this, along with the others of the abovesaid traitors, as a traitor and enemy of the king and the realm, set fires in the abovesaid town of Burton and feloniously burned down part of the houses and goods of the same town. Thereafter the abovesaid earl, together with others of the abovesaid traitors, left the town for the field there, with standards unfurled, and with hostility, anticipating the arrival of the said lord king in the same field, organized his martial forces against the same lord king, an action which was contrary to his homage, fealty and lineage, by which the earl was bound to the king. And on account of this, when the said Thomas the earl understood that the same lord king would come, and confront them with a great force, the same Thomas the earl fled in disarray together with his co-conspirators. And even, in flight with the lord king in strong pursuit, he caused diverse destructions until the same Thomas the earl, with standards unfurled, came to Boroughbridge. There the supporters of the lord king, with the full authority of the king to resist the enemies and traitors of the lord king with every means and way they possessed, rallied for the lord king. And the abovesaid Thomas the earl, along with the other traitors, with horses and arms, and with standards unfurled, attacked the supporters of the king who were there with hostility, and he killed some of those supporters feloniously, and he fought them, until the same Thomas the earl, along with the abovesaid traitors, in disarray, was captured. And some of the traitors were captured, and certain others were killed, and others fled. And so no one remained with Thomas the earl, save himself, together with his other fellow traitors, that might overthrow and vanquish the same lord king. And these traitorous acts and homicides, arsons, depredations and hostile acts of war, with horses and arms, and with standards unfurled, are manifest and well known to the earls and barons and other magnates of the realm. Therefore, it is considered that the abovesaid Thomas the earl, as a traitor, should be drawn, and for the abovesaid homicides, depredations, arsons and robberies should be hanged, and for the abovesaid flight in that part should be beheaded. And in addition to this the abovesaid earl, in previous times, had committed against the lord king many ills wretchedly and maliciously contrary to his homage, faith and lineage. Namely, when the lord king happened to be at

Newcastle-upon-Tyne with supplies, horses, armour, jewels and other various goods, of great quantity and worth, the abovesaid Thomas the earl, with horses and arms, and with a great armed force, seized [the same] and damaged and carried them off. The same lord king, by his special grace, had pardoned and set aside those damages and transgressions caused by the abovesaid Thomas the earl and other causers of the same damages; and this was done in order to return the said Thomas to the best course of life. Beyond this, the abovesaid Earl Thomas, gathering to him various men, came with force and arms to diverse parliaments of the lord king and on many occasions prevented the same lord king from holding his parliaments, as he should have done according to his office. And, frequently, he [Thomas] did not deign to come to such parliaments, against the mandate of the king; instead, he showed contempt and also frequently organised various gatherings and illegal meetings against the lord king, in various places and contrary to the order of the lord king. Also, with many malefactors and disturbers of the lord king's peace, gathered and collected together by the said Thomas, they committed murders and depredations and various other felonies for which they deserved to be put to death; and the same Thomas, by receiving and maintaining them, merited the same judgment, according to the laws and customs of the realm. Also, when Thomas the earl, after he had come with a great force of armed men to the parliament of the lord king at York,[26] he caused the said king to pardon suit for breach of the peace levelled against him and the above said malefactors for previous acts, of around a thousand persons, and this despite the fact the same Earl Thomas earlier took an oath to observe certain of the Ordinances, namely that the lord king should not set aside suits for breach of the peace in cases involving the deaths of men.[27] Also even when the lord king, as was mentioned above, in order to steer the same Earl Thomas on a better course as best he could, offered various large gifts of land, lordships and liberties, in many exchanges and certain gifts, various grants and pardons, and through charters made for the benefit of the same Earl Thomas, the same Earl

26 Maddicott, *Lancaster*, p. 312, suggests this is the York parliament of 1318. The Bridlington chronicler also laments similar demands for pardon of malefactors when discussing the 1321 parliament at Westminster, but also makes reference to the 1318 York parliament [**36c**].

27 This relates especially to Ordinance, cl. 28: 'As the people feel much aggrieved that men are emboldened to kill and rob people because the king by evil counsel so lightly gives them his peace contrary to the form of law, we ordain that no felon or fugitive be henceforth sheltered or protected for any sort of felony by the king's charter of his peace being granted to him…', *EHD 1189–1327*, n. 100, pp. 535–6.

Thomas encouraged rebelliousness against the king and, disobedient, persevered in his wickedness. Also, the same Thomas the earl sent certain knights of his household to the city of York in order to lure the community of the same city and custody of the same into the control of the same Earl Thomas. And also the same Earl Thomas usurped royal authority to himself in various ways and sought to usurp in order to reduce through his efforts in this way the lord king. Also when the lord king, at that time established at York, ordered various magnates and others of the realm with whom he wished to seek counsel that they should come to York in order to discuss a campaign of the same lord king into Scotland, the said Earl Thomas, then in his castle at Pontefract with a great multitude of armed men, sent his men to prevent ease of transit near to Pontefract, both by roads and by bridges, so that the counsellors of the lord king, mandated by the same, could not reach York. And when the lord king had left the area of York and headed south, and, with his household, had come near to Pontefract, the said Earl Thomas and his men came out of the castle and, in order to disrespect the lord king, subjected the same lord king to vile and contemptible abuse with a great tumult, to the greatest contempt of the same lord king as if the lord king should be their enemy, and neither the king nor their lord. Also, the said Earl Thomas, together with the Earl of Hereford and others of his co-conspirators, sought to have and to make a confederacy and alliance with Robert Bruce, Thomas Randolph, James Douglas and other enemies of the lord king and of the realm, and the mode and form of the same confederacy was discovered in a certain indenture found with the said Earl of Hereford at the time that he was killed, and in the following words:

> The agreement which John Denom ought to deliver to Robert, king of Scotland, and to Sir Thomas Randolph, Earl of Moray, seneschal of Scotland, and to Sir James Douglas, or to those soonest found, on behalf of the earls of Lancaster and of Hereford and their allies. That is to say, that the said king of Scotland and the said Earl of Moray, the seneschal, and Sir James Douglas, with their forces, shall come to the said earls of Lancaster and of Hereford, and to their allies, at whatever hour they shall be warned thereto, at a certain place, where they may assemble; and they shall injure all those whom the said Earl of Lancaster and ⌈Earl⌉ of Hereford, and their allies may wish to injure; and save all those from injury, whom they may wish to have saved, to the best of their power. Also, they shall come to the said earls of Lancaster and of Hereford in all places where they may wish to come, in England, in Wales and in Ireland, to live and die with them in maintenance of their quarrel, without claiming conquest or lordship in the said lands. And if the said king of Scotland, or his other persons before

> named, for them and their resources, may wish to assure this thing and do it; or if the king of Scotland be prevented himself by illness, or by other great cause, by reason whereof he cannot come in his proper person, then the before-named Earl of Moray the seneschal, and Sir James Douglas, with their forces aforesaid, assure and do what is before said; the aforesaid earls of Lancaster and of Hereford shall give assurance that they will never make raid upon them in aid of the king of England. And at such time as the aforesaid earls of Lancaster and of Hereford, and their allies, shall have brought their quarrel to an end, they shall use [all] lawful pains, that good peace be made between the two lands of England and of Scotland, to the best of their power; so that they shall keep their land of Scotland, as peaceably, as they shall do with their land of England.

And what is more, after the abovesaid traitors of the same Thomas the Earl of Lancaster had made an entrance, by force and arms, into the castle and town of the lord king at Gloucester, with his army, and had occupied the same castle and town contrary to the will of the lord king, and had carried out depredations, arsons, murders and other enormities in the town of Bridgnorth, the same traitors, fearing the imminent arrival of the lord king against them, gave up the said castle and town. Thereafter they fled hurriedly towards the abovesaid Thomas the earl in order to gain the refuge of their leader and captain; the which Thomas the earl, his sedition and support notorious in this region, received those traitors and encouraged them in military activity against the lord king and to bring civil war[28] in his realm, as already described. And he sent his men, together with the same co-conspirators, to besiege the castle of the lord king at Tickhill, and certain machines to launch great stones against the abovesaid castle and against the men of the lord king found within the same castle. So, these traitors continuously besieged that castle for three weeks, with attacks and acts of war, and killed certain men of the king who were there. And afterwards the abovesaid Thomas the earl, with the abovesaid evil deeds, felonies and crimes perpetrated, as also mentioned above, fled, heading towards the Scots, enemies of the lord king and of the realm, until he reached Boroughbridge. There he was captured, as is also mentioned above. Whence the lord king, having regard for such deeds and iniquities of the said Thomas, as well as his enormous ingratitude, found no cause to show mercy to the same Thomas the earl in relation to the abovesaid punishments passed against him. However, as the earl was the product of excellent and most noble parents, the lord king, out of respect for the

28 The Latin word is *Guerra*, which is often taken to signify civil or 'private' war rather than war (Latin: *bellum*) per se; see, for instance, Bartlett, *'Mortal Enmities'*, p. 15.

said parents, through his special grace, remitted execution of two of the punishments adjudged to him, as was described: namely, that the same Thomas the earl should not be drawn nor hanged but that the execution should be in such a way upon him that he should be beheaded.

[There then follows a shorter account of the misdeeds of an identified number of Lancaster's followers, namely Warin de Insula, William Tochet, Thomas Mauduit, Henry de Bradebourne, William fitz William, William Cheine, a list that includes some also identified in the Sherburn Indenture [**32c**]; unlike their leader, they were spared neither drawing nor hanging. The conclusion to the record is as follows:]

... But we, in great awareness of the enmities and rebellions of the abovesaid Thomas and others of our abovesaid enemies and so that others of our subjects should in future fear greatly to undertake such acts, we aim to make an example throughout the abovesaid record and the present process. In proof of such matters, we openly publish these our letters. Witnessed by me at York, the second day of May, in the fifteenth year of our reign [1322].

36 Thomas of Lancaster: the assessment of the chroniclers

Chroniclers, a number of whom such as the St Albans chronicler, John de Trokelowe, were pro-Lancastrian,[29] *described the lineage and exalted position of Lancaster. The near-contemporaneous account of the reign in the* Vita *allows us to see how the career of the earl was perceived, at least by one observer prepared to shift their view of him according to events and rumour.*[30]

(a) *Trokelowe*, pp. 72–3

Concerning the instructions of the Earl of Lincoln and the marriage of his daughter.

Thomas, the Earl of Lancaster, in the fullness of time, married the only daughter of the noble Earl of Lincoln. The Earl of Lincoln, in his time, was strong in military matters and wise in counsel, and instructed the said Thomas in the ways of war and decorum, as his son and heir.

29 Gransden, *Historical Writing*, p. 6.

30 Given-Wilson, '*Vita Edwardi Secundi*: memoir or journal?'

So, realising his time had nearly come, Lincoln called Thomas to him, so that he could reduce his weakness by the other's strength and offer him his last benediction, and spoke these words,

'My son, husband of my only daughter; my inheritance falls to you. You are the son of a fine father, from whom you hold three earldoms and now, through your wife, you will obtain two more, namely Lincoln and Salisbury; thus you will control five earldoms. Remember therefore that the Lord has made you wealthy above all of the magnates in England; therefore you owe honour to Him for such riches. You perceive faithfully that the church in England, which should be free, is no more than a servant, burdened by the oppressions of Rome and the unjust exactions wholly extorted by rulers. Also the people of our land, who should enjoy great freedoms, are led into servitude by various vexations and tallages imposed upon them by kings. On account of which I urge you, for the blessing of God and of myself, when the time presents itself, release and defend, by your strength, the church and the people from such oppressions to the honour of God. Show to your king, who is your lord and also your cousin, the honour that is due and, you should ensure with all care and promptness that he remove from his court the evil counsellors and aliens, and keep the Great Charter and the other articles ...'

With this said, and having given his benediction and having received the sacrament of the church with piety, and having disposed of his temporal possessions wisely, he returned to Christ and was buried with honour in the church of St Paul in London. Into his inheritance, on the part of his wife, Thomas entered. The admonishment of his father-in-law was not forgotten ...

(b) *Vita*, pp. 51, 169–71, 215

1312

This Earl Thomas was related to the lord king in the second degree of kinship, for they were descended from two brothers in the first degree, namely from the elder King Edward and his brother Edmund, Earl of Lancaster. His mother was queen of Navarre, his sister queen of France, and his sister's daughter is now queen of England. As each parent was of royal birth, he is clearly of nobler descent than the other earls. You may assess his power by the size of his patrimony. For he had five earldoms in England, namely the earldoms of Lancaster, Leicester and Ferrers from his father, and the earldoms of Lincoln and Salisbury from his wife. See how the lordship of so many noble earldoms is now reduced to one. Now Thomas alone can do as much as formerly Earl Edmund, Lord Longespée, Lord Lacy and Lord Ferrers, each singly, could do. I do not believe that any militarily active duke or count under the Roman empire could do as much from the profits of his lands as Thomas Earl of Lancaster.

1319

This extensive lament at the failings of the Earl of Lancaster, only a section of which is offered here,[31] *follows the aborted siege of Berwick in 1319, at which point widespread rumours linked Lancaster to a treacherous plot with the Scots.*

That the king raised the siege was blamed on the Earl of Lancaster; he was also blamed for the Scots coming to seize the queen, and the king's enemies returning unscathed to their own country. Some evidence of treachery was openly spoken of, from which the reputation of the earl and his followers was seriously damaged. For it was commonly said that the earl received forty thousand pounds from Robert Bruce to help him and his men secretly, and that at the siege, while everyone was attacking the wall, none of the earl's retinue assaulted it, and that the town of Berwick would have surrendered if the earl's scheming had not hindered this, and that James Douglas on his way back to Scotland passed through the earl's lines, and that the earl went unarmed through the midst of the Scots.

Oh! Earl of Lancaster, whose riches are so great, why for such a sum of money have you lost your reputation and your name for constancy? Would that that money had never been, for which your reputation died and dishonour was born! There is great damage when reputation is in danger, the cost of which is immeasurable, because once injured it can scarcely ever be regained. Indeed if you scattered all your riches in gifts, you would never recover your former reputation. Oh! What paeans of praise you had while you were courageously upholding the Ordinances! The goodwill of the people is turned to hatred, and your fame is changed to infamy. Thus although Joab performed many brave deeds, his treachery towards Abner and Amasab thoroughly tarnished all his renown.[32]

Oh! noble earl, why do you not recall to mind the 'chosen generation',[33] your royal family which you disgrace! Why do you not take thought,

31 The full text of the lament is in *Vita*, pp. 169–75.

32 See 2 Kings (2 Sam.) 3:27, 20:10.

33 1 Pet. 2: 9.

distinguished earl, how great a charge is the crime of broken faith! For, although the deeds of guilty men are punished in a variety of ways, nevertheless traitors justly suffer the extreme penalty. For it is proper that traitors should undergo the worst fate, and who has ever committed such a deed with impunity? … What then are you doing, Earl of Lancaster? If you intend to take the path of wickedness, the whole world will rise against you, and you will not be able to escape the due punishment. Therefore you should either convict the deceitful lips [of rumour] of falsehood, or quickly turn your evil deeds into better actions.

1322

Oh, what a sight! To see the Earl of Lancaster, who was recently the terror of the whole country, receiving judgment in his own castle and home. Then the earl was led out from the castle, and, mounting some worthless beast of burden, was led to the Capitol. Then the earl stretched forth his head as if in prayer, and the executioner cut off his head with two or three blows. And these things happened in March in the fifteenth year of the reign.[34]

Oh! Earl of Lancaster! Where is your power, where are your riches, with which you hoped to subdue all, and that no one could resist you? If you had been steadfast in your early faith, you would never have come to be forsaken. If Samson had remained cautious and Solomon devout, the one would not have been deprived of his strength nor the other of his wisdom. Perhaps a hidden cause, not immediate but in the past, brought punishment upon the earl. The Earl of Lancaster once cut off Piers Gaveston's head, and now by the king's command the Earl of Lancaster has lost his head. Thus, perhaps not unjustly, the earl received like for like, as it is written in Holy Scripture: 'for with the same measure that you shall mete withal it shall be measured to you again'.[35]

(c) *Bridlington*, pp. 72–3

Also in the same parliament[36] the following was made known by the earls:

34 On 22 March 1322.

35 Luke 6:38.

36 Westminster parliament, May–July 1321.

Since recently many chief men of the kingdom had charged the lords Despenser, Hugh the father and Hugh the son, with many misdeeds done by them against the estate of the king and the crown, to the disinheritance of the magnates and the destruction of the people; and, in proceeding against the said misdeeds and overcoming by force what could not be achieved by process of law, the aforesaid earls had made an alliance between themselves by written oath and by another means, although they had not sought permission from the king; and then, in proceedings against the aforesaid father and son and their allies and those supporting them, the aforesaid magnates and others of the same opinion had ridden out with the king's banners and their own unfurled, had taken and seized castles, and likewise taken towns, manors, tenements, goods and chattels, and had imprisoned men of allegiance to the king and to others, certain of whom they had killed, and others they had released for ransom; and they had done many other things in the destruction of the aforesaid Hugh and Hugh and their friends in England, Wales and the Marches, of which action some could be called trespasses and some felonies; and on this account the aforesaid magnates had begged our lord king, for the good of peace, the tranquillity of the people and the soothing of rancour, and to draw together the hearts of the great men, that they should be absolved and cleared of all alliances, trespasses and felonies, it was agreed in the same parliament that none of them, whatsoever their estate might be, on account of the trespasses, made by oath, in writing or otherwise, because of the expeditions with the king's and others' banners unfurled, and because of the seizures, occupations and detentions of castles, towns, manors and of other things, and also because of imprisonments, ransoms, homicides, plunderings, felonies and some other actions which can be called trespasses, made against the peace of our lord king in the said proceeding, from 1 March last past until the Wednesday next after the feast of the Assumption following [19 August], that none should be accused, charged, arrested, imprisoned or otherwise oppressed, nor summoned to trial in the king's court before him himself or elsewhere, but that they should be quit of all trouble, offence and accusation; excepting that the aforesaid Hugh and Hugh should be for ever debarred from all action or right of recovering their goods or chattels noted above or restitution of their losses; and that all who were in the same proceedings when it was being done, both greater and lesser men supporting the aforesaid lords, should have general charters under the king's great seal in the terms expressed above.

Look now how lawmakers are made lawbreakers! For, in the York parliament[37] the Earl of Lancaster persuaded the lord king to pardon liability of prosecution for breach of his peace against [the earl] himself and his other wrongdoers to the number of about a thousand; and yet the same earl had earlier sworn upon the keeping of certain Ordinances that the lord king might not pardon liability to prosecution for breach of the peace in cases arising from any man's death. Alas! that such an error blinded so many noble men; they torture and condemn others, so they say, for their offences, while they think to absolve, to whitewash and to cover up themselves and their accomplices, charged with the greatest crimes, just as a short time before, through their recognizances made in parliament, when they sought from our lord king the benefit of pardon and acquittal for their own immeasurable faults.

37 Thomas of Lancaster: death and 'martyrdom'

*Just as verse in parody of hymns was produced to celebrate the death of Gaveston [**5c**], so replication of 'rhymed offices' lamented the death and celebrated the life of Lancaster. This adoration was taken up by the populace through pilgrimage and other forms of pious expression.*

(a) *Political Songs*, pp. 268–71

The office of St Thomas of Lancaster[38]
Anthem: Rejoice, Thomas, the glory of chieftains, the light of Lancaster,
who by thy death imitates Thomas of Canterbury;
whose head was broken on account of the peace of the church,
and thine is cut off for the cause of the peace of England;
Be to us an affectionate guardian in every difficulty.
Prayer: O God, who, for the peace and tranquillity of the inhabitants of England, willed that the blessed Thomas thy martyr and earl

37 A reference to the York parliament of October 1318, Maddicott, *Lancaster*, p. 53.

38 Page, 'The rhymed office'. Page associates the rhymed office with prayers intended for liturgical use at Hereford Cathedral in honour of SS Thomas and Ethelbert of Hereford and the Virgin Mary, and suggests that those hearing the rhymed office sung would immediately grasp the implied association between these saints, the Virgin and Thomas of Lancaster.

should fall by the sword of the persecutor, grant propitious, that all who devoutly reverence his memory on earth, may merit to obtain worthy reward along with him in Heaven, through our Lord.

Prosa: The pouring out of prayers to Thomas restores the sick to health;
The pious earl comes immediately to the aid of those who are feeble;
They are relieved from their infirmities by the suffrage of one who was infirm.
So that it is shown by the miracles of St Thomas,
That the royal vessel is beheaded for the cure of the kingdom.
Oh, how the cure of diseases declares the sainted leader!
Sequence: Let us honour the highest king,
For the memory of the sweet martyr,
Whom we join in praising with the utmost reverence.
He is called Earl Thomas, of an illustrious race;
He is condemned without cause,
Who was born of a royal bed.
Who when he perceived that the whole commons were falling into wreck,
Did not shrink from dying for the right,
In the fatal commerce.
O royal flower of knights,
Preserve ever from evils this thy family, bringing them to glory. Amen.

[Further and concluding stanzas of the Office, as gathered in Wright's edition, repeat similar themes regarding Lancester's piety, his sacrifice and the miracles associated with prayer at his tomb. In an additional observation, it is noted that 'he is deserted by the company of his knights, while he is treacherously deserted by Robert de Hoyland', Lancaster's most senior retainer.]

(b) *Anonimalle*, p. 109

And the body of the noble Earl of Lancaster was handed over by the king's order to the monks of the same town where his body lies buried in their church close to the high altar. And soon after, on the fourth day before the kalends of April [29 March 1322], Our Lord Jesus Christ did many miracles for love of him.

(c) *Court Rolls of Walsham le Willows*, pp. 133–5

+Memorandum: The inventory of the goods of William Lene, on the day on which he died, *viz.* Saturday before the feast of All Saints [28 October 1329].

[There follows an inventory of Lene's goods, the details and sum total of which suggest a reasonably prosperous unfree tenant.]

Sum £26 9s. 11d.
From which – [there then follows a series of bequests arising from the inventory, an unusual record of what is effectively a peasant will from this period; after bequests to family members, payment of formal obligations to the lord of the manor and to the church, as well as certain charitable donations, the final particular bequest is as follows:]

Item for the expense of one going to [the shrine of] St Thomas of Lancaster, an unknown amount …

38 The treatment of the king's opponents

Edward's vengeful assault upon the defeated contrariants attracted considerable attention from the chroniclers and was dismissed as 'shameful' by the Westminster monk Robert of Reading, the probable author of the Flores Historiarum, *the most vehemently anti-royalist of the near-contemporary chronicles. As well as a slew of executions and financial penalties, Edward's officers began to account for the land and property that had come into the king's hands, as, for instance, orders to manage the new royal estate make clear.*

(a) *Flores Historiarum*, pp. 207–8

At last, to the following shameful acts and to the perpetual confusion of the realm, the cruel tyrants (*tyranni*) brought forth to be drawn and hanged innocent barons, renowned and famous, that is lords Warin de Lisle, William Tuchet, Thomas Mauduit, Henry de Bradbourn, William fitz William, William de Cheney, together with a certain chosen chief [servant] John Page; they were all led to the slaughter in front of the said earl, their lord, and were hanged, commending their souls and cause to the divine disposition of Christ. And by similar tyranny[39] the

39 The Latin word used here for 'tyranny' is *dominatio.*

sons of the devil, judges of iniquity, dispatched illustrious nobles, more distinguished than the rest by virtue of their heroic deeds, throughout various parts of the realm to be beheaded [*ad decollationem*][40]; that is at York John de Mowbray, Roger de Clifford, Joslin de Deyvile; at Canterbury Bartholomew de Badlesmere and Bartholomew de Ashburnham; at Bristol Henry de Montfort and Henry de Willington; at Gloucester Roger de Elmerugge and John Giffard; at Cardiff William Fleming; at Winchelsea Thomas Colpepper; at London Henry Tyes; at Windsor Francis de Aldenham; at Gower Stephen Baret; and at Auckland John de Eure. Those beheaded all decided rather to submit to death in the interest of truth, than shamefully to violate the faith they had promised. And the king, as he wretchedly acquired the mark of infamy and the name of tyrant, apart from those he had ordered to be killed by the most ugly death, also ordered to be fettered by iron feet-shackles and manacles worthy knights to the number of ninety, to be tormented for a long time in the filth of prison. By their absence and the death of the others, the realm was deprived of the counsel and defence of noble and leading men, and will hardly or never again recover its former position of honour. Further, he increased the miserable slaughter and capture of the nobles so much by the abhorrent savagery of his cruel actions, that whomsoever of them in his perversity by unfair means he saw as a rebel, of whatever condition or rank or generally of benefit to truth he was, they were carried off to savage punishments and death, or driven to extreme poverty by paying ransoms, all except the supporters of the criminals. With the heirs of the dead and the captured wretchedly delivered up to the filth of prisons, the wickedness of the perverse threw out their wives and daughters, plundered of their lands, possessions and all their things, to be wandering paupers. Alas! the grief and groaning, the unexpected lamentation and beating of breasts is drawn forth by personal recollections, when they see the bodies of illustrious military leaders and barons each dismembered and scattered, and pavements flowing and earth reddening with their blood, whose nobility of counsel and whose memorable bravery for a long time up to now used to repel enemies from the realm. Delighting in these previously described deaths of the faithful and in subsequent other evils, the sons of the devil and their supporters, imitating the father, employed fraud and deception, falsity and inconstancy among the just; all their virtue so withered away, that no people seemed equal

40 The author may be using *decollatio* as a general word for execution, since all except Lancaster were drawn and hanged, and some were quartered.

to them in treachery. For they had looked with prejudice on nothing except piety and justice: not honour, nor civil war, impiety and the shedding of the blood of innocents.

(b) *Anonimalle*, pp. 109–11

The king had enquiries made throughout the region as to where those whom he held to be his enemies were; and they were in justice his friends, but he would not listen. And for that he had them drawn and hanged wherever they were best known and had their lordship: Sir Bartholomew Badlesmere, who was the king's steward and formerly a man of his oath, was drawn and hanged and beheaded at Canterbury. And the headless body was again hanged near his nephew Sir Bartholomew Ashburnham. On the Wednesday before Easter [7 April 1322] a certain Henry Tyes was drawn and hanged at London; on the Saturday before Palm Sunday [3 April 1322], a certain Sir Francis Aldenham was drawn and hanged at Windsor; on Wednesday after Palm Sunday [7 April 1322], Sir John Mowbray the noble youth, Sir Roger Clifford, and Sir John Dayville were drawn and hanged at York, and hung there a long time in iron chains, but then with the king's permission they were taken down and are buried in the church of the Dominicans at York. Sir Henry Montfort and Sir Henry Willington were drawn and hanged at Bristol. Sir Roger Elmerigge, and several others, lords and esquires, some franklins and others (were captured), of whom some were released for a heavy ransom, some died in prison, and some were outlawed. After the said vengeance had been thus cruelly taken and exacted, the king in the same year turned his attention with all his forces to Scotland.

(c) *CPR 1321–1324*, p. 161

May 18 [1322]. York. Mandate to Roger Beler, keeper of the castles, manors, towns and lands late of Thomas, sometime Earl of Lancaster, and of other rebels in the counties of Leicester, Stafford and Derby, which are in the king's hands, to make an extent thereof, to wit, of the yearly value in demesnes, villeinages, homages, service, rents and all other issues; and to enquire what lands are forfeitures to the king without claim, and what have claims lodged against them; what are worth keeping in the king's hands for stock and other profits, what would be better let to farm to tenants and at what rates and terms; also as to those lands kept in the king's hand, at what farm they would let; also how much great wood and underwood could be sold without waste or destruction and what other profits could be made thereof; and he is to certify the king hereof this side of the quinzaine of Midsummer. By K. and C.

The like to the following touching the castles, manors, towns, lands and tenements of rebels in the following counties:

[There then follows a list of nineteen separate commissions relating to lands across the country. A further commission for the county of Lincoln was also issued in June 1322.[41]]

(d) *CFR 1319–1327*, p. 152

1322. July 30. Newcastle-upon-Tyne.

Be it remembered that the king on 8 July in the beginning of the sixteenth year at York ordained and enjoined on John, bishop of Norwich, the chancellor, that he, taking with him Henry le Scrope, chief justice of the king, William de Bereford, chief justice of the Common Bench, William de Ayremynne, keeper of the rolls of chancery, and Geoffrey le Scrope, king's serjeant, should proceed in the following form to the delivery of the prisoners in the Marshalsea and in the castle of York, of whom some were taken against the king in the war waged of late in the realm by certain magnates thereof, and some surrendered themselves to the king's will, whose names also the king caused to be delivered to the chancellor; to wit that from the more important prisoners he should receive security by their oath and bond of loyal behaviour, and that they should come to the king to have delivery of their lands; and that from the less important prisoners he should receive like security by oath and other things contained in the said bond or letters, and cause enrolment to be made by way of record on the rolls of chancery of their loyal behaviour towards the king and their ransoms to be paid to the king, and that he should likewise receive by mainprise security from them of their behaviour under a certain penalty, and of their ransom to be paid, and that after such securities have been received he should cause their bodies to be delivered from prison and their lands to be delivered to them; and that he should cause poor persons, who

41 *CPR 1321–1324*, p. 161

have nothing, to be delivered of the king's alms; by pretext whereof the chancellor, associated with said Henry and others, proceeded to the delivery of the following persons:

[There then follows the record of a fine for 2,000 marks[42] paid by Richard le Waleys of the country of York 'to save his life and to have his lands'; the fine is recorded in the form of 'letters obligatory', effectively a bond which begins in the following form:]

Notification by Richard Waleys, 'chivaler', dated at York, 11 July, 16 Edward II [1322], that whereas of late in a war waged in the land by certain magnates against the king he was with the said magnates against the king and for that reason has rendered himself to the will and forfeiture of and to the king of his body, lands and tenements, and the king has granted him his life, lands and tenements by ransom, he … has made an oath on the Holy Gospels to be obedient, intendant and of aid to the king as his liege lord in all things …[43]

[There then follows a series of general obligations associated with loyalty to the king, a record of Richard Waley's formal acknowledgement of the same and the identification of sureties (mainpernors) for Richard's future loyalty and good behaviour. A series of further names follows, all of whom entered into similar agreements. The Fine Rolls also include a schedule which records that all such fines were subsequently annulled and cancelled in the first parliament of Edward III's reign, January 1327.[44]]

39 The York Parliament of May 1322 and the Statute of York

(a) An agenda for the York parliament

Davies, *Baronial Opposition*, p. 582, Appendix no. 93, pp. 582–3; Ormrod, 'Agenda', pp. 26–7 (from which the translation is taken)

To establish first the statute for the repeal of the Ordinances

Also to place the good points in a statute

…

42 I.e. £1,332, a very large sum in the early fourteenth century. A mark is 13s. 4d. or 160d., or two-thirds of a pre-decimal pound.

43 For a fuller version of this entry, see Fryde, *Tyranny*, p. 71.

44 *CFR 1319–1327*, p. 154; *PROME*, January 1327; see also *CCR 1327–1330*, p. 98.

[A series of other agenda items follows relating to such matters as the false returns of officers, the treatment of the chattels of felons, the administration of crimes across counties, the creation of wool staples to encourage domestic cloth production and so on.[45] The agenda concludes as follows:]

And let it be known that the king wishes that each learned person of his council consider these matters … in such a way as to adjust the law for the profit of the king and of the people … What will be agreed will be put into the form of a statute where there is need for a statute or for other form of remedy there or other remedy will suffice and that such things shall be put before the king so that he can plan before parliament so that the people who come to parliament might be released earlier.

(b) The Statute of York, 1322

Statutes, I, pp. 189–90; also *EHD*, III, no. 103, pp. 543–4; the statute is available online at www.legislation.gov.uk/aep/Edw2/15/1 (last accessed 19 June 2021)

Whereas our lord King Edward, son of King Edward, on the sixteenth day of March in the third year of his reign [1310], to the honour of God, and for the good of himself and his realm, granted to the prelates, earls and barons of his realm, that they could choose certain persons from the prelates, earls and barons, and of other lawful men whom they considered sufficient to be called to them in order to ordain and establish the state of the household of our said lord the king, and of his realm, according to right and reason, and in such a way that their Ordinances should be made to the honour of God, and to the honour and profit of holy church, and to the honour of the said king, and to his profit and to the profit of his people, in accordance with right and reason, and to the oath which our said lord the king made at his coronation, and the archbishop of Canterbury, primate of all England, the bishops, earls and barons chosen for this purpose, did make certain Ordinances which begin thus: 'Edward by the grace of God, king of England, lord of Ireland, and duke of Aquitaine, to all to whom these letters shall come, greeting. Know that whereas on the sixteenth day of March in the third year of our reign, to the honour of God, &c.' and

45 Ormrod, 'Agenda', argues that these items, not all necessarily discussed and resolved at the York parliament of 1322, reflected commons petitions and the wider agenda of the political community.

ends thus, 'Given at London the fifth day of October in the fifth year of our reign.'[46]

The which Ordinances our said lord the king, at his parliament at York, in three weeks from Easter in the fifteenth year of his reign [2 May 1322],[47] did, by the prelates, earls and barons, among whom were the more part of the said Ordainers who were then living, and by the commonalty of the realm, there by his command assembled, cause to be rehearsed and examined: and forasmuch as upon that examination it was found, in the said parliament, that by the matters so ordained the royal power of our said lord the king was restrained in divers things, contrary to what ought to be, to the weakening of his royal sovereignty, and against the estate of the crown; and, also, forasmuch as, in time past, by such ordinances and provisions, made by subjects concerning the royal power of the ancestors of our lord the king, troubles and wars have happened in the realm, whereby the land had been in peril, it is agreed and established, at the said parliament, by our lord the king, and by the said prelates, earls and barons, and the whole commonalty of the realm, at this parliament assembled, that all the things, by the said Ordainors ordained and contained in the said Ordinances, shall from henceforth for the time to come cease and shall lose their name, force, virtue and effect for ever; the statutes and establishments duly made by our lord the king and his ancestors, before the said Ordinances, abiding in their force: and that forever hereafter, all manner of ordinances or provisions, made by the subjects of our lord the king or of his heirs, by any power or authority whatsoever, concerning the royal power of our lord the king or of his heirs, or against the estate of our said lord the king or of his heirs, or against the estate of the crown, shall be void and of no avail or force whatever; but the matters which are to be established for the estate of our lord the king and of his heirs, and for the estate of the realm and of the people, shall be treated, agreed and established in parliaments, by our lord the king, and by the assent of the prelates, earls and barons, and the commonalty of the realm; as has been accustomed formerly.

46 See above [**3c**].

47 The date of the commencement of the York parliament, *PROME*, May 1322.

(c) *CCR 1318–1323*, pp. 557–8

The king in his parliament at York in three weeks from Easter, in the 15th year of his reign [2 May 1322], desiring to ordain and establish a matter that should be to the honour of God and of holy church, to the profit of himself and his realm, the good keeping of his peace and the tranquillity of his people, made the following establishments by the assent of the archbishops, bishops, abbots, priors and other prelates, earls, barons and the commonalty of his realm, there assembled:

[There then follow, as well as grants and establishments from other articles and statutes, notably *Articuli super Cartas* (the Article upon the Charters) of 1300 in relation to the levying of prises,[48] versions of the 1311 Ordinances in relation to the preservation of the rights of holy church (Ordinance 1), the keeping of the king's peace (Ordinance 2), the limits on the extent to which stewards and marshals may hold pleas (Ordinance 26; also *Articuli super Cartas,* 1300, restated in the Statute of Stamford, 1309, and the 'Household Ordinances', 1311, for which see [**3a**], [**3d**]), the limits of the statute of merchants made in the reign of Edward I at Acton Burnell (Ordinance 33), outlawry (Ordinance 35) and felony (Ordinance 36).]

48 Repeated in the Statute of Stamford, 1309; see [**3a**], first clause.

VII: THE FRENCH WAR

Introduction

Edward's French war was unnecessary, fairly small-scale and unsuccessful, but became disastrous for him only because it gave the opportunity for his exiled opponents to coalesce around his wife and son in France. His domestic problems migrated to France and ran out of control.

England's cross-Channel landholdings had long been a major irritant between England and France. They had reached their greatest extent in Henry II's reign (1154–89) when he inherited Normandy from his great-grandfather and Maine, Touraine and Anjou from his father, and acquired Aquitaine at his marriage with Eleanor. The northern areas were steadily lost in the thirteenth century and the Treaty of Paris (1259) was intended to clarify and stabilise the Anglo-French relationship [**40a**]. By the treaty Henry III surrendered his claim to the northern lands in return for a clear acknowledgement of his right to Aquitaine. The territory remained important to the English crown, as an embodiment of family inheritance and prestige, as England's main source of wine, and also as an important source of royal revenue[1] and thus a useful guarantee for repaying the king's Italian bankers.

Unfortunately, the Treaty of Paris did not settle the problems. If anything it worsened them. A number of the land exchanges that guaranteed the treaty were conditional on information still to be determined and in the end were not fully carried out. More importantly, Henry III had agreed to do liege homage for the southern lands, although until then Gascony had had a claim to be alod not fief, but the precise terms of homage and the 'appropriate' services were not fully defined in the treaty, and when Edward II did homage in 1320 there was still room for sharp words over the terms [**40b**].[2] What rankled was that English kings, equal in royal status to kings of France, had to bend the knee to French kings for their duchy and had to accept that their Gascon

1 See [**12**].

2 Pole-Stuart, 'Interview', pp. 414–15; Cuttino, *English Medieval Diplomacy*, pp. 54–74, 82; Vale, *Origins*, pp. 48–62.

subjects had the right to appeal beyond their immediate lord's officials to the French king's court; English kings then might be summoned to the same courts as vassals. This was ever more likely in a period of increasingly efficient administration, which revealed problems of inconsistent rights and jurisdictions at porous borders. In addition, internal instability in Gascony and discontent with the English administration (as much in need of reform there as in England)[3] added to the number of potential appeals to Paris. This was an uncomfortable position for English kings.

These problems touched sovereignty. They were in essence insoluble, and Charles IV's negotiators overtly rubbed salt into the wound in 1324 by emphasising his superiority to Edward in France, being 'emperor in his kingdom' while Edward was only his vassal [**41b**]. Nonetheless war was not inevitable. Although the problems had led to war in 1294, the French marriages of Edward I and Edward II since then were meant to bring the royal families closer together,[4] Edward II's state visits to France in 1313 and 1314 had kept communications open, and the popes, both the Gascon Clement V (d. 1314) and John XXII (elected 1316), actively encouraged peace. With tolerance and constant discussion a *modus vivendi* might be worked out, as it was (for all practical purposes) from 1303 to 1324. Discussions at Montreuil and Perigueux showed the high-powered and knowledgeable delegations the English could call on.[5] Such détente was a 'fudge' perhaps, but it kept the peace. The deaths of French kings in 1314, 1316 and 1322 made the situation more tense, but the ceremonies were often postponed[6] and there was little advantage to either side in fighting. War could not make Edward II sovereign in Gascony nor destroy his legitimate claim to the duchy, and domestic problems in both countries made war unappealing. When war came in 1324 it followed a series of coincidences that were badly handled.

So what went wrong? In 1323–4 the problems of homage, appeals and porous borders coalesced at a time when some of the mediating voices were missing. Henri de Sully (often an intermediary with England) had been dismissed by Charles IV, who relied more on his Anglophobe uncle, Charles de Valois, and an experienced voice was lost at a critical

3 Tout, *Edward II*, pp. 199–201.

4 Brown, 'Political repercussions', pp. 573–89.

5 Cuttino, *Diplomatic Administration*, pp. 89–91.

6 No homage was paid to Louis X who died before the ceremony took place; homage to Philip V was delayed until 1319 (by proxy) and 1320 (in person).

point with the death of Aymer de Valence, the Earl of Pembroke, on 23 June 1324.[7] Nonetheless, it was still a slow-burning crisis and a solution was ultimately available in the transfer of the duchy to Prince Edward.[8]

Homage had become due again at Charles IV's accession on 3 January 1322 and Edward as usual asked for delays. Twenty-one months later, in November 1323, he was still seeking this when cross-border problems arose at St Sardos (Lot-et-Garonne). The incident at St Sardos illuminates the complexity of cross-border landholdings, but need not have proved more dangerous than other clashes at Marsan and on the Ile d'Oléron. In this case the abbey of Sarlat, a 'privileged' house directly under the French king and situated fully in French territory, claimed that all its dependencies, wherever they lay, were to be treated as similarly 'privileged', including one of its dependent territories at St Sardos, which was within the Agenais and under English jurisdiction. The abbey's intention to build a bastide there offended the local lord, Raymond Bernard of Montpezat, and resulted on 16 October 1323 in the hanging of a French serjeant. Bernard was deemed responsible and Ralph Basset, seneschal of Gascony, was suspected of collusion. When both ignored three summonses to appear before French courts between December 1323 and February 1324, they were banished from French territory and Bernard's lands and castle (all in English-held territory) were declared forfeit.[9] In letters to Edward of 29 December 1323 Charles IV was firm but still fairly conciliatory [**41a**], but by 5 May 1324 he was impatient. Edward's envoys wrote to him then that, although he might find it difficult to believe, Charles was now prepared to use force to execute the judgment against Montpezat [**41b**]; and, indeed, when their negotiations failed, Charles proclaimed a preliminary summons to arms to deal with Montpezat for 10 June.[10] An experienced negotiator might have defused the situation, but Pembroke died en route to Paris on 23 June. On 10 July the English envoys reported they had been brusquely received, that Charles had declared all Edward's French lands forfeit, and that his forces, sent south under Charles de Valois, were expected in Gascony before

7 Vale, *Origins*, pp. 228–9.

8 For details of events in 1324, see Vale, *Origins*, pp. 230–40; Phillips, *Edward II*, pp. 455–69; Haines, *Edward II*, pp. 314–21; Chaplais, *Saint-Sardos*, pp. 186–7, 190 n. 1, 191 n. 2. For Pembroke's death, see also Phillips, *Aymer de Valence*, p. 233.

9 Vale, *Origins*, pp. 230–6.

10 Chaplais, *Saint-Sardos*, p. 187; Vale, *Origins*, p. 236.

5 August [**41c**]. Edward II retaliated on 21 July with orders to arrest all French subjects and their goods in his lands.[11]

During August Edward's lands in the Agenais and Saintonge (except Saintes) accepted French occupation and were steadily lost, but Gascony generally supported English rule and Bordeaux and most ports along the Garonne remained in English hands. On 25 August, however, Valois joined the siege of La Réole and on 22 September the Earl of Kent was forced to surrender it in return for a six-month truce to 14 April 1325.[12] The terms were poor, but Gascon lords defended those who had surrendered against their critics.[13] The difficulties of fighting a war in Gascony and the many points at issue in the negotiations are visible in letters and instructions. For example, letters between the younger Despenser and Ralph Bassett in October and November 1324 show the problems of knowing what was going on, sending the right forces and supplies, and coping with the weather when all communications depended on sea transport [**42a–b**]; and negotiations by Edward's envoys in November 1324 had to cover homage, a possible marriage, lands still held despite the Treaty of Paris, the legal rights to Montpezat Castle, what to do with those sentenced in this affair, whether the duchy might be granted to Prince Edward, the status of the truce between Kent and Valois, pardons for those fighting on both sides (Mortimer always excepted), and possible expenses for the king of France, for which the pope would be mediator [**41d**].

At this point Isabella was drawn into negotiations.[14] She landed at Wissant on 9 March 1325 and stayed in France for the next sixteen months. She complained that negotiations were hard and by 31 March had negotiated only an extension of Kent's truce to 9 June [**43a**]. Further negotiations were concluded on 31 May, which halted the war and further loss of land, but the terms were not good [**43b**]. Gascony was to be surrendered to the French king before being received back; a French official would confirm Edward's appointments there; he could not raise a Gascon army; the status of the Agenais would be reviewed and Edward would be liable for French war costs there.

11 Gascon Roll Project online, C61/36 m. 30 no. 19.

12 Chaplais, *Saint-Sardos*, no. 47, pp. 61–3.

13 *PROME*, Parliament of October 1324, E30/1582 m. 2; Chaplais, *Saint-Sardos*, pp. 95–8.

14 For events in 1325, see Vale, *Origins*, pp. 241–2; Phillips, *Edward II*, pp. 471–500; Haines, *Edward II*, pp. 321–9.

Homage was arranged for 15 August, but on 1 June it was postponed until 29 August and then Edward postponed his passage on 24 August, claiming illness.[15] A suitable solution was found when Charles IV, for a relief of £60,000 *parisis*, permitted Edward to grant his French lands to his son.[16] Prince Edward left for France on 12 September and did homage on 24 September. Edward II would act as 'governor and administrator' for his son, a minor, at first with Henri de Sully as the French-appointed seneschal, then with his own appointment of Oliver Ingham.[17] Problems, however, continued. Charles IV still held the lands that the French had occupied, claims for compensation came from all sides, and Edward II complained that his son was acting on the counsel of French advisers to undermine him.[18] Conflict threatened again and on 18 July 1326 Edward complained that the French king was waging open war against him.[19]

Militarily this was a small war, although it cost Edward c. £65,000.[20] Its significance lay in how badly it was handled and the humiliating loss of inherited lands, which added another accusation to those against Edward II in 1327. But worse was the opportunity it gave to the English exiles in France. Letters between Edward, Isabella, the bishops, the prince, the French king and the pope between December 1325 and June 1326 show the steady alienation of Isabella and Edward.[21] Edward's and the bishops' letters in December[22] and Isabella's reply in February ⌜**44a**⌝ highlight her declared fear of Despenser, the king's amazement, and his belief that someone had turned her against Hugh. By 8 February 1326 he had heard of her association with Mortimer,[23] and his letters of March and June expressed growing anger at this inappropriate public liaison and at Mortimer's wearing Prince Edward's livery at the French

15 *Foedera*, II.i, pp. 601–3, 606.

16 *Foedera*, II.i, pp. 607–8; *CPR 1324–1327*, pp. 173–4.

17 *Foedera*, II.i, 609; Chaplais, *Saint-Sardos*, nos 212–16.

18 Letter to Prince Edward, 19 June, ⌜**44c**⌝ below; letter to Gascon cities, 27 June (*Foedera*, II.ii, pp. 631–2; Gascon Roll Project, C61/38, no. 110).

19 Vale, *Origins*, pp. 241–4; Chaplais, 'Le Duché-Pairie de Guyenne', p. 157; Gascon Roll Project online: C61/38 m. 3 no. 110, m. 2 no. 123; *CPR 1324–1327*, p. 296.

20 Vale, *Origins*, pp. 236–46; Haines, *Edward II*, pp. 328–9.

21 *CCR 1323–1327*, pp. 576–82 (*Foedera*, II.i, pp. 615–16, 622–3, 630–1).

22 *CCR 1323–1327*, pp. 580–1; *Vita*, pp. 242–7.

23 *CCR 1323–1327* p. 543. There is little evidence that Isabella was close to Mortimer before this time (Phillips, *Edward II*, pp. 488–91; Doherty, *Isabella*, pp. 81, 84–5, 86–8), but for an argument that their romantic association began earlier, see Mortimer, *Traitor*, pp. 140–9.

queen's coronation.[24] His letter to the pope on 10 June rehearsed all his complaints against Isabella [44b] and his angry letters to the prince and Charles on 19 June became threatening [44c–d]. Isabella's position in France, however, was becoming difficult. Possibly her association with Mortimer irritated the French king, possibly Despenser was bribing the French peers against her,[25] and by 3 August she had moved to Hainault. On 27 August she betrothed Prince Edward to Philippa of Hainault. Rumours of invasion abounded. Most of Edward's preparations were directed to the south coast and his defences for the east coast were quite inadequate to stop Isabella and her supporters landing near Orwell on 24 September.[26]

40 Homage

(a) Treaty of Paris: ratification by Henry III, 13 October 1259

The treaty still left points open to dispute. Clause 3 shows that many rights and services were unknown or unclear and services would be 'appropriate' until clarified; moreover, not all land exchange conditions were fulfilled. Thus there was still room for argument under Edward II about exactly what was due: whether English kings must do homage in person or not, and whether they must also give an oath of fealty (Vale, Origins, *pp. 51–4).*

Layettes du Trésor des Chartes, III, no. 4554; trans. *EHD*, III, no. 41, pp. 376–9

Henry, by the grace of God, king of England, lord of Ireland and duke of Aquitaine.

We make known to all and all who are to come in future that we, by God's will, have made and ratified peace with our dear cousin, the noble king Louis of France, in this manner:

1 [Louis to give up rights in three bishoprics of Limoges, Cahors and Périgueux.]
2 [Lands in Agen, Quercy and Saintonge to return to the English kings under certain conditions.]

24 *CCR 1323–1327*, pp. 576–9.

25 *Anonimalle Chronicle*, pp. 122–3; *The Brut*, p. 234; *Scalacronica*, pp. 190–3; Phillips, *Edward II*, p. 499.

26 Phillips, *Edward II*, pp. 500–4.

3 And for what he shall give us and our heirs in fief and domain, we and our heirs will do him and his heirs, kings of France, liege homage (*homage lige*), and also for Bordeaux, Bayonne and Gascony, and for all the land that we hold beyond the English Channel in fief and domain, and for the islands, if there are any, that we hold that are of the kingdom of France; and we will hold of him as a peer of France and as duke of Aquitaine. And for all these things we will do him our appropriate services (*servises avenable*) until it is found what services are due for these things, and then we shall be bound to do them, exactly as they have been found. Concerning homage for the county of Bigorre, for Armagnac and for Fezensac, let what is right be done about them. And the king of France absolves us if we or our ancestor ever wronged him by holding his fief without doing him homage and without doing his service, and all arrears.

4 [Louis to pay the costs of 500 knights for two years.]

5 [Henry and his sons renounce all claims to rights in Normandy, Anjou, Touraine, Maine and the land of Poitiers.]

6 [Henry renounces all claims on people in those lands (para. 5), saving rights claimed for the English kings in Agen and Quercy (para 2).]

7 [Both sides renounce claims on each other over disputes, wars and arrears.]

8 [Sureties are given and oaths sworn.]

(b) Edward's homage to Philip V, 1320

Philip V succeeded in 1316, but homage was delayed until 1320. The ceremony was fractious. Edward paid liege homage but sharply refused the demand of the French lawyers to swear fealty. The document below, describing the event, was drawn up after Philip's death in 1322 and probably before 1324 to inform the English clerks on precedents for the homage now due to Charles IV. A similar report appears in the Winchester Chartulary, which records the five acts of homage for Gascony made in 1259, 1279, 1286, 1308 and 1320 and appends the 'false and prejudicial' claim of the French on 30 June 1320 that Edward had explicitly stated 'that he was bound and that he became our man for the duchy' (Goodman, Chartulary, *nos 127, 128).*

TNA PRO C47/29/9 (no. 25): published in Pole-Stuart, 'Interview', pp. 414–15; Chaplais, *Diplomatic Practice*, I, pp. 359–60 (no. 199)

Memorandum that when our lord king and Philip, recently king of France, brother of the present king, were gathered at Amiens, three or four days after the homage done in the great church, in the chamber of the said king of France with many prelates and nobles and others of their council to renew and swear the articles of an alliance recently made between their fathers for them and their heirs and successors to last for ever, one of the council of the said king of France, speaking to his said lord proposed the following words or some to similar effect: 'My lord, when the king of England, your brother, did you homage, he made protestation that the peace treaties formerly made between your ancestor and his should be maintained for him, and that the said homage is done according to these peace treaties. And as my lord wishes well that the said peace treaties should be maintained for him as before, as they could and should be done, let him do his homage as it ought to be done. And, my lord, he should do fealty to you.'

And then our said lord the king said to the king of France, 'He said that we are held to do fealty'; and the said king replied to him, 'You are held to do us fealty.' And our said lord turned towards the prelates and nobles of his council, speaking to them in secret, to take advice on this demand; in this way he was advised by those who saw his face but they could not hear the words that he spoke to them in private. And when some of the prelates and nobles were leaning towards our said lord and began to discuss, our said lord now turned towards the said king without taking their advice and announced the following words or ones similar in effect: 'And we know well that the homage that we did at Boulogne was done according to the form of the peace treaties between our ancestors and according to the form in which our ancestors did it; and your father agreed this form; and we have his letters in relation to that; and we have done it now in the same form, nor can anyone demand another form from us by right, nor do we intend to do that. And as for the fealty we are certain that we do not do it at all, nor was it asked of us and we cannot believe that if this fealty had had to be given that it would not have been demanded at that time.'

And then the king of France looked towards the people of his council and they all remained silent against the response of our said lord; and then one of the court remembrancers spoke in private to the one who had first made the proposal and he advised him a little, and then spoke to his lord the king and said, 'My lord, the perpetual alliance of friendship and aid against all men and to have enemies and banned men deported ought to be renewed and sworn now after the homage.' And then our said lord replied gladly and with an amiable countenance said, 'We wish willingly that this should be done and it is right.'

And he [the king of France] was shown by our said lord's face that he was angry that they wanted to oblige him to do homage in a form other than his ancestors had been obliged. And then our said lord had the articles of the said alliance read out and had them sworn on the Psalms by Sir Hugh Despenser the father. And the said king of France had them sworn in the same way by his marshal. And then it was said that letters would be made on both sides on the making of the alliance and the said homage. And therefore the clerks of our said lord who went towards the chancellor of France to have the letters on the aforesaid deed ...

41 Negotiations

The delayed homage to Charles IV and the fracas over the bastide at St Sardos increased tensions. Letters, reports and instructions show Charles's increasing impatience and the difficulties of Edward's envoys.

(a) Charles IV to Edward II, 29 December 1323

Chaplais, *Saint-Sardos*, no. 167, pp. 180–1

Dearest and well-beloved brother,

We have heard your envoys on what they have said on your behalf, all of which they have explained well and wisely, about why you have sent them to us, and they have asked us on your behalf that we would postpone the homage which you owe to us during your predicament.

Dear brother, we wish you to know that we will always do whatever we can well do for you and you should know that, as long as you have had the business of the Scottish war and your other great matters to deal with over there, we have refrained from pressing you for the said homage for the love that we have of you. But, dear brother, we do not see that currently, thank God, you have such great difficulties or such obvious cause for which you ought to request such postponement and that you cannot come here to do the said homage; and you should know that we have already restrained ourselves for a long time and, if we further delay it, we could be blamed for it, which you ought not to want. Thus we have replied on the matter to your envoys that they should tell you that you should be at Amiens on the octave of the next Nativity of St John the Baptist [1 July 1324] to do us the said homage. And we, dear brother, beg you to our utmost that you do not fail to come there.

With regard to this issue of the bastide of St Sardos, concerning which your aforesaid envoys have spoken to us and [said] that what was done was not in any way with your knowledge or consent, certainly, dear brother, in this matter we do not believe that such evil-doers came from you, nor at your command, nor that you would wish in any way to support them, for always we have assumed and assume that you would not wish to do anything that was to our hurt or prejudice, nor that you would want us to do so against you.

And as for the lawsuit which is under way against Arnaud Caillou, which your envoys asked to be revoked or suspended until you and we should meet together, you should know, dear brother, that our council does not consider that we ought or could rightly revoke it, but, dear brother, for love of you we will willingly revoke the banishment made against him, as long as he will stand trial in our court. And we beg you not to receive or allow to be received in your kingdom nor in your other lands those banned in our kingdom, any more than you would want that we should receive your banished men. And, dear brother, at your mere request we have had banned from our entire kingdom certain of your banished men and again we have had this [order] renewed and kept according to the request of your envoys.

Concerning the injuries that our people do to yours, according to what you have given us to understand, we have ordered and do order that they should be addressed, if there are any, and that they should cease doing them. And, dear brother, we will not allow in any way that our people do any injuries to yours, and if there were any [done], always we wish to have the matter addressed as is right and will be reasonable, and we suppose that in this matter you will wish to have things done towards you as to our people.

On certain other articles, dear brother, concerning which your said envoys have spoken to us, we are not fully advised, but always we will do what will be right.

Given at Limoges, Thursday after Christmas [29 December].

(b) English envoys in France to Edward II, 5 May 1324

The envoys were the Earl of Kent and the archbishop of Dublin. Their report shows Charles's mounting irritation.

Chaplais, *Saint-Sardos*, no. 167 (pp. 184–7)

Dearest Sire,

May it please your noble lordship to know that we received your letter by Donevald, your envoy, on Sunday 29 April, from which we have heard the good news about your health, by which we are most heartily comforted and pray God that He will maintain it to the increase of joy and honour.

And on the point, dearest Sire, that you cannot believe that the king of France wishes to send an army and a force to any part of your duchy, as your letters suppose, we believe for sure that, by our other letters and by M. Elis de Joneston who carries them, you have now learned the truth.

And, Sire, the following Monday we came to the said king at the meeting he arranged at Bois de Vincennes, where he had had the wisest men of his council assembled in a great number to hear our message. And after the delivery of your letters and our recommending and notifying him of your estate, Sire, and of my lady the queen and of his nephews and nieces, your children, and thanking him for the postponement to continue with your affairs until his next parlement, we exonerated you for your ignorance of each kind of trespass which they say was done against him at the place of St Sardos, to which you never assented or commanded. And, Sire, emphasising the various alliances and close kinship between you, and the perils and profits and all the causes by which we thought we could win him over, we asked him, according to our letters of credence, that he might be pleased to revoke the lawsuit begun in the case of the said bastide, which actions were done only by officials, in order to hear his will and seek his good grace and, with these and your other affairs concerning him expedited, we could go to the region to enquire about the truth of the deed and have all the wrongs done everywhere against him and his people put right in such a way that he would be content.

And we were told to go into a chamber close by while they consulted and we were recalled in a bit and, before the king and his council, his chancellor replied to us that they were amazed that his brother wished to make such a request to him, since he had already replied fully by letters and messengers, that the king could not do so without being dishonoured and that he would not dare do all that he [Edward] wished him [Charles] to do, for the offence to God and the outcry of his people, that such great and horrible rebellions, injuries and offences done against the estate of his crown have been left unpunished for nothing; Sire, they affirmed to us that you are informed and cognisant of this, and that you ought to be ashamed to ask and to speak of a deed so notoriously wrong and treacherous. And, Sire, the king up to now has held you excused from the deed, but now, at our embassy, it seems much more to him to be with your agreement, since those he banished, while piling up their misprisions more and more, continue variously in their positions and use their power as before, although we can affirm and witness to him to the contrary.

And because, Sire, they do not wish that we should lack any detail or knowledge of the deed, they recounted the whole process before us:

[Here the chancellor rehearsed the history of St Sardos from the time of King Louis to the recent murder of the royal official.]

And besides this, Sire, they strongly reproved our simple-mindedness and foolishness in being willing to undertake to speak or promise to address the wrongs done against his royal majesty on your behalf – you who are Duke of Guienne, vassal and subject to the king of France, who is emperor in his kingdom and has no sovereign under God, since law does not permit that he be judged by his subject – and he does not want to take any emendations except in accordance with his own lordship.

And we, Sire, finding their wills so strange and their words so unpleasant took a respite until the next day, and because it seems to us the case made is so prejudicial to your lordship we strongly requested that he would postpone all things until a suitable time when they might be fully settled and redressed by your and his councils. This point, Sire, we put into writing to deliver to them, but they finally refused, replying that such a request has often before been seen and refused. And then we heard that the king is sending us his chancellor, his marshal and Alphonse Despaigne to ask what power we have to undertake these matters, and we said that your brother, the Earl of Kent, had the authority to hear and determine all trespasses and to remove ministers and to appoint others. Concerning which, Sire, they charged us in this manner: that since they have heard from us of your displeasure about the wrongs and rebellions mentioned above, they command us, as soon as we should go to Gascony where you are, Sire, duke and man of the king of France, by the power that we have from you, that we should have these men who are banished for this deed arrested and seized and deliver them to his prison to answer to him for their castles. We would not want to authorise this, so we promised to use our power, if we should come there, to do what it would seem to us should rightly be done for his honour. And besides that, Sire, we were charged and commanded that we allow him to execute the sentences made on Montpezat Castle, so that, if his people who come there to do that should be impeded, we should give permission to evict the garrison. Unless we do that, Sire, it was bluntly said to us that the king would never grant or discuss the revocation, cessation, interview or anything else that concerns you. And, hearing such strong opinion, we firstly begged and then charged Lords Clermont and Croune to sound out the will of the king's privy counsellors about a delay of only twenty days with the intention of consulting you, and that in the meantime nothing should be done with his summoned host, which is summoned to be here at the octave of Pentecost [Sunday 10 June], which things were finally all followed up; but they then told us they would bring forward this host by eight days earlier than the summons and that the king would sooner give you three of the best castles in his power than suffer such wrongs and such wicked deeds against him to go unpunished, and if we did not respond to him fully concerning the things in the next four days, he would never speak with you concerning this matter or anything else touching you. Sire, we have discussed this situation with all your friends in France who were there and with your council in Gascony. And having heard every opinion, we cannot agree at all, having regard on the one hand to the dishonour and mischief which would occur, for it seems very hard to us to authorise the removal of the obstacle mentioned above, namely from the castle, which they say is in your hand and garrisoned by your people, on which, Sire, we have no orders from you; and having regard on the other hand to the danger that would arise from the departure of the said army for fear of secret plotting and especially because of the small comfort we have from the great men of the said duchy and by word of mouth from all others in the country who know of it and to whom we have spoken; that all the greatest want to avoid war at this time, supposing above all that the wrong will dissolve and go away among your people.

Most honoured lord, this is the state in which your affairs are with us, and we ourselves are in the utmost anxiety with the harshness that we find here; therefore, dear lord, may it please you to discuss these matters in the presence of your council diligently and as quickly as you can, so that we can be certified without delay of your will. Afterwards we will have a trustworthy eloquent man sent to you, who has heard the matters, in order to inform you more fully on the truth of this matter; he will hasten to you, Sire, as fast as he can after these things are clarified.

Most honoured lord, God in his power give you a good life, long, honourable and blessed. Written at Paris, Saturday 5 May in the evening.

(c) English envoys in France to Edward, 10 July 1324

The envoys were M. Richard of Eryom, canon of York and doctor of both laws, M. John of Shoreditch and M. Richard of Gloucester. They found no one at Amiens on 1 July and reached Charles on 5 July at Anet where he married Jeanne of Evreux. Charles was still displeased and they were brusquely received.

Chaplais, *Saint-Sardos*, no. 167, pp. 189–90

... We were rather curtly replied to in this manner: although you have disavowed the events of St Sardos by words, it appears otherwise by your deeds, for there has never been any punishment or redress of the trespass done there, but during the delays that you, dear lord, have had from the king of France you have made alliances, restored castles, towns and diverse other possessions against him, have notoriously received and receive those banished by him in England and elsewhere; because of this he will do none of those things that you asked him. But, because he found no man for the lands of the duchy of Guienne and the county of Ponthieu,[27] he had them taken into his own hand before we came to him, and so he intends to keep them, claiming that he will do justice to you when you come before him.

And, most honourable lord, although we began to give your reasons for the said matters, they told us that they would hold us in scorn for the present, because of which we can have no other answer.

And, most noble lord, from what we can see, they are very ready to go against Gascony with force. Lord Charles, Count of Valois, will be the leader of those who go, and several counts and other nobles who will go had left for Paris before our departure from the king, and they will be at Orleans next Sunday [14 July] and at Gascony in the

27 That is, he considered them vacant, as homage had not been done.

fortnight after St Mary Magdalene [5 August].[28] And they commonly say amongst themselves that if you order any people from England to Gascony to strengthen those who are there, you, dear lord, for your disobedience and rebellion will lose your lands in France for ever without any recovery ...

And if any messengers should come from you to the said king it is best that they be with him quickly and with sufficient power to do the things that please him, for they say that they do not want to be served any longer just with parchment and words (*parchemen et paroles*) as they have been. We tell you these things as we have heard them, so that you can be better advised. Dearest lord, we pray it please God to save and keep you and increase your honour.

Written at Abbeville, Tuesday after St Thomas [10 July].

(d) Edward's instructions to his envoys to France, 15 November 1324

The envoys were the bishops of Norwich and Winchester and the Earl of Richmond.

Chaplais, *Saint-Sardos*, no. 167, pp. 192–4

First, as the king of France has occupied by force against the king of England several cities, castles, towns and lands in the duchy of Guienne and the county of Ponthieu, because the king of England did not do his homage as he ought, the envoys are to excuse the king of England, because he was not summoned or given notice properly to do homage, according to the reasons and memoranda that will be given to them. And they are to ask that the places occupied against the king of England be returned and to offer that the said king of England will come, given sufficient surety and safe conduct, to do his duty of homage to the king of France correctly. And let the safe conduct be such that neither the king of England nor those who come with him should be hindered by anything else in any matter by a lawsuit or *ex officio*; and if they can achieve that, then they should do fealty in the name of the said king by the power that will be given them, and set a day and place to do homage. And if the king of France should possibly want to say that the occupied places are forfeit to him for any cause, for which reason he might want to retain them wholly or in part for ever, the said envoys

28 Valois's forces had originally been ordered to muster at Moissac on 8 July, Chaplais, *Saint-Sardos*, p. 190 n. 1.

should deny every manner of forfeiture by the said memoranda and evidence and should not in any way assent to such retention of the land by the king of France; thus they will say that they would want to consult the king of England. And if it is the case that the king of France will not agree to make actual restitution but will promise restitution, then the said envoys should do fealty, but the king of France should give surety by his letters that after homage is done, he would make actual restitution of the said occupied places without delay.

Item, if the king of France speaks of having or making any marriage with the king of England the said envoys should sound out what marriage he would like and on what condition and take a delay to consult the king of England.

Item, if the king of France wishes to ask for release and quitclaim of the three cities and bishoprics, that is Limoges, Cahors and Perigord, which have been demanded by the king of England since the peace made between King Louis of France and King Henry of England, the said envoys should first examine the detail and take a delay and consult the king.

Item, if the king of France among other things speaks of taking Montpezat Castle as a lawful action within his right and of making and having a bastide at St Sardos according to the judgment of his court the said messengers should strive to turn the king away from these demands. And if they do not agree on the two things then it should be agreed that after restitution is made to the king of England of all the things occupied by the king of France, he will be ready to stand trial on these matters in the court of the king of France by the judgment of his peers. And it would be good to sound out whether the king of France would give up his challenge in return for money and to make clear that, if so, it would not prejudice any similar case in future. And if they cannot agree on this form then they should agree, if the king of France agrees, that the debate on this should be put to the pope, as a private person, wise and discreet.

[Six further instructions concerned the following:

1 sentences of banishment against Basset and other English ministers;
2 on what terms Charles would allow the grant of Aquitaine to Prince Edward;
3 conditions for extending the truce between Charles Valois and the Earl of Kent;
4 extending the truce (whether the old one or new) until Michaelmas;

5 arrangements for returning supporters of both kings to the peace of the other (Roger Mortimer and others banished from England expressly excepted);
6 terms of restitution of French-occupied areas, French expenses and the pope as arbitrator.]

42 War

Running a war in Gascony from England was difficult. Situations could change quickly and supplies could be delayed. Letters between Despenser and Basset in October and November 1324 are given below as examples of the difficulties. They emphasise the importance of spending money wisely and of the most impressive following that the king might use. For other news letters, see Chaplais, Saint-Sardos, *nos 64–7, 69–70, 72–8, 81–91, 93, 95, 97–8, 102–7.*

(a) Hugh Despenser the younger to Ralph Basset, early October 1324

Chaplais, *Saint-Sardos*, no. 57, pp. 75–7

Dear cousin

It grieves us most strongly regarding your misfortune and the anguish you are in; and know that better counsel and a better company of men and necessities for Gascony would have been sent out if it had not been that it was assumed there would be peace, through the great offers and reasonable course of action offered to the king of France and the negotiations there between our lord king and him; [and know] that the small company of men that was sent to those parts (which were provided only to secure places and to be captains in certain towns and castles during the negotiations between the king and those of France) and the silver which comes with them, could not have a [favourable] wind to sail over until recently, and we understand that you have been told of this more fully by now. But if those of the realm had imagined that the king of France had wanted war, a much greater and better force would have come to you and will come as soon as the winter weather has passed, which prevents any fleet passing over the sea, as Arnaud Caillou will be able to tell you more fully and you can see also by the letters which come to Bayonne. And because the said Arnaud

Caillou is charged to tell you of some alliances and to execute these with your counsel and to take your oath to seal these, so we ask you that you do this when he asks you. And dear cousin, we beg you not to be discomforted by anything and to work loyally and hard on the affairs of our lord the king to save his honour and land, for know for certain that God has ordained this to the confusion of the French.

And understand that we are in sure hope that, even if nothing should remain to us except Bayonne alone, we will soon recover all that is ours and even more to the great honour of him and of all of you, who are now in misfortune and great distress for him and the good friends that the king has and will have; and in so far as he himself and all those of his realm take this thing to heart, they are preparing to bring the place relief from one day to another, as you will see and be aware of for a fact.

And know that the king will have a truce day with those of Scotland on the octave of St Martin [18 November], so that at this next summer the king will come to Gascony with a large and noble company, and Lord Robert de Bruce with him (if affairs can be put right between them) and for this we are in certain hope, from some men familiar with these parts who have spoken with us. And keep this matter secret.

And send us quickly your advice by the next messenger, whether it is worth more that the king should come with all the people he can have from England, Wales, Ireland and any other part where he can have them, or to come with a few sound people and to have soldiers from Spain and Aragon and other countries on his arrival there, for it seems to us that it would be better to have people of Spain and Aragon and those parts to attract hearts to us and they will know better how to succeed in bringing great people from outside the region to you, and at least cost to the king and the people, and strangers never know at all how to succeed like those of the same land. For that and for the victuals and all other things touching those parts and the arrival of the king there we ask for your counsel quickly, for you should know better than we do. And we will arrange this according to what you advise us and more, if we can improve on what you tell us; and let us know every day by all the messengers, clearly and openly, all the preparations and all the things which can turn to the advantage of the land and to the nuisance of the French, for be sure that we will go to great trouble and effort in this business, unceasingly and without fail, as if the matter touches the safety of our own life. And you will be aware of this daily and will see it in truth, since one has perceived all their malice and their evil plotting and sudden attack against us (which things no one amongst us would have expected to find, if they had not seen them in actual fact); and soon, with the help of God, that will turn to their own confusion.

And dearly loved cousin, take good comfort to yourself and be glad and happy, and work so courageously and so well now in the king's affairs in this wrong and this sudden surprise attack, so that it will be to your honour and that of your lineage for ever, and with the sure hope in the good relief that the king and his people will provide with the help of God, as soon as they can, which is much greater than you would believe. And good cousin, when one is in trouble by evil plotting and by treason and one thinks about good relief, then one ought to be of good heart and glad and work vigorously, for from this comes honour.

Well-loved cousin, we beg you that if you lack money or victuals or other things that can be of service and that we can provide, tell us about it by your letter (making mention of the sum) and we will ourselves quickly, either from the king or from our own, do what we can for you, so that nothing is lacking for you in such matters, if God pleases. And strive to work vigorously and we will also do the same for you, for the relief of his land and of you and of the good people of those parts, and be in no doubt of that. And good cousin, we know well that you are wise and foresighted, and for that, think well and wisely how to keep safe the king's money and to use it wisely to his profit, for he wishes that it should be spent by your advice and you know well that since this war has started, it is important that one is vigilantly careful with it, that it is saved to the right time and never foolishly spent, for without money one can do nothing, and on the other hand that it should never be spared where it can be of use to the profit and honour of the king and to the injury of his enemies. And we hold you so wise and so prudent that you will do it well with the help of God to the honour of the king and the safety of this land. Sire, may the Holy Spirit help you, etc.

(b) Ralph Basset to Hugh Despenser, 9 November 1324

Chaplais, *Saint-Sardos*, no. 79, pp. 94–5

[On the forces the king should bring] ... for when our lord king has come and sees that he can have enough other people, then he can discharge them at will, for they will be glad to return by sea without taking anything from the king. Because of this, sir, for God's sake, do not omit anything just [to save] a small amount of costs and so make the arrival of our said lord less noble, strong and honourable.

And it seems so to me, sir, that it would be for [his] great honour and great security that our lord king should bring with him a section of the men-at-arms of Scotland and Ireland, and two chiefs of the best family connections from each region of Wales and that those of Wales bring with them footmen to such a number as will seem to you appropriate. And thus you will have two benefits: first, that they will serve you in your affairs and secondly, that you will be sure that you will have no war in Wales while they are away, and thus it would be worth more than if they were to give hostages. And, sir, if an accord is made between the Scots and you, then it would be good to have chieftains of the men-of-arms of Scotland brought with you and you will thus have great service from them and will be sure not to have war in those parts while they are away and with you. And if the accord is not made, then nothing that I have said above is valid, for I would not dare in any way to advise that our lord king should leave his kingdom if he was not very sure of the land behind him.

Sir, it is worth more to have a host of England, Scotland, Ireland and Wales than of England alone, for if there is a host of so many countries and diverse languages, such a host will be renowned through all lands as good, strong and noble and three times greater than it is and so would be more honourable and profitable for us, and because the French strengthen themselves by having men from Germany and other divers countries so that men may say that they are noble and of great power and that they lead people of various languages.

Sir, I have made Arnaud Caillou my lieutenant in my seneschausy and the said Arnaud has appointed his lieutenant to keep Blaye, and he himself will be going between them whenever there is a need ...

[A list of other appointments is reported here.]

Sir, because I know well that you have so much to do that you will hardly have the opportunity to look at these things and think about them, I have sent the same things to Master Robert Baldock and have begged him to mention them to you again every day. Sir, please do not take ill that I now send you so little, for from day to day, as I may think of it and as business increases, I will send [news] to you by all those travelling between us. Sir, God keep you and keep your good lordship in honour. Written at Bordeaux, 9 November.

43 Isabella's negotiations

(a) Isabella to Edward II, 31 March 1325

Chaplais, *Saint-Sardos*, no. 167, pp. 199–200

Most honoured heart, etc., greetings.

As regards the matters concerning us, may it please you to know, my most honoured heart, that I came to Poissy to my lord and brother the king of France Thursday next before the Annunciation of Our Lady [21 March] and on the advice of those of your council who were with me I begged him for his support in the matters for which I had come here and I found him obdurate. And finally he replied to me that it pleased him that his council and yours should treat on the said matters because it was appropriate that this procedure should be followed. And so it was done and in the negotiations my brother's people remained so obdurate that between them and your council there could be no manner of agreement. And on this the envoys of our holy father the pope, who were always present at the negotiations and behaved and behave well and diligently to their utmost power, who saw that the said matters were about to break down, began to negotiate with the people of my lord brother on the matters and in this negotiation there came so many difficulties and alterations that the agreement hoped for one day was despaired of another day ...

[Isabella describes disagreements on whether the truce should be extended or new and reports a new one to last from 14 April to 9 June.]

My most honoured heart, with the assent of your council I am remaining here until I have your orders, and the bishop of Norwich and my cousin Richmond are staying with me. By the advice of the papal envoys and of us all the bishop of Winchester and Sir William Airmyn are coming to you to inform you more fully of these affairs ...

My most honoured heart I beg you ... please to accept the uncertainty and the dissension that have been found here as the excuse for my and the others, who are with me at your command, not having written to you earlier since I came to my brother. We could not write earlier to you with any certainty and we dared not write to you on other things until we should write to you on this matter.

My most honoured heart, may the Holy Spirit save you and keep you always by its grace

Given at Poissy, the last day of March.

(b) Isabella's agreement made at Paris, 31 May 1325

Edward II ratified this agreement on 13 June 1325. It was an interim solution and the problem of homage was only temporarily solved. Moreover, not all lands were returned to Edward and his son (as his proxy), and the French king claimed the right to appoint the seneschal, to keep the lands occupied by French troops and to claim expenses from Edward.

Foedera, II.i, pp. 601–2

Edward by the grace of God, king of England, lord of Ireland and duke of Aquitaine, to all those who will see or hear these present letters, greetings. Know that we have seen and looked at these letters patent of our envoys and proctors and the counsellors of the king of France, written below in the form that follows:

To all those who will see or hear these present letters. We, Pierre, bishop of Viviers, Alfons d'Espeigne, Gaucher, constable of France, Jean Cherchemont, chancellor, Hugh de Chalencon, cantor of Clermont, and Gaillie Flote, lord of Revel, knight, counsellors and proctors of the king of France, our very dear and very revered lord, and we, John, bishop of Norwich, John of Brittany, Earl of Richmond, and William Airmyn,[29] canon of York, envoys and proctors of the king of England, our very dear and very revered lord, make it known that we, counsellors and proctors of the said king of France, in his name and for him on the one part and we, the aforesaid envoys and proctors of the said king of England, in his name and for him on the other part, have made agreement, for the good of peace, with our very high and very noble lady, Lady Isabella, queen of England, sister of the said king of France, and the reverend fathers in God, Monsieur Guillaume, archbishop of Vienne, and Monsieur Hugues, bishop of Orange, envoys of our very holy father the pope, we, the counsellors, envoys and proctors aforesaid, having full power for this from the said kings, our lords, according to what is contained in the letters patent, sealed with their seals, the tenor of which letters is contained here above.

First that the king of France aforesaid will be able to and will hold in his hand the land that the said king of England holds in the duchy of Guienne in the following manner: that is to say:

29 Given as Airmin here. On Airmyn's role in the negotiations and its consequences for his subsequent ecclesiastical career, see Grassi, 'William Airmyn', pp. 553–5, 558–61.

That the king of France will appoint there a seneschal, a good and sufficient person, and not untrusted by the said king of England; the which seneschal will be able to and will govern the said land in the name of the said king of France and will appoint there judges, bailiffs, sergeants and other officials and the accustomed ministers.

And will govern the said land according to how it has been and is accustomed to be governed; castellans and other keepers of castles, wherever they are, and of fortified houses outside the towns, deputed by the said king of England, retaining their custody in sufficient numbers according to the ordinance of the said seneschal; which will be done with the counsel and advice of the castellans and other keepers of the said castles and fortified houses.

And so that the said seneschal may be able to govern the country better and more peacefully, the men-at-arms who are in the country because of the king of England will retire into Bayonne completely and immediately.

And we, the aforesaid envoys and proctors of the said king of England, have promised and covenanted that we will procure, as far as is in our power in relation to our lord the said king of England, that the said men-at-arms will come to the country [i.e. of Bayonne] as soon as they well can.

And also the men-at-arms of the king of France will withdraw, save those in the castles wherever they are and the fortified houses outside the towns, in one part and another; they will stay garrisoned at the ordinance of the seneschal aforesaid with the counsel and advice of the castellans and other keepers of castles and fortified houses as is said above in order that these cannot be captured or taken.

And those who will be castellans and all keepers of the said castles and fortified houses will swear on the Holy Gospels to the said seneschal that they will not go out, nor allow their people to go out carrying arms outside the said castles and fortified houses without the permission of the said seneschal, nor will they do or bring damage to anyone, in order the better keep the peace.

And if some or others who remain in the said castles and fortified houses offend against the form of their oath, the seneschal will be able to correct and duly punish them according to their offence; no less the keepers of the said castles and fortified houses to whom the king of England will have given permission, following this, staying on behalf of the said king of England.

And that, these things being done, the said king of England will give permission in good faith and will not put up any impediment by himself nor by any other openly or secretly.

And if anyone wishes to put up impediments, he will not give him aid, counsel or comfort; nor suffer that any impediment is done by him or by his officials.

And so that all the things may be done in good faith the seneschal, a prudent man who will be appointed as is said, will take an oath to the king of France that he will govern the said land well and loyally, especially keeping the points of this accord.

And so that no one may make accusations that any rough treatment should occur for past actions, we, the counsellors and proctors of the king of France, will and order on behalf of the said king of France that the said seneschal will not interfere with criminal acts that have been done in times past, nor interfere in the practices of official duties.

And because we, the aforesaid counsellors, envoys and proctors of the kings, our said lords, have the firm hope that the things said above will be done and accomplished before the next feast of the Assumption of Our Lady [15 August], we have agreed that, if the king of England comes to Beauvais at the said feast of the Assumption, the king of France will be there; and if the king of England offers to do homage to him the king of France will receive it; with a protestation made on behalf of the king of France that no prejudice should be made by this to the said king of France, in the right that he says he has in the land which he holds at present.

And if either of the kings is prevented by illness or by any other clear impediment by which he cannot come nor be there at the day, he who is aware that he will be prevented will notify the other king as soon as he well can before the said day; and then there should be agreed another day quickly and sufficiently, to do the said homage at the said place of Beauvais and the other things which are appropriate to be done there.

And we, the aforesaid counsellors and proctors of the said king of France, for him and in his name, make an agreement that the said king of France for the love and consideration of his said sister, the queen of England, once the homage is done, will return to the said king of England or at his command the said land which the king of France will have or had by the permission of the said king of England, with the county of Ponthieu, and will put in such officials as the king of England would like.

And, with this, we agree in the name of the said king of France that, once the said homage is done in the manner said above, he, for the love of his said sister, will not ask the king of England for anything from the land, which the king of France will have held with the permission of the said king of England, as is said above, because of the forfeiture of the past time, if there should be any; but the land that the said king of France holds at present in the said duchy, the king of France will hold in peace by such right as he has. Save that in the said affair, no new right is acquired by the king of France by reason of this agreement, nor prejudice done to the king of England, in possession or ownership; and concerning this the aforesaid parties may make formal protestation at the offering and the reception of the said homage and at their protestations the said parties will make agreement.

And if the king of England or his proctor for him asks justice of the king of France on the land that the king of France holds at present in the said duchy, the king of France will do it for him well and speedily, summarily and completely.

And at the meeting the proctor of the said king of France will be heard and justice will be done to him in relation to the expenses, outlay and costs that the king of France will have made and sustained because of the difficulty that he says and maintains that the king of England and his people have put the king of France and his people to, which he can hardly truly calculate.

And, in the case that it should be considered and judged by right, by the said king of France that the said land should be rendered to the king of England and that the king of England should be held to render and restore to the said king of France the expenses, outlay and costs above said, once the amount is clarified, the said king of England will be bound to render and pay them to the said king of France or at his command, within one year from the time of the declaration.

And if he does not do it the king of France will undertake due execution on the land that the king of England will hold in the realm of France. On which matter we, the above said envoys and proctors of the said king of England, promise to see and procure that the said king of England will give permission in good faith and will put no impediment by himself nor by another, either openly or secretly, nor suffer that this is done on his behalf.

And in the case that it is considered and judged by right that the said land that the king of France holds at present in the said duchy ought to remain with the king of France, we, the aforesaid counsellors and proctors of the said king of France, agree in the name of the said king that, for consideration of his said sister, the king of England will not be held to render to him anything for the expenses, outlay and costs mentioned above.

Also we, the aforesaid counsellors, messengers and proctors, have agreed in the names of our aforesaid lords the kings and for them, that all people taken or arrested by one side and the other at the instigations of the aforesaid two kings should be returned and freed completely; that is to say the people taken and arrested in Gascony as soon as the said permission is granted, and peace proclaimed there; and the people taken and arrested because of it in France and England to be also returned and delivered as soon as it will come to the attention of the said parties that permission has been granted and the said peace proclaimed in Gascony as is said.

And all the matters said above and each of them we, the aforesaid counsellors, envoys and proctors of the aforesaid kings of France and England have promised in good faith in the name of our said lords and on their behalf to hold, keep and complete point by point in good faith all things in the manner in which they are contained above and not to do nor go against it nor suffer anyone to do so.

And, so that among these things there will be good accord and good friendship between the two kings, decisions will be made at the meeting of the two kings above-said regarding those who have been supporters and who have been made subject or others, on one side and the other; and regarding our lords the two kings, we, the aforesaid counsellors, envoys and proctors, have promised to ensure and procure in good faith that each of them will issue, before the next feast of the Nativity of St John the Baptist at the latest, their letters patent sealed with their seal by which they will agree, ratify and approve all and each of the things written above.

[The letters empowering both groups to negotiate are then cited.]

In witness of which things we, the counsellors, envoys, and proctors above said, have put our seals to these letters. Given at Paris the last day of May in the year of grace 1325.

We agree, ratify and approve all the things written above and each of them. In witness of which we have had these our letters patent made. Given at Westminster, 13 June, in the year of grace 1325 and of our reign 18.

44 Letters of Isabella and Edward

Edward's letters written on 1–2 December 1325, 18 March 1326 and 19 June 1326 to Isabella, Prince Edward, Charles IV and others are extensively calendared in CCR 1324–1327, *pp. 576–82 and printed fully in* Foedera, *II.i, pp. 615–16, 622–3, 630–1. They illustrate the changing situation, from Isabella's initial refusal to return (blamed on her fear of Despenser in her letter of 5 February [**44a**]) to her liaison with Mortimer. Edward's letter to the pope on 10 June 1326 provides a succinct resumé of his complaints against her [**44b**]. By June Charles's failure to return the French lands had also become an acute irritant to Edward [**44c–d**].*

(a) Isabella to Archbishop Reynolds, 5 February 1326

*This is probably a reply to the bishops' letters sent at the king's request in December to ask her to return (*Vita, *pp. 242–7). It has survived as part of Hereford's* Apologia *written in defence against charges brought against him in 1334 as part of a campaign to prevent his preferment to the bishopric of Winchester.*

Twysden, *Scriptores X*, cols. 2767–8

Reverend Father in God

We have carefully looked at your letters by which you request us to return to the company of our dearest and most sweet lord and friend. And you make known to us that Sir Hugh Despenser does not wish us ill, on the contrary he would wish us well, according to what you say. Regarding this we are greatly surprised, for neither you nor anyone of a holy bent of mind ought to believe that we would leave the company of our said lord without the greatest and most reasonable cause, unless it was to avoid physical danger and for fear of the said Hugh, who has the governance of our said lord and his whole kingdom and who would like to dishonour us as much as he can, of that we are very certain and have well proved it, although we have dissimulated it for a long time in order to escape danger. And certainly we desire nothing more, after God and the salvation of our soul, but to be in and to live and to die in the company of our said lord. So we beg you with all our might to have us excused, because we cannot do what you request in this case, for in no way could we return to the company of our said lord without putting ourselves in mortal danger; regarding which we are in the greatest distress, so that we cannot write, etc.

Given at Paris, the Wednesday after Candlemas [5 February 1326].

(b) Edward to Pope John XXII, 10 June 1325

Edward's letter to the pope was addressed through the papal nuncios, the archbishop of Vienne and the bishop of Orange. It mainly concerned church matters: arrears of the annual census, repayment of a loan, complaints about the bishops of Hereford, Lincoln, Norwich and the archbishop of Dublin, and recommendation for Baldock, but Edward also included a schedule explaining his complaints about Isabella.

Foedera, II.i, pp. 629–30

Schedule to Edward's letter

Lords, you have mentioned to us on behalf of the most Holy Father the matter of the return of our wife: we reply to you:

The most Holy Father, who is true and just and wants all reasonable things, has himself well understood, and it is well known, that at your command and encouragement and that of many others, in the hope of firm and good peace, we sent our wife to France, in all sweetness of true love of heart and mind, as God knew. And afterwards she stayed a long time there, beyond two parts of a year, and negotiations with the king of France were nearly finished; we, who so missed her company, ordered her many times, through the venerable father ... the bishop of Winchester and by our letters, that, in the faith and affection by which she was bound to us, ceasing and leaving all other excuses, she should come to us with all speed. And she would not come but withdrew herself from us, right up until now. And she received into her company our mortal enemy and the convicted and judged traitor, Mortimer, and others of our enemies and notoriously has, and up to now does, adhere to them. And she detains our eldest son and heir, Edward, to whom we have often sent saying that he should come to us. But she does not allow him to come to us and makes him associate and adhere to the said enemy and traitor, Mortimer, who has worn the livery of our said son before all the people in Paris in the solemnity of the coronation at the feast of Pentecost last past,[30] to the great contempt and disparagement of us and all our people. And now more is rumoured, that she makes alliances with magnates of those part to enter and invade our realm with hostile intent against our will. Nevertheless, when she comes, if she does what she ought in obedient and due fashion towards us, we will do what we ought towards her; nor do we believe that our said most Holy Father or the king of France or any good man should want us to do anything else in this matter.

(c) Edward II to Prince Edward, 19 June 1326

This letter and the following one to Charles have become more threatening than those of December and March. Edward II also complained to Gascon cities on 27 June of Prince Edward's independent actions which undermined his authority as his son's governor in Gascony (Gascon Roll Project, C61/38, no. 110).

Foedera, II.i, pp. 630–1; *CCR 1323–1327*, pp. 576–7

... it seems to us that you do not keep the agreement and do not obey our commands humbly as a good son should do to his father, since you have not come to us to be under our government as you ought to be ... but, along with your mother, you have notoriously kept company with and adhered to Mortimer, our traitor and mortal enemy, in the company of your mother and elsewhere; and he has publicly worn at Paris your livery at the celebrations of the coronation at Whitsuntide last, in such great despite of us and in such great dishonour of us and you, although you have informed us untruthfully that he is not an adherent of your mother or you; whereby we consider ourselves very evilly paid.

We have also understood that you, by counsel contrary to us and contrary to your benefit, have made many orders, ordinances and divers things, without advising us and contrary to our orders and wishes, concerning the duchy of Guyenne ... these matters are very unbecoming and may be very damaging.

We therefore order, command and charge you, firmly enjoining you in the faith and love that you owe us, and if you desire our blessing, and under pain of everything you can forfeit to us, and as you wish that we

30 The queen of France was crowned on 11 May 1326: Lord, 'Queen Isabella', p. 47.

shall hold you for our dear and well-loved son, as we have always done, that, putting aside all excuses ... you should come to us with all speed ... if you have done anything [concerning marriage or the Duchy] you should have it revoked, as is appropriate.

Edward, dear son, as you are of tender age, take our commands tenderly to heart, and fulfil them humbly and completely, if you wish to avoid our wrath and great anger and as you love your own advantage and your honour. And do not trust any counsel contrary to the will of your father, as the wise King Solomon teaches; and inform us speedily of what you will do, understanding for certain that if we find you hereafter contrary or disobedient to our will by whatsoever counsel it may be, we will ordain in such wise that you shall feel it all the days of your life and so that all other sons shall take from it an example of disobeying their lords and fathers.

(d) Edward II to Charles IV, 19 June 1326

Edward rehearses Isabella's refusal to return and her adherence to Mortimer 'to our great dishonour and that of all her blood', and asks that Prince Edward be sent home. He then demands the swift return of his lands 'without having regard to the strictness of the words of any covenant that, in the opinion of some people, seems to be intended for our disinheritance' (a reference to the disadvantageous terms of the agreement). The letter ends threateningly.

Foedera, II.i, p. 631; *CCR 1323–1327*, p. 577

Therefore ... we beg you ... that you will understand and graciously fulfil and expedite our said requests and with full effect, for the profit and honour between us and so that we may not be dishonoured, nor we and our said son disinherited ... but you must understand from us, as from every man of our estate, that it is, as it should be, very burdensome for us to bear such shameful despites and great damages for so long; and, indeed, dear brother, we will be unable to suffer them for long.

VIII: TYRANNY AND DEPOSITION

Introduction

After his success at Boroughbridge and the annulment of the Ordinances, Edward II was back in control of his kingdom. In 1321–2, despite dislike of the Despensers, it was clear that the majority of Edward's subjects were not yet prepared to rebel against their anointed king and, with care, a return to stability might have been possible. Two things, however, destroyed long-term peace: the harshness of the punishments after Boroughbridge and Edward's continued reliance on favourites. Failure in Scotland and war with France further undermined his reputation and less than five years later he lost his throne.

The fear and distrust after the unprecedented scale of executions in 1322 is easy to understand. Earlier rebellions had led to confiscated lands, fines, imprisonment and exile, but rarely execution.[1] Moreover, there was continued pressure even on loyal subjects,[2] so it is not surprising that the author of the *Vita* could write in 1325 that the nobles were terrified and 'let the king's will have free rein ... whatever pleases the king, though lacking in reason, has the force of law' [**49a**, 1325.]. This comes close to the contemporary definition of tyranny. That word itself was not, however, used in the *Vita*, and rarely elsewhere in contemporary writing. John of Trokelowe (probably writing after 1323) saw Edward as 'intent on tyranny' in his earlier attack on Langton in 1307,[3] but only the author of the *Flores* used the word explicitly and frequently. He called the king and the Despensers 'tyrants' for the actions after Boroughbridge, wrote of Edward's 'insane tyranny' and the 'cruelty of the tyrant' in 1323, and stated that the Gascons in 1324 preferred French rule to the 'tyranny, greed, and folly of the king

1 The *Flores* (pp. 207–8) provides the longest list of those executed in addition to Lancaster (twenty-two); the Boroughbridge Roll (*Complete Peerage*, II, App. C) lists twenty-one, as do Cotton MS Cleo D IX (Haskins, 'A chronicle', pp. 79–80) and the *Chroniques de Londres* (p. 44). The accusations against Despenser in 1326 list eighteen. Fryde's list of twenty-six (*Tyranny*, p. 61) includes some who died in battle.

2 Ormrod, 'Agenda', p. 17.

3 Trokelowe, p. 63.

of England' [**49b**].[4] Orleton, who was accused in 1334 of describing Edward as tyrant and sodomite in his Oxford sermon in 1326, denied it, saying that the word 'could not in any way be sensibly applied by the judgement of any man of wisdom to the father of the lord king', and was 'never said or put forward by me', but he admitted using it of Hugh Despenser the Younger, 'who tyrannically presumed to rule the ... kingdom'.[5] 'Tyrancie' was indeed used in the accusations against Hugh in 1326 [**46b**], but is not used in the accusations against Edward [**48**].

Contemporary perceptions of Edward's harshness at this time were also increased by his actions against the city of London and six individual churchmen. London was always restless and the eyre of 1320–1, blamed on Despenser and Stapeldon, stoked opposition that flared into violence as the queen approached in 1326 [**51**].[6] Edward's relationship with the church as an institution, on the other hand, was generally good. There was no clash over principle as there had been under Edward I and, with their rights intact, both the English church and the papacy willingly made financial grants to the king. English prelates might bargain, as in 1316 for the *Articuli Cleri*, but these were not a protest of principle, rather a request for necessary administrative reforms.[7] Similarly, although both Clement V and John XXII refused to annul the Ordinances and John XXII was unco-operative over Edward's request to be re-anointed with the holy oil of St Thomas, the popes generally supported him, sending cardinal legates to his negotiations with Lancaster and Bruce.[8] Nonetheless, individual bishops who angered the king might find themselves punished. John Stratford and William Airmyn (promoted respectively to the sees of Winchester in 1323 and Norwich in 1325) waited months for their temporalities, but Edward's irritation with them was largely because he wanted promotion to a see for his trusted chancellor, Robert Baldock.[9] Political suspicions informed his anger against others. John Hotham, bishop of Ely since 1316, was disliked for 'certain causes', which (given the date of 1321) were almost certainly political;[10]

4 See also *Flores*, pp. 207–8, 220.

5 Twysden, *Scriptores X*, col. 2765.

6 Williams, *Medieval London*, pp. 290–9; Fryde, *Tyranny*, pp. 165–75; Phillips, *Edward II*, pp. 506–8.

7 *Statutes*, I, p. 171; see above Chapter II: The king's wealth.

8 Tout, *Edward II*, pp. 195–7, 205–10; Fryde, *Tyranny*, p. 138; Phillips, *Edward II*, pp. 340–1, 450–2.

9 Haines, *Stratford*, pp. 136–49; Grassi, 'William Airmyn', pp. 556–61; Phillips, *Edward II*, pp. 449–51, 480.

10 *Bridlington*, p. 73; Haines, *Orleton*, pp. 158–9.

John Droxford (Bath and Wells since 1309) may have been suspected of supporting the rebels when Edward asked the pope to transfer him to Europe in 1323.[11] Henry Burghersh of Lincoln was certainly politically suspect as the nephew of the executed contrariant Bartholomew Badlesmere and lost his temporalities for two years after 1322.[12] Adam Orleton (bishop of Hereford since 1317), suspected of favouring the Mortimers in 1321–2, lost his temporalities when the accusations were revived in 1324.[13] All but Orleton returned to a normal relationship with the crown, but, nonetheless, clerical dissatisfaction was enough to add the accusation that Edward had destroyed the holy church to the accusations against him in 1327 and few bishops stood up for Edward wholeheartedly at his deposition.

The king's harshness against individuals and London was exacerbated by general financial pressures as exchequer reforms facilitated the collection of old debts, and by the Despensers' accumulation of land and power. The depth of hatred for both Despensers is evident in plots against them,[14] and in their swift trials and executions. Contemporary views differed on which Despenser was worse [**47a–d**], but Hugh the Younger was generally seen as the most rapacious and was blamed for Edward's harshness [**49a**, re 1325]. The formal accusations against each reflect these views: those against Hugh the Elder were short and generic, while those against his son were long, explicit and mentioned tyranny [**46a–b**].

The general unease in these years is revealed in pilgrims flocking to Lancaster's cult, attempts to free those imprisoned and unrest in London.[15] It is not, therefore, surprising that when Isabella arrived in September 1326, she found quick support for her stated plan to remove the Despensers from Edward's side. Her next step, however, – to remove the king – was more controversial. Although political theory allowed the removal of unsuitable kings, there were in England no precedents, no processes, nor any institutions with the authority to do it. The declaration on homage in 1308 opened a justification for resistance, but not for removal; the Ordinances had merely limited certain specific prerogatives; and earlier threats to Edward in 1310–12 may simply have been to remove homage and obedience to make government difficult. Even the more extreme threats in 1321 did not

11 'John Droxford', *ODNB*, accessed 12 April 2018.

12 'Henry Burghersh', *ODNB*, accessed 19 December 2018.

13 Haines, *Orleton*, pp. 144–52; *Select Cases in ... King's Bench*, IV, pp. 143–6.

14 *Select Cases in ... King's Bench*, IV, pp. 154–7.

15 Given-Wilson, *Edward II*, pp. 84–6.

threaten to choose another king (*rex*), but a *rector* [**45**].[16] Exactly when deposition began to be seriously discussed remains unknown, but the rebels' range of actions must have been discussed quite early, as they considered what might happen if Edward welcomed Isabella and sent Despenser away or stood his ground and turned out to have solid support or fled and they captured him. Moreover, by now his eldest son was a teenager and, if Edward was removed, a minority would be short. Once the decision to remove him had been taken, Edward's opponents quickly and effectively devised justification and process.[17]

Theories of kingship running back into classical times, infused with Christian teaching and elements of contractual lordship, led to a mixture of sometimes contradictory ideas. Kings were under no man, but they were under God and (as the thirteenth-century jurist Henry de Bracton emphasised) under the law. Kings had great power but also clear duties of justice and defence. If they failed to rule well, they forfeited their claim to kingship and might be removed. The practical politics of the thirteenth century, like the theories, tugged in both directions: Magna Carta, the Song of Lewes, the Articles on the Charters, the words of Bracton and the Ordinances laid out limits for royal actions; but Pope Innocent III's declaration that Magna Carta was illegal,[18] the Dictum of Kenilworth and Edward I's increasing punishments for treason instead of *diffidatio*, effectively defiance or renunciation of allegiance, pushed arguments in the opposite direction. To remove a king, there were two possible justifications: incapacity or tyranny. Incapacity was most obviously shown through immaturity or illness, and by the early fourteenth century there were instances of deposition for incapacity in Portugal and Germany through papal intervention; but if a king was simply weak or easily led, could he be removed? And in England who had the right to decide if the king was incapable or tyrannous and who had the authority to remove him?[19] In Edward's case this question was never publicly answered. When he announced the deposition, Mortimer declared that he was simply a spokesman for arrangements made by common assent of the magnates [**50c**]. Parliament was an excellent forum for the announcement, spreading responsibility widely and

16 Childs 'Resistance', pp. 184–5.

17 Valente, 'Deposition', passim; Phillips, *Edward II*, pp. 520–39.

18 On which see, for instance, Helmholz, 'Pope Innocent III'.

19 Dunbabin, 'Government', pp. 493–7, 517; Peters, *Shadow King*, pp. 138–40, 156–9, 215, 232–45. For similar problems at the time of Richard II, see Caspary, 'Deposition of Richard II', pp. 194–201.

ensuring legitimacy, but this was not a 'parliamentary' deposition, nor did Edward III consider it so. A century later Henry IV expended much effort to avoid admitting a parliamentary title, but as Gwilym Dodd has pointed out, the role of parliament caused less anxiety in 1327: parliament did not yet look like a threat to royal power and Edward III was quite clearly the legitimate direct heir.[20]

There is no surviving official record of the deposition procedure. For both narrative and process we have to rely on chronicle accounts (one of which includes what may be an official or semi-official memorandum) [**50c**] and Adam Orleton's *Apologia* of 1334, which records the accusations against Edward [**48**]. These accusations are exaggerated to justify the doubtful legality of removing the king, but they are not fiction and it is easy to see to what the charges apply. Domestic problems bulk largest, with failure in Scotland and France adding weight to the charges. The accusations blame the king's pride, cruelty and harshness, but also refer to 'insufficiency', inability to understand good and evil, and control by others. The balance of his offences weighs more heavily on the side of a 'useless' king than a tyrant, and the sermon texts chosen for the deposition confirm inadequacy rather than tyranny. Edward's incorrigibility added further justification for removal. Throughout his reign he had faced warnings and open opposition and had heeded none. The accusations were given a deliberate legal form and the 'indictment' was 'proved' by notoriety (an established if increasingly archaic legal form).

The chronicles have significant differences in details of chronology and personnel, but tally reasonably well on the general progression of events with the crucial events unfolding on 12–13 January.[21] On 12 January, after news of Edward II's refusal to attend parliament arrived, the bishop of Hereford asked those present if they wanted Edward II or his son as king, but the decision was postponed overnight; that evening the accusations were drawn up (or more likely revised); and the Londoners asked the prelates and magnates to join them in swearing loyalty to Isabella and young Edward. On 13 January the decision to remove Edward was announced, three sermons were preached, the accusations were read, and the people's acclamation of the young Edward was orchestrated. A second delegation, now representative of all political ranks, went to Kenilworth to tell Edward of his deposition

20 Dodd, 'Political legitimacy', pp. 168–70, 174–9.

21 The clearest analyses of the narrative are in Valente, 'Deposition', pp. 853–62, and Phillips, *Edward II*, pp. 524–39.

and renounce fealty. It arrived there on 20 or 21 January and returned to report Edward's resignation to parliament on 25 January (from which date Edward III's regnal year is formally reckoned to start), but the news had already reached London and the peace of Edward III had been publicly proclaimed on 24 January.[22]

With no constitutional authority and procedure to guide them, Edward's opponents had devised a process that drew on the law, the church, the magnates and the people. They combined the appearance of legal procedures (indictment, breach of feudal oath and renunciation of homage) with the support of the church (shown through apposite sermons) and the acclamation of the people, elements that had been equally prominent in the coronation. The oaths at the London Guildhall on 12 and 13 January further strengthened the appearance of popular support [**51**], and for extra security Edward III's proclamation of his succession in London on 24 January emphasised his father's formal and willing resignation.[23]

Edward's deposition was a highly successful political manoeuvre, but there were dissenters. London had not initially responded wholeheartedly to Isabella's request for support [**51**]; dissenters at the deposition included the archbishop of York and the bishops of London, Carlisle and Rochester; not all those summoned to parliament agreed to take the London oaths;[24] and later plots to release Edward reveal others who were uneasy at what had been done. Questions have also been raised as to its nature: whether what happened might be better called a coup or an abdication. Since its success depended on the willing leadership of the queen and prince, it could be seen as a palace coup; since Edward II resigned, it could be seen as an abdication (but his resignation was under duress and occurred after the declaration of the deposition). Whatever the constitutional anomalies, however, most chroniclers then and most historians since have accepted it as a deposition and,

22 *CCR 1327–1330*, p. 1. Although Edward III's regnal year began on 25 January and he was crowned on 1 February 1327, news of his accession was slow in reaching Ireland, where he was not proclaimed until 13 May, for which see Phillips, *Edward II*, p. 511.

23 For the precise wording indicating that Edward II had removed himself from government (*s'en est ouste del gouvernement*), see *Foedera*, II.ii, p. 683. For the Westminster parliament, see also *PROME*, Westminster Parliament of 1327, Introduction and Texts.

24 Phillips, *Edward II*, pp. 537. For the names of those who did take the oaths, see *CPMR 1323–64*, pp. 12–14.

despite some dissent and unease, the removal of Edward II took place remarkably peacefully.

45 Threats to remove the king before 1327

The author of the Vita *records threats under 1310, 1311, 1312 and 1321 (pp. 18–21, 32–3, 58–9, 186–7, 192–3). Some may be simply echoes from the genre of* Specula Regis, *but others suggest possible action: of withdrawal of obedience or appointment of a* rector.[25] *Since the author almost certainly had no knowledge of Edward's deposition, the reports indicate that Edward's removal, although not necessarily his deposition, was not unthinkable before then.*

Vita, pp. 186–7, 192–3

1321

[The barons demand the dismissal of Hugh Despenser] ... otherwise they would no longer have the king for king, but would utterly renounce their homage and fealty and whatever oath they had sworn to the king, and as men without a king, without a ruler, and without a judge, they would proceed to take vengeance upon Hugh on their own authority for lack of justice.

... [If the king failed to respond to their petitions] ... they would utterly renounce their homage and set up another ruler [*rector*] to do justice to all and make the guilty and the arrogant bow their necks ... At this time Earl Aymer is said to have uttered these words in the presence of the king: 'Consider, lord king,' he said, 'the power of the barons; pay heed to the looming danger; neither brother nor sister should be dearer to you than yourself. Do not therefore for any living soul lose your kingdom.'

46 Judgments against the Despensers, 1326

(a) Judgment on the Elder Despenser

This is also recorded in Trinity Coll. Camb. MS R.5.41 fo. 123v (Phillips, Edward II, *p. 513 n.).*

25 Effectively a replacement ruler.

Annales Paulini, pp. 317–18

[27 October 1326] at Bristol Lord Hugh Despenser the elder, Earl of Winchester, was brought before Sir William Trussell, knight and justice appointed to this hearing, and Lords Henry, Earl of Lancaster, Thomas of Brotherton, Earl of Norfolk and marshal of England, Edmund, Earl of Kent, Roger Mortimer, Thomas Wake and other magnates sitting in judgment there to hear the sentence, and so he was brought to account and accused in the French language in these words:

> Lord Hugh, from the start this court forbids you all manner of reply: because you made a law that a man could be condemned without reply, let that law be applied to you and your supporters, and [let it be applied to you] as one who is an attainted traitor, because formerly with the assent of the king and all the baronage you were banished and exiled from the land as a traitor, and were not reconciled except through force against the law of the land, usurping royal power for yourself and advising the king to disinherit and rob his loyal subjects, and particularly my lord Thomas of Lancaster, whom you had put to death without any reason; you are a robber and have robbed the land by your cruelty, so that all the people beg and pray for public vengeance against you; you have advised the king treacherously to rob the prelates of the holy church, not permitting the holy church its rightful liberties; for these offences the court adjudges that you be drawn for treason, hanged for robbery and beheaded because you have committed crimes against the holy church, and that your head be taken to Winchester of which you were earl against law and reason. And because you sought such a dignity and honour there, the court wills that your head be put up there to your dishonour; and because you formerly dishonoured the order of chivalry in so far as you had good men hanged in quartered tunics, the court determines that you be hanged in a tunic quartered with your arms and that the arms be destroyed for ever.

(b) Judgment on the Younger Despenser

The accusations survive in several document collections and chronicles, indicating wide distribution. The Durham text (printed by Holmes, 'Judgement on the Younger Despenser', pp. 261–7) has copying errors in the list of executions.

Taylor, 'The Judgment on Hugh Despenser, the Younger', pp. 73–7

Hugh Despenser, in the parliament of our Lord King Edward, son of King Edward, son of King Henry, held at Westminster in the fifteenth year of his reign [1321], by examination of the prelates, earls, barons and all the community of the realm, it was notoriously found that your father and you, Hugh, were traitors and enemies of the realm. For which, with the assent and commandment of our lord king and the assent of all the baronage, your father and you, Hugh, were exiled from the realm, never to return, unless with the assent and leave of our lord king and all the community of the realm, and that in full parliament duly summoned to do this; against which judgement and exile your father and you, Hugh, returned to the realm and were found at court without authority. And you, Hugh, while returning, feloniously robbed two dromonds[26] to the value of 60,000 pounds sterling, to the great dishonour of the lord king and his realm and to the peril of the merchants who go often to foreign countries.

After you committed these felonies, Hugh, you came to our lord king and had him ride out in force with men-at-arms against the peers of the realm and others of his loyal men and liege people to destroy and disinherit them against the Great Charter and the Ordinances; and thus riding out in force and arms, usurping royal power, you, Hugh, and your father and your supporters feloniously robbed the good people of the realm. By Andrew Harclay and other traitors, you and your supporters had the good Earl of Hereford, Sir William de Sully and Sir Roger Burghfield feloniously murdered, and the very honourable lord, the good Earl of Lancaster, seized, who was cousin germane of our lord king and his brothers, uncle to the very honourable king of France and to his sister, the very honourable lady, queen of England. You had him falsely imprisoned and robbed of all his property, and you had him judged in his own hall in his castle at Pontefract, by your royal power which you had usurped from our lord king, and by false record, against law and reason and the Great Charter, and also without right of reply, you had him martyred and murdered with a harsh and piteous death.

And this wickedness, cruelty and tyranny done to such a worthy person could not satisfy your spilling of Christian blood, thus on the same day, to further torment my said lord, you had six barons, his knights, drawn and hanged, and judged to death by this false record against law and reason and hanged, harshly and without mercy, Sir Warin de l'Isle, Sir William Touchet, Thomas Mauduit, Sir Henry de Bradebourne, Sir William Cheney, Sir William fitz William the younger; at York Sir Roger de Clifford, Lord de Mowbray and Sir Goselin Dayville; at Canterbury Lord Badlesmere and Sir Bartholomew de Ashburnham;

26 A dromond or dromon was a form of Mediterranean galley, well known for its speed and military benefit.

at Windsor Sir Francis de Aldeham; at London Sir Henry Tyes; at Gloucester Sir John Giffard and Sir Roger de Elmbridge; at Bristol Sir Henry de Willington and Sir Henry de Montford; at Winchelsea Sir Thomas Colpeper; and you had several other great men put in harsh imprisonment to murder them without cause for covetousness of their lands; such as Lord Mortimer, and Lord Mortimer the uncle, and Lord Berkeley and Sir Hugh Daudley, father and son. The children of Hereford, who were nephews of the king, and great ladies, wives of the lords, and their children, you held in prison and infamy and as orphans after the death of their lords. And the widowed ladies, like Lady Baret, who followed you to seek mercy, you, like a tyrant, had beaten by your servants, and her arms and legs broken most harshly, against the order of chivalry and law and reason, because of which the good lady is for ever insane and lost; and several of these you have made follow the court on foot in great poverty without pity or mercy, who used to be ladies of great honour, and you always used them in this outrageous way until God in His mercy sent to the realm our good gracious lady and her son and the good people who came to help her, by whom the realm was saved.

Hugh, after this destruction of our noble liege lord and other people of the realm, done falsely, harshly and traitorously, you, Hugh, and your father and Robert Baldock, who had between you treacherously and corruptly taken royal power from our lord king, led him and his people into Scotland against his enemies, where you by your traitorous advice made him lose more than 20,000 of his people, who died piteously by privation, to the great dishonour and damage of our lord king and all his people and had him return without any success. And during the return, you, Hugh, and your father and Robert Baldock falsely and traitorously counselled our lord king to leave our lady queen in bodily peril in Tynemouth Priory in Northumberland, in the war area; you advised the king to flee from there as far as Blackhow Moor, where his Scottish enemies, by your traitorous advice, surprised him to the great dishonour and damage of the king and his people as appeared that day by those who were taken and the deaths of others; and in such great danger and difficulty and bodily peril, my lady, who was your liege lady, by your traitorous deed would have been lost, to the perpetual dishonour and damage of the king and his realm, if God had not sent her help at sea, on which she had to venture to save her life and honour, in such great difficulty and peril of body and soul, which until now had never happened to any good lady of her noble estate.

Hugh, this treason and cruelty could not satisfy you, thus by the royal power which you usurped from our lord king, you had the liberties of the holy church destroyed; prelates such as Hereford, Lincoln, Ely, Norwich, you feloniously robbed of their goods within the holy church and outside; you had them robbed and plundered of their horses, and plate, and harness, thus you made them go on foot; and you had them robbed of their lands and possessions by force and without law and reason. As if it was not sufficient for you to make war on the ministers of holy church, you took on God and his saints, like a false Christian, renegade and traitorous, since, when you knew that God did miracles for my good lord whom you had murdered so cruelly without law and reason, you, Hugh, like a false Christian, sent men-at-arms into the holy church and had it closed for use, and ordered and forbade that any be so rash as to enter the Church to adore God or his saints, for whose merit God did grace and miracles, despite you.

Hugh, after this wickedness, you counselled our lord king, falsely and treacherously, to the disinheritance of his crown and his heirs, to give the earldom of Winchester to your father, who was a false traitor, and the earldom of Carlisle to Andrew Harclay, who was a notorious and attainted traitor, and the land of Cantref Mawr and others which belong to the crown to you, Hugh. And your father and you and Robert Baldock had my lady queen removed from her land which had been given and assigned her by the king; and put her on a daily wage against the dignity of her high standing and estate; always inciting and causing discord between the lord king and her, to the utmost of your power, like false and disloyal traitors. And Hugh, when my lady queen and her son, by command of our lord king crossed the sea to save the land of Gascony, which was on the point of being lost by your traitorous counsel, you sent by sea a great sum of silver to some evil people, your supporters, to destroy my lady and her son, who was rightful heir to the realm, and to impede their return to this country; which would have been to their damage and destruction if you had succeeded in doing so. Hugh, your father, Robert Baldock, and the other false traitors, your supporters, went about the realm by land and sea usurping royal power, by force making great and lesser men swear and take an oath to you, to maintain you in your false quarrels against all people, without having regard that these confederations were false and traitorous and against the liege homage of the estate of the king and his crown. And those not wishing to do this, by your royal power you had put into harsh prison, like Sir Henry Beaumont and others who did not wish to do it, nor swear to you, nor be accomplices in your wicked deeds.

And when you, Hugh, and the other false traitors knew that my lady and her son had arrived in this land, by your evil counsel you had our lord king go away from them, and you took him outside his realm in great personal peril and to his great dishonour and that of his people, feloniously taking the treasure of the realm and the great seal with you.

Lord Hugh, with all the good people of the realm as witnesses, great and small, rich and poor, by common assent you are found and attainted a robber, for which you will be hanged; and you are found a traitor, for which you will be drawn and quartered and [the parts] sent about the realm; and because you were outlawed by our lord king and common assent and came back to court without common assent and without authority, you will be beheaded; and because you were at all times disloyal and inciting discord between our lord king and our very honourable lady the queen and between others of the realm, so you will be disembowelled and then they will be burned.

Repent, traitor, tyrant, renegade; so go to take your judgment, traitor, evil-doer and attainted wretch.

47 The Despensers in the chronicles

Chroniclers are less united in condemnation of the Despensers than of Gaveston. While the author of the Flores *strongly condemns both, the authors of the* Vita *and the Bridlington chronicle recognise the Elder's strengths, although the* Vita's *author disliked the Elder as Forester (pp. 74–7, 190–1 and in the extract from 1321 below). The* Annales Paulini *record the Younger's humility in death.*

(a) *Flores Historiarum*, p. 194

1320

And behold 'one woe is past, and another woe follows hereafter',[27] worse than the first. For Hugh Despenser the Younger, who had been chamberlain [*custos capitis regis*] 'was turned aside as a crooked bow'[28] and, kindled within by the fire of greed, strove with all his burning desires to obtain the whole honour of the earldom of Gloucester ...

27 Rev. 9:12.

28 Ps. 77:57.

excessively burned up by the fire of disloyalty, Hugh not only arrogantly and violently attacked the holders of the [other] two parts of the inheritance,[29] but also, to add to his shame, was trying falsely to drive out all the Marcher barons and many northerners, accusing them of homicides and shameful crimes, offering falsehoods about them to the king, for which (if they had been true) they ought by right for ever to leave the honours of their lordships ... By the disturbances of these wicked deeds of Hugh Despenser the Younger and by the evil counsels of Hugh his father, such jealousies and disorders arose in the realm that they were leading the unpropitious times towards civil war for lack of good government ...

(b) *Vita*, pp. 194–5, 238–9

1321

But in truth, in the opinion of many, this misfortune fell upon them justly. For the cruel and greedy father had in the past wronged many, and obtained the excommunication of many. For when he was justice of the forest he accused many of illegal hunting, he wretchedly disinherited many, forced some into exile, extorted unjust ransoms from many, collected a thousand pounds' worth of land by means of threats, and behold now he feels the hand of God coming to correct him ... But according to some the son's wickedness outweighed the father's harshness. For, confident of the royal favour, he did everything on his own authority, grabbed everything, had no regard for the authority of anyone whomsoever, set traps for his co-heirs ...

1325

For though Hugh Despenser, Earl of Winchester, shrewder than all and more experienced, had to be put in charge of such a business, yet he was hated by everyone and even by the king's son ...

29 On the death of the Earl of Gloucester in 1314, the lands were split between his three sisters: Hugh Despenser married Eleanor de Clare, 1306; Hugh d'Audley the younger married Margaret, widow of Gaveston, 1317; Roger d'Amory married Elizabeth, widow of the Earl of Ulster, 1317.

(c) *Annales Paulini*, pp. 319–20

1326

Then [the younger Despenser] was condemned to death by the said justice, to be drawn through the whole city of Hereford, then hanged then beheaded. He bore all these with humility and patience and said before all the people that he deserved a heavier sentence, and he often sought forgiveness from those standing near and around him ...

(d) *Bridlington*, p. 87

1326

On the last day before the vigil of the apostles Simon and Jude [27 October], Hugh Despenser the father was taken at Bristol, drawn, hanged and finally beheaded. What sadness! That such a great man pre-eminent in his time and strong in understanding and uprightness should act foolishly at the end ...

48 The accusations against Edward II, 1327

This text survives through Orleton's Apologia *or* Responsiones *written in 1334 as a denial of charges made against him to block his move to the bishopric. The Lambeth MS copy used by Twysden (*Scriptores *X, cols. 2763–8) and Wilkinson (*Constitutional History, *II, pp. 170–1) is defective and is corrected in Valente.*

Valente, 'Deposition', pp. 879–81 (from Winchester Cathedral Archives, Cartulary, no. 234)

Those matters which had been agreed and ordained against the said king by the common counsel and assent of all the prelates, earls and barons, and the whole community of the said kingdom, in order to remove him from the government of his realm were contained in public instruments conceived and dictated in the presence[30] of the reverend father, Lord John, then bishop of Winchester and treasurer of England,

30 *Presente* omitted in Lambeth MS.

now by God's grace archbishop-elect of Canterbury,[31] written by the hand of Master William Mees, clerk, his secretary and a public notary, and redacted in public form. This agreement I brought forward to insert with the present matters in my apology, and it goes thus:

It has been decided that Prince Edward, the eldest son of the king, shall have the governance of the realm and shall be crowned king for the following reasons:

First, because the king is incompetent to govern in person. Throughout his reign he has been controlled and governed by others who have counselled him badly, to his own dishonour and to the destruction of the holy church and of all his people, without his being willing to see or understand what is good or evil, or to make amendment, or his being willing to do what was required by the great and wise men of his realm, or to allow amendment to be made.

Also, throughout his reign he has not been willing to listen to good counsel or adopt it, or to give himself to the good government of his realm; but he has always given himself up to unseemly works and occupations, neglecting to satisfy the needs of his realm.

Also, through lack of good government he has lost the realm of Scotland and other lands and lordships in Gascony and Ireland, which his father left him in peace; and he has lost the friendship of the king of France and of many other great men.

Also, by his pride and cruelty and by evil counsel, he has destroyed the holy church and imprisoned some of the persons of the holy church and brought distress and uncertainty[32] to others; and also he has put many and noble men of his land to a shameful death, imprisoned, exiled and disinherited [others].

Also, whereas he was bound by his oath to do justice to all, he has not been willing to do it, for the sake of his own profit and from his greed and that of the evil counsellors who have been about him; nor has he kept the other points of his oath, which he made at his coronation, as he was bound to do.

31 John Stratford was provided to Canterbury 26 November 1333 and received his temporalities 5 February 1334.

32 *Et doute* omitted in Lambeth MS.

Also, he has abandoned his realm, [and left it without a governor and has gone out of the realm with the notorious enemies of his realm],[33] and done all that he could do to ruin his realm and his people, and what is worse, by his weakness[34] and lack of character he has shown himself incorrigible and without hope of amendment; which things are so notorious and known to all that they cannot be denied.

49 The character of Edward II in the chronicles

Chroniclers were critical of Edward, but he was not universally condemned. The most balanced view is from the author of Vita, *probably someone quite close to the court and writing before 1326. The most virulent view is expressed by the author of the continuation of the* Flores Historiarum, *especially around 1323–4. A relentless critic of Edward, he openly calls Edward's rule 'tyranny'. Le Baker, writing in the 1340s, was sympathetic to Edward, reflecting the current cult and writing of him as a martyr. Higden's character sketch, also written in the 1340s, rejected the cult. For modern assessments of Edward's character, see Tout,* Edward II, *pp. 9–11; Haines,* Edward II, *pp. 25–48; Phillips,* Edward II, *pp. 607–14; Given-Wilson,* Edward II, *pp. 3–6.*

(a) *Vita*, pp. 68–71 (1313), 152–3 (1318), 230–1 (1325)

1313

Behold, our King Edward has now reigned six full years and up until now he has achieved nothing praiseworthy or memorable, except that he has made a splendid marriage and has produced a handsome son and heir to the kingdom ... Oh! If our King Edward had borne himself as well at the outset of his reign, and not accepted the counsels of wicked men, not one of his predecessors would have been more renowned than he. For God had endowed him with gifts of every virtue, and had made him equal to or indeed more excellent than other kings. Certainly if anyone cared to describe those qualities which ennoble our king, he could not find his like in the land. His ancestry, reaching back to the tenth generation, shows his nobility.

33 The words within brackets were omitted in the Lambeth MS; in their absence *deguerpist* ('abandoned') was translated as 'stripped' by Wilkinson.

34 *Frelete* here; *crualte* in Lambeth MS.

At the beginning of his reign he had wealth, a land of abundance and the goodwill of his people. He became the son-in-law of the king of France, and was closest kin to the king of Spain.[35] If he had followed the advice of the barons, he would have humbled the Scots with ease. Oh! If he had practised the use of arms, he would have exceeded the prowess of King Richard. Physically this would have been inevitable, for he was tall and strong, a handsome man with a fine figure. But why linger over this description of him? If only he had given to arms the attention that he expended on rustic pursuits,[36] he would have raised England on high; his name would have resounded through the land. Oh! What hopes he raised as Prince of Wales! All hope vanished when he became king of England ...

1318

Nebuchadnezzar, that most powerful king of the Assyrians, before the twelfth year of his reign did, we are told, nothing memorable, but in that twelfth year of his reign he began to flourish and to conquer nations and kingdoms. He overcame Arphaxat, king of the Medes, in war, and out of many kingdoms constructed one powerful monarchy.[37] Neither has our King Edward who has reigned eleven years and more, done anything that ought to be preached in the marketplace or from the roof-tops. Would that, following the example of King Nebuchadnezzar, he would now at least try to attack his enemies, so that he might repair the damage and disgrace, which he has borne so long.

1325

The king also sent letters to every county commanding and ordering that all who had returned from the army to their homes without leave should be arrested and hanged forthwith without trial. The king's harshness has indeed increased so much today that no one, however great and wise, dares to cross the king's will. Thus parliaments, consultations and councils decide nothing these days. For the nobles of the realm, terrified by threats and the penalties inflicted on others, let the king's will have free rein. Thus today will conquers reason.

35 Edward's mother, Eleanor of Castile, was sister to Alfonso VIII of Castile. In 1313 Edward was thus first cousin twice removed to the reigning king, Alfonso XI.

36 If this passage was written in 1313, it is the earliest voiced criticisms of Edward's pastimes, but the author may have been writing a year or two in arrears. Otherwise the earliest recorded reference is in the crown's prosecution in 1315 of Robert le Messager's words in 1314 after Bannockburn: [**49e**].

37 See Judith 1:1, 5, 11, 13.

For whatever pleases the king, though lacking in reason, has the force of law.[38]

(b) *Flores Historiarum*, pp. 214–15 (1323), 217–19 (1323), 221 (1324), 226 (1324)

It has been suggested that this chronicle was written as an apologia for Isabella and Mortimer's deposition of the king, but this poses problems, since the narrative for the end of the reign and of the deposition itself (where the writer might be expected to become even more critical) is instead more factual and draws heavily on Adam Murimuth.

1323

... the king did not cease from committing insane tyranny, oppressions of the people and of the church, and other wicked deeds against God and truth. But by his behaviour whatever it might be, he procured for himself eternal dishonour and the hissing of contempt, with news of it being carried back to every people under the heavens. In this deplorable state of dishonour, the king set out from York to the north, where he applied himself immediately to spilling the blood of the innocent and other wicked deeds; making for the south, having proceeded through the territories of various regions, raging, he arrived in London, staying a short but rough time there, taking away with him by force four leading citizens of the city, to suffer continually destructive penalties causing extreme poverty before redeeming themselves into the counsel of the king. He ordered certain knights, strong in valour, whom the cruelty of the tyrant had shortly before thrown into the confines of prison, to be put to the abominable sufferings of tortures, so that through excessive kinds of punishments they falsely confessed themselves traitors to the king and the realm, and through the same fabrications of falsity, they dishonoured the reputation and life of others for ever by the legal record of such a charge. From the number of those who were afflicted, indeed, certain knights, always behaving to the utmost of their ability with excellent courage, chose rather to end their life under the vengeful punishments, than with risk of damnation to implicate themselves or others in the chain of falsehood.

38 *Inst.* 1.2.6, *Corpus Iuris Civilis*, I, p. 1. For the author's views on kingship, see *Vita*, pp. 38–9, 58–61, 64–5, 128–31.

1323

Having reduced the chief men of the land to nothing by the abominable sufferings of torments and frequent death by secret treachery, the king's madness flared strongly towards the rest of the people, so that his sight could not look well on anyone of the middling or lower orders. Indeed the passion of greed and avarice grew in him day after day, concerning which things, with unexpected speed, together with his justices – but more truly his torturers – about Michaelmas and thereafter, shamelessly crossing the counties of Chester, Lancaster, Nottingham, Derby, Warwick, Stafford, Worcester, Gloucester and Hereford he reduced them to such want and servitude by devilish plundering and extortions, that they will hardly or never recover to their former state. For against the path of law and justice, by false lies, he savagely tore and took away from some of the counties £900, from others £800 or £700, and yet others £600 or at least £500, whence, with these aforesaid actions and other accursed spoils, having violated the oath taken at his coronation to the realm and the church, he unjustly in a short time had heaped up such an abundance of treasure to himself, that none of the preceding kings had enjoyed such a similar multitude of things in times past; for he laid up inestimable amounts of treasure; rich in these things he did not understand he was as a poor man, bereft of friends. The king, drunk on the blood of the just, and with a thirsty heart striving for the ruin of the rest, the depth of whose greed could not be satiated by the immensity of the treasure of the realm accumulated by his own barbarity, so that he stretched forth 'his hand to afflict' not 'some of the church'[39] but to confound all the bishops with his wicked ferocity and to drive them mercilessly from the realm. For in these times, in contempt of Christ and the church and the Apostolic See, not beyond the reproach of excommunication, he wrongly deprived churches of their rights and liberties, and especially he forcibly despoiled the bishops of Lincoln, Winchester and Hereford of the totality of their temporalities and their other goods; concerning which things, secretly he repeatedly reconciled the theatrical and laughable with the wicked and raging.

1324

... the king did not fear to provoke divine anger, because his deadly rage did not spare holy places and temples, prelates or other lower churchmen, sex or age, those of noble blood, the freely born followers of the most renowned leaders, the revered grey hair of old age, the brisk

39 Acts 12:1.

action of young manhood, the want of women and widows, the neediness of wards and orphans, the losses and wretchedness of the imprisoned, but savage and pitiless to all, adding anguish to lamentable torments, he did good to no one, but harmed everyone except the unjust, in truth, savagely withdrawing grace and mercy from all seeking their face.

1324

[in the margin: O how badly the king treats his queen]

People are going to be not too much disturbed, I suppose ... if the king in his rage brought numerous injuries to peoples of foreign regions and unknown tongue, since he has cruelly imposed more grievous damages on the noble queen, his consort. For, as it was truly believed, contemptuously, in rage, he deprived her of her children, all her goods and her household without cause, and condemned her, like a maidservant deprived of favour, to the watchful keeping of those jealous of her.

(c) Le Baker, *Chronicon*, pp. 28–9, 30, 31, 32

Le Baker's sympathy for Edward is visible throughout his narrative, especially in pp. 27–34 (pp. 26–32 of the translation by Preest).

1327

And so the noble Lord Edward, formerly the king, suffered with patience the loss of his royal crown and his liberty for love for Jesus Christ, the poor crucified one, and remained with his kinsman Henry, the Earl of Leicester, lacking nothing that a monk-like recluse might need. This servant of God, even when he had sunk to the depths, lamented no misfortune, except that his wife, whom he was not able not to love, did not want to see him, without whose embraces he had lived as a widower for more than a year ... How many songs of love this second Orpheus sang with pleading voice, but in vain ... The love of this suffering man, patient in the rest of his adversities, awoke such pity in the earl, his keeper, and all those in their households, that they did not forego sending messages of the despairing love of the noble knight for his wife to a heart harder than an unyielding anvil.

... He was a man best endowed with natural strengths; brave in the face of hardships, bearing all his sufferings by the grace of God, he overcame all the deceitful actions of the evildoers by nature or by grace ... as

I more truly believe, the Almighty kept his confessor for a more public martyrdom.

... At length they came to Berkeley Castle, where the noble Edward was shut up to exercise the virtue of patience like an anchorite, where, robbed like the Blessed Job of his temporal kingdom, though not by foreigners but by his own wife, servants and maidservants, deprived of the control exercised through honours and advantages, he waited for the heavenly kingdom to replace the earthly.

... Thus the heavenly kingdom of the angels received one hated by the world, as it had hated his master Jesus Christ before him, first the teacher, rejected by the kingdom of the Jews, and then the disciple, stripped of the kingdom of the English.

(d) Higden

Polychronicon, VIII, pp. 298–300

This passage was copied by the canon of Bridlington (p. 91) with minor changes, noted here.

This Edward was a fine figure of a man, outstanding in strength, but very unreliable in his way of life, so it is commonly believed. For, setting little store by the companionship of noble men, he made friends with dandies, singers, actors, carters, ditch-diggers, oarsmen, sailors and other craftsmen of this sort, indulging in drinking, lightly betraying secrets, striking those nearby for little cause; following rather someone else's counsel than his own; lavish in giving, splendid in feasting, ready in speech and contradictory in actions,[40] unlucky against his enemies, cruel to those in his household; passionately close to one of his friends, whom he greatly cherished, enriched, preferred and[41] honoured. From this came dishonour to the lover, abuse to the one loved, scandal to the people and damage to the kingdom. Also he promoted unworthy and unsuitable men to ecclesiastical offices, who afterwards were thorns in his eyes and spears in his side.

40 *Sermone* ('in words') in Bridlington.

41 Bridlington adds 'from whose presence he could not bear to be away and, above the others' before 'honoured'.

(e) Edward's rustic pursuits

In 1315 Robert le Messager of Newington was accused of 'irreverently uttering indecent words' about the king the previous year after the battle of Bannockburn. Robert denied it, but was found guilty and imprisoned. The Vita *records similar criticism under 1313 [**49a**], other chroniclers repeated the criticisms later [**49d**], and some linked them to the story of the imposter in 1317 (Childs, '"Welcome my brother"', pp. 160–1).*

Johnstone, 'The eccentricities', p. 267 (from TNA: LTR Memoranda Roll E368/86 m. 32d)

[7 November 1315] And the chosen jurors, in the presence of the said Robert, said on their oath that Saer Kaym, under-bailiff of the vill of Newington, at Newington recently, that is at the beginning of July in the eighth year of the king [1314], asked the said Robert if he had recently had any news of the lord king; he said yes, and it was bad, adding that the king had withdrawn from Scotland, defeated by the Scots. And when the same Saer showed amazement at this, Robert asserted that it was no surprise because the lord king did not willingly hear Mass. And questioned further by Saer as to what the king did in the time when he should hear Mass, etc., Robert asserted that he spent time applying himself to making ditches and digging and also to other inappropriate things etc.

50 The deposition

There is no surviving official record of the deposition, as it did not fall within the responsibility of any institution or department of government. Most information comes from chronicles, which provide many corroborative details, but also reveal differences. Some, such as Murimuth, provide only short reports, others, such as the Historia Roffensis, *Trinity College Cambridge MS R.5.41, the Lanercost chronicle and so-called Pipewell chronicle offer much more detail. The* Annales Paulini *emphasise the role of London. The fullest recent analyses of the form and possible chronology are in Valente 'Desposition', pp. 852–81 and Phillips,* Edward II, *pp. 524–39.*

(a) Murimuth, *Continuatio Chronicarum*, pp. 51–2

The queen travelled with her son and Roger Mortimer and others to London, where soon after Epiphany she had a parliament held, in which it was proclaimed on behalf of the whole kingdom that three bishops, two earls, two abbots, four barons, two knights from each county in England, and a certain number of persons from London and other cities and great towns, and especially from the ports, should be sent to the king at Kenilworth, and should tell him and urgently request him to renounce the royal dignity and the crown and to allow his eldest son to rule for him; otherwise they would withdraw their homage to him and elect another as their king. When he heard this, with tears and weeping, he replied that he grieved immensely that he deserved so ill of the people of his kingdom; but because it could not be otherwise, he said that it pleased him that his son was so accepted by the whole people that he should succeed him and rule in his stead. The envoys returning to the parliament in London brought back the king's reply fully, and even more fully than it had been given. When this reply was accepted, the whole community of the realm most promptly acknowledged as king the young Edward, third from the conquest, and on 1 February AD 1327 they had him crowned at Westminster by Archbishop Walter. On that day three of Roger Mortimer's sons and many others were knighted. Also a dower was assigned to the queen of such a size that hardly one-third of the kingdom remained for the king, her son.

(b) *Historia Roffensis* of William Dene

BL Cotton MS Faustina B. V, fos 49r–50r [Latin text printed in Haines, *Edward II*, pp. 344–5]

The day after Epiphany, that is on Wednesday [7 January], at Westminster, all the prelates, earls and barons and the people in a great crowd and especially the London citizens, came together with a great noise at the parliament of the queen, who was ruling then. In this it was stated by the bishop of Hereford, with many other bishops supporting him, that if the queen should stay with the king she would be killed by him. And after some time they were asked whom they would prefer to reign, the father or the son; and this was done on the first day of parliament. And those gathered in parliament were charged by the same bishop that each should go to his own lodging and on the following day, after having eaten and drunk, all should return and answer the bishop's question, at the third hour. When they had returned and the same question had been asked, they did not want to reply to the question, some from a fullness of heart, some led by fear, and some secretly from fear of the Londoners. In the end, with one voice for all, the son was raised to be king; when homage had been made to him, they led the new king into the great hall, saying 'Behold your king.' Walter, archbishop of Canterbury, publicly preached, 'The voice of the people, the voice of God.'[42] The bishop of Winchester added, 'When the head is sick, the other limbs suffer.'[43] Hereford further added: 'Woe to thee, O land, when thy king is a child.'[44] And with peace made among the people by Thomas Wake and the Londoners supporting him, the 'Ave rex in excelsis' was proclaimed. In which proclamation, the bishop of Rochester, standing on high with other prelates and great men of the kingdom, because he did not sing with the others nor agree to sing the 'Gloria laus et honor' to the new king, was badly harassed and threatened with death. The bishop of Rochester, although he was pressed by the justices to do his fealty to the king like the rest of the prelates, nevertheless did not do so, but he sent the archbishop to answer on his behalf. The archbishop of York, the bishops of London, Rochester and Carlisle, with others, did not give consent.

And so, when these things had been completed, the bishops of London, Ely and Hereford, two earls, two barons, ⌜and⌝ certain messengers from the counties, cities and Cinque Ports combined were sent on behalf of the entire kingdom to the father, who had been king, to Kenilworth, where the king was detained in prison and in the custody of the Earl of Lancaster, to give him back his homage, and they did give it back; there the king, having fallen on his knees with his hands raised, begged forgiveness from those sent and humbly beseeched that they should allow him to live and not kill him. In responding to him, penitent and seeking forgiveness, the bishop of Hereford showed himself to be severe, harsh and cruel. Having returned homage to the king, who was detained in custody, the messengers returned to parliament

42 A popular saying at least from the eighth century in the time of Alcuin (letter 132), who warned against it: *MGH*, *Epistolae IV*, p. 199.

43 A vernacular French proverb from at least the twelfth century: Steiner, 'Vernacular proverbs', pp. 51, 62; used in England at least from the thirteenth century: Wright, *Political Songs*, p. 31; Matthew Paris, *Chron. maj.*, i. 231.

44 Ecclesiastes 10:16.

in London. Soon it was decided to crown the new king on Sunday, the day before the Purification [1 February 1327].

(c) Trinity College Cambridge MS R.5.41, fos 125–6

Valente ('Deposition', 870–5) has convincingly argued that the 'Form of deposition', beginning with the formal memorandum quod, *was an interpolated official or semi-official document. The text was almost certainly written to support the position of Isabella and Mortimer and places the renunciation by Edward II before the deposition, a sign perhaps of unease and a perceived need to emphasise the importance of Edward's voluntary resignation.*

From the Latin text printed in Haines, *Edward II*, pp. 343–4

Parliament at London with the king absent

At the same time, 7 Ides January [7 January], parliament began in London, with the king absent, in the presence of the queen and her son. Here the Londoners made the bishops, the earls and similarly the barons and knights and as many as were there take an oath to them, and the archbishop of Canterbury offered them fifty tuns of wine before they would receive him into their friendship, and afterwards he took the oath. In this parliament with the unanimous assent of the bishops and nobles and all the people, Lord Edward II, king of England, was deposed from the government of his land, and his eldest son, Edward, Duke of Aquitaine, was put in his place, as follows.

Form of the deposition of Edward king of England, II since the Conquest

Memorandum that on the day of St Hilary, bishop and confessor [13 January], AD 1327, in the parliament at Westminster, when mutual consultation had taken place between the prelates and magnates of almost the whole of the kingdom in the royal palace in the great hall at Westminster, these things written below were done before the prelates and magnates of the realm gathered together in the common hall mentioned before.

First Lord Roger Mortimer who had been told by the magnates that he should announce to the people what had been arranged, excused himself [for doing this], saying that he should not be held culpable at law over an announcement of this sort, because this had been enjoined on him by common assent. In these circumstances he set forth before the people what had been unanimously agreed among the magnates: that the king should not henceforth have the government of the realm, because he was insufficient and the destroyer of the nobles of the realm and of the holy church against his oath and the crown, and had acquiesced in bad counsel. And therefore his eldest son, the Duke of Aquitaine, should reign instead of him, if the people assented.

And Lord Thomas Wake replied, raising his hand: 'I say for myself he will never reign.'

And the Lord Bishop of Hereford took as a theme Proverbs chapter 13[45]: 'where there is no governor, the people shall fall.' Having proposed that, he explained why he and the other magnates had gone to the king at Kenilworth Castle and what the king was told. Indeed, having set out the preamble of his speech, that is: 'Hear the prayers of your people,' 2 Chronicles, chapter 6,[46] he made clear the many, great and intolerable faults of the king in his government, that is that he clung to evil and treacherous counsel, that he also destroyed the nobles of the realm, and he had wretchedly lost the lands of his crown, which his father the illustrious Edward, king of England, had left him entire. Because of this the prelates and nobles of the realm wanted to put his son in his place in the government of the realm, if he himself should agree. He, although he replied that he took such counsel as the magnates had ordained for him, nonetheless, expressing sorrow for his actions, gave assent to those things that the messengers demanded, and the homage of the magnates, previously made to him and then revoked, was annulled.

Following that, the Lord Bishop of Winchester, wishing to address the people, began thus: 'My head aches,' 4 Kings chapter 4,[47] and in developing this, understanding by 'the head' the king himself who is head of the kingdom, he asserted that the kingdom suffered pain because of the evil government of that head, which deflected the illness of this head back to become its own pain, just like that poetic saying, 'When the head is sick the other limbs suffer,'[48] and, openly attacking many other unseemly things and evils visited on God's church and the realm, he concluded that by the unanimous agreement of the nobles his

45 *Recte* 11:14.

46 2 Chronicles 6:21.

47 4 Kings 4:19.

48 See n. 43 above.

eldest son should be substituted in the government of the realm, if the people agreed to this arrangement made by the prelates and nobles.

When this had been done, Lord Thomas Wake, with arms outstretched and waving his hands, asked the people whether they consented to this arrangement, and they in like manner shouted approbation with a loud voice.

Then the Lord Archbishop of Canterbury began speaking to the people thus: 'The voice of the people, the voice of God.'[49] Speaking in French, he said before all the people, 'Most beloved people, you know well that you have now been afflicted for a long time by various oppressions committed by the king and his evil counsellors. And therefore you eagerly cry out to God for a remedy. Your voice has clearly now been heard, because by the unanimous consent of all the magnates, Lord King Edward has been deprived of the government of the realm, and his son has been put in his place, if you unanimously agree and provided that he sticks to the wise counsel of wise men; the inadequacies of the king and the troubles visited by him on the church of God and on the realm have been set out as above.'

Hearing this, the whole people with unanimous consent, once again with hands outstretched as before, shouted 'Let it be, let it be, Amen.'

(d) *Lanercost*, pp. 257–8 (trans. Maxwell, pp. 254–6)

After Christmas, by common advice of all the nobles of England, a parliament was held in London, at the beginning of which two bishops, Winchester and Hereford, were sent to the king at Kenilworth, begging him humbly and urgently on the part of my lady the queen, and her son, the Duke of Aquitaine, and all the earls, barons and commonalty of the whole country assembled in London, that he would be pleased to come to the parliament to perform and ordain with his liegemen what ought to be done for the crown of England and what justice demanded. When he had heard this request he utterly refused to comply, but cursed them contemptuously, declaring that he would not come among his enemies – or rather, traitors. The aforesaid envoys returned, therefore, and on the vigil of the octave of Epiphany [12 January 1327] they entered the great hall of Westminster, where the aforesaid parliament

49 See n. 42 above.

was being held, and publicly recited the reply of the two envoys before all the clergy and people.

On the next day, that is on the feast of St Hilary, the bishop of Hereford preached, and took for his text that passage in Ecclesiasticus, 'An unwise king shall be the ruin of his people.'[50] dwelt heavily upon the king's lack of wisdom and folly, and upon his childish doings (if indeed they deserved to be spoken of as childish), and upon the many and divers disasters that had happened in England in his time. And all the people answered with one voice, 'We do not wish this man to reign over us any longer.'

Then, on the next day following, the bishop of Winchester preached and took for his text against the king that passage in Kings 4,[51] 'My head aches'; he sorrowfully explained what a weak head England had had for many years. The archbishop of Canterbury preached on the third day and took for his text, 'The voice of the people, the voice of God'; and at the end he announced to all his hearers that, by the unanimous consent of all the earls and barons, and of the archbishops and bishops, and all the clergy and people, Lord Edward was deposed from his earlier rank, so that he should reign no longer nor govern the people of England any more; and he added that all the above-mentioned, both people and clergy, unanimously agreed that Lord Edward, his first-born son, should succeed his father in the kingdom.

When this had been done, all the great men, with the assent of the whole community, sent solemn envoys to his father at Kenilworth to renounce their homage, and to inform him on behalf of the whole kingdom that he had been deposed from the royal dignity and that he should govern the people of England no more. The aforesaid envoys were two bishops, Winchester and Hereford; two earls, Lancaster and Warenne; two barons, de Ros and de Courtenay; two abbots, two priors, two justices, two friars preachers, two Carmelite friars. But at the instance of my lady the queen, Minorite friars were not sent, so that they should not be bearers of such a displeasing message, for he greatly loved the Minorites. Also there were two knights from beyond Trent, and two from this side of Trent; two citizens of London and two from the Cinque Ports; so that altogether there were twenty-four important persons appointed to bear that message.

50 Ecclesiasticus 10:3.

51 Kings 4:19.

(e) The Pipewell Chronicle

BL Cotton Julius A i, fos 56–56v in Clarke, *Medieval Representation*, pp. 193–5, with amendments from *EHD*, III, no. 14, pp. 287–8

And on the feast of St Hilary [13 January] in the year of our lord 1326 [1327] there came to the great hall at Westminster the archbishops, bishops, earls and barons, abbots and priors and all the others from cities and boroughs alike, together with the whole community of the land. There by common assent of all it was solemnly declared by the archbishop of Canterbury how the good king Edward when he died had left his son the lands of England, Ireland, Wales, Gascony and Scotland in good peace and how the son had as good as lost the lands of Gascony and Scotland through bad counsel and bad custody, and how likewise through bad counsel he had caused a great part of the noble blood of the land to be destroyed to the great dishonour and loss of himself, his realm and the whole people, and had done many other astonishing things. Therefore, it was agreed by absolutely all the aforesaid that he ought no longer to reign but that his eldest son, the Duke of Guyenne, should reign and wear the crown in his stead. For when the bishop of Hereford and the bishop of London, who had been sent to him at Kenilworth on behalf of the community of the land to ask him to come to the parliament, bore witness that he remained as cruel and malevolent as before, it was accordingly ordained and agreed that great folk such as bishops, abbots, priors, earls, barons, knights, justices and others should go to him and renounce entirely their homage to him and on behalf of the whole land; and so it was done. It was further ordained that our lady the queen, for the great anxiety and anguish she had suffered as well on this side as overseas, should stay queen all her life, and that our lord the king who now is should take to wife the daughter of the Count of Hainault.

On the feast of Saints Fabian and Sebastian [20 January] in the aforesaid year, according to the English style and dominical letter D, there came to Kenilworth the under-mentioned, namely: the bishops of London, Winchester and Hereford, the abbots of Glastonbury and Dover, the earls Warenne and of Lancaster, the barons Sir Hugh de Courtenay, Sir Richard de Grey, the justices Sir Geoffrey le Scrope and John de Bourser,[52] two [?] barons of the Ports, four burgesses of

52 The name is nearly illegible but begins 'Bou...'. John de Bourser was one of the judges sworn in on 13 January 1327 at London (*CPMR 1323–64*, p. 13).

London and four knights on behalf of the community of the land. And they recited to our lord the king the aforementioned shortcomings as they had been charged to do. He before them all freely admitted that he had governed them and the land badly and with tears and on his knees he begged their mercy for this and asked them to pardon him and to ask in full parliament for them to pardon his trespasses against them. He also granted and ordained that Sir Edward, his eldest son, should be king in his place and wear the crown on Sunday, the eve of the Purification [1 February] and that every kind of homage and service should in no wise be [omitted] to him. And on this there came Sir William Trussell of Petling and knelt before our lord the king and begged him for mercy, begging him to pardon him his trespasses against him, and he pardoned him and gave him the sign of peace in front of them all.

51 The role of London

Although they report little of the official business of the deposition (except the renunciation of homage by Trussell), the annals are valuable for events in London before and during the deposition. They show some dissension over Isabella's letters to London, the high level of violence there and the oaths demanded in support of Isabella. Texts of the oaths and lists of the large numbers of laymen and clergy who took the oath of 13 January are to be found in London records: CPMR, *I, pp. 12–15; Hartrich, 'Urban Identity', pp. 94–7.*

Annales Paulini, pp. 315, 321–4

The queen and her son Edward sent letters, sealed with their seals, to the mayor and community of London seeking their help in the cause for which they had come to England.[53] When this was done, although some in the city spoke against it, all the people of the city rose up quickly together and promised their willingness to defend to the death the queen's cause and to destroy traitors and enemies of the realm. On the same day, namely Wednesday 15 October, they first seized from his home John Marshal, a London citizen who was the servant and secretary of Lord Hugh Despenser the son and who revealed what was said at the city's assembly, and beheaded him in the middle of the marketplace of West Cheap at about the ninth hour.

53 The text of the second letter is given in *Anonimalle Chronicle*, pp. 124–7.

[pp. 316–21 report the murders of Stapeldon and his esquires, removal of Baldock to Newgate gaol, and the murder of Arnald de Hispania, wine merchant]

… In the same year, from that day when the bishop of Exeter was killed, such cruelty and wickedness spread through the young men of the city of London that the mayor, aldermen and older burgesses of the city had neither the strength nor the courage to resist the young men's demands and deeds; so that it came about that they seized Master Robert Baldock's treasure from St Paul's church; and the Earl of Arundel's treasure, which had been placed in the priory of Holy Trinity in London, was similarly carried off. Even the Bardi company, where, as it was said Lord Hugh Despenser the son had his treasure, was plundered during the night and all the goods found there were carried away. Similarly John Charlton, Lord William Cliff. And so they carried out many wicked deeds in the city and other neighbouring places. The robbery of this period was called at the time 'Rifflinge' and the robbers were called 'Riffleres'.

Throughout this same time so much fear and anxiety filled the London officials and commissioners of every area of jurisdiction that they dared not hold any chapters or consistories. The court of Arches, the consistory of St Paul's and the chapter of the archdeacon of London were empty for almost the whole year and no business of any kind was carried out. Nor for the whole of the said time did the mayor or sheriffs of London in any way dare to hold pleas and their courts, as is customary; and obstructions of this sort had never been seen before then.

In the same year on the day before the nones of December [4 December], Lord Hugh Despenser's head was brought to London with the greatest public commotion and blowing of horns, and on through the middle of the city to London Bridge, with the mayor and London citizens accompanying it; and it was fastened to the top of the bridge.

In the same year, on the day after Epiphany [7 January 1327], a parliament began in London at Westminster, which all the greater men of the kingdom of England, both clergy and laity, attended. And there the Lord King Edward, through proceedings brought against him, was deposed. Many good things, however, were ordered and established there. All those who had fled and been disinherited were restored to the lands, properties and fiefs of their fathers in the said parliament. They also granted, confirmed and increased the liberties of the city of London.

In the same year on the ides of January [13 January 1327], Lord Roger Mortimer came to the Guildhall with a great company, and presented himself to the citizens of London promising that he would defend the queen's cause and would maintain the liberties of the said city. Likewise Lord Walter, archbishop of Canterbury, Lord Alexander, archbishop of Dublin, and the bishops, Roger Martival of Salisbury, Henry Burghersh of Lincoln, John Hotham of Ely, John Droxford of Bath, Roger Northburgh of Coventry, John Langton of Chichester, Hamo Frendsbury of Rochester, came to the Guildhall and promised to support Lady Isabella, the queen, and her son Edward and to support their cause and the liberties of the city of London, as is set out more fully below. A certain clerk of the sheriff of London, Roger Depham, holding a certain schedule written in French in his hand, charged the said bishops and many earls and barons thus:

> You swear that with all your might and main you will help to preserve and keep safe the bodies of Isabella queen of England and of Edward now king of England,[54] and you will help them with all your might and main in the cause the said king and queen have against Hugh Despenser the son and Master Robert Baldock, their enemies, and their supporters, and that you will faithfully give the counsel which will be asked of you, and that you will faithfully keep silent about what you know of that counsel; and you will preserve and keep the franchises of the city of London, and you will maintain with all your might and main the matters concerning this cause and also all the things which are ordained and will be ordained in this parliament by the peers of the land and the community of the realm, for the honour of God and the holy church and for the common profit of all the people; and you will not depart from this in life or death as God helps you and yours.

When the schedule had been read through, all and every one of the bishops and magnates, each for himself, swore on the Gospels that he would maintain and keep every single thing the document contained, in the presence of Richard Bethune, mayor of London, Andrew Horn, chamberlain of the said Guildhall, and a very great crowd from the city. The lord archbishop of Canterbury moreover declared publicly before the people gathered there, that if he should offend against them in some way, he would submit to their ordinances totally, and finally at the request of certain men he offered to the aforesaid community fifty tuns of wine in order to have their peace and goodwill, but he did this with a great feeling of shame.

54 The reference to 'Edward now king' suggests that this was the oath taken not on 13 January, but on 20 January, when the young prince was already regarded as king: *CPMR 1323–64*, pp. 11–12.

About the same time all the earls and barons of the kingdom of England withdrew their homage from the deposed king through a proctor, namely William Trussell, knight, in these words:[55]

> I, William Trussell, proctor for the prelates, earls and barons, and other people named in this procuration, having by this full and sufficient power, relinquish and return to you, Edward, the homage and fealty due to you as Edward king of England before this time from the people named in my said procuration, and I make free and quit the persons named above in the best way that law and custom allows; and I make protestation in the name of all and every one of them that they do not wish henceforth to be in your fealty nor liegeance, nor to hold anything from you as king, thus considering you henceforth a private person with no manner of dignity.

55 The renunciation is copied into several chronicles. This version is very close to the best copies in semi-official collections: *Rotuli Parliamentorum Anglie Hactenus Inediti*, ed. Richardson and Sayles, pp. 100–1.

IX: THE DEATH AND 'AFTERLIFE' OF EDWARD II

Introduction

The deposition was not the end of the story. The major difficulty for Isabella and Mortimer and Edward III's new government was what to do with Edward. The sentence on him had been perpetual imprisonment and the intention seems to have been to make him reasonably comfortable at Kenilworth Castle with an allowance of £5 a day for his maintenance.[1]

Edward, however, was dangerous to the new regime. Support for his deposition had not been unanimous. There were still those who had sympathy for him, those who had severe reservations about the rights of deposing an anointed king, and those who found the new regime less appealing than they had hoped. Edward inevitably became the focus of plots. These seem to have centred on Warwickshire and South Wales, where Mortimer was not popular, and especially among the Dominicans. Arrests in March to May and an attack on Berkeley Castle in July, which succeeded in penetrating the castle, indicate the level of conspiracies. In early September the government was worried by news of another conspiracy emanating from Wales and on 21 September Edward was dead. He lay at Berkeley for a month, was moved to Gloucester Abbey on 21 October, and was finally buried there on 20 December 1327. Gloucester was chosen because it was close to where he died, already had royal associations through the coronation of Henry III, and avoided the need to transport his body across the country, which might have encouraged visible opposition to the government. Arrangements for the funeral were lavish and royal. A fine tomb was set up, probably in the late 1330s.[2]

1 Phillips, *Edward II*, p. 541; the correct reference for the £5 per day is *CCR 1327–1330*, p. 284. See also Phillips, 'Kings in captivity.'

2 Phillips, *Edward II*, pp. 554–8; Welander, *Gloucester Cathedral*, pp. 147–50; Bryant et al., *The Tomb of Edward II*, passim (reprinted in Barlow et al., *Edward II*, chapter 2).

Even dead, Edward remained a problem for the government. He became the focus of a cult and of rumours. Popular cults were not unusual outcomes of violent political drama, and Edward's favour to the Dominicans and interest in the Holy Oil gave him sufficient pious aura. The cult is reflected in Le Baker's sympathetic portrayal of Edward as a martyr, a tormented but patient man with a crown of hay.[3] Pilgrims flowed into Gloucester Abbey, the fabric of which benefited from their donations [**52b**].[4] The cult, however, like that for Thomas of Lancaster, was highly criticised by Ranulph Higden [**52a**] and was locally contained.

The rumours were twofold and contradictory: that his death was murder and that he still lived. There is no doubt that Edward's death was very opportune for the government and Mortimer was directly accused of Edward's murder at his own fall in 1330 [**54b**], but the evidence for murder remains circumstantial. Many contemporary chronicles reported Edward's death without comment. A few, however, hinted at the possibility of unnatural death and the fully embellished murder story appeared in popular chronicles such as *The Brut* and Higden's *Polychronicon* [**53a–i**]. From the mid-fourteenth century Edward's murder became part of the accepted historical narrative.[5] Le Baker's testimony of murder carries some weight because of his use of a local witness, Sir Thomas More, but his account is clearly highly coloured. The pursuit of Thomas Gurney suggests that he was seen to have responsibility for the king's death (whether murder or not), but Edward III's leniency to Isabella and ambivalence to Mautravers have led to doubts about murder (and even Edward's death).

The different question of whether Edward really died in September 1327 is raised by rumours both that he was alive in prison at Corfe Castle and that he was living abroad. Political imprisonment and death often spawn such rumours and subsequent plots, as they would do later with the death of Richard II and the so-called 'Princes in the Tower'. The rumour that Edward was alive culminated in England in 1330 in a plot by his half-brother, the Earl of Kent, to release him. Few contemporary writers believed the rumours; some explicitly described them as fantasy [**54a i–v**]. At his fall Mortimer was accused of deliberately

3 *Le Baker*, pp. 28–34 (trans. Preest, pp. 27–32).

4 Phillips, *Edward II*, pp. 21–2, 600–5; Phillips, 'Edward II and the prophets', pp. 196–201; Welander, *Gloucester Cathedral*, pp. 144–7, 150–63.

5 For the chronology of reporting in the chronicles, see Mortimer, 'Sermons of sodomy', table 1, pp. 58–60.

deceiving Kent [**54b**] and in the context of Kent's plot, the pope strenuously denied that he had any belief that Edward was living.[6] Most modern historians have been equally sceptical, but the rumour that Edward escaped abroad lives on. Two elements in this survival story can be dismissed. It is clear that the alleged tomb of Edward II in Italy was far earlier than the fourteenth century and it is extremely unlikely that William de Galeys, brought before Edward III in 1338 at Koblenz, was any more Edward II than had been the delusional impostor, John of Powderham, who claimed to be Edward II during his lifetime.[7] The Fieschi letter provides more of a problem because some of its circumstantial detail is correct and its precise origin and purpose are unclear, although it may be placed within the diplomatic manoeuvrings of the mid- to late 1330s [**55**]. The letter has been examined sympathetically by Cuttino and Lyman (1978), Fryde (1979) and Mortimer (2003, 2005, 2010),[8] and more sceptically by Haines (1996, 2003), Phillips (2010) and King (2016).[9] Phillips provides a full survey of the recent literature and King directly addresses Ian Mortimer's latest argument. Despite the rumours of Edward's survival, the normal narrative of England's history during the Middle Ages and into the modern period remains that of Edward's imprisonment and death, probably by murder.

Edward in the reign of Richard II

At the end of the fourteenth century Edward's reign became the focus of renewed political interest. On the one hand, Richard II, wanting to strengthen and even exalt his own position, formally urged Edward's canonization.[10] On the other hand, dissatisfaction with Richard's rule made his subjects search the records for precedents to limit his power or even remove him.

6 Phillips, *Edward II*, p. 570.

7 *Wardrobe Book of William Norwell*, pp. 212, 214; King, 'Death of Edward II revisited', pp. 17–19; Phillips, *Edward II*, pp. 594–5; Childs, '"Welcome my brother"', passim.

8 Cuttino and Lyman, 'Where is Edward II?', pp. 525–30; Fryde, *Tyranny*, pp. 201–6; Mortimer, *Traitor*, pp. 244–64; Mortimer, Death of Edward II'; Mortimer, 'Edward III, his father and the Fieschi', pp. 175–234.

9 Haines, 'Edwardus redivivus'; Haines, *Edward II*, pp. 219–38; Phillips, *Edward II*, pp. 582–600; King, 'Death of Edward II revisited', pp. 1–22.

10 Thielmann, 'Political canonization', pp. 252–9.

Richard's visit to Edward's tomb in 1378 and his arrangement in 1383 for annual masses for Edward are not exceptional, but his interest quickened. In 1385 he made his first request for canonization and, as political conflict grew, his interest intensified. After the Wonderful Parliament in 1386–7 he asked the pope for an inquiry into Edward's miracles [**56a i–ii**]. The inquiry began in 1389, a book of miracles was submitted in 1395, and in 1397 Richard followed this up with an embassy to Rome, but nothing more happened.[11]

Richard's opponents also looked closely at Edward's reign for precedents to use against Richard. At the Wonderful Parliament the Earl of Gloucester and Archbishop Arundel, meeting Richard II as representatives of the parliamentary community, claimed that kings were limited by law (*ex antiquo statuto*) in terms of annual parliaments and parliament's power of dissolution and that a third allowed deposition [**56b i**]. This is a clear reference to Edward's reign, although he was not mentioned by name and no such law existed.[12] The continual council imposed on Richard at this parliament so outraged him that he questioned the judges in 1387 about punishments for those who limited royal prerogative, and the wording of question 9 to the judges indicates that Richard's opponents may have seen the appointment of the Ordainers in 1310 as a precedent for the council [**56b iii**].[13] This is probably also the 'statute' by which, as the continuator of the *Eulogium* writes, Edward was 'adjudged' [**56b ii**]. In c. 1389–90 Richard himself had records searched for any statutes of Edward I and Edward II that affected royal prerogative.[14] He also ensured affirmations of his regality in parliament in 1390 and 1391, the second of which explicitly referred back to Edward II [**56b iv**]. The accusations against the Appellants in 1397 drew specific attention to their search in 1387 for records on Edward's deposition [**56b v**]. In 1399 Richard's opponents looked carefully at Edward's deposition for precedents to remove Richard, but they did not, in the end, follow the same procedure.[15]

11 Phillips, *Edward II*, pp. 603–5; Given-Wilson, 'Richard II, Edward II', pp. 567–8; Saul, *Richard II*, p. 323.

12 *Knighton*, pp. 354–62; Saul, *Richard II*, pp. 157–8.

13 Clementi, 'Richard II's ninth question', pp. 103–8.

14 Saul, *Richard II*, p. 237.

15 *Ibid.*, pp. 418–19, 430–1.

52 The cult of Edward II

(a) The cult

*Higden was also highly critical of the cult of Thomas of Lancaster [*Polychronicon*, VIII, pp. 312–14], for a discussion of which, see Edwards, 'The cult of "St" Thomas'.*

Higden, *Polychronicon*, VIII, pp. 324–6: written or revised in the 1340s

Concerning his merits, whether he should be numbered among the saints, there was frequent dispute among the people, as [there had been] once about Thomas of Lancaster. But in truth neither foul prison nor vile death (since those things are duly meted out to evil men), nor the frequency of offerings, nor the appearance of miracles (since such things are indifferent to good and evil) prove anyone a saint, unless the holiness of his previous life accords with these; for it is good for everyone if, with contrition, such things wash away his guilt or diminish the merited punishment, although they may not bring about an immediate entry to heaven. But the boldness of the importunate, foolishly hoping for safety from punishment for himself and for others like him, and the excessive desire of women, who love to wander around, greatly increase and spread around the rumour of such worship, until the building erected on sand totters and falls.

(b) Pilgrimages to Gloucester

Historia et Cartularium monasterii Sancti Petri Gloucestriae, I, pp. 44–5, 46[16]

After his death certain neighbouring monasteries, namely St Augustine's Bristol, St Mary of Kingswood, St Adelm of Malmesbury feared to accept his worthy body for terror of Roger Mortimer and Queen Isabella and other accomplices. Nevertheless, this abbot[17] brought him from Berkeley Castle on his own honourably adorned carriage, painted with the arms of his own church, and he was brought to the monastery at Gloucester; he was honourably received by the abbot with the whole community dressed in solemn vestments and with a procession of all the citizenry, and he was borne to his burial there in the church in the northern part near the great altar...

16 See also Welander, *Gloucester Cathedral*, pp. 144–60, 628–9.

17 Abbot John Thoky, d. 1329.

In his[18] time the offerings of the faithful and the devotion which [the people] had for King Edward, who had been buried in the church, began; so that within a few years the crowd of common people was such that the city of Gloucester scarcely held the multitude of people flowing together there from various cities, towns and villages of England. As a result, out of the offerings made there in six years of his prelacy, St Andrew's aisle was completed from beginning to end, as may now be seen.

53 Was Edward murdered?

Most chronicles written close to the event offer a plain statement that Edward died, although some hint at unnatural death. The long version of The Brut, *however, disseminated the story of murder, which was elaborated later by Le Baker. Edward's murder soon became part of the normal historical narrative.*

(a) *Annales Paulini*, p. 338

[This part of the annals may have been written in the early 1330s.]

p. 338 In the same year on the day before the feast of the apostle St Mathias [21 September], King Edward, who was called 'of Caernarfon' because he was born there, died in Berkeley Castle, where he was held in custody, and he was interred in Gloucester Abbey, in the presence of Lord Edward the king, his eldest son, and other great men of the land on the thirteenth day before the kalends of January [20 December].

(b) *Anonimalle*, pp. 134–5

[A short continuation of *The Brut*: written c. 1333.]

It so happened that soon afterwards the king became ill there and died on the day of St Matthew the Apostle before Michaelmas [21 September] and was buried at Gloucester on the eve of St Thomas [20 December], after he had reigned nineteen years, three months and two weeks, on whose soul may God have mercy, Amen.

18 Abbot John Wigmor, elected 1329.

(c) *The Brut*, pp. 252–3

[A long continuation of *The Brut*, written c. 1333; the English translation was made in the mid-fourteenth century.]

And this Edward of Caernarfon was at Berkeley Castle ... and they took and led him to Corfe Castle,[19] which the king hated like any death; and they kept him there safely until St Matthew's day in September [21 September] in the year of grace 1327, that the foresaid Sir Roger Mortimer sent the manner of his death, how and in what manner he should be done to death. And anon, as the foresaid Thomas and John had seen the letter and the command, they made King Edward of Caernarfon good cheer and good solace as they might at that supper; and the king knew nothing of their treachery. And when it was time to go to bed, the king went to his bed and lay and slept fast. And as the king lay and slept, the traitors, false, foresworn against their homage and fealty, came secretly to the king's chamber with their company with them, and laid a huge table on his stomach and, with men, pressed and strongly held down the four corners of the table upon his body. Wherewith the good man woke and was terribly frightened of being killed there and slain, and his body was turned upside-down. Then the false tyrants, as traitors, took a horn and put it into his fundament as deep as they could and took a spit of burning copper and put it through the horn into his body and often rolled his bowels with it; and so they killed their lord, and nothing was perceived; and after he was interred at Gloucester.

(d) Murimuth, *Continuatio Chronicarum*, pp. 52, 53–4

[This part was written some time before c. 1337.]

Afterwards, because it seemed to some that Lord Edward, the king's father, was treated extremely indulgently at Kenilworth, it was ordained that Lord Thomas Berkeley and Lord John Mautravers should take custody of him; so, about Palm Sunday, he was secretly taken to Berkeley. And because they feared people might come to set him free, he was taken from the said place at night to various places, that is to Corfe and to some other secret places, so that it was hard to know where he was, but finally they took him back to Berkeley. But

19 *The Brut* is the only chronicle to make this error.

always Lord Berkeley had custody of him for one month and treated him humanely, and Lord Mautravers the other month and treated him quite otherwise. The queen sent him luxurious clothing and sweet letters, but did not want to see him, pretending that the community of the realm would not allow it. However, he had his expenses, that is 100 marks a month. And so at Berkeley and elsewhere he existed not as he would have liked, but as Lord Mautravers wished, until the time to be noted below...

... Afterwards, on the tenth day before the kalends of October [22 September], AD etc. 27, Edward, king of England, died in Berkeley Castle, where, as has been shown, he was held and detained unwillingly in prison. And although many abbots, priors, knights, burgesses of Bristol and Gloucester were called to view the whole body, and looked at it superficially [*superficialiter*], nonetheless it was rumoured that he was deceitfully killed on the order of Lords John Mautravers and Thomas Gurney. Because of this those two and others fled. But Lord Thomas Gurney was found and captured abroad three years later and sent to England to receive punishment for his crimes; but he was beheaded at sea, under a certain pretext, in case, perhaps, he should accuse magnates, prelates and others of England of consenting to and conniving in the royal death. But Lord John Mautravers went to Germany and to other places and stayed there, and is still there at the present time.[20]

(e) *Bridlington*, p. 97

[First written sometime before c. 1339.]

Also in the same year on the eleventh day before the kalends of October, the feast day of St Matthew the apostle and evangelist [21 September], King Edward called 'of Caernarfon' died in Berkeley Castle where he had been placed in custody, and on the eve of St Thomas the apostle which followed [21 December] he was buried at Gloucester. He reigned for nineteen years, two months and nineteen days, in which he always lived in dread, he feared his intimates, he was frightened of his friends as if of enemies.

20 Gurney was captured and died in 1333; Mautravers was finally allowed back to England in 1352: Phillips, *Edward II*, p. 575.

(f) *Lanercost*, p. 260 [Maxwell trans. p. 259]

[Written before 1346.]

The deposed king died soon after, either by a natural death or inflicted violently by others, and was buried at Gloucester among the monks on the feast of St Thomas the Apostle [21 December 1327] and not at London with the other kings, because he had been deposed so that he should not reign.

(g) Higden, *Polychronicon*, VIII, p. 324

[Written or revised in the 1340s.]

On the third day before the nones of April [3 April 1327] the former king was transferred from Kenilworth to Berkeley Castle where, however, since many plotted to free him, about the feast of St Matthew the Evangelist [21 September 1327], he was shamefully killed, pierced with a red-hot spit through his privy parts.

(h) *Chroniques de Londres*, p. 53

[Compiled between 1343 and 1346.]

Then Sir Edward de Caernarfon had these warders, Sir Thomas de Berkeley and Sir John Mautravers, to keep him securely in perpetual imprisonment. And with the abetting of certain persons and the assent of his false custodians, false and deceitful perjurers, treacherously by night he was vilely murdered.

(i) Le Baker, *Chronicon*, pp. 28–9, 31, 32, 33–4

[Written after c. 1348. Le Baker emphasised Edward's torment and sanctity. The full narrative of his imprisonment and death can be read in translation in Preest, *Geoffrey Le Baker*, pp. 27–32.]

And so the noble Lord Edward, formerly the king, suffering with patience the loss of his royal crown and liberty for love of Jesus Christ, the poor crucified one, remained with his kinsman Henry, Earl of Leicester, lacking nothing that a recluse, like a monk, might need.

... William Bishop, still alive after the Great Plague, told me this [the story of Edward being shaved in cold water]; he had been in charge of Edward's escort but, confessed and contrite, he repented in hope of divine mercy.

... They also intimated to [Edward's keepers], but only half-clearly, that Edward's death would please them, whether natural or violent. Here the deceit of the sophists flourished through the bishop, who wrote, '*Edwardum occidere nolite timere bonum est*: To kill Edward do not fear it is good.' This sophism can be divided into two propositions, the first of them being the first three words, namely '*Edwardum occidere nolite*; do not kill Edward', and the second being the other three words, '*timere bonum est*: to fear is good', in this case it does not seem to suggest any treachery. But the letters' recipients, to whom what was in the bishop's mind was not unknown, changed the sophism, that is into this sense: '*Edwardum occidere nolite timere*: do not fear to kill Edward', and then added the reading '*bonum est*: it is good', well knowing the wickedness, they wickedly emphasised the wicked message, but not openly saying it.

... Those tyrants ... at night on [22 September] suddenly seized him as he lay in bed and held him down and choked him with great featherbeds, of a massive weight of more than fifteen strong men. Then with a plumber's iron, made red hot, and thrust through a guiding tube, leading to the secret parts of his bowels they burnt, after his inner parts, his heart and lungs. For they were afraid that if a wound were found on the king's body, where any friends of justice are wont to look for wounds, his tormentors would be forced to answer for a visible injury and suffer punishment for it. Thus this strongest of knights was destroyed; his loud cries, heard both inside and outside the castle, gave sufficient notice that someone was suffering a violent death. The screaming of the dying man woke many people in Berkeley and some in the castle, as they themselves asserted, to compassion and to prayers for the holy soul of one leaving this world.

54 Did Edward die?

All government records and contemporary chroniclers accepted that Edward died in 1327, whether his death was natural or not. Nonetheless, the question of his possible survival, based on Kent's plot in 1330, the appearance of William le Galeys in Koblenz in 1338 and the Fieschi letter has recently been reopened.

(a) Kent's plot in 1330

The Earl of Kent was persuaded that Edward continued to live at Corfe Castle and planned to release him. He was arrested on 16 March, interrogated and executed on 19 March 1330. Chroniclers who reported the rumours that Edward lived discounted them and saw Kent as deceived. Murimuth explicitly stated that the rumours were fantasy. The Lanercost chronicle, Le Baker and The Brut *(at great length pp. 263–7) provide much detail.*

i Adae Murimuth, *pp. 59–60*

... about mid-Lent the king held parliament at Winchester, where, at the instigation of the queen and Roger Mortimer, the Earl of Kent, the king's uncle, was accused with many others of plotting to free him and put him back into his position in the realm, since certain people claimed that the king's father was alive, although this was quite false and a fantasy, as the outcome of the matter afterwards proved. Nonetheless, the said earl was beheaded there, because of certain confessions he made and certain letters found with him, although none of those confessions and letters (even if they were true) ought to provide cause for his death. Indeed others of the accused were sent away on bail, such as the bishop of London; yet others were put in prison, such as Robert of Taunton and certain others. However, the said earl was little lamented by the people, because he had a wicked household, taking things from the people on his own authority as he went around through the country and paying little or nothing to them.

ii Annales Paulini, *p. 349*

In the following Lent the king held his parliament at Winchester; in this parliament Lord Edmund, Earl of Kent, was wretchedly condemned to death and beheaded. There were at this time certain wicked spies who asserted to men throughout the whole English realm that the king, who had recently died, was alive abroad and would come back soon if he should have the assent and help of the nobles of the realm; and many believed this to be true. Because of this several of the prelates and magnates suffered many injuries and from that arose the occasion of the said earl's ruin.

iii Bridlington, *p. 100*

Also in the same year Edmund of Woodstock, Earl of Kent, the king's uncle, was beheaded at Winchester because he worked continuously for the release of his brother, Edward the imprisoned king. And he was accused of this by certain of his rivals.

iv Lanercost, *pp. 264–5 (trans. Maxwell pp. 264–5)*

On 16 March my lord Edmund of Woodstock, Earl of Kent ... was taken at Winchester as a traitor to the king, and there before many nobles of the realm he acknowledged that, both by command of my lord the pope and at the instigations of certain bishops of England (whom he named expressly) and by the advice of many great men of the land (whom he also named and proved by sure tokens) and especially at the instigation of a certain preaching friar of the convent of London, to wit, Thomas of Dunheved (who had told the said earl that he had raised up the devil, who asserted that my lord king Edward, lately deposed, was still alive) and at the instigation of three other friars of the aforesaid order (to wit, Edmund, John and Richard), he intended to act and did act with all his power, so that the said Lord Edward, the deposed king, should be delivered from prison and restored to the kingdom; and for such a purpose my lord the pope and the said lord bishops and nobles aforesaid had promised him plenty of money besides advice and aid in carrying it out. In consequence of this confession, the said Edmund, Earl of Kent was condemned to death and cruelly beheaded. Moreover it was said that his death was procured chiefly through the agency of Sir Roger de Mortimer, Earl of March ...

v Le Baker, Chronicon, *pp. 43–4 (trans. Preest pp. 39–40)*

[The description of the deceit is peculiar to Le Baker, but the trial repeats Murimuth almost verbatim.]

... certain men, wishing to discover what friends Edward II, the recently murdered king of England, had, pretended that he was living in splendour in Corfe Castle, but did not wish to be seen during the day. Because of this they had dancing take place for many nights on the walls and towers of the castle, carrying wax candles and lit torches, as if they had the custody of some great king to whom they were paying court, so that they should be seen by country halfwits. The news spread through all England that the king's father was alive. The Earl of Kent, therefore, sent there a certain Dominican friar to spy out the truth, who, thinking he had corrupted the castle's doorkeeper with bribes, was himself deceived. He was let in to stay in the doorkeeper's chamber by day, so that he might see whom he wanted to see by night. At night he was let into the hall, told to dress in secular cloths lest he should be noticed, and it seemed to him that he saw Edward, the king's father, sitting in splendour at dinner. He told the Earl of Kent what he believed he had seen. So the earl swore, in the presence of certain people in whom he should not have had trust, that he would work to see that his brother should be freed from the prison where he was detained.

(b) Accusations against Mortimer, 1330

PROME, Parliament of November 1330, C65/2 m.7, no. 1

Also, whereas the father of our lord the king was at Kenilworth by the ordinance and assent of the peers of the realm, to stay there at their pleasure in order to be provided for as was appropriate for such a lord, the said Roger by the royal power usurped by him was not satisfied until he had him at his will, and ordained that he be sent to Berkeley Castle where he was traitorously, feloniously and falsely murdered and killed by him and his followers.

. . .

Also, although the said Roger knew well that the father of our lord the king was dead and buried, he, with others of his faction, in a deceitful manner gave the Earl of Kent to believe that the said father of our lord the king was alive. Whereupon the said Earl of Kent was most desirous to know the truth, whether he was alive or not. And he set about finding this out by all the good means that he knew, until the said Roger, by his said usurped royal power, had the said Earl of Kent arrested at the parliament held at Winchester, and so arranged matters, and had him prosecuted by his said royal power, that the earl was put to death at the said parliament.

55 The Fieschi letter

*Recent studies of Edward's reign by Phillips (*Edward II, *pp. 582–4), Haines (*Edward II, *pp. 221–2) and Mortimer (*Traitor, *pp. 251–62) provide lengthy up-to-date commentaries on the letter and its context. The letter was* *discovered in the departmental archive of Hérault in France in a cartulary of the bishop of Maguelonne, dated c. 1368. It was published in France in 1878, in England in 1883 (*Chronicles*, ed. Stubbs, II, pp. civ–cvi) and again in 1978 (see Cuttino and Lyman, 'Where is Edward II?'). There is now another translation of the letter supported by photographs of the manuscript.*[21] *The letter is authentically fourteenth century, but its purpose and reliability are matters of debate. The letter purports to be written by Manuel Fieschi, a papal clerk, who held English benefices, although he may never have been resident in England. It was addressed to Edward III and has been associated with diplomatic manoeuvring in the 1330s; it was certainly written before 1345 when Fieschi became bishop of Vercelli.*

Cuttino and Lyman, 'Where is Edward II?', pp. 537–8

In the name of God: Amen. I have written down by my own hand those things that I have heard from your father's confession and accordingly I have taken care to make them known to your lordship.

First, he says that, feeling that England was in rebellion against him, accordingly at your mother's warning he withdrew from his household in the Earl Marshal's castle by the sea that is called Chepstow (Gesosta). Later, driven by fear, he embarked on a vessel (*barcham*) together with the lords Hugh Despenser and the Earl of Arundel and some others and landed at Glamorgan on the coast, and there he was captured together with the said Lord Hugh and Master Robert Baldock; and they were captured by Lord Henry of Lancaster; and they took him to Kenilworth (Chiongurda) Castle and others were taken elsewhere to other places; and there, at the demand of many people, he lost the crown. Subsequently, afterwards, you were crowned at the very next feast of the Blessed Mary of Candlemas [2 February]. Finally they sent him to Berkeley Castle.

Afterwards, after some time, the attendant who guarded him said to your father, 'Sire, Lord Thomas Gourney and Lord Simon *d'Esberfort*,[22] knights, have come to kill you. If it pleases you, I shall give you my clothes, so that you can better escape.' Then, dressed in these clothes, he came out of prison around the time of twilight and when he had reached the last door, without opposition because he was not recognised, he found the doorkeeper sleeping whom he immediately killed. Having taken the door keys, he opened the door and left, together with his keeper, who had been guarding him. The said

21 Smith, 'Fieschi letter'.

22 Barford or Bereford or Beresford?

knights who had come to kill him, seeing that he had thus escaped, fearing the queen's anger and, indeed, personal danger, decided to put that said porter in a chest, having first cut out his heart; and wickedly they presented the heart and body of the porter to the queen as the body of your father, and the said porter's body was buried at Gloucester as the body of the king.

And after he left the prisons of the aforesaid castle he was received at Corfe Castle together with his companion who had guarded him in the prisons, by Lord Thomas, the castellan, without the knowledge of the lord of the said castle, Lord John Maltravers, the lord of the said Thomas; in which castle he remained secretly for a year and a half. Later, having heard that the Earl of Kent, who had said that he was alive, had been beheaded, he embarked on a ship with his aforesaid keeper and by the will and counsel of the said Thomas, who had received him; he crossed into Ireland where he stayed nine months. Afterwards, afraid that he might be recognised there, assuming the habit of a hermit, he returned to England and landed[23] at the port of Sandwich, and in the same habit he crossed the sea to Sluys. Afterwards he travelled into Normandy, and from Normandy, as many do, crossing the Languedoc he came to Avignon, where, having given a florin to a papal servant, he sent a note to Pope John by the same servant. The pope had him summoned to him and kept him secretly and honourably for more than fifteen days. Finally after various discussions, reflecting carefully on all matters, having received permission to depart, he went to Paris, and from Paris into Brabant, from Brabant to Cologne, so that out of devotion he might see the three kings.[24] And leaving Cologne he crossed through Germany and so headed out to Milan in Lombardy and from Milan he entered a certain hermitage of the castle Mulazzo,[25] where he remained for two and a half years. And because this castle became involved in war he moved to the castle of Cecima[26] in another hermitage in the diocese of Pavia in Lombardy. And he was in this last hermitage for two years or thereabouts, remaining in seclusion, doing penance and praying to God for you and other sinners.

23 *Applico* is commonly used for the arrival of ships; so he presumably travelled by sea.

24 The shrine of the three kings at Cologne Cathedral.

25 *Milasci*; either Melazzo, in Alessandria province, Piedmont, 70 km south-east of Turin, 35 km south-west of Alessandria; or Mulazzo (which has Fieschi connections), in Massa and Carrara province, Tuscany, 35 km north-west of Massa.

26 *Cecima*; in Pavia province, Lombardy, 70 km south of Milan, 35 km south of Pavia: south of Voghera.

In testimony of which things, for your lordship's consideration, I have appended [my] seal.

Your Manuel de Fieschi, notary to the lord pope, your devoted servant.

56 Memories in the reign of Richard II

(a) Richard's attempt at canonization

i Westminster Chronicle, 1385 and 1390, pp. 158–9 (1385), 436–9 (1390)

1385

In the year of our lord 1385 the king of England sent special letters to the lord pope in favour of the canonization of King Edward II who lies at Gloucester; but he did not get his wish.

1390

The king proceeded to Gloucester, the resting place of his great grandfather, whose translation he was very anxious to effect. Here he was met by the archbishop of Canterbury and the bishop of London and other bishops, with clergy and lawyers in attendance, to consider dispatching to the pope testimony about miracles after having first discussed among themselves whether the miracles were genuine or fictitious. The pope had earlier addressed a bull concerning this matter to the bishop of London, directing him to inquire into the genuineness of these miracles and to certify to the pope the true facts of the case.

ii Richard II's letter to Urban VI (date uncertain: 1385–9)

Perroy, *Diplomatic Correspondence*, no. 95 (pp. 62–3)

Most blessed Father we have not forgotten that we have asked Your Holy Clemency before, because of the merits of the glorious King Edward our dearest [great] grandfather, whose body honourably rests interred in the monastery of St Peter at Gloucester, and also because of the very many signs of miracles which omnipotent God has wonderfully worked from day to day to the honourable renown of the glory of our said grandfather, so that the most celebrated news runs through in public to the glory of God, that the Apostolic Providence might deign to order an inquiry concerning these things;

so that if they [the miracles] are sufficiently proved his name should be ascribed to the catalogue of saints. Therefore, at the instance of our supplication, it has pleased Your Holiness, so we have heard, to have the foresaid matter recommended in this manner and to have ordered an inquiry on the premises by commissioners deputed by the Apostolic Authority. But nevertheless, most benevolent Father, because we have not yet heard for sure by the letters of this commission, whose arrival we await daily, we most humbly beg Your same Holiness from the Apostolic Benevolence to confirm what still remains to be done in this matter of the premises and of our consideration. And that you deign to receive Brother William Brut, a monk of the said monastery, coming now to Your Holiness's presence for the said discussed matter of the said canonization and any other business of the monastery advanced in Your Holiness's court by the said monk. Your Holiness, etc.

(b) References to Edward II's reign in the political narrative

*Knighton recorded Richard's opponents' claim in the 'Wonderful' parliament of 1386–7 that kings were limited by law in terms of annual parliaments, parliament's dissolution and possible deposition (Knighton, pp. 356–7, 360–1: below [**56b i**]). The continuator of the* Eulogium *also recorded that Edward was subject to procedures imposed upon him by statute (below [**56b ii**]). In this context* statutum *should be read as 'the law of the land'; it did not yet have the exclusive meaning of the modern word 'statute'.*[27] *In turn, Richard made specific reference to Edward II's reign when he took legal advice against the threats of 1386–7 (below [**56b iii**]). His attempt to have Edward canonized and the statements on regality (below [**56b iv**]) were also meant to undermine his opponents' references to Edward's reign.*

i The Wonderful Parliament in Knighton's Chronicle, pp. 360–1

Yet there remains one other thing of our message for us to tell you on behalf of your people. They have it from an ancient law (*ex antiquo statuto*), which in fact not very long ago was lamentably invoked, that if the king from any evil counsel or foolish stubbornness or contempt or through his violent will or in any improper way should estrange himself from his people and will not be governed and guided by the laws, statutes and laudable ordinances of the kingdom, with the wholesome

27 Clementi, 'Richard II's ninth question', pp. 98–9.

counsel of the lords and nobles of the kingdom, but should obstinately by his own mad counsels recklessly exercise his own individual will, then it would be lawful for them, with the common assent and consent of the people of the kingdom, to depose the king himself from the royal throne, and to raise some near kinsman of royal lineage to the royal throne in his place.

ii The Wonderful Parliament in Eulogium, pp. 359–60

Here 'adjudged' (adjudicatus) *means that he had a judgment imposed on him. The author probably had in mind the appointment of the Ordainers or the Ordinances, as in questions to the judges (Clementi, 'Richard II's ninth question', pp. 100–1).*

The king did not want to come to parliament. They, however, sent for the statute (*statuto*) by means of which Edward had been adjudged, and under pain of that statute they compelled the king to come.

iii Question 9 to the judges

The questions to the judges were Richard's response to the attacks on his prerogative. The 'adjudgement' of Edward II in this question was, sometimes rather tentatively, interpreted as a reference to his deposition; however, given the context of the appointment of the continual council in 1387, it makes more sense as a reference to the appointment of the Ordainers in 1310 (Clementi, 'Richard II's ninth question', 96–113).

PROME, parliament roll for 28 January 1398, no. 47, Shrewsbury.[28] See also Stat. 21 Richard II, c. 12; *Statutes*, II, p. 103; also copied at 1387 into *Westminster Chronicle*, pp. 200–1 and Knighton, pp. 398–9

Also it was asked of them how he is to be punished who has moved in parliament that the statute by which King Edward, son of Edward the great-grandfather of the present king, was at some time adjudged in parliament, should be sent for; by the inspection of which statute, the new statute and ordinance and commission were conceived in parliament. To which question they unanimously replied that both he who moved the act and any other who by pretext of such a motion brought that statute into parliament deserve to be punished as criminals and traitors.

28 The parliament commenced at Westminster in September 1397 and was then adjourned until the following January, when it was held at Shrewsbury.

iv On the regality of the king: parliament, 1391

Commons petitions (no doubt planted by the king) in the parliaments of 1390 (item 15) and 1391 (item 13) supported the king's regality, and this petition of 1391 specifically mentioned Edward II. See Saul, Richard II, *p. 255; Tuck,* Richard II, *pp. 71, 103–4; McKisack,* Fourteenth Century, *p. 467.*

PROME, parliament roll for 3 November 1391, Westminster, no. 13

The regality of our king.

In this parliament on 2 December [1391], the commons prayed openly in full parliament that our lord the king should be and remain as free in his regality, liberty and royal dignity in his time as any of his noble progenitors, once kings of England, were in their times: notwithstanding any statute or ordinance made before this time to the contrary, and likewise in the time of King Edward the Second who lies at Gloucester. And that if any statute was made at the time of the said King Edward to the derogation of the liberty and franchise of the crown, that it should be annulled and of no force. And then all the prelates and lords temporal prayed in the same manner. Whereupon our said lord the king thanked the said lords and commons for the great tenderness and affection they had for the salvation of his honour and of his estate. And because their said prayers and requests seemed honest and reasonable to him, he fully assented and agreed to the same.

v Accusations against the Appellants: parliament, 1397

Among the accusations against the Appellants is that in 1387 they searched the records for the process of deposition of Edward II.

PROME, Pleas of the Crown held at Westminster,
17 September 1397, no. 7

Also the aforesaid duke, earls of Arundel and Warwick, and Thomas Mortimer, continuing their malicious, false and treacherous purpose, and with the force of the said people, at Huntingdon, on the Thursday next after the feast of St Nicholas in the said eleventh year [12 December 1387] treacherously planned and agreed to go to you with their said force, in whatsoever place they might have found you within your kingdom, to withdraw from you their liege homage, and then to have you deposed from your royal estate and majesty, and to take your crown into their keeping. And they would have treacherously performed the said plan, if they had not been prevented by

Henry of Lancaster, Earl of Derby, and Thomas Mowbray, Earl of Nottingham. And the said duke, the earls of Arundel and Warwick continuing their treacherous purpose and force aforesaid, by common agreement amongst them, caused the records in your treasury to be searched, from the time of King Edward your great-grandfather, to see how your said great-grandfather was deprived of his crown. And they explained in writing to you, most redoubtable lord, in your royal palace of Westminster at the said parliament in the eleventh year the reason for the loss of his aforesaid crown. And they said falsely and treacherously that they had adequate reason to depose you, but that out of reverence for the very noble king your grandfather, and your noble father (whom God absolve) and in hope of your better governance they would suffer you to continue your royal estate and regality.

BIBLIOGRAPHY

Primary printed sources

Adae Murimuth Continuatio Chronicarum. Robertus de Avesbury de Gestis Mirabilibus Regis Edwardi Tertii, ed. E. M. Thompson, RS 93 (London, 1889).

Annales Londonienses, in *Chronicles of the Reigns of Edward I and Edward II*, ed. W. Stubbs, 2 vols., RS 76 (London, 1882–3), vol. 1.

Annales Paulini, in *Chronicles of the Reigns of Edward I and Edward II*, ed. W. Stubbs, 2 vols., RS 76 (London, 1882–3), vol. 1.

The Anonimalle Chronicle, 1307–1334 from Brotherton Collection MS 29, ed. W. R. Childs and J. Taylor, YAS Record Series 147 (1991).

Avesbury: see *Adae Murimuth.*

Bridlington: see *Gesta Edwardi de Carnarvan.*

The Brut, ed. F. W. Brie, Early English Texts Society, original series 131 (1906).

Calendar of Close Rolls, 1307–1330 (HMSO, London, 1892–8).

Calendar of Fine Rolls, 1307–1327 (HMSO, London, 1912–13).

Calendar of Letter Books ... of the City of London. Letter Book E (circa AD 1314–1337), ed. R. R. Sharpe (London, 1903).

Calendar of Patent Rolls, 1307–1330 (HMSO, London, 1894–1904).

Calendar of Plea and Memoranda Rolls ... of the City of London, 1323–64, ed. A. H. Thomas (Cambridge, 1926).

Chaplais, P., ed., *The War of Saint-Sardos*, Camden Society 3rd series 87 (London, 1954).

Chronicon Galfridi le Baker de Swynebroke, ed. E. M. Thompson (Oxford, 1899); now trans. by D. Preest as *The Chronicle of Geoffrey Le Baker* (Woodbridge, 2012).

Chronicon Henrici Knighton, ed. J. R. Lumby, 2 vols., RS 92 (London, 1889–95), vol. 1.

Chronicon de Lanercost, 1201–1346, ed. J. Stevenson (Maitland Club, Edinburgh, 1839); the section for 1272–1346 trans. by Sir H. Maxwell (Glasgow, 1913).

Chroniques de Londres, ed. G. J. Aungier, Camden Society old series 28 (1844).

Corpus Iuris Civilis, vol. I, ed. P. Krüger and T. Mommson (Berlin, 1902).

Court Rolls of the Manor of Wakefield, vol. IV: 1315–17, ed. J. Lister, YAS 78 (1930).

The Court Rolls of Walsham le Willows, 1303–50, ed. R. Lock, Suffolk Records Society 41 (1998).

English Historical Documents, vol. III: 1189–1327, ed. H. Rothwell (London, 1975).

Eulogium Historiarum, ed. F. S. Haydon, 3 vols., RS 9 (London, 1858), vol. III.
Flores Historiarum, ed. H. R. Luard, 3 vols., RS 95 (1890), vol. III.
Foedera: see Rymer.
Gesta Edwardi de Carnarvan Auctore Canonico Bridlingtoniensi, in *Chronicles of the Reigns of Edward I and Edward II*, ed. W. Stubbs, 2 vols., RS 76 (London, 1882–3), vol. II.
Goodman, A. W, ed., *Chartulary of Winchester Cathedral* (Winchester, 1927).
Handbook of British Chronology, ed. E. B. Fryde, D. E. Greenway, S. Porter and I. Roy, 3rd ed., Royal Historical Society (1986).
Higden: see *Polychronicon*.
Historia et Cartularium Monasterii Sancti Petri Gloucestrie, ed. W. H. Hart, 3 vols., RS 33 (1863), vol. I.
Jenks, S., *The Enrolled Customs Accounts*, part 1, 12 vols., List and Index Society 303 (Kew, 2004).
Knighton: see *Chronicon Henrici Knighton*.
Lanercost: see *Chronicon de Lanercost*.
Layettes du Trésor des Chartes, vol. III, ed. J. de Laborde (Paris, 1875); accessed online 2019 at: digi.ub.uni-heidelberg.de/diglit/teulet1875bd3/0005.
Le Baker: see *Chronicon Galfridi le Baker*.
Letter Book E: see *Calendar of Letter Books*.
Matthew Paris, *Matthaei Parisiensis, Monachi Sancti Albani, Chronica Majora*, vol. I, ed. H. R. Luard, RS 57 (1872).
MGH: *Monumenta Germaniae Historica, Epistolae IV*, ed. E. Duemmler (1895).
Mun. Gild. Lond.: *Munimenta Gildhallae Londoniensis*, ed. H. T. Riley, 3 vols., RS 12 (London 1849–62), vol. II: *Liber Custumarum* (London, 1860).
Murimuth: see *Adae Murimuth Continuatio Chronicarum*.
Ormrod, W. M., H. Killick and P. Bradford, eds, *Early Common Petitions in the English Parliament, c. 1290–c. 1420*, Camden Society 5th series 52 (2017).
Oxford Dictionary of National Biography: online edition.
Parl. Writs: *Parliamentary Writs and Writs of Military Summons*, ed. Sir F. Palgrave, 2 vols. (London, 1827–34), vol. II.
Perroy, E., ed., *Diplomatic Correspondence of Richard II*, Camden Society 3rd series 48 (1933).
Polychronicon Ranulphi Higden Monachi Cestrensis ed. J. R. Lumby, 9 vols., RS 41 (London, 1865–6), vol. VIII.
PROME: *The Parliament Rolls of Medieval England, 1275–1504*, gen. ed. C. Given-Wilson, 16 vols. (Woodbridge, 2005), vol. III.
Pronay, N. and J. Taylor, ed., *Parliamentary Texts of the Later Middle Ages* (Oxford, 1980).
The Red Book of the Exchequer, ed. H. Hall, 3 vols., RS 99 (London, 1896), vol. III.
Regesta Regum Scottorum, vol. V: The Acts of Robert I, King of Scots, 1306–1329, ed. A. A. M. Duncan (Edinburgh, 1988).
The Register of Richard de Kellawe, Lord Palatine and Bishop of Durham, 1311–1316, ed. T. D. Hardy, 4 vols. (HMSO, London, 1873).

The Register of Thomas Cobham, Bishop of Worcester, 1317–27, ed. E. H. Pearce, Worcestershire Historical Society 40 (1930).

The Register of Walter de Stapledon, Bishop of Exeter, 1307–1326, ed. F. C. Hingeston-Randolph (London and Exeter, 1892).

Return of Members: Return of the Name of Every Member of Parliament of the Lower House of the Parliaments of England, Scotland and Ireland ... 1213–1874 (London, 1878).

Rotuli Parliamentorum, 6 vols. (HMSO, London, 1783).

Rotuli Parliamentorum Anglie Hactenus Inediti, ed. H. G. Richardson and G. Sayles, Camden Society 3rd series 51 (1935).

Rymer, T., *Foedera, Conventiones, Litterae*, ed. A. Clarke et al., Record Commission, 4 vols. (London, 1816–69), vol. II.

Scalacronica: Sir Thomas Gray, *Scalacronica, 1272–1363*, ed. A. King, Surtees Society 209 (2005).

Scotichronicon by Walter Bower, Vol. VI, Books XI and XII, ed. N. F. Shead et al. (Aberdeen, 1991).

Select Cases in the Court of King's Bench under Edward II, vol. IV, ed. G. O. Sayles, Selden Society 74 (1955).

Statutes of the Realm, ed. A. Luders et al., 11 vols. (London, 1810–28).

Stones, E. L. G., ed., *Anglo-Scottish Relations, 1174–1328* (Oxford, 1965).

Thomas Wright's Political Songs of England from the Reign of John to that of Edward II, ed P. R. Coss (Cambridge, 1996).

Trokelowe: *Johannis de Trokelowe et Henrici de Blaneforde, Chronica et Annales*, ed. H. T. Riley, RS 28 (London, 1866).

Tupling, G., ed., *South Lancashire in the Reign of Edward II* (Chetham Society, 1949).

Twysden, Roger, *Historiae Anglicanae Scriptores X* (London, 1652).

Vita: *Vita Edwardi Secundi*, ed. and trans. W. R. Childs, Oxford Medieval Texts (Oxford, 2005).

Vita Edwardi Secundi, ed. N. Denholm-Young (London, 1957).

The Wardrobe Book of William de Norwell, 1338–1340, ed. M. Lyon, B. Lyon, H. S. Lucas and J. de Sturler (Brussels, 1983).

Westminster Chronicle, 1381–1394, ed. L. C. Hector and B. F. Harvey, Oxford Medieval Texts (Oxford, 1982).

Wright, *Political Songs*: see *Thomas Wright*.

Primary internet sources

The Anglo-American Legal Tradition, University of Houston (digitised legal and administrative records for the reign): http://aalt.law.uh.edu/EdwardII.html

The Gascon Rolls Project (1317–1468): accessible at www.gasconrolls.org

PROME: The Parliament Rolls of Medieval England, 1275–1504: accessible at www.sd-editions.com

Statutes of the Realm: accessible at www.legislation.gov.uk

Secondary works

Barlow, J., R. Bryant, C. Heighway, C. Jeens, D. Smith, with G. Fowlie and L. Keen, *Edward II: His Last Months and his Monument* (Bristol, 2015).

Barratt, N., 'Tout and the exchequer', in *Thomas Frederick Tout (1855–1929): Refashioning History for the Twentieth Century*, ed. C. M. Barron and J. T. Rosenthal (London, 2019), pp. 171–84.

Barrow, G. S., *Robert the Bruce and the Community of the Realm of Scotland* (Edinburgh, 1988).

Bartlett, R., *'Mortal Enmities': the Legal Aspect of Hostility in the Middle Ages* (Aberystwyth, 1998).

Britnell, R. H., *The Commercialisation of English Society, 1000–1500* (Cambridge, 1993; 2nd edition Manchester, 1996).

Britnell, R. H., 'Forstall, forestalling and the Statute of Forestallers', *EHR* 102 (1987), pp. 89–102.

Britnell, R. H. and B. M. S. Campbell, eds, *A Commercialising Economy: England, 1086 to c. 1300* (Manchester, 1995).

Brown, E. A. R., 'The political repercussions of family ties in the early fourteenth century: the marriage of Edward II of England and Isabelle of France', *Speculum* 63 (1988), pp. 573–95; 64 (1989), pp. 373–9.

Bryant, R. M., G. N. H. Bryant and C. M. Heighway, *The Tomb of Edward II: a Royal Monument in Gloucester Cathedral* (Stonehouse, 2007).

Buck, M. C., *Politics, Finance and the Church in the Reign of Edward II. Walter Stapeldon Treasurer of England* (Cambridge, 1983).

Buck, M. C., 'The reform of the exchequer, 1316–1326', *EHR* 98 (1983), pp. 241–60.

Carus-Wilson, E. M. and O. Coleman, *England's Export Trade, 1275–1547* (Oxford, 1963).

Caspary, G., 'The deposition of Richard II and the canon law', *Proceedings of the Second International Congress of Medieval Canon Law 1963* (Vatican, 1965), pp. 189–201.

Chaplais, P., 'Le Duché-Pairie de Guyenne: l'homage et les services féodaux de 1301 à 1337', *Annales du Midi* 68 (1957), pp. 5–38; repr. in P. Chaplais, *Essays in Medieval Diplomacy and Administration* (London, 1981).

Chaplais, P., *English Medieval Diplomatic Practice* (London, 1982).

Chaplais, P., *Piers Gaveston: Edward II's Adoptive Brother* (Oxford, 1994).

Cheney, C. R., ed., *Handbook of Dates for Students of English History* (London, 1978).

Childs, W. R., *Anglo-Castilian Trade in the Later Middle Ages* (Manchester, 1978).

Childs, W. R., 'Anglo-Portuguese relations in the fourteenth century', in *The Age of Richard II*, ed. J. L. Gillespie (Stroud, 1997), pp. 27–49.

Childs, W. R., 'Finance and trade under Edward II', in *Politics and Crisis in Fourteenth Century England*, ed. J. Taylor and W. Childs (Gloucester, 1990), pp. 19–37.

Childs, W. R., 'Government and market in the early fourteenth century', in *Ruling Fourteenth-Century England: Essays in Honour of Christopher Given-Wilson*, ed. R. Ambühl, J. Bothwell and L. Tompkins (Woodbridge, 2019), pp. 37–57.

Childs, W. R., 'Resistance and treason in the *Vita Edwardi Secundi*', in *Thirteenth Century England VI*, ed. M. Prestwich, R. H. Britnell and R. Frame (Woodbridge, 1997), pp. 177–91.

Childs, W. R., '"Welcome my brother": Edward II, John of Powderham and the chronicles, 1318', in *Church and Chronicle in the Middle Ages: Essays Presented to John Taylor*, ed. I. Wood and G. A. Loud (London, 1991), pp. 149–63.

Clark, G., 'The long march of history: farm wages, population, and economic growth, England, 1209–1869', *Economic History Review* 60 (2007), pp. 97–135.

Clarke, M. V., *Medieval Representation and Consent: a Study of Parliaments in England and Ireland, with Special Reference to the Modus Tenendi Parliamentum* (London, 1936).

Clementi, D., 'Richard II's ninth question to the judges, 1387', *EHR* 86 (1971), pp. 96–113.

The Complete Peerage, new ed., V. Gibbs, 14 vols. (London, 1910–59).

Cowan, E. J., *For Freedom Alone: the Declaration of Arbroath, 1320* (Edinburgh, 2003; 2014).

Cuttino, G. P., *English Diplomatic Administration, 1259–1339* (Oxford, 1971).

Cuttino, G. P., *English Medieval Diplomacy* (Bloomington, 1985).

Cuttino, G. P. and Thomas W. Lyman, 'Where is Edward II?', *Speculum* 53 (1978), pp. 522–43.

Davies, J. C., *The Baronial Opposition to Edward II: Its Character and Policy. A Study in Administrative History* (Cambridge, 1918).

Davies, J.C., 'The Despenser war in Glamorgan', *Transactions of the Royal Historical Society*, 3rd series, 9 (1915), pp. 21–64.

Davis, J., *Medieval Market Morality: Life, Law and Ethics in the English Market Place, 1200–1500* (Cambridge, 2012).

Denton, J. H., 'The clergy and parliament in the thirteenth and fourteenth centuries', in *The English Parliament in the Middle Ages*, ed. R. G. Davies and J. H. Denton (Manchester, 1981), pp. 88–108.

Dodd, G., 'Parliament and political legitimacy in the reign of Edward II', in *The Reign of Edward II: New Perspectives*, ed. G. Dodd and A. Musson (Woodbridge, 2006), pp. 165–89.

Doherty, P., *Isabella and the Strange Death of Edward II* (London, 2003).

Dunbabin, J., 'Government', in *The Cambridge History of Medieval Political Thought, c. 350–c. 1450*, ed. J. H. Burns (Cambridge, 1988), pp. 477–519.

Edwards, J., 'The cult of "St" Thomas of Lancaster and its iconography', *YAJ* 64 (1992), 103–22; *YAJ* 67 (1995), pp. 187–91.

Edwards, J. G., 'The personnel of the commons in parliament under Edward I and Edward II', in *Historical Studies of the English Parliament*, ed. E. B. Fryde and E. Miller, 2 vols. (Cambridge, 1970), I, pp. 150–67: first printed in *Oxford Essays in Medieval History Presented to Thomas Frederick Tout* (1925).

Edwards, J. G., 'The *Plena Potestas* of English Parliamentary representatives', in *Historical Studies of the English Parliament*, ed. E. B. Fryde and E. Miller, 2 vols. (Cambridge, 1970), I, pp. 136–49: first printed in *Oxford Essays in Medieval History Presented to Herbert Edward Salter* (1934).

Farmer, D. L., 'Crop yields, prices and wages in medieval England', *Studies in Medieval and Renaissance History* 6 (1983), pp. 117–55.

Farmer, D. L., 'Prices and wages', in *The Agrarian History of England and Wales, vol. II: 1042–1350*, ed. H. E. Hallam (Cambridge, 1988).

Frame, R. F., *Ireland and Britain, 1170–1450* (London, 1998).

Fryde, N., 'Antonio Pessagno of Genoa, king's merchant of Edward II of England', in *Studi in Memoria di Federigo Melis*, vol. II (Naples, 1978), pp. 159–78.

Fryde, N., *The Tyranny and Fall of Edward II, 1321–1326* (Cambridge, 1979).

Fuller, E.A., 'The tallage of 6 Edward II, and the Bristol rebellion', Transactions of the Bristol and Gloucestershire Archaeological Society 19 (1894/5), pp. 171–278.

Given-Wilson, C., *Edward II: the Terrors of Kingship* (London, 2016).

Given-Wilson, C., *The English Nobility in the Middle Ages: the Fourteenth-Century Political Community* (London, 1987).

Given-Wilson, C., 'Richard II, Edward II, and the Lancastrian inheritance', *EHR* 109 (1994), pp. 553–71.

Given-Wilson, C., '*Vita Edwardi Secundi*: memoir or journal?', in *Thirteenth Century England VI*, ed. M. Prestwich, R. H. Britnell and R. Frame (Woodbridge, 1997), pp. 165–76.

Goronwy Edwards, J., *Calendar of Ancient Correspondence Concerning Wales* (Cardiff, 1935).

Gransden, A., *Historical Writing in England, c. 1307 to the Early Sixteenth Century* (London, 1982).

Gras, N. S. B., *The Early English Customs System* (Cambridge, MA, 1918).

Grassi, J., 'William Airmyn and the bishopric of Norwich', *EHR* 70 (1955), pp. 550–61.

Hadwin, J. F., 'The last royal tallages', *EHR* 96 (1981), pp. 344–58.

Haines, R. M., *Archbishop John Stratford: Political Revolutionary and Champion of the Liberties of the English Church, ca. 1275/80–1348* (Toronto, 1986).

Haines, R. M., *The Church and Politics in Fourteenth Century England: the Career of Adam Orleton, c. 1275–1345* (Cambridge, 1978).

Haines, R. M., '*Edwardus Redivivus*: the 'Afterlife' of Edward of Caernarvon', *Transactions of the Gloucestershire Archaeological Society* 114 (1996), pp. 65–86.

Haines, R. M., *King Edward II: His Life, his Reign, and its Aftermath, 1284–1330* (Montreal, 2003).

Haines, R. M., 'Looking back in anger: a politically inspired appeal against John XXII's translation of Bishop Adam Orleton to Winchester (1334)', *EHR* 116 (2001), pp. 389–404.

Hamilton, J. S., *Piers Gaveston, Earl of Cornwall, 1307–1312: Politics and Patronage in the Reign of Edward II* (London, 1988).

Harriss, G., *King, Parliament and Public Finance in Medieval England to 1369* (Oxford, 1975).

Hartrich E., 'Urban identity and political rebellion', in *Fourteenth Century England VII*, ed. W. M. Ormrod (Woodbridge, 2012), pp. 94–7.

Haskins, G. L., 'A chronicle of the civil wars of Edward II', *Speculum* 14 (1939), pp. 73–81.

Haskins, G. L., 'The Doncaster Petition, 1321', *EHR* 53 (1938), pp. 478–85.

Hatcher, J. and M. Bailey, *Modelling the Middle Ages: the History and Theory of England's Economic Development* (Oxford, 2001).

Helmholz, R. H., 'Pope Innocent III and the annulment of Magna Carta', *Journal of Ecclesiastical History* 69 (2018), pp. 1–14.

Holmes, G. A., 'Judgement on the Younger Despenser, 1326', *EHR* 70 (1955), pp. 261–7.

Holmes, G. A., 'A protest against the Despensers, 1326', *Speculum* 30 (1955), pp. 207–12.

Hutchison, H. F., *Edward II* (New York, 1972).

James, M. K., *Studies in the Medieval Wine Trade* (Oxford, 1971).

Johnstone, H., 'The eccentricities of Edward II', *EHR* 48 (1933), pp. 264–7.

Jurkowski, M., C. L. Smith and D. Crook, *Lay Taxes in England and Wales, 1188–1688*, PRO Handbooks 31 (Kew, 1998).

Kaeuper, R. W., *Bankers to the Crown: the Riccardi of Lucca and Edward I* (Princeton, NJ, 1973).

Kaeuper, R. W., 'The Frescobaldi of Florence and the English crown', *Studies in Medieval and Renaissance History* 10 (1973), pp. 45–97.

King, A., 'The death of Edward II revisited', in *Fourteenth Century England IX*, ed. J. Bothwell and G. Dodd (Woodbridge, 2016), pp. 1–22.

Lapsley, G., 'Knights of the shire in the parliaments of Edward II', *EHR* 34 (1919), pp. 25–42.

Legg, J. W., The Sarum Missal (Oxford, 1916).

Lloyd, T. H., *Alien Merchants in England in the High Middle Ages* (Brighton, 1982).

Lloyd, T. H., *England and the German Hanse, 1157–1611: a Study of their Trade and Commercial Diplomacy* (Cambridge, 1991).

Lloyd, T. H., *The English Wool Trade in the Middle Ages* (Cambridge, 1977).

Lloyd, T. H., *The Movement of Wool Prices in Medieval England*, EcHR Supplement 6 (1993).

Lopez, R. S., 'Majorcans and Genoese on the North Sea route in the thirteenth century', *Revue Belge de Philologie et d'Histoire* 29 (1951), pp. 1163–79.

Lord, C., 'Queen Isabella at the court of France', in *Fourteenth Century England II*, ed. C. Given-Wilson (Woodbridge, 2002), pp. 45–52.

Lunt, W. E., *Financial Relations of the Papacy with England to 1327* (Cambridge, MA, 1939).

McKisack, M., *The Fourteenth Century* (Oxford, 1963).

McKisack, M., *The Parliamentary Representation of the English Boroughs during the Middle Ages* (London, 1932).

McNamee, C. J., *The Wars of the Bruces: Scotland, England and Ireland, 1306–1328* (East Linton, 1997).

Maddicott, J. R., *The English Peasantry and the Demands of the Crown, 1294–1341*, Past and Present supplement 1 (1975).

Maddicott, J. R., *The Origins of the English Parliament, 924–1327* (Oxford, 2010).

Maddicott, J. R., 'Parliament and the constituencies, 1271–1377', in *The English Parliament in the Middle Ages*, ed. R. G. Davies and J. H. Denton (Manchester, 1981), pp. 61–87.

Maddicott, J. R., *Thomas of Lancaster, 1307–1322: a Study in the Reign of Edward II* (Oxford, 1970).

Mate, M., 'High prices in early fourteenth century England: causes and consequences', *Economic History Review*, 2nd series 28 (1975), pp. 1–16.

Mills, M. H., 'Exchequer agenda and estimate of revenue, Easter term 1284', *EHR* 40 (1925), pp. 229–34.

Mortimer, I., 'The death of Edward II in Berkeley Castle', *EHR* 120 (2005), pp. 1175–214.

Mortimer, I., 'Edward III, his father and the Fieschi', in *Medieval Intrigue* (London, 2010).

Mortimer, I., *The Greatest Traitor: the Life of Sir Roger Mortimer, Ruler of England 1327–1330* (London, 2003).

Mortimer, I., 'Sermons of sodomy: a reconsideration of Edward II's sodomitical reputation', in *The Reign of Edward II: New Perspectives*, ed. G. Dodd and A. Musson (Woodbridge, 2006), pp. 48–60.

Ormrod, W. M., 'Agenda for legislation, 1322–c.1340', *EHR* 105 (1990), pp. 1–33.

Ormrod, W. M., 'The crown and the English economy, 1290–1348', in *Before the Black Death: Studies in the Crisis of the Early Fourteenth Century*, ed. B. M. S. Campbell (Manchester, 1991), pp. 149–83.

Ormrod, W. M., 'Political theory in practice: the forced Loan on English overseas trade of 1317–18', *Historical Research* 64 (1991), pp. 204–15.

Ormrod, W. M., 'The sexualities of Edward II', in *The Reign of Edward II: New Perspectives*, ed. G. Dodd and A. Musson (Woodbridge, 2006), pp. 22–47.

Page, C., 'The rhymed office for St Thomas of Lancaster: poetry, politics and liturgy in fourteenth century England', *Leeds Studies in English* 14 (1983), pp. 134–51.

Perkins, C., 'The wealth of the Knights Templar', *American Historical Review* 15 (1910), pp. 252–63.

Peters, E., *The Shadow King: Rex Inutilis in Medieval Law and Literature, 751–1327* (New Haven, 1970).

Phillips, J. R. S., *Aymer de Valence, Earl of Pembroke, 1307–1324: Baronial Politics in the Reign of Edward II* (Oxford, 1972).

Phillips, J. R. S., *Edward II* (New Haven and London, 2010).

Phillips, J. R. S., 'Edward II and Ireland (in fact and in fiction)', *Irish Historical Studies* 33 (May 2002), pp. 1–18.

Phillips, J. R. S., 'Edward II and the prophets', in *England in the Fourteenth Century: Proceedings of the 1985 Harlaxton Symposium*, ed. W. M. Ormrod (Woodbridge, 1986), pp. 189–201.

Phillips, J. R. S., 'Kings in captivity: the case of Edward II of England, "the Island King"', *Quaestiones Medii Aevi Novae* 18 (2013), pp. 37–58.

Phillips, J. R. S., 'Parliament in the reign of Edward II', in *Fourteenth Century England X*, ed. G. Dodd (Woodbridge, 2018), pp. 25–46.

Phillips, J. R. S., 'Tout and the reign of Edward II', in *Thomas Frederick Tout (1855–1929): Refashioning History for the Twentieth Century*, ed. C. M. Barron and J. T. Rosenthal (London, 2019), pp. 107–21.

Phillips, J. R. S., 'Some afterthoughts on Edward II', in *People, Power and Identity in the Late Middle Ages: Essays in Memory of W. Mark Ormrod*, ed. G. Dodd , H. Lacey and A. Musson (London, 2021), pp. 285–304.

Pole-Stuart, E., 'The interview between Philip V and Edward II at Amiens in 1320', *EHR* 41 (1926), pp. 412–15.

Powicke, M., *Military Obligation in Medieval England: a Study in Liberty and Duty* (Oxford, 1962).

Prestwich, M., *Edward I* (London, 1988).

Prestwich, M., *War, Politics and Finance under Edward I* (London, 1972).

Ramsay, J. H., *A History of the Revenues of the Kings of England, 1066–1399*, 2 vols (Oxford, 1925).

Robinson, C., 'Was Edward II a degenerate?', *American Journal of Insanity* 66 (1910), pp. 445–64.

Roskell, J. S., 'The problem of the attendance of the lords in medieval parliaments', *Bulletin of the Institute of Historical Research* 29 (1956), pp. 153–204.

Ruddock, A. A., *Italian Merchants and Shipping in Southampton, 1270–1600* (Southampton, 1951).

Saaler, M., *Edward II, 1307–1327* (London, 1997).

Saul, N., *Richard II* (New Haven, 1997).

Schriber, C. P., 'Edward II and the tactics of kingship', *Journal of the Rocky Mountain Medieval and Renaissance Association* 13 (1992), pp. 1–23.

Sharp, B., *Famine and Scarcity in Late Medieval and Early Modern England: the Regulation of Grain Marketing, 1256–1631* (Cambridge, 2016).

Simkin, D., 'The English army and the Scottish campaign of 1310–11', in *England and Scotland in the Fourteenth Century: New Perspectives*, ed. A. King and M. Penman (Woodbridge, 2007), pp. 14–39.

Slavin, P., 'The fate of the former Templar estates in England, 1308–1338', in *Crusades XIV*, ed. B. Z. Kedar, J. Phillips and J. Riley-Smith, Society for the Study of the Crusades and the Latin East (London, 2015), pp. 209–35.

Smith, D., 'The Fieschi letter', in J. Barlow, R. Bryant, C. Heighway, C. Jeens, D. Smith, with G. Fowlie and L. Keen, *Edward II: His Last Months and his Monument* (Bristol, 2015), pp. 127–36.

Smith, J. B., 'Edward II and the allegiance of Wales', *Welsh History Review* 8 (1976–7), pp. 139–71.

Smith, J. B., 'Gruffydd Llwyd and the Celtic alliance, 1315–1318', *Bulletin of the Board of Celtic Studies* 26 (1976), pp. 463–78.

Smith, J. B., 'The rebellion of Llywelyn Bren', in *Glamorgan County History, vol. III: The Middle Ages*, ed. T. B. Pugh (Cardiff, 1971), pp. 72–86.

Spufford, P., *Origins of the English Parliament* (London, 1967).

Steiner, A., 'Vernacular proverbs in medieval Latin prose', *American Journal of Philology* 65 (1944), pp. 37–68.

Stubbs, W., *The Constitutional History of England in its Origins and Development*, 3 vols. (Oxford, 1880).

Taylor, J., 'The judgment on Hugh Despenser, the Younger', *Medievalia et Humanistica* (1958), pp. 73–7.

Thielmann, J. M., 'Political canonization and political symbolism in medieval England', *Journal of British Studies* 19 (1990), pp. 241–66.

Tout, T. F. 'The captivity and death of Edward of Carnarvon', *Bulletin of the John Rylands Library* 6 (1921–2), pp. 69–114.

Tout, T. F., *Chapters in the Administrative History of Medieval England*, 6 vols. (Manchester, 1920–33).

Tout, T. F., *The Place of the Reign of Edward II in English History*, 2nd ed. (Manchester, 1936).

Tout, T. F., 'The study of medieval chronicles', *Bulletin of the John Rylands Library* 6 (1921–2), pp. 414–38.

Tristram, E. W., *English Wall Painting of the Fourteenth Century* (London, 1955).

Trueman, J. H. 'The privy seal and the English Ordinances of 1311', *Speculum* 31 (1956), pp. 611–25.

Tuck, A., *Richard II and the English Nobility* (London, 1973).

Vale, M., *The Origins of the Hundred Years War: the Angevin Legacy, 1250–1340* (Oxford, 1996).

Valente, C., 'The deposition and abdication of Edward II', *EHR* 113 (1998), pp. 852–81.

Vernon Harcourt, L. W., *His Grace the Steward and the Trial of Peers* (London, 1907).

Walker, S., 'Political saints in later medieval England', in *The MacFarlane Legacy: Studies in Late Medieval Politics and Society*, ed. R. H. Britnell and A. J. Pollard (Stroud, 1995), pp. 77–106.

Warner, K., *Edward II: the Unconventional King* (Stroud, 2014).

Weber, W. C., 'The purpose of the English *Modus Tenendi Parliamentum*', *Parliamentary History* 17 (1998), pp. 149–77.

Welander, D., *The History, Art, and Architecture of Gloucester Cathedral* (Stroud, 1991).

Wells-Furby, B., 'The Gower prelude to the Marcher rising of 1321: a question of evidence', *Welsh History Review* 27 (2014), pp. 4–27.

Wilkinson, B., *Constitutional History of Medieval England, 1216–1399*, vols II–III (London, 1952–8).

Wilkinson, B., 'The Sherburn indenture and the attack on the Despeners, 1321', *EHR* 63 (1948), pp. 1–28.

Willard, J. F., *Parliamentary Taxes on Personal Property, 1290–1334: a Study in English Financial Administration* (Cambridge, MA, 1934).

Williams, G. A., *Medieval London from Commune to Capital* (London, 1963).

Wolff, B. P., *The Royal Demesne in English History: the Crown Estate in the Governance of the Realm from the Conquest to 1509* (London, 1971).

INDEX